AWS for Solutions Architects

Design your cloud infrastructure by implementing DevOps, containers, and Amazon Web Services

Alberto Artasanchez

BIRMINGHAM—MUMBAI

AWS for Solutions Architects

Group Product Manager: Wilson D'souza

Publishing Product Manager: Rahul Nair

Senior Editor: Arun Nadar

Content Development Editor: Pratik Andrade, Sayali Pingale

Technical Editor: Yoginee Marathe

Copy Editor: Safis Editing

Project Coordinator: Neil Dmello

Proofreader: Safis Editing

Indexer: Rekha Nair

Production Designer: Prashant Ghare

First published: January 2021

Production reference: 1210121

Published by Packt Publishing Ltd.

Livery Place

35 Livery Street

Birmingham

B3 2PB, UK.

ISBN 978-1-78953-923-3

www.packt.com

To my mother, Laura Loy, from whom I got my balance. To the memory of my father, Alberto Artasanchez Sr., from whom I got my passion for life and determination. And most importantly, to my wife, Karen Artasanchez, who supports me no matter how crazy my ideas are.

– Alberto Artasanchez

`Packt.com`

Subscribe to our online digital library for full access to over 7,000 books and videos, as well as industry leading tools to help you plan your personal development and advance your career. For more information, please visit our website.

Why subscribe?

- Spend less time learning and more time coding with practical eBooks and Videos from over 4,000 industry professionals

- Improve your learning with Skill Plans built especially for you

- Get a free eBook or video every month

- Fully searchable for easy access to vital information

- Copy and paste, print, and bookmark content

Did you know that Packt offers eBook versions of every book published, with PDF and ePub files available? You can upgrade to the eBook version at `packt.com` and as a print book customer, you are entitled to a discount on the eBook copy. Get in touch with us at `customercare@packtpub.com` for more details.

At `www.packt.com`, you can also read a collection of free technical articles, sign up for a range of free newsletters, and receive exclusive discounts and offers on Packt books and eBooks.

Contributors

About the author

Alberto Artasanchez is a solutions architect with expertise in the cloud, data solutions, and machine learning, with a career spanning over 28 years in various industries. He is an AWS Ambassador and publishes frequently in a variety of cloud and data science publications. He is often tapped as a speaker on topics including data science, big data, and analytics. He has a strong and extensive track record of designing and building end-to-end machine learning platforms at scale. He also has a long track record of leading data engineering teams and mentoring, coaching, and motivating them. He has a great understanding of how technology drives business value and has a passion for creating elegant solutions to complicated problems.

I want to thank my wife, Karen Artasanchez, for her continuous support on all my projects. I also want to thank the Packt editors. Without them, this book would never have happened. In particular, I want to thank Pratik Andrade, Vaidehi Sawant, Arun Nadar, and Rahul Nair.

About the reviewers

Umair Hoodbhoy is a cloud architect with nearly 20 years of experience in enterprise IT. He spent 10 years at Cisco, Hewlett-Packard Enterprise, and Juniper Networks in a variety of roles, including product management for 7 years. Earlier in his career, he obtained the Cisco Certified Internetwork Expert (CCIE Routing & Switching #11857) and **Certified Information Systems Security Professional** (**CISSP**) certifications. More recently, he earned cloud certifications in AWS, Google Cloud Platform, and Aviatrix Systems. Umair is currently a solutions architect in the multi-cloud networking space.

Arunabh Sahai is a results-oriented leader who has been delivering technology solutions for more than 16 years across multiple industries around the globe. He is also a forward-thinking technology enthusiast and a technology coach, helping learners to polish their technology skills. Arunabh holds a master's degree in computer science and has in-depth knowledge of cloud (AWS/Azure/GCP) technologies. He holds multiple certifications attesting to his cloud technology knowledge and experience. He is also passionate about intelligent automation using predictive analytics. You can connect with him on his LinkedIn, and he will be happy to help you with your technology questions.

Packt is searching for authors like you

If you're interested in becoming an author for Packt, please visit `authors.packtpub.com` and apply today. We have worked with thousands of developers and tech professionals, just like you, to help them share their insight with the global tech community. You can make a general application, apply for a specific hot topic that we are recruiting an author for, or submit your own idea.

Table of Contents

2
Leveraging the Cloud for Digital Transformation

Section 2:
AWS Service Offerings and Use Cases

3
Storage in AWS – Choosing the Right Tool for the Job

4

Harnessing the Power of Cloud Computing

5

Selecting the Right Database Service

6

Amazon Athena – Combining the Simplicity of Files with the Power of SQL

7

AWS Glue – Extracting, Transforming, and Loading Data the Simple Way

8

Best Practices for Application Security, Identity, and Compliance

Section 3:
Applying Architectural Patterns and Reference Architectures

9
Serverless and Container Patterns

10
Microservice and Event-Driven Architectures

11

Domain-Driven Design

12

Data Lake Patterns – Integrating Your Data across the Enterprise

13

Availability, Reliability, and Scalability Patterns

Section 4: Hands-On Labs

14
Hands-On Lab and Use Case

Other Books You May Enjoy

Index

Preface

Often, when a new technology emerges, it is touted as the most important technology to come along. Cloud computing is no exception. It may not be the most important technological innovation to come along, but few people will disagree that it is an important step in the evolution of computing. More than a breakthrough by itself, it builds on other technologies such as virtualization, the internet, redundant storage, and so on. Part of its magic is putting it all together.

Another key aspect of the cloud is the power and cost savings that come from allowing multiple users to share the same resources while keeping the environment and the users' data secure.

The rate of adoption of cloud technologies keeps on accelerating and the question is no longer if cloud computing will be the dominant paradigm but rather how fast it will be adopted by companies of all sizes.

AWS is at the forefront of cloud adoption and is the undisputed leader. Enterprises are trusting their workloads to AWS because of its scalability, reliability, flexibility, and breadth of service offerings.

In this book, we will do a deep dive into the most important services available in AWS and many of their features. We will also assist you in deciding when to use one service over another, as well as recommended best practices when using a particular service. Finally, in the last chapter, we will put many of the technologies together and review a real-world use case.

Who this book is for

If your job involves making architectural decisions and making technology recommendations on how the cloud and AWS should be used, this book is for you.

What this book covers

Chapter 1, Understanding AWS Cloud Principles and Key Characteristics, describes the ubiquity of cloud computing, AWS' market share, its revenue, and its adoption across industries.

Chapter 2, Leveraging the Cloud for Digital Transformation, begins to describe the AWS infrastructure and its services as well as how it can be used to achieve digital transformation across your enterprise.

Chapter 3, Storage in AWS – Choosing the Right Tool for the Job, goes through common storage use cases and the AWS services that support them.

Chapter 4, Harnessing the Power of Cloud Computing, visits common compute use cases and the AWS services that support them.

Chapter 5, Selecting the Right Database Service, visits common database (relational and NoSQL) use cases and the different AWS database services.

Chapter 6, Amazon Athena – Combining the Simplicity of Files with the Power of SQL, presents an overview of an important service offered by AWS called Amazon Athena. Amazon Athena is a powerful service that enables you to use standard SQL to access file content.

Chapter 7, AWS Glue – Extracting, Transforming, and Loading Data the Simple Way, shows how the AWS Glue service can simplify the creation of data lakes and data warehouses and their population.

Chapter 8, Best Practices for Application Security, Identity, and Compliance, goes through the common security, identity, and compliance use cases and the AWS services that support them.

Chapter 9, Serverless and Container Patterns, explains the concepts behind, and illustrates, microservice and container cloud architectures and use cases.

Chapter 10, Microservice and Event-Driven Architectures, illustrates serverless and event-based cloud architectures and their use cases.

Chapter 11, Domain-Driven Design, describes domain-driven design as well as bounded patterns and their use cases.

Chapter 12, Data Lake Patterns – Integrating Your Data across the Enterprise, explains the benefits and challenges of implementing an enterprise data lake. It also explores best practices and how to measure the success of your data lake implementation.

Chapter 13, Availability, Reliability, and Scalability Patterns, describes high availability, reliability, scalability, and operations cloud architectures and when to use them.

Chapter 14, Hands-On Labs and Use Cases, revisits many of the concepts from previous chapters and combines them to build a practical, generic web UI serverless architecture.

To get the most out of this book

The book's focus is on best practices and architectural patterns. It focuses on what AWS services to use and when rather than focusing on how to use AWS services. It does not have any computing language prerequisites and it contains little to no code examples.

Download the color images

We also provide a PDF file that has color images of the screenshots/diagrams used in this book. You can download it here: `http://www.packtpub.com/sites/default/files/downloads/9781789539233_ColorImages.pdf`.

Get in touch

Feedback from our readers is always welcome.

General feedback: If you have questions about any aspect of this book, mention the book title in the subject of your message and email us at `customercare@packtpub.com`.

Errata: Although we have taken every care to ensure the accuracy of our content, mistakes do happen. If you have found a mistake in this book, we would be grateful if you would report this to us. Please visit `www.packtpub.com/support/errata`, selecting your book, clicking on the Errata Submission Form link, and entering the details.

Piracy: If you come across any illegal copies of our works in any form on the Internet, we would be grateful if you would provide us with the location address or website name. Please contact us at `copyright@packt.com` with a link to the material.

If you are interested in becoming an author: If there is a topic that you have expertise in and you are interested in either writing or contributing to a book, please visit `authors.packtpub.com`.

Reviews

Please leave a review. Once you have read and used this book, why not leave a review on the site that you purchased it from? Potential readers can then see and use your unbiased opinion to make purchase decisions, we at Packt can understand what you think about our products, and our authors can see your feedback on their book. Thank you!

For more information about Packt, please visit `packt.com`.

Section 1: Exploring AWS

In this section, you'll get an understanding of the basics of cloud computing. We will also explore the basics of AWS, a few fundamental services, and the business value that can be gained by leveraging AWS.

This part of the book comprises the following chapters:

- *Chapter 1, Understanding AWS Cloud Principles and Key Characteristics*
- *Chapter 2, Leveraging the Cloud for Digital Transformation*

1
Understanding AWS Cloud Principles and Key Characteristics

You would be hard-pressed to talk to someone today that has not heard of the cloud. For most of its history, Amazon did not advertise, but when it did begin advertising on television, the first commercials were for **Amazon Web Services** (**AWS**) and not for its e-commerce division.

Even though the term cloud is pervasive today, not everyone understands what the cloud is. One reason this is the case is that the cloud can be different things for different people. Another reason is that the cloud is continuously evolving.

In this chapter, we will put our best foot forward and attempt to define the cloud, and then we will try to define the AWS cloud more specifically. We will also cover the vast and ever-growing influence and adoption of the cloud in general and AWS in particular. After that, we'll start introducing some elementary cloud and AWS terms to start getting our feet wet with the lingo.

We will then try to understand why cloud computing so popular. Assuming you buy the premise that the cloud is taking the world by storm, we will then learn how we can take a slice of the cloud pie and build our credibility by becoming certified. Finally, toward the end of the chapter, we will look at some tips and tricks you can use to simplify your journey to obtain AWS certifications, and we will look at some frequently asked questions about the AWS certifications.

In this chapter, we will cover the following topics:

- What is cloud computing?
- What is AWS cloud computing?
- The market share, influence, and adoption of AWS
- Basic cloud and AWS terminology
- Why is cloud computing so popular?
- The five pillars of a well-architected framework
- Building credibility by becoming certified
- Learning tips and tricks to obtain AWS certifications
- Some frequently asked questions about AWS certifications

Let's get started, shall we?

What is cloud computing?

Here's a dirty little secret that the cloud providers may not want you to know. Cloud providers use cryptic acronyms and fancy terms such as EC2 instances and S3 services (in the case of AWS), or Azure VMs and blobs (in the case of Azure), but at its most basic level, the cloud is just a bunch of servers and other computing resources managed by a third-party provider in a data center somewhere.

But we had data centers and third party-managed servers long before the term cloud became popular. So, what makes the cloud different from your run-of-the-mill data center?

Before we try to define cloud computing, let's analyze some of the characteristics that are common to many of the leading cloud providers.

Cloud elasticity

One important characteristic of the leading cloud providers is the ability to quickly and frictionlessly provision resources. These resources could be a single instance of a database or a thousand copies of the same server, used to handle your web traffic. These servers can be provisioned within minutes.

Contrast that with how performing the same operation may play out in a traditional on-premises environment. Let's use an example. Your boss comes to you and asks you to set up a cluster of computers to host your latest service. Your next actions probably look something like this:

1. You visit the data center and realize that the current capacity is not enough to host this new service.

2. You map out a new infrastructure architecture.

3. You size the machines based on the expected load, adding a few more terabytes here and a few gigabytes there to make sure that you don't overwhelm the service.

4. You submit the architecture for approval to the appropriate parties.

5. You wait. Most likely for months.

It may not be uncommon once you get the approvals to realize that the market opportunity for this service is now gone, or that it has grown more and the capacity you initially planned will not suffice.

It is difficult to overemphasize how important the ability to deliver a solution quickly is when you use cloud technologies to enable these solutions.

What do you think your boss would say if after getting everything set up in the data center and after months of approvals, you told them you made a mistake and you ordered an *X213* server instead of an *X312*, which means you won't have enough capacity to handle the expected load and getting the right server will take a few more months? What do you think their mood will be like?

In a cloud environment, this is not necessarily a problem, because instead of needing potentially months to provision your servers, they can be provisioned in minutes.

Correcting the size of the server may be as simple as shutting down the server for a few minutes, changing a drop-down box value, and restarting the server again.

Hopefully, the unhappy boss example here drives our point home about the power of the cloud and the pattern that is emerging. The cloud exponentially improves time to market. And being able to deliver quickly may not just mean getting there first. It may be the difference between getting there first and not getting there at all.

Another powerful characteristic of a cloud computing environment is the ability to quickly shut down resources and, importantly, not be charged for that resource while it is down. Being able to shut down resources and not paying for them while they are down is not exclusive to AWS. Many of the most popular cloud providers offer this billing option.

In our continuing on-premises example, if we shut down one of our servers, do you think we can call the company that sold us the server and politely ask them to stop charging us because we shut the server down? That would be a very quick conversation and depending on how persistent we were, it would probably not be a very pleasant one. They are probably going to say, "*You bought the server; you can do whatever you want to do with it, including using it as a paperweight.*" Once the server is purchased, it is a sunk cost for the duration of the useful life of the server.

In contrast, whenever we shut down a server in a cloud environment, the cloud provider can quickly detect that and put that server back into the pool of available servers for other cloud customers to use that newly unused capacity.

Cloud virtualization

Virtualization is the process of running multiple virtual instances on top of a physical computer system using an abstract layer sitting on top of actual hardware.

More commonly, virtualization refers to the practice of running multiple operating systems on a single computer at the same time. Applications that are running on virtual machines are oblivious to the fact that they are not running on a dedicated machine. These applications are not aware that they are sharing resources with other applications on the same physical machine.

A **hypervisor** is a computing layer that enables multiple operating systems to execute in the same physical compute resource. These operating systems running on top of these hypervisors are **Virtual Machines** (**VMs**) – a component that can emulate a complete computing environment using only software but as if it was running on bare metal.

Hypervisors, also known as **Virtual Machine Monitors** (**VMMs**), manage these VMs while running side by side. A hypervisor creates a logical separation between VMs, and it provides each of them with a slice of the available compute, memory, and storage resources.

This allows VMs to not clash and interfere with each other. If one VM crashes and goes down, it will not make other VMs go down with it. Also, if there is an intrusion in one VM, it is fully isolated from the rest.

Definition of the cloud

Let's now attempt to define cloud computing.

The **cloud computing** model is one that offers computing services such as compute, storage, databases, networking, software, machine learning, and analytics over the internet and on demand. You generally only pay for the time and services you use. The majority of cloud providers can provide massive scalability for many of their services and make it easy to scale services up and down.

Now, as much as we tried to nail it down, this is still a pretty broad definition. For example, in our definition, we specify that the cloud can offer software. That's a pretty broad term. Does the term software in our definition include the following?

- Code management
- Virtual desktops
- Email services
- Video conferencing

These are just a few examples of what may or may not be included as available services in a cloud environment. When it comes to AWS and other major cloud providers, the answer is yes. When AWS started, it only offered a few core services, such as compute (Amazon EC2) and basic storage (Amazon S3). As of 2020, AWS offers 212 services, including compute, storage, networking, databases, analytics, developer and deployment tools, and mobile apps, among others. For the individual examples given here, AWS offers the following:

- **Code management** – AWS CodeCommit, AWS CodePipeline, and AWS CodeDeploy
- **Virtual desktops** – AWS Workspaces
- **Email services** – Amazon SES and Amazon WorkMail
- **Video conferencing** – Amazon Chime

As we will see throughout the book, this is a tiny sample of the many services that AWS offers. Additionally, since it was launched, AWS services and features have grown exponentially every year, as shown in the following figure:

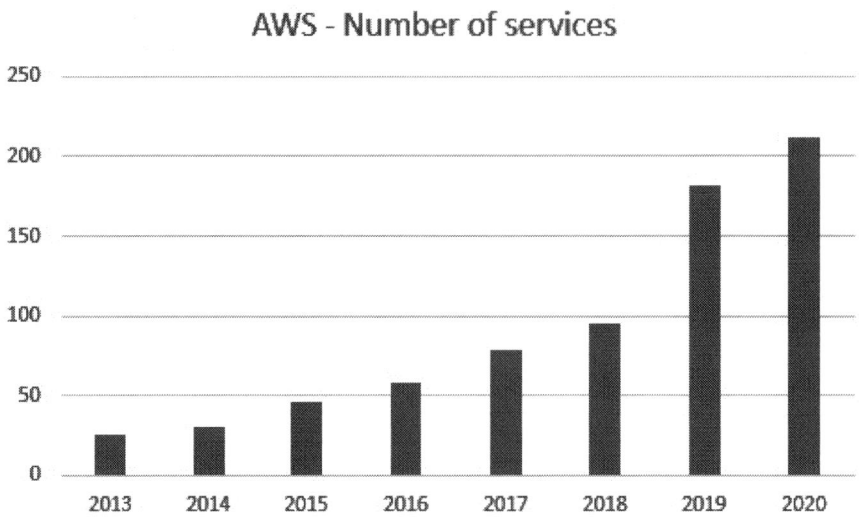

Figure 1.1 – AWS – number of services

There is no doubt that the number of offerings will continue to grow at a similar rate for the foreseeable future. Having had the opportunity to work in the AWS offices in Seattle, I can report that AWS is hard at work creating these new services and eating their own dog food by using their existing services to create these new services.

Private versus public clouds

Up until a few years ago, one of the biggest and most common objections to hamper cloud adoption on a massive scale was the refrain that *the cloud is not secure*. To address this objection, cloud providers started offering private clouds: a whole infrastructure setup that only one company can access and is completely private to them. However, this privacy and security comes at a price. One of the reasons why the cloud is so popular and affordable is that any resources that you are currently not using can be used by other customers that do need the capacity at that time, meaning they share the cost with you. Whoever uses the resources the most, pays the most. This cost-sharing disappears with private clouds.

Let's use an analogy to gain further understanding. The gig economy has great momentum. Everywhere you look, people are finding employment as contract workers. There are Uber drivers, people setting up Airbnbs, people doing contract work for Upwork. One of the reasons contract work is getting more popular is that it enables consumers to contract services that they may otherwise not be able to afford. Could you imagine how expensive it would be to have a private chauffeur? But with Uber or Lyft, you almost have a private chauffeur who can be at your beck and call within a few minutes of you summoning them.

A similar economy of scale happens with a public cloud. You can have access to infrastructure and services that would cost millions of dollars if you bought it on your own. Instead, you can have access to the same resources for a small fraction of the cost.

A private cloud just becomes a fancy name for a data center managed by a trusted third party, and all the elasticity benefits wither away.

Even though AWS, Azure, GCP, and the other popular cloud providers are considered mostly public clouds, there are some actions you can take to make them more private. As an example, AWS offers Amazon EC2 dedicated instances, which are EC2 instances that ensure that you will be the only user for a given physical server. Again, this comes at a cost.

Dedicated instance costs are significantly higher than on-demand EC2 instances. On-demand instances may be shared with other AWS users. As mentioned earlier in the chapter, you will never know the difference because of virtualization and hypervisor technology. One common use case for choosing dedicated instances is government regulations and compliance policies that require certain sensitive data to not be in the same physical server with other cloud users.

Truly private clouds are expensive to run and maintain, and for that reason, many of the resources and services offered by the major cloud providers reside in public clouds. But just because you are using a private cloud does not mean that it cannot be set up insecurely, and conversely, if you are running your workloads and applications on a public cloud, you can use security best practices and sleep well at night knowing that you are using state-of-the-art technologies to secure your sensitive data.

Additionally, most of the major cloud providers' clients use public cloud configurations, but there are a few exceptions even in this case. For example, the United States government intelligence agencies are a big AWS customer. As you can imagine, they have deep pockets and are not afraid to spend. In many cases with these government agencies, AWS will set up the AWS infrastructure and services on the premises of the agency itself. You can find out more about this here:

```
https://aws.amazon.com/federal/us-intelligence-community/
```

Now that we have gained a better understanding of cloud computing in general, let's get more granular and learn about how AWS does cloud computing.

What is AWS cloud computing?

Put simply, AWS is the undisputed market leader in cloud computing today, and even though there are a few worthy competitors, it doesn't seem like anyone will push them off the podium for a while. Why is this, and how can we be sure that they will remain a top player for years to come? Because this pattern has occurred in the history of the technology industry repeatedly. Geoffrey A. Moore, Paul Thompson, and Tom Kippola explained this pattern best a long time ago in their book *The Gorilla Game: Picking Winners in High Technology.*

Some important concepts covered in their book are listed here:

- There are two kinds of technology markets: Gorilla Games and Royalty Markets. In a Gorilla Game, the players are dubbed gorillas and chimps. In a Royalty Market, the participants are kings, princes, and serfs.

- Gorilla Games exist because the market leaders possess proprietary technology that makes it difficult for competitors to compete. This proprietary technology creates a moat that can be difficult to overcome.

- In Royalty Markets, the technology has been commoditized and standardized. In a Royalty Market, it's difficult to become a leader and it's easy to fall off the number one position.

- The more proprietary features a gorilla creates in their product and the bigger the moat they establish, the more difficult and expensive it becomes to switch to a competitor and the stronger the gorilla becomes.

- This creates a virtuous cycle for the market leader or gorilla. The market leader's product or service becomes highly desirable, which means that they can charge more for it and sell more of it. They can then reinvest that profit to make the product or service even better.

- Conversely, a vicious cycle is created for second-tier competitors or chimps. Their product or service is not as desirable, so even if they charge as much money as the market leader, because they don't have as many sales, their research and development budget will not be as large as the market leader.

- The focus of this book is on technology, but if you are interested in investing in technology companies, the best time to invest in a gorilla is when the market is about to enter a period of hypergrowth. At this point, the gorilla might not be fully determined and it's best to invest in the gorilla candidates and sell stock as it becomes obvious that they won't be a gorilla and reinvest the proceeds of that sale into the emerging gorilla.

- Once a gorilla is established, most often, the way that a gorilla is vanquished is by a complete change in the game, where a new disruptive technology creates a brand new game.

To get a better understanding, let look at an example of a King Market and an example of a Gorilla Game.

Personal computers and laptops – Back in the early 1980s when PCs burst onto the scene, many players emerged that sold personal computers, such as these:

- Dell

- Gateway

- IBM

- Hewlett Packard

I don't know about you, but whenever I buy a computer, I go to the store, see which computer is the cheapest and has the features I want, and pull the trigger regardless of the brand. This is the perfect example of a King Market. It is difficult to differentiate yourself and stand out and there is little to no brand loyalty among consumers.

Personal computer operating systems – Whenever I buy a new computer, I make sure of one thing: that the computer comes with Microsoft Windows, the undisputed market leader in the space. Yes, the Macintosh operating system has been around for a long time, Linux has been around for a while making some noise, and the Google Chrome operating system is making some inroads, especially in the educational market. But ever since it was launched in November 1985, Microsoft Windows has kept the lion's share of the market (or should we say the gorilla's share?).

Of course, this is a subjective opinion, but I believe we are witnessing the biggest Gorilla Game in the history of computing with the advent of cloud computing. This is the mother of all competitive wars. Cloud vendors are not only competing to provide basic services, such as compute and storage, but are continuing to build more services on top of these core services to lock in their customers further and further. Vendor lock-in is not necessarily a bad thing. Lock-in, after all, is a type of golden handcuffs. Customers stay because they like the services they are being offered. But customers also realize that as they use more and more services, it becomes more and more expensive to transfer their applications and workloads to an alternate cloud provider.

Not all cloud services are highly intertwined with their cloud ecosystems. Take these scenarios, for example:

- Your firm may be using AWS services for many purposes, but they may be using WebEx, Microsoft Teams, Zoom, or Slack for their video conference needs instead of Amazon Chime. These services have little dependency on other underlying core infrastructure cloud services.

- You may be using Amazon Sagemaker for artificial intelligence and machine learning projects, but you may be using the TensorFlow package in Sagemaker as your development kernel, even though TensorFlow is maintained by Google.

- If you are using Amazon RDS and you choose MySQL as your database engine, you should not have too much trouble porting your data and schemas over to another cloud provider that also supports MySQL, if you decide to switch over.

With some other services, it will be a lot more difficult to switch. Here are some examples:

- Amazon DynamoDB is a NoSQL proprietary database only offered by AWS. If you want to switch over to another NoSQL database, porting it may not be a simple exercise.

- If you are using CloudFormation to define and create your infrastructure, it will be difficult if not impossible to use your CloudFormation templates to create infrastructure in other cloud provider environments. If the portability of your infrastructure scripts is important to you and you are planning on switching cloud providers, Terraform by *HashiCorp* may be a better alternative since Terraform is cloud-agnostic.

- If you have a graph database requirement and you decide to use using Amazon Neptune (which is the native Amazon graph database offering), you may have a difficult time porting out of Amazon Neptune, since the development language and format can be quite dissimilar if you decide to use another graph database solution such as Neo4j or TigerGraph.

As far as we have come in the last 15 years with cloud technologies, I believe and I think vendors realize that these are the beginning innings, and locking customers in right now while they are still deciding who their vendor is going to be will be a lot easier than trying to do so after they pick a competitor.

A good example of one of those make-or-break decisions is the awarding of the **Joint Enterprise Defense Infrastructure** (**JEDI**) cloud computing contract by the Pentagon. JEDI is a $10 billion 10-year contract. As big as that dollar figure is, even more important is the fact that it would be nearly impossible for the Pentagon to switch to another vendor once the 10-year contract is up.

For that reason, even though Microsoft was initially awarded the contract, Amazon has sued the US government to potentially get them to change their mind and use AWS instead.

Let's delve a little deeper into how influential AWS currently is and how influential it has the potential to become.

The market share, influence, and adoption of AWS

It is hard to argue that AWS is not the gorilla in the cloud market. For the first 9 years of AWS's existence, Amazon did not break down their AWS sales and their profits. As of January 2020, Microsoft does not fully break down its Azure revenue and profit. As of 2019, in its quarterly reports, they were disclosing their Azure revenue growth rate without reporting the actual revenue number and instead burying Azure revenues in a bucket called *Commercial Cloud*, which also includes items such as Office 365 revenue. Google for a long time has been cagey about breaking down its **Google Cloud Platform** (**GCP**) revenue. Google finally broke down its GCP revenue in February 2019.

The reason cloud providers are careful about reporting these raw numbers is precisely because of the Gorilla Game. Initially, AWS did not want to disclose numbers because they wanted to become the gorilla in the cloud market without other competitors catching wind of it. And if Microsoft and Google disclosed their numbers, it would reveal the exact size of the chasm that exists between them and AWS.

Even though AWS is the gorilla now, and it's quite difficult to debunk the gorilla, it appears the growth rates for GCP and Azure are substantially higher than AWS's current growth rate. Analysts have pegged the growth rate for GCP and Azure at about 60% year on year, whereas AWS's recent year-on-year revenue growth is closer to 30% to 40%. But the revenue for Azure and GCP is from a much smaller base.

This practice of most cloud providers leaves the rest of us guessing as to what the exact market share and other numbers really are. But, analysts being analysts, they still try to make an educated guess.

For example, one recent analysis from Canalys Cloud Channels in 2019 puts AWS's share of the market at around 33% and the market share for its closest competitor, Azure, at around 17%.

Up until this point, AWS has done a phenomenal job of protecting their market share by adding more and more services, adding features to existing services, building higher-level functionality on top of the core services they already offer, and educating the masses on how to best use these services. It is hard to see how they could lose the pole position. Of course, anything is possible, including the possibility of government intervention and regulation, as occurred in the personal computer chip market and in the attempt the government made to break up Microsoft and their near monopoly on the personal operating system market.

We are in an exciting period when it comes to cloud adoption. Up until just a few years ago, many C-suite executives were leery of adopting cloud technologies to run their mission-critical and core services. A common concern was that they felt having on-premises implementations was more secure than running their workloads on the cloud.

It has become clear to most of them that running workloads on the cloud can be just as secure, if not more secure, than running them on the cloud. There is no perfectly secure environment, and it seems that almost every other day we hear about sensitive information being left exposed on the internet by yet another company. But having an army of security experts on your side, as is the case with the major cloud providers, will often beat any security team that most companies can procure on their own.

The current state of the cloud market for most enterprises is a state of **Fear Of Missing Out (FOMO)**. Chief executives are watching their competitors jumping on the cloud and they are concerned that they will be left behind if they don't take the leap as well.

Additionally, we are seeing an unprecedented level of disruption in many industries propelled by the power of the cloud. Let's take the example of Lyft and Uber. Both companies rely heavily on cloud services to power their infrastructure and old-guard companies in the space, such as Hertz and Avis, that rely on older on-premises technology are getting left behind. In fact, on May 22 2020, Hertz filed for Chapter 11 bankruptcy protection. Part of the problem is the convenience that Uber and Lyft offer by being able to summon a car on demand. Also, the pandemic that swept the world in 2020 did not help. But the inability to upgrade their systems to leverage cloud technologies no doubt played a role in their diminishing share of the car rental market.

Let's continue and learn some of the basic cloud terminology in general and AWS terminology in particular.

Basic cloud and AWS terminology

There is a constant effort by technology companies to offer common standards for certain technologies while providing exclusive and proprietary technology that no one else offers.

An example of this can be seen in the database market. The **Standard Query Language (SQL)** and the ANSI-SQL standard have been around for a long time. In fact, the **American National Standards Institute (ANSI)** adopted SQL as the SQL-86 standard in 1986.

Since then, database vendors have continuously been supporting this standard while offering a wide variety of extensions to this standard in order to make their products stand out and to lock in customers to their technology.

The cloud is no different. Cloud providers provide the same core functionality for a wide variety of customer needs, but they all feel compelled to name these services differently, no doubt in part to try to separate themselves from the rest of the pack and make it more difficult to switch out of their environments once companies commit to using them.

As an example, every major cloud provider offers compute services. In other words, it is simple to spin up a server with any provider, but they all refer to this compute service differently:

- AWS uses **Elastic Cloud Computing (EC2)** instances.
- Azure uses **Azure Virtual Machines**.
- GCP uses **Google Compute Engine**.

The following tables give a non-comprehensive list of the different core services offered by AWS, Azure, and GCP and the names used by each of them:

Service	AWS	Azure	GCP
Compute	• Amazon EC2 • Lightsail	• Azure Virtual Machines • Virtual Machine Scale Sets	• Google Compute Engine • Graphics Processing Unit (GPU)
Containers	• Amazon Elastic Container Service (ECS) • Amazon Fargate • Elastic Container Service for Kubernetes • Elastic Container Registry • Batch • Amazon EMR	• Azure Kubernetes Service (AKS) • Container Instances • Batch • Service Fabric • Cloud Services	• Google Kubernetes Engine • Knative • Container Security

Figure 1.2 – Cloud provider terminology and comparison (part 1)

These are some of the other services, including serverless technologies services and database services:

Service	AWS	Azure	GCP
Serverless Technologies	• AWS Lambda	• Azure Functions	• Google Cloud Functions
Relational Databases	• Amazon Relational Database Service (RDS) • Aurora • Redshift	• Azure SQL Database • Data Warehouse • Server Stretch Database • Table Storage • Redis Cache • Data Factory	• Google Cloud SQL • Cloud Spanner
NoSQL Databases (Key Value)	• Amazon DynamoDB	• Azure Table Storage	• Google Cloud Datastore • Google Cloud Bigtable
NoSQL Databases (Indexed)	• Amazon SimpleDB	• Azure Cosmos DB	• Google Cloud Datastore
Object Storage	• Amazon Simple Storage Service (S3)	• Azure Blob Storage	• Google Cloud Storage
File Storage	• Amazon Elastic Block Store (EBS) • Snowball • Snowball Edge • Snowmobile • Amazon Elastic File System (EFS)	• Azure Managed Disks • Azure File Storage	• Google Compute Engine Persistent Disks • Persistent Disk • ZFS/Avere • Transfer Appliance • Transfer Service
Archival Storage	• Amazon Glacier	• Azure Archive Storage	• Google Cloud Storage Nearline and Coldline

Figure 1.3 – Cloud provider terminology and comparison (part 2)

These are additional services:

Service	AWS	Azure	GCP
Domain Name Service (DNS)	• Amazon Route 53	• Azure DNS	• Google Cloud DNS
Peering	• Amazon DirectConnect	• Azure ExpressRoute	• Google Cloud Interconnect
Virtual Networking	• Amazon Virtual Private Cloud (VPC)	• Azure Virtual Networks (VNets)	• Google Virtual Private Cloud
Elastic Load Balancing	• Amazon Elastic Load Balancer	• Azure Load Balancer	• Google Cloud Load Balancing
PaaS services	• AWS Elastic Beanstalk • VMware Cloud on AWS	• App Service and Cloud Services	• Google App Engine
Machine Learning	• SageMaker • Machine Learning • Rekognition • Lex • Polly • Comprehend • Translate • Transcribe • DeepLens • Deep Learning AMIs	• Machine Learning • Azure Bot Service • Cognitive Services	• Google Cloud Machine Learning Engine • Dialogflow • Google Cloud Natural Language • Google Cloud Speech API • Google Cloud Translation API • Google Cloud Video Intelligence • Google Cloud Job Discovery

Figure 1.4 – Cloud provider terminology and comparison (part 3)

If you are confused by all the terms in the preceding tables, don't fret. We will learn about many of these services throughout the book and when to use each of them.

In the next section, we are going to learn why cloud services are becoming so popular and in particular why AWS adoption is so prevalent.

Why is cloud computing so popular?

Depending on who you ask, some estimates peg the global cloud computing market at around USD 370 billion in 2020, growing to about USD 830 billion by 2025. This implies a **Compound Annual Growth Rate** (**CAGR**) of around 18% for the period.

There are multiple reasons why the cloud market is growing so fast. Some of them are listed here:

- Elasticity
- Security
- Availability
- Faster hardware cycles
- System administration staff
- Faster time to market

Let's look at the most important one first.

Elasticity

Elasticity may be one of the most important reasons for the cloud's popularity. Let's first understand what it is.

Do you remember the feeling of going to a toy store as a kid? There is no feeling like it in the world. Puzzles, action figures, games, and toy cars are all at your fingertips, ready for you to play with them. There was only one problem: you could not take the toys out of the store. Your mom or dad always told you that you could only buy one toy. You always had to decide which one you wanted and invariably, after one of two weeks of playing with that toy, you got bored with it and the toy ended up in a corner collecting dust, and you were left longing for the toy you didn't choose.

What if I told you about a special, almost magical, toy store where you could rent toys for as long or as little as you wanted, and the second you got tired with the toy you could return it, change it for another toy, and stop any rental charges for the first toy? Would you be interested?

The difference between the first traditional store and the second magical store is what differentiates *on-premises* environments and cloud environments.

The first toy store is like having to set up infrastructure in your own premises. Once you purchase a piece of hardware, you are committed to it and will have to use it until you decommission it or sell it at a fraction of what you paid for it.

The second toy store is analogous to a cloud environment. If you make a mistake and provision a resource that's too small or too big for your needs, you can transfer your data to a new instance, shut down the old instance, and importantly, stop paying for that instance.

More formally defined, elasticity is the ability of a computing environment to adapt to changes in workload by automatically provisioning or shutting down computing resources to match the capacity needed by the current workload.

In AWS as well as with the main cloud providers, resources can be shut down without having to completely terminate them, and the billing for resources will stop if the resources are shut down.

This distinction cannot be emphasized enough. Computing costs in a cloud environment on a per-unit basis may even be higher when comparing them with on-premises prices, but the ability to shut resources down and stop getting charged for them makes cloud architectures cheaper in the long run, often in a quite significant way. The only time when absolute on-premises costs may be lower than cloud costs is if workloads are extremely predictable and consistent. Let's look at exactly what this means by reviewing a few examples.

Web store front

A popular use case for cloud services is to use it to run an **online store front**. Website traffic in this scenario will be highly variable depending on the day of the week, whether it's a holiday, the time of day, and other factors.

This kind of scenario is ideally suited for a cloud deployment. In this case, we can set up resource load balancers that automatically start and shut down compute resources as needed. Additionally, we can set up policies that allow database storage to grow as needed.

Apache Spark and Hadoop workloads

The popularity of Apache Spark and Hadoop continues to increase. Many Spark clusters don't necessarily need to run consistently. They perform heavy batch computing for a period and then can be idle until the next batch of input data comes in. A specific example would be a cluster that runs every night for 3 or 4 hours and only during the working week.

In this instance, the shutdown of resources may be best managed on a schedule rather than by using demand thresholds. Or, we could set up triggers that automatically shut down resources once the batch jobs are completed.

Online storage

Another common use case in technology is file and object storage. Some storage services may grow organically and consistently. The traffic patterns can also be also consistent.

This may be one example where using an on-premises architecture may make sense economically. In this case, the usage pattern is consistent and predictable.

Elasticity is by no means the only reason that the cloud is growing in leaps and bounds. Having the ability to easily enable world-class security for even the simplest applications is another reason why the cloud is becoming pervasive. Let's understand this at a deeper level.

Security

The perception of *on-premises* environments being more secure than cloud environments was a common reason that companies big and small would not migrate to the cloud. More and more enterprises are now realizing that it is extremely hard and expensive to replicate the security features that are provided by cloud providers such as AWS. Let's look at a few of the measures that AWS takes to ensure the security of their systems.

Physical security

You probably have a better chance of getting into the Pentagon without a badge than getting into an Amazon data center.

AWS data centers are continuously upgraded with the latest surveillance technology. Amazon has had decades to perfect the design, construction, and operation of their data centers.

AWS has been providing cloud services for over 15 years and they literally have an army of technologists, solution architects, and some of the brightest minds in the business. They are leveraging this experience and expertise to create *state-of-the-art* data centers. These centers are in nondescript facilities. You could drive by one and never know what it is. If you do find out where one is, it will be extremely difficult to get in. Perimeter access is heavily guarded. Visitor access is strictly limited, and they always must be accompanied by an Amazon employee.

Every corner of the facility is monitored by video surveillance, motion detectors, intrusion detection systems, and other electronic equipment.

Amazon employees with access to the building must authenticate themselves four times to step on the data center floor.

Only Amazon employees and contractors that have a legitimate right to be in a data center can enter. Any other employee is restricted. Whenever an employee does not have a business need to enter a data center, their access is immediately revoked, even if they are only moved to another Amazon department and stay with the company.

Lastly, audits are routinely performed and part of the normal business process.

Encryption

AWS makes it extremely simple to encrypt data at rest and data in transit. It also offers a variety of options for encryption. For example, for encryption at rest, data can be encrypted on the server side, or it can be encrypted on the client side. Additionally, the encryption keys can be managed by AWS, or you can use keys that are managed by you.

Compliance standards supported by AWS

AWS has robust controls in place to allow users to maintain security and data protection. We'll be talking more about how AWS shares security responsibilities with their customers, but the same is true with how AWS supports compliance. AWS provides many attributes and features that enable compliance with many standards established big different countries and standards organizations. By providing these features, AWS simplifies compliance audits. AWS enables the implementation of security best practices and many security standards, such as these:

- ITAR
- SOC 1/SSAE 16/ISAE 3402 (formerly SAS 70)
- SOC 2
- SOC 3
- FISMA, DIACAP, and FedRAMP
- PCI DSS Level 1
- DOD CSM Levels 1-5
- ISO 9001 / ISO 27001 / ISO 27017 / ISO 27018
- MTCS Level 3
- FIPS 140-2
- HITRUST

In addition, AWS provides enables the implementation of solutions that can meet many industry-specific standards, such as these:

- **Criminal Justice Information Services (CJIS)**
- **Family Educational Rights and Privacy Act (FERPA)**
- **Cloud Security Alliance (CSA)**
- **Motion Picture Association of America (MPAA)**
- **Health Insurance Portability and Accountability Act (HIPAA)**

Another important thing that can explain the meteoric rise of the cloud is how you can stand up high-availability applications without having to pay for the additional infrastructure needed to provide these applications. Architectures can be crafted in such a way that additional resources are started when other resources fail. This ensures that we only bring additional resources when they are necessary, keeping costs down. Let's analyze this important property of the cloud in a deeper fashion.

Availability

When we deploy infrastructure in an on-premises environment, we have two choices. We can purchase just enough hardware to service the current workload, or we can make sure that there is enough excess capacity to account for any failures that may occur. This extra capacity and the elimination of single points of failure is not as simple as it may first seem. There are many places where single points of failure may exist and need to be eliminated:

- Compute instances can go down, so we need to have a few on standby.
- Databases can get corrupted.
- Network connections can be broken.
- Data centers can flood or burn down.

This last one may seem like a hypothetical example but there was a fire reported in the suburb of Tama in Tokyo, Japan, that apparently was at an AWS data center under construction. Here is a clip of the incident:

```
https://www.datacenterdynamics.com/en/news/aws-building-site-
burns-in-fatal-tokyo-fire-reports-say/
```

Using the cloud simplifies the *"single point of failure"* problem. We already determined that provisioning software in an on-premises data center can be a long and arduous process. In a cloud environment, spinning up new resources can take just a few minutes. So, we can configure minimal environments knowing that additional resources are a click away.

AWS data centers are built in different regions across the world. All data centers are *"always on"* and delivering services to customers. AWS does not have *"cold"* data centers. Their systems are extremely sophisticated and automatically route traffic to other resources if a failure occurs. Core services are always installed in an N+1 configuration. In the case of a complete data center failure, there should be the capacity to handle traffic using the remaining available data centers without disruption.

AWS enables customers to deploy instances and persist data in more than one geographic region and across various data centers within a region.

Data centers are deployed in fully independent zones. Each data center is constructed with enough separation between them such that the likelihood of a natural disaster affecting two of them at the same time is very low. Additionally, data centers are not built in flood zones.

To increase resilience, data centers have discrete **Uninterruptable Power Supplies (UPSes)** and onsite backup generators. They are also connected to multiple electric grids from multiple independent utility providers. Data centers are connected redundantly to multiple tier-1 transit providers. Doing all this minimizes single points of failure.

Faster hardware cycles

When hardware is provisioned on-premises, from the instant that it is purchased it starts becoming obsolete. Hardware prices have been on an exponential downtrend since the first computer was invented, so the server you bought a few months ago may now be cheaper, or a new version of the server may be out that's faster and still cost the same. However, waiting until hardware improves or becomes cheaper is not an option. At some point, a decision needs to be made and a purchase needs to be made.

Using a cloud provider instead eliminates all these problems. For example, whenever AWS offers new and more powerful processor types, using them is as simple as stopping an instance, change the processor type, and starting the instance again. In many cases, AWS may keep the price the same even when better and faster processors and technology becomes available.

System administration staff

An on-premises implementation may require a full-time system administration staff and a process to ensure that the team remains fully staffed. By using cloud services, many of these tasks can be handled by the cloud providers, allowing you to focus on core application maintenance and functionality and not have to worry about infrastructure upgrades, patches, and maintenance.

By offloading this task to the cloud provider, costs can come down because instead of having a dedicated staff, the administrative duties can be shared with other cloud customers.

The five pillars of a well-architected framework

That all leads us nicely into this section. The reason the cloud in general and AWS in particular are so popular is that they simplify the development of well-architected frameworks. If there is one *must-read* white paper from AWS, it is the paper titled *AWS Well-Architected Framework*, which spells out the five pillars of a well-architected framework. The full paper can be found here:

```
https://d1.awsstatic.com/whitepapers/architecture/AWS_Well-
Architected_Framework.pdf
```

In this section, we will summarize the main points about those five pillars.

First pillar – security

In both on-premises and cloud architectures, security should always be a high priority. All aspects of security should be considered, including data encryption and protection, access management, infrastructure security, monitoring, and breach detection and inspection.

To enable system security and to guard against nefarious actors and vulnerabilities, AWS recommends these architectural principles:

- Always enable traceability.
- Apply security at all levels.
- Implement the principle of least privilege.
- Secure the system at all levels: application, data, operating system, and hardware.
- Automate security best practices.

Almost as important as security is the next pillar – reliability.

Second pillar – reliability

Another characteristic of a well-architected framework is the minimization or elimination of single points of failure. Ideally, every component should have a backup, and the backup should be able to come online as quickly as possible and in an automated manner, without the need for human intervention. Another applicable concept to support reliability is the idea of self-healing systems. An example of this is how Amazon S3 handles data replication. At any given time, there are at least six copies of any object stored in Amazon S3. If, for some reason, one of the resources storing one of these copies fails, AWS will automatically recover from this failure, mark that resource as unavailable, and create another copy of the object using a healthy resource to keep the number of copies at six. When using AWS services that are not managed by AWS and are instead managed by you, make sure that you are following a similar pattern to avoid data loss and service interruption.

The well-architected framework paper recommends these design principles to enhance reliability:

- Continuously test backup and recovery processes.

- Design systems so that they can automatically recover from a single component failure.

- Leverage horizontal scalability whenever possible to enhance overall system availability.

- Use automation to provision and shutdown resources depending on traffic and usage to minimize resource bottlenecks.

- Manage change with automation.

Whenever possible, changes to the infrastructure should occur in an automated fashion.

Third pillar – performance efficiency

In some respects, over-provisioning resources is just as bad as not having enough capacity to handle your workloads. Launching an instance that is constantly idle or almost idle is a sign of bad design. Resources should not be at full capacity, but they should be efficiently utilized. AWS provides a variety of features and services to assist in the creation of architectures with high efficiency. However, we still have a responsibility to ensure that the architectures we design are suitable and correctly sized for our applications.

When it comes to performance efficiency, the recommended design best practices are as follows:

- Democratize advanced technologies.
- Take advantage of AWS's global infrastructure to deploy your application globally with minimal cost and to provide low latency.
- Leverage serverless architectures wherever possible.
- Deploy multiple configurations to see which one delivers better performance.

Efficiency is closely related to the next pillar – cost optimization.

Fourth pillar – cost optimization

This pillar is related to the third pillar. If your architecture is efficient and can accurately handle varying application loads and adjust as traffic changes, it will follow that your costs will be minimized if your architecture can downshift when traffic slows down.

Additionally, your architecture should be able to identify when resources are not being used at all and allow you to stop them or, even better, stop these unused compute resources for you. In this department, AWS also provides you with the ability to turn on monitoring tools that will automatically shut down resources if they are not being utilized. We strongly encourage you to adopt a mechanism to stop these resources once they are identified as idle. This is especially useful in development and test environments.

To enhance cost optimization, these principles are suggested:

- Use a consumption model.
- Leverage economies of scale whenever possible.
- Reduce expenses by limiting the use of company-owned data centers.
- Constantly analyze and account for infrastructure expenses.

Whenever possible, use AWS-managed services instead of services that you need to manage yourself. This should lower your administration expenses.

Fifth pillar – operational excellence

The **operational excellence** of a workload should be measured across these dimensions:

- Agility

- Reliability

- Performance

The ideal way to optimize these metrics is to standardize and automate the management of these workloads. To achieve operational excellence, AWS recommends these principles:

- Provision infrastructure through code (for example, via CloudFormation).

- Align operations and applications with business requirements and objectives.

- Change your systems by making incremental and regular changes.

- Constantly test both normal and abnormal scenarios.

- Record lessons learned from operational events and failures.

- Write down and keep standard operations procedures manual up to date.

AWS users need to constantly evaluate their systems to ensure that they are following the recommended principles of the *AWS Well-Architected Framework* paper and that they comply with and follow architecture best practices.

Building credibility and getting certified

It is hard to argue that the cloud is not an important technology shift. We have established that AWS is the clear market and thought leader in the cloud space.

Comparing the cloud to an earthquake, we could say that it started slowly as a small rumbling that started getting louder and louder, and we are now at a point where the walls are shaking and it's only getting stronger.

In the *The market share, influence, and adoption of AWS* section, we introduced the concept of FOMO. There, we mentioned that enterprises are now eager to adopt cloud technologies because they do not want to fall behind their competition and become obsolete.

Hopefully, by now you are excited to learn more about AWS and other cloud providers, or at the very least, you're getting a little nervous and catching a little FOMO yourself.

We will devote the rest of this chapter to showing you the path of least resistance for how to become an AWS guru and someone that can bill themselves as an AWS expert.

As with other technologies, it is hard to become an expert without hands-on experience, and it's hard to get hands-on experience if you can't demonstrate that you're an expert. The best method, in my opinion, that you use to crack this chicken-and-egg problem is to get certified.

Fortunately, AWS offers a wide array of certifications that will demonstrate to your potential clients and employers your deep AWS knowledge and expertise.

As AWS creates more and more services, they continue to offer new certifications (and render some of them obsolete) aligned with these new services.

Let's review the certifications available as of August 2020.

AWS Certified Cloud Practitioner – Foundational

This is the most basic certification offered by AWS. It is meant to demonstrate a broad-strokes understanding of the core services and foundational knowledge of AWS. It is also a good certification for non-technical people that need to be able to communicate using the AWS lingo but are not necessarily going to be configuring or developing in AWS.

This certification is ideal to demonstrate a basic understanding of AWS technologies for people such as salespeople, business analysts, marketing associates, executives, and project managers.

AWS Certified Solutions Architect – Associate

> **Important note**
> There is a new exam version (SAA-C02) as of March 22, 2020

This is the most popular certification offered by AWS. Many technically minded developers and administrators skip taking the Cloud Practitioner certification and start by taking this certification instead. If you are looking to demonstrate technical expertise in AWS, obtaining this certification is a good start and the bare minimum to demonstrate AWS proficiency.

AWS Certified Developer – Associate

Obtaining this certification will demonstrate your ability to design, develop, and deploy applications in AWS. Even though this is a Developer certification, do not expect to see any code in any of the questions during the exam. However, having knowledge of at least one programming language supported by AWS will help you to achieve this certification. Expect to see many of the same concepts and similar questions to what you would see in the Solutions Architect certification.

AWS Certified SysOps Administrator – Associate

Obtaining this certification will demonstrate to potential employers and clients that you have experience in deploying, configuring, scaling up, managing, and migrating applications using AWS services. You should expect the difficulty level of this certification to be a little bit higher than the other two Associate-level certifications, but also expect quite a bit of overlap in the type of questions that will be asked with this certification and the other two Associate-level certifications.

AWS Certified Solutions Architect – Professional

This certification together with the DevOps Engineer – Professional certification is at least two or three times harder than the Associate-level certification. Getting this certification will demonstrate to employers that you have a deep and thorough understanding of AWS services, best practices, and optimal architectures based on the particular business requirements for a given project. Obtaining this certification shows to potential employers that you are an expert in the design and creation of distributed systems and applications on the AWS platform. It used to be that having at least one of the Associate-level certifications was a prerequisite in order to sit for the professional-level certifications, but AWS has eliminated that requirement.

AWS Certified DevOps Engineer – Professional

This advanced AWS certification validates knowledge on how to provision, manage, scale, and secure AWS resources and services. Obtaining this certification will demonstrate to potential employers that you can run their DevOps operations and that you can proficiently develop solutions and applications in AWS.

AWS Certified Advanced Networking – Specialty

This AWS specialty certification demonstrates that you possess the skills to design and deploy AWS services as part of a comprehensive network architecture and that you know how to scale using best practices. Together with the Security – Specialty certification, this is one of the hardest certifications to obtain.

AWS Certified Security – Specialty

Possessing the AWS Certified Security – Specialty certification demonstrates to potential employers that you are well versed in the ins and outs of AWS security. It shows that you know security best practices for encryption at rest, encryption in transit, user authentication and authorization, penetration testing, and generally being able to deploy AWS services and applications in a secure manner that aligns with your business requirements.

AWS Certified Machine Learning – Specialty

This is a good certification to have in your pocket if you are a data scientist or a data analyst. It shows to potential employers that you are familiar with many of the core machine learning concepts, as well as the AWS services that can be used to deliver machine learning and artificial intelligence projects, such as these:

- Amazon SageMaker
- Amazon Rekognition
- Amazon Comprehend
- Amazon Translate
- Amazon Lex
- Amazon Kinesis
- Amazon DynamoDB

AWS Certified Alexa Skill Builder – Specialty

This is a focused certification. It tests for a small subset of services that are used to deliver Alexa Skills.

AWS Certified Database – Specialty

Having this certification under your belt demonstrates to potential employers your mastery of the persistence services in AWS and your deep knowledge of the best practices needed to manage them.

> **Important note**
> This is a brand new certification as of April 6, 2020.

Some of the services tested are these:

- Amazon RDS
- Amazon Neptune
- Amazon DynamoDB
- Amazon Kinesis
- Amazon DocumentDB

AWS Certified Data Analytics – Specialty

Completing this certification demonstrates to employers that you have a good understanding of the concepts needed to perform data analysis on petabyte-scale datasets.

> **Important note**
> This has a new certification name and exam version as of April 13, 2020 (formerly AWS Certified Big Data – Specialty).

This certification shows your ability to design, implement, and deploy analytics solutions that can deliver insights by enabling the visualization of data and implementing the appropriate security measures. Some of the services covered are listed here:

- Amazon QuickSight
- Amazon Kinesis
- Amazon DynamoDB

Learning tips and tricks to obtain AWS certifications

Now that we have learned about the various certifications offered by AWS, let's learn about some of the strategies we can use to get these certifications with the least amount of work possible and what we can expect as we prepare for these certifications.

Focus on one cloud provider

Some enterprises are trying to adopt a cloud-agnostic or multi-cloud strategy. The idea behind this strategy is to not have a dependency on only one cloud provider. In theory, this seems like a good idea, and some companies such as Databricks, Snowflake, and Cloudera offer their wares so that they can run using the most popular cloud providers.

However, this agnosticism comes with some difficult choices. One way to implement this strategy is to choose the least common denominator, for example, only using compute instances so that workloads can be deployed on various cloud platforms. Implementing this approach means that you cannot use the more advanced services offered by cloud providers. For example, using AWS Glue in a cloud-agnostic fashion is quite difficult if not impossible.

Another way that a multi-cloud strategy can be implemented is by using the more advanced services, but this means that your staff will have to know how to use these services for all the cloud providers you decide to use. To use the common refrain, you will end up being a *jack of all trades and a master of none.*

Similarly, it is difficult to be a cloud expert across vendors at an individual level. It is recommended to pick one cloud provider and try to become an expert on that one stack. AWS, Azure, and GCP, to name the most popular options, offer an immense amount of services that continuously change and get enhanced, and they keep adding more services. Keeping up with one of these providers is not an easy task. Keeping up with all three, in my opinion, is close to impossible.

Pick one and dominate it.

Focus on the Associate-level certifications

As we mentioned before, there's quite a bit of overlap between the Associate-level certifications. In addition, the jump in difficulty between the Associate-level certifications and the Professional-level ones is quite steep.

I highly recommend sitting down for at least two, if not all three, of the Associate-level certifications before attempting the Professional-level certifications. Not only will this method prepare you for the Professional certifications, but having multiple Associate certifications will make you stand out against others that only have one Associate-level certification.

Get experience wherever you can

AWS recommends having 1 year of experience before taking the associate-level certifications and 2 years of experience before you sit for the professional-level certifications. This may seem like a *catch-22* situation. How can you get experience if you are not certified?

There are a couple of loopholes in this recommendation. First, it's a recommendation and not a mandatory requirement. Second, they mention that experience is required, but not necessarily work experience. This means that you can get experience as you are training and studying for the exam.

I can tell you from personal experience that work experience is not required. I personally passed the two professional certifications before I engaged in my first AWS project.

Let's spend some time now addressing some of the questions that frequently come up while preparing to take these certifications.

Some frequently asked questions about the AWS certifications

I have had the opportunity to take and pass 9 of the 12 certifications offered by AWS. In addition, as part of my job, I have had the good fortune of being able to help hundreds of people to get certified. The next section will have a list of frequently asked questions that you will not find in the AWS FAQ section.

What is the best way to get certified?

Before we get to the best way to get certified, let's look at the worst way. Amazon offers extremely comprehensive documentation. You can find this documentation here:

```
https://docs.aws.amazon.com/
```

This a great place to help you troubleshoot issues you may encounter when you are directly working with AWS services or perhaps to correctly size the services that you are going to be using. It is not, however, a good place to study for the exams. It will get overwhelming quickly and much of the material you will learn about will not be covered in the exams.

The better way to get certified is to use the training materials that AWS specifically provides for certification, starting with the roadmaps of what will be covered in each individual certification. These roadmaps are a good first step to understanding the scope of each individual exam.

You can begin to learn about all these roadmaps, or learning paths, as AWS likes to call them, here: `https://aws.amazon.com/training/learning-paths/`.

In these learning paths, you will find a combination of free online courses as well as paid intensive training sessions. While the paid classes may be helpful, in my opinion, they are not mandatory for you to pass the exam.

Before you look at the learning paths, the first place to go to find out the scope of each certification is the study guides available for each certification. In these study guides, you will learn at a high level what will and what won't be covered for each individual exam.

For example, the study guide for the AWS Cloud Practitioner Certification can be found here:

```
https://d1.awsstatic.com/training-and-certification/docs-
cloud-practitioner/AWS-Certified-Cloud-Practitioner_Exam-
Guide.pdf
```

Now, while the training provided by AWS may be sufficient to pass the exams and I know plenty of folks that have passed the certifications using only those resources, there are plenty of third-party companies that specialize in training people with a special focus on the certifications. The choices are almost endless, but there are a couple of companies that I can recommend and have a great reputation in this space.

Acloud.guru

Acloud.guru has been around since 2015, which is a long time in cloud years. Acloud.guru has courses for most of the AWS certifications. In addition, they also offer courses for Azure and GCP certifications. Finally, they have a few other courses unrelated to certifications that are also quite good.

They constantly update and refresh their content, which is a good thing because AWS is also constantly changing their certifications to align with new services and features.

The company was started in Melbourne, Australia, by Sam and Ryan Kroonenburg, two Australian brothers. Initially, Ryan was the instructor for all the courses, but they now have many other experts on their staff to help with the course load.

They used to charge by the course, but a few years back they changed their model to a monthly subscription, and signing up for it gives you access to the whole site.

The training can be accessed here: `https://acloud.guru/`.

Acloud.guru is the site that I have used the most to prepare for my certifications. This is how I recommend tackling the training:

1. Unless you have previous experience with the covered topics, watch all the training videos at least once. If it's a topic you feel comfortable with, you can play the videos at a higher speed, and then you will be able to watch the full video faster.

2. For video lessons that you find difficult, watch them again. You don't have to watch all the videos again – only the ones that you found difficult.

3. Make sure to take any end-of-section quizzes.

4. Once you are done watching the videos, the next step is to attempt some practice exams. One of my favorite features of Acloud.guru is the exam simulator. Keep on taking practice exams until you feel confident and you are consistently correctly answering a high percentage of the questions (anywhere between 80 and 85%, depending on the certification).

The questions provided in the exam simulator will not be the same as the ones from the exam, but they will be of a similar difficulty level and they will all be in the same domains and often about similar concepts and topics.

By using the exam simulator, you will achieve a couple of things. First, you will be able to gauge your progress and determine whether you are ready for the exam. My suggestion is to keep on taking the exam simulator tests until you are consistently scoring at least 85% and above. Most of the real certifications require you to answer 75% of the questions correctly, so consistently scoring a little higher than that should ensure that you pass the exam.

Some of the exams, such as the Security Specialty exam, require a higher percentage of correct answers, so you should adjust accordingly.

Using the exam simulator will also enable you to figure out which domains you are weak on. After taking a whole exam in the simulator, you will get a list detailing exactly which questions you got right and which questions were wrong, and they will all be classified by domain.

So, if you get a low score on a certain domain, you know that's the domain that you need to focus on when you go back and review the videos again.

Lastly, you will be able to learn new concepts by simply taking the tests in the exam simulator. Let's now learn about another popular site that I highly recommend for your quest toward certification.

Linux Academy

Linux Academy was created even earlier than Acloud.guru. It was founded in 2012. They are currently headquartered in Texas and they also frequently refresh their courses and content to accommodate the continuously changing cloud landscape. They also offer courses for the Azure and GCP certifications. True to their name and their roots, they also offer courses for Linux.

They claim to get over 50,000 reviews a month from their students with a user satisfaction rating of over 95%.

Acloud.guru bought them in 2019, but they still provide different content and training courses. The content often does not overlap, so having access to both sites will improve your chances of passing the certification exams.

I don't necessarily recommend signing up for multiple training sites for the lower-level certifications such as Cloud Practitioner and the associate-level certifications. However, it may not be a bad idea to do it for the harder exams. The more difficult exams are for the professional-level certifications and, depending on your background, some of the specialty certifications. I found the Security and Advanced Networking certifications especially difficult, but my background does not necessarily align with these topics, so that may have been part of the problem.

Whizlabs

Whizlabs was founded by CEO Krishna Srinivasan after spending 15 years in other technology ventures. In addition to AWS, it also offers certification courses for the following technologies:

- Microsoft Azure
- Google Cloud Platform

- Salesforce
- Alibaba Cloud

Whizlabs divides the charges for their training between their online courses and their practice tests.

One disadvantage of Whizlabs is that unlike the exam simulator with Acloud.guru, where they have a bank of questions and they randomly combine them, the Whizlabs exam questions are fixed and they will not be shuffled to create a different exam.

They also have a free version of their practice exams for most of the certifications, with 20 free questions.

The same strategy as mentioned before can be used with Whizlabs. You don't need to sign up for multiple vendors for the easier exams, but you can combine a couple when it comes to the harder exams.

Jon Bonso's Udemy courses

Jon Bonso on Udemy can be considered the new kid on the block but his content is excellent, and he has a passionate and growing following. For example, as of August 2020, his Solution Architect Associate practice exams has over 75,000 students with over 14,000 ratings and a satisfaction rating of 4.5 stars out of a possible 5 stars.

The pricing model used is also similar to Whizlabs. The practice exams are sold separately from the online courses.

As popular as his courses are, it is worth noting that Jon Bonso is a one-man band and does not offer courses for all the available AWS certifications, but he does focus exclusively on AWS technologies.

How long will it take to get certified?

A question that I am frequently asked is about how many months you should study before sitting down for the exam. I always answer it using hours instead of months.

As you can imagine, you will be able to take the exam a lot sooner if you study 2 hours every day instead of only studying 1 hour a week. If you decide to take some AWS-sponsored intensive full-day or multi-day training, that may go a long way toward shortening the cycle.

I had the good fortune of having the opportunity to take some AWS training. To be honest, even though the teachers were knowledgeable and were great instructors, I found that taking such courses was a little like drinking out of a firehouse. I much prefer the online AWS and third-party courses, where I could watch the videos and take the practice exams whenever it was convenient.

In fact, sometimes, instead of watching the videos, I would listen to them in my car or while on the train going into the city. Even though watching them is much more beneficial, I felt like I was still able to embed key concepts while listening to them, and that time would have been dead time anyway.

You don't want to space the time between study sessions too much. If you do that, you may find yourself in a situation where you start forgetting what you have learned.

The number of hours it will take you will also depend on your previous experience. If you are working with AWS for your day job, that will shorten the number of hours needed to complete your studies.

The following subsections will give you an idea of the amount of time you should spend preparing for each exam.

Cloud Practitioner certification

Be prepared to spend anywhere from 15 to 25 hours preparing to successfully complete this certification.

Associate-level certifications

If you don't have previous AWS experience, plan to spend between 70 and 100 hours preparing. Also keep in mind that once you pass one of the associate certifications, there is considerable overlap between the certifications, and it will not take another 70 to 100 hours to obtain the second and third certifications. As mentioned previously in this chapter, it is highly recommended to take the two other associate-level certifications soon after you pass the first one.

Expect to spend another 20 to 40 hours studying for the two remaining certifications if you don't wait too long to take them after you pass the first one.

Professional-level certifications

There is quite a leap between the associate-level certifications and the professional-level certifications. The domain coverage will be similar, you will need to know how to use the AWS services covered in much more depth, and the questions will certainly be harder.

Assuming you took at least one of the associate-level certifications, expect to spend another 70 to 100 hours watching videos, reading, and taking practice tests to pass this exam.

AWS removed the requirement of having to take the associate-level certifications before being able to sit for the professional-level certifications, but it is still probably a good idea to take at least some of the associate exams before taking the professional-level exams.

As is the case with the associate-level exams, once you pass one of the professional-level exams, it should take much less study time to pass the other Professional exam as long as you don't wait too long to take the second exam and forget everything.

To give you an example, I was able to pass both Professional exams a week apart from each other. I spent the week taking practice exams and that was enough, but your mileage may vary.

Specialty certifications

I am lumping all the Specialty certifications under one subheading, but there is great variability in the level of difficulty between all the Specialty certifications. If you have a background in networking, you are bound to be more comfortable with the Advanced Networking certification than with the Data Science certification.

When it comes to these certifications, unless you are collecting all certifications, you may be better off focusing on your area of expertise. For example, if you are a data scientist, the Machine Learning Specialty certification and the Alexa Skills Builder certification may be your best bet.

In my personal experience, the Security certification was the most difficult one. Something that didn't help is that AWS does set a higher bar for this certification than with the other certifications.

Depending on your experience, expect to spend about these amounts of time:

- Security Specialty – 40 to 70 hours
- Alexa Skill Builder Specialty – 20 to 40 hours
- Machine Learning Specialty – 40 to 70 hours
- Data Analytics Specialty (previously Big Data Specialty) – 30 to 60 hours
- Database Specialty – 30 to 60 hours
- Advanced Networking Specialty – 40 to 70 hours

What are some last-minute tips for the days of the exam?

I am a runner. I mention that not to boast but because I found a lot of similarities between preparing for races and preparing for the AWS exams. A decent half marathon time is about 90 minutes, which is the time you get to take the Associate-level exams, and a good marathon time is about 3 hours, which is how long you get to take the Professional-level exams.

Keeping focus for that amount of time is not easy. For that reason, you should be well rested when you take the exam. It is highly recommended to take the exam on a day when you don't have too many other responsibilities; I would not take it after working a full day. You will be too burnt out.

Make sure you have a light meal before the exam – enough so that you are not hungry during the test and feel energetic, but not so much that you actually feel sleepy from digesting all that food.

Just as you wouldn't want to get out of the gate too fast or too slow in a race, make sure to pace yourself during the exam. The first time I took a Professional exam, I had almost an hour left when I completed the last question, but when I went back to review the questions, my brain was completely fried and I could not concentrate and review my answers properly, as I had rushed through the exam to begin with. Needless to say, I did not pass. The second time I took it, I had a lot less time left but I was much more careful and thoughtful with my answers, so I didn't need as much time to review and I was able to pass.

You also don't want to be beholden to the clock, checking it constantly. The clock will always appear in the top-right part of the exam, but you want to avoid looking at it most of the time. I recommend writing down on the three sheets you will receive where you should be after every 20 questions and checking the clock against these numbers only when you have answered a set of 20 questions. This way, you will be able to adjust if you are going too fast or too slow but you will not spend an inordinate amount of time watching the clock.

Let's now summarize what we have learned in this chapter.

Summary

In this chapter, we were able to piece together many of the technologies, best practices, and AWS services we covered in the book. We weaved it all together into a generic architecture that you should be able to leverage and use for your own projects.

As fully featured as AWS has become, it is all but certain that AWS will continue to provide more and more services to help enterprises, large and small, to simplify the information technology infrastructure.

You can rest assured that Amazon and its AWS division are hard at work creating new services and improving the existing services by making them better, faster, easier, more flexible, and more powerful, as well as adding more features.

As of 2020, AWS offers a total of 212 services. That's a big jump from the two services it offered in 2004. The progress that AWS has made in the last 16 years has been nothing short of monumental. I personally cannot wait to see what the next 16 years will bring for AWS and what can kind of solutions we will be able to deliver with their new offerings.

We also covered some reasons that the cloud in general and AWS in particular are so popular. As we learned, one of the main reasons for the cloud's popularity is the concept of elasticity, which we explored in detail.

After reviewing the cloud's popularity, we have hopefully convinced you to hop aboard the cloud train. Assuming you want to get on the ride, we covered the easiest way to break into the business. We learned that one of the easiest ways to build credibility is to get certified. We learned that AWS offers 12 certifications. We learned that the most basic one is AWS Cloud Practitioner and that the most advanced certifications are the Professional-level certifications. In addition, we learned that, as of 2020, there are six Specialty certifications for a variety of different domains. We also covered some of the best and worst ways to obtain these certifications.

Finally, we hope you became curious enough about potentially getting at least some of the certifications that AWS offers. I hope you are as excited as I am about the possibilities that AWS can bring.

In the next chapter, we will cover in broad strokes how the AWS infrastructure is organized, as well as understanding how you can use AWS and cloud technologies to lead a digital transformation.

2
Leveraging the Cloud for Digital Transformation

AWS has come a long way since Amazon started in 2006, when it offered just two basic services. In this chapter, we will highlight the scale of Amazon's infrastructure. We will also learn how today's businesses are using AWS to completely transform their technology infrastructure, operations, and business practices.

Enterprises today have become exponentially more agile by leveraging the power of the cloud. In this chapter, we will first talk about Regions, **Availability Zones (AZs)**, and **Local Zones (LZs)**. We will then learn about the AWS Global Infrastructure and learn how to implement a digital transformation program.

In this chapter, we will cover the following topics:

- Learning about the AWS Global Infrastructure
- Implementing a digital transformation program

Without further ado, let's get down to business.

Learning about the AWS Global Infrastructure

The infrastructure offered by AWS is highly secure and reliable. It offers over 175 services. Most of them are available in all AWS Regions around the world. Regardless of the type of technology application you are planning to build and deploy, AWS is sure to provide a service that will facilitate its deployment.

AWS has millions of customers and tens of thousands of consulting and technology partners around the world. Businesses large and small across all industries rely on AWS to handle their workloads. To give you an idea of the breadth of the scale that AWS provides, here are some statistics. AWS provides the following:

- 24 launched Regions

- 3 announced Regions

- 77 AZs

- Services in 245 countries

- 97 Direct Connect locations

- 205 edge locations

- 216 Points of Presence

- 11 Regional Edge Caches

> **Important note**
> These numbers are accurate as of the writing of this book. By the time you are reading this, it would not be surprising for the numbers to have changed. All of the major cloud providers are in an arms race to provide more services, more features, and more data centers.

Yet another confirmation of the dominance of AWS are the results for the last 10 years based on the prestigious Gartner report. Gartner publishes reports on many technology verticals, including cloud technologies. These reports often include a Magic Quadrant chart where leaders are identified in these technology verticals. For the last 9 years, AWS has been chosen as a leader in *Gartner's Magic Quadrant for Cloud Infrastructure*, obtaining a higher score than any other cloud provider.

The full report can be accessed here: `https://pages.awscloud.com/Gartner-Magic-Quadrant-for-Infrastructure-as-a-Service-Worldwide.html`.

Now that we have covered how the AWS infrastructure is organized at a high level, it is time to move on to another important topic. We have all these great services and toys in all these places around the world. How do we leverage them and stitch them together to add value to our business, reduce costs, and increase operational efficiencies? Your boss is not going to care that you can spin up 1,000 servers in 5 minutes. What they are going to want to know is: How do we use these 1,000 servers to better assist our customers and increase our revenue, reduce our costs, and fatten up our bottom line?

Regions, Availability Zones, and Local Zones

How can Amazon provide such reliable service across the globe? How can they offer reliability and durability guarantees for some of their services? The answer reveals why they are the cloud leaders and why it's difficult to replicate what they offer. Amazon has billions of dollars of infrastructure deployed across the world. These locations are organized into different Regions and zones. More formally, Amazon calls them the following:

- AWS Regions
- AZs
- LZs

AWS Regions exist in separate geographic areas. Each AWS Region comprises several independent and isolated data centers that provide a full array of AWS services dubbed **AZs**.

LZs can be thought of as mini-AZs that provide core services that are latency sensitive.

You can leverage LZs to ensure that resources are in close geographic proximity to your users.

Amazon is continuously enhancing its data centers to provide the latest technology. Amazon's data centers have a high degree of redundancy. Amazon uses highly reliable hardware, but hardware is not foolproof. Occasionally, a failure can happen that interferes with the availability of resources in each data center. If all instances are hosted in only one data center, the possibility exists that a failure can occur with the whole data center and then none of your resources will be available. The following diagram illustrates how Regions, AZs, and LZs are organized:

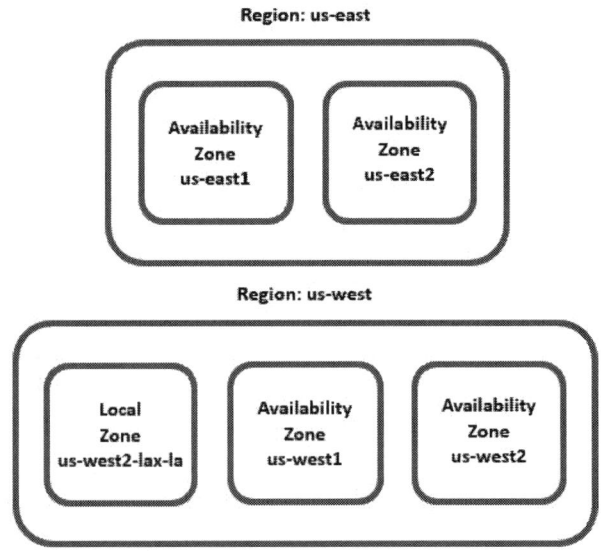

Figure 2.1 – Example of Regions, AZs, and LZs

Notice that Regions can contain both **AZs** as well as **LZs**. It is important to highlight that AWS Regions are independent of each other. For example, all Amazon RDS activity and commands such as the creation of a database instance or listing which databases are available can only run in one Region at a time. By default, there will always be a designated default Region. This default can be changed in one of two ways:

- It can be modified via the console by changing the EC2_REGION environment variable.

- By changing the region parameter using the **AWS Command Line Interface (AWS CLI)**.

You can obtain more information about how to change and maintain AWS environment variables using the AWS CLI by visiting this link: https://docs.aws.amazon.com/cli/latest/userguide/cli-configure-envvars.html.

In the following subsections, we will look at AWS Regions in greater detail and see why they are important.

AWS Regions

AWS Regions are groupings of data centers in one geographic location that are specially designed to be independent and isolated from each other. This independence promotes availability and enhances fault tolerance and stability.

For most services, when you log into the AWS console, you will see the services that are available specifically for that Region. As AWS builds out their infrastructure, there may be cases here and there where a specific service is not available in a certain Region. Usually, this is a temporary situation as the service propagates across all Regions. This can happen when a service is still not **generally available** (**GA**) and still in the Beta stage.

A few select services are available globally and are not Region specific. Some examples are **Simple Storage Service** (**S3**) and **Identity Management Service** (**IAM**).

Other services allow you to create inter-Region fault tolerance and availability. For example, Amazon RDS allows the creation of read replicas in multiple Regions. To find out more about it, visit `https://aws.amazon.com/blogs/aws/cross-region-read-replicas-for-amazon-rds-for-mysql/`.

One of the advantages of using such an architecture is that resources will be closer to users and will therefore increase access speed and reduce latency.

Another obvious advantage is that you will be able to serve your clients without disruption even if a whole Region becomes unavailable, and you will be able to recover faster if something goes terribly wrong. These read replicas can be automatically converted to the primary database if the need arises.

As of August 2020, there are 24 AWS Regions and 3 announced Regions. The naming convention that is usually followed is to list the country code, followed by the geographic region, followed by a number. For example, the US East Region in Ohio is named as follows:

- **Location**: US East (Ohio)

  Name: us-east-2

Regardless of where you live in the world, if you live in a populated area there is bound to be an AWS Region within at most 500 miles or so from you. If you live in Greenland, it may be a little further away from you (however, you will still be able to connect as long as you have an internet connection).

In addition, AWS has two dedicated Regions just for the US government:

- **Location**: AWS GovCloud (US-East)

  Name: us-gov-east-1

- **Location**: AWS GovCloud (US)

  Name: us-gov-west-1

If the work that you are doing becomes huge, maybe you too can get a dedicated Region.

The full list of available Regions can be found here: `https://docs.aws.amazon.com/AWSEC2/latest/UserGuide/using-regions-availability-zones.html#concepts-available-regions`.

AWS GovCloud

In case there was any doubt about the clout of the US government, consider this. AWS provides a complete Region specifically and exclusively for US government agencies and customers that allows them to run highly sensitive applications in this environment. This environment is known as **AWS GovCloud**. It offers the same services as other Regions, but it specifically complies with requirements and regulations specific to the needs of the US government.

As AWS continues to grow, do not be surprised if it offers similar Regions to other governments around the world, depending on their importance and the demand they can generate.

Obvious candidates based on sheer size are the European Union and China. However, due to political sensitivity, it is possible that most of the workloads coming from the Chinese government will instead go to companies such as Alibaba, with their Alibaba Cloud offering. In the case of Europe, there isn't a European domiciled 800-pound gorilla in that region so it is highly probable that that business will instead go to AWS or Azure.

Availability Zones

As we discussed earlier, AZs are components of AWS Regions. An AZ is fancy lingo by AWS for a data center. AZs are state of the art. To ensure independence, AZs are always at least 60 miles away from each other. They have multiple power sources, redundant connectivity, and redundant resources. All this translates into unparalleled customer service and allowing them to deliver highly available, fault tolerant, and scalable applications.

AZs within an AWS Region are interconnected. These connections have the following properties:

- Fully redundant
- High bandwidth
- Low latency
- Scalable
- Encrypted
- Dedicated

Depending on the service you are using, if you decide to perform a multi-AZ deployment, an AZ will automatically be assigned to the service, but for some services, you may be able to designate which AZ is to be used.

Local Zones

LZs are new components in the AWS infrastructure family.

LZs place select services close to end users and allow them to create AWS applications that can deliver single-digit millisecond responses.

You can think of them as a subset of an AZ. They offer some but not all of the services an AZ provides. A VPC can be extended in any AWS Region into an LZ if a subnet is created and assigned to the LZ. Subnets in an LZ operate like any other subnets created in AWS.

AWS allows the creation of database instances in an LZ. LZs provides connections to the internet and they can use AWS Direct Connect.

The naming convention for LZs is to use the AWS Region followed by a location identifier, for example: us-west-2-lax-2a.

AWS Direct Connect

AWS Direct Connect is a low-level infrastructure service that enables AWS customers to set up a dedicated network connection between their on-premise facilities and AWS. By using AWS Direct Connect, you can bypass any public internet connection and establish a private connection linking your data centers with AWS. This solution provides higher network throughput, increases the consistency of connections, and, counterintuitively, can often reduce network costs.

However, it is important to note that by default AWS Direct Connect does not provide encryption in transit. To encrypt the data traversing AWS Direct Connect, you will need to use one of the transit encryption options available for that service. For example, you can combine AWS Direct Connect with AWS Site-to-Site VPN to deliver an IPsec-encrypted private connection while at the same time lowering network costs and increasing network bandwidth throughput.

To encrypt the traffic, you can also use an AWS technology partner such as Aviatrix Systems as an alternative solution to encrypt this network traffic.

AWS Direct Connect uses the 802.1q industry standard to create VLANs. These connections can be split up into several virtual interfaces. This enables us to leverage the same connection to reach publicly accessible services such as Amazon S3 by using an IP address space and private services such as EC2 instances running in a private **Virtual Private Cloud** (**VPC**) within AWS. Doing this will enable a clear and distinct separation between public and private environments. Virtual interfaces can dynamically be changed quickly to adapt to changing requirements.

AWS Direct Connect can reduce costs when workloads require high bandwidth. It can reduce these costs in two ways:

- It transfers data from on-premises environments to the cloud, directly reducing cost commitments to **Internet Service Providers** (**ISPs**).

- The costs of transferring the data using a dedicated connection are billed using the AWS Direct Connect data transfer rates and not the internet data transfer rates, which are normally lower.

Network latency and responses to requests can be extremely variable. Workloads that use AWS Direct Connect have a much more homogenous latency and consistent user experience.

AWS Direct Connect works with any AWS service that can be accessed over the internet, including VPCs, EC2 instances, and S3. In the next section, we will summarize what we have learned so far regarding AWS infrastructure and list the current components.

Implementing a digital transformation program

We spent some time in *Chapter 1, Understanding AWS Cloud Principles and Key Characteristics*, on how we can make the transformation as individuals to become cloud experts. In this section, we will spend some time learning how to perform the transformation from legacy on-premises technologies into the cloud.

As you can imagine, this can be a difficult exercise, especially for large enterprises that have a long history of using old technologies and have made big investments in them.

Deciding to start migrating applications and on-premises services to the cloud is not a decision that can be made lightly. A complete migration will likely take years and potentially can cost millions of dollars just on migration, transformation, and testing costs.

For this reason, important decisions need to be made along the way. Some of the most important decisions that need to be made are as follows:

- Should we perform the bare minimum amount of tasks to achieve the migration, or do we want to use this change as an opportunity to refactor, enhance, and optimize our services? Doing the bare minimum (which is basically only migrating our workloads to the cloud) will mean that any problems and deficiencies that exist in the current environment will brought over to the new environment.

- Should the migration be purely technological, or should we use this opportunity to transform our current business processes? We could take this opportunity to do a complete assessment of how we do business today and figure out how we can improve it. This will potentially create efficiencies, cut costs, and increase customer satisfaction. However, this option will inherently have a higher upfront cost and it may or may not work. If the new methods and processes that we come up with are worse than the previous ones, not only will we have spent more money to migrate to the cloud but we are now stuck with a worse solution than we had previously.

In the previous section, we got a 30,000 ft view of the infrastructure of the cloud. In *Chapter 1, Understanding Cloud Principles and Key Characteristics*, we spent some time learning why the cloud is important and why so many companies are migrating their workloads to the cloud. In this section, we will start learning the basic strategies for migration to the cloud and weigh up some of the options.

Cloud migration

As we have started to discover, there are additional tasks we can perform in addition to migrating workflows to the cloud. What tasks should be performed and when they should be done is going to be dependent on a variety of factors, such as available budget, staff technical expertise, and leadership buy-in.

It is hard to create discrete cohorts to classify these tasks since they are more of a continuum. Having said this, and without further ado, let's attempt to create a classification nonetheless. Keep in mind that this classification is not meant to be dogmatic. You may run into other ways to classify this migration. Additionally, you may be able to mix and match the approaches, depending on your needs. For example, your CRM application may be moved without changing it. But perhaps your accounting software was built in-house and now you want to use a vendor-enabled solution such as QuickBooks Online.

Let's review the most common options when migrating to the cloud and learn when to pick one over the others.

Rehost in the cloud

This method is also commonly known as *lift and shift*. By rehosting your application in the cloud, you are performing the least amount of work to move your workloads to the cloud. Applications are simply being rehosted as they are in a different environment. Services are simply migrated. Let's say, for example, that you are hosting a simple three-tier application on your on-premises environment that is using the following:

- A web server
- An app server
- A database server

Using the *lift and shift* strategy, you would simply set up three similar servers on the cloud, install the applicable software on each server, and migrate the necessary data. Therefore, this approach will have the lowest migration costs. Obviously, this simplicity comes at a cost. Any problems in the existing applications will come along during the migration. If the existing applications are obsolete and suboptimal, they will remain obsolete and suboptimal.

This strategy aligns best with an *Infrastructure as a Service* architecture, which we will learn more about in *Chapter 4, Harnessing the Power of Cloud Computing*.

Have you ever had to move from one house to another? It's a painful process, right? In broad strokes, there are two ways that you can pack for the move:

- You can just put everything in a box and move it to the new house.

- You can be judicious and sort through what you have, item by item, and decide if you are going to toss, sell, recycle, or take the item with you.

Packing everything and going is a quick way because you avoid sorting through everything, but as you well know it can be more expensive because you will be moving more things, and it is painful because you may realize later that you should have not moved some items to begin with.

The move to the cloud is not very different. It is a good idea to use *lift and shift* if you are already confident that your processes and workflows are solid and do not need to be changed. This is rarely the case.

Refactor in the cloud

Refactoring your services to run in the cloud entails not only migrating the applications as they are but also changing the underlying infrastructure architecture. However, the code of the higher-level services will not be changed. This way, you can leverage your existing code base, languages, and the frameworks you are currently using. It may be a good balance between taking advantage of some of the properties inherent to the cloud, such as elasticity and scalability, without having to make wholesale changes to your existing applications. The architecture that best aligns with this approach is known as **Platform as a Service** (**PaaS**). We will learn more about PaaS in *Chapter 4, Harnessing the Power of Cloud Computing*.

It is advisable to use this method when you are comfortable with your current set of applications, but you want take advantage of certain cloud advantages and functionality. For example, you may want to add fail-over to your databases without having to buy the software that would be needed to run this setup in a dedicated manner. If you were implementing this functionality *on-premises*, you would have to own all the infrastructure. A specific example is Oracle Data Guard, which allows you to implement this failover but not without having to install the product, and you need enough expertise to ensure that the product is configured correctly. Instead, when we are in a cloud environment, we can leverage the virtualization nature of the cloud and costs can be shared with other cloud customers.

Revise before migrating to the cloud

Another potential strategy is to modify, optimize, and enhance the existing applications and code base before migrating to the cloud in preparation for migrating to the cloud. Only then do you rehost or refactor the applications to the cloud. In the long run, this may be a good strategy and provide business continuity and business enhancement. The downside of this approach is the cost associated with changing and testing the code upfront. In addition, changing the code in the on-premises environment may not allow you to take advantage of all the features that creating the code in the cloud would offer. For example, you may want to create reports using AWS QuickSight. AWS QuickSight is a great tool for creating dashboards and reports. However, AWS QuickSight can only be used when in a cloud environment and not in your on-premises environment because QuickSight is only supported within AWS.

This method is good to use when you know that your applications are suboptimal and they need to be revised, and you take the cloud migration as an opportunity to enhance and fix your applications. Using this approach, you will only need to test your application once. The drawback is that if things go south, it may be difficult to ascertain if the problems that cropped up are because of new bugs in the code or because we migrated to the cloud.

Rebuild in the cloud

Yet another option is to completely rewrite the existing code and rearchitect the existing applications. This will enable us to use all the features of the cloud and to fully take advantage of them. This will allow you to use state-of-the-art technologies to create new services and reinvent your existing business workflows. There will be considerable work to accomplish this rewrite. In many cases, especially for established enterprises that find themselves being disrupted by new start-ups, if they don't reinvent themselves, they will soon find themselves relegated to a footnote in history. Another disadvantage of this approach is potential vendor lock-in.

This approach is even more radical than revising your application. In this case, you are making wholesale changes and starting from scratch to create your new applications and workflows. It is quite important to have subject matter experts and business experts involved in the design process because you may want to make changes even to the way that you do business and upend all your current beliefs about how things should be done.

Replace in the cloud

One final possibility, instead of rebuilding your applications, is to still get rid of them but replace them with commercially available SaaS alternatives such as Salesforce, Workday, ServiceNow, or SAP. Depending on how deep and talented your talent pool is and what their areas of expertise are, this option may or may not be more expensive than rebuilding your application. Using this option, your software costs will likely be higher, but they will be offset by lower development and maintenance costs. If you decide to rebuild, you will not have to pay for CRM and commercial software licenses, but development cycles will likely be longer, you will have a higher number of defects, and higher maintenance may apply.

The previous methods of migration implied that all development was done in house. One difference with this approach is that we are migrating from systems that were built in house to software built by professional vendors. As with the other approaches, this approach has advantages and disadvantages. One of the advantages is that the learning curve and the development life cycle will be potentially shortened. Not as much development will be needed. However, a disadvantage is that the software will more than likely require additional licenses.

Now that we have reviewed the different ways that you can migrate to the cloud, let's understand a little bit better why we might want to migrate to the cloud to begin with. We'll gain this understanding by learning about the concept of digital transformation.

Migration assessment tools

As you migrate your workloads and projects from your current environment to the cloud, you don't have to reinvent the wheel. As you can imagine, many others have already started this journey. To facilitate this process, AWS, as well as third-party vendors, offers a wide variety of tools to facilitate this migration. A few examples of services and tools that are worth exploring are as follows:

- **AWS Migration Hub**: AWS Migration Hub is a central repository that can be used to keep track of a migration project

- **AWS Application Discovery Service**: AWS Application Discovery Service automates the discovery and inventory tracking of different infrastructure resources, such as servers, and any dependencies among them.

- **AWS Migration Pattern Library**: This is a collection of migration templates and design patterns that can assist in the comparison of migration options and alternatives.

- **CloudEndure Migration**: CloudEndure Migration is a product offered by AWS that simplifies cloud migration by automating many of the steps necessary to migrate to the cloud.

- **AWS Data Migration Service**: This service can facilitate the migration of data from your on-premises databases to the cloud, for example, into Amazon RDS.

This by no means is not a comprehensive list. There are many other AWS and third-party services that can assist in your migration.

What exactly is a digital transformation?

The term "digital transformation" is harder and harder to define because it is being overloaded to the point that it has become a nebulous concept. Like many amazing technology trends, it is over-hyped and over-used. Some studies report that up to 40% of tech spending will be allotted to digital transformation, while enterprises are planning to spend over $2 trillion by 2019, according to **International Data Corporation** (**IDC**). The source of these details is the following website: `https://www.idc.com/`.

The term "digital transformation" has become something that simply means platform modernization, which can include migrating on-premises infrastructure to the cloud. You can blame CIOs, consultants, and third-party vendors for this confusion. They are all trying to convince the C-Suite that their solution can cover today's enterprise infrastructure and business requirements.

But savvy high-level executives understand that there is no magic bullet, and a digital transformation will require planning, strategizing, testing, and a great deal of effort to accomplish.

Let's try to nail it down and define it.

Digital Transformation Definition

Digital transformation involves using the cloud and other advanced technology to create new or change existing business flows. It often involves changing the company culture to adapt to this new way of doing business. The end goal of digital transformation is to enhance the customer experience and to meet ever-changing business and market demand.

A digital transformation is an opportunity to reconsider everything, including the following:

- The current structure of teams and departments
- Current business flows
- The way new functionality is developed

For digital transformation to succeed it should not be limited to one single aspect of the business, such as marketing, operations, or finance. It should eventually be all-encompassing and cover the whole gamut of how you engage with your customers. It should be an opportunity to completely transform how you interact with your potential and existing customers. It should go well beyond simply swapping one server in one location for another more powerful or cheaper one in the cloud.

In some regards, start-ups have a big advantage over their bigger, more established rivals because they don't have to unlearn and reimagine their processes. Start-ups have a clean slate that can be filled with anything in the AWS service catalog, as well as other technologies. Existing players must wipe the slate clean while keeping their existing client base and finding a way to keep the trains running while they perform their digital transformations.

Digital transformation goes well beyond changing an enterprise's technology infrastructure. For a digital transformation to be successful it must also involve rethinking processes, using your staff in new ways, and fundamentally changing the way business is done.

Disruptive technological change is usually undertaken in pursuit of new revenue sources or to increase profits by creating efficiencies. Today's customers continue to raise the bar of expectations driven by so many successful businesses that have been able to deliver on the execution of their digital transformations.

Many companies across industries that are normally not thought of as technology companies are wolves in sheep's clothing, meaning they are really technology companies under the covers even though they operate in non-technology areas. A few examples are as follows:

- **Biotech**: They use computational chemistry and machine learning to create new drugs.
- **Banking**: Countless examples of fintech companies, such as SoFi, Lending Club, Marcum, and Prosper, use technology to disrupt the current players.

- **Lodging**: Companies such as Airbnb and VRBO rely heavily on the cloud and new technologies to compete against existing entrenched competitors quite successfully.

- **Insurance**: More than ever, companies in this space are taking advantage of technology to improve underwriting and reduce costs. An example here is a company called Lemonade, which recently went public.

- **Health care**: Doctors are using technology to finally streamline their back-office operations and to digitize all their paper records. In addition, a trend that is gaining more and more traction is the concept of telemedicine, which is the ability to consult a doctor without visiting their office and, instead, conducting the appointment in a videoconference session. One of the leaders in this space is Teledoc.

In the next section, we will learn about some of the forces that push companies into embarking on digital transformation. The status quo is a powerful state. Most companies will find it difficult to move from what's already working even though they may realize that the current approach is not ideal. It normally takes significant pressure to finally bite the bullet and migrate to the cloud.

Digital transformation drivers

One of the most important reasons companies are finally beginning to migrate their workloads to the cloud and transform their business is because they realize if they don't disrupt themselves, someone else will do it for them.

They are seeing competition from start-ups that can start with a clean slate and without legacy baggage, or they also see incumbent competitors embarking on digital transformation initiatives.

Take the examples of Uber and Lyft. Both companies have upended the transportation business. Taxi companies, rental car companies, and even trucking companies have been put on notice and have realized that they must adapt or die. A big reason for Uber's and Lyft's success is that they are using the cloud to host their operations.

One famous example of a competitor that had to file for bankruptcy is Hertz. Up until 2020, Hertz had been in business for 102 years. This year it had to file for bankruptcy. It is a reorganization bankruptcy, so it may still rise from the ashes, but it demonstrates the pressure that businesses are under to transform themselves.

Another obvious example is none other than Amazon's e-commerce operations. In this case, many of its competitors failed to adapt and have been forced to declare bankruptcy. A partial list of famous retailers that had to file for bankruptcy in 2020 is as follows:

- Tailored Brands
- Lord & Taylor
- Brook Brothers
- Lucky Brand
- GNC
- J.C. Penney
- Neiman Marcus
- J. Crew
- Modell's Sporting Goods
- Pier 1

In some ways, you can think of Amazon's impressive e-commerce operations as simply just another use case of AWS.

Let's now look at some examples of companies that have been able to survive and thrive by migrating to the cloud or by creating their applications in the cloud to begin with.

Digital transformation examples

Digital transformation without tangible positive business outcomes will inevitably result in a short stay with your employer or in the marketplace. Innovation for the sake of innovation might be fine in academia and research institutions, but in the business world, innovation must always be tied to improvement in business metrics such as increased sales or higher profits.

Keep in mind that digital transformation could mean more than just moving your operations to the cloud. As we saw in the previous section, it may involve refactoring and replacing existing processes. Furthermore, it could also mean involving other technologies that were previously not being used, such as robotics, **Internet of Things** (**IoT**), and mobile apps.

As an example, how many restaurants now offer the ability to order in advance through the web or via a mobile app?

A few more concrete examples are as follows:

- TGI Fridays is using virtual assistants to enable mobile ordering.
- McDonalds is performing test trials using voice recognition technology in their drive-throughs.
- Chipotle restaurants in the US have completely changed their ordering model during the Covid-19 pandemic. Instead of allowing customers to come into the restaurant and order, customers had to put in their orders via the Chipotle mobile app. Customers would get a time when they could come up and pick up their order or, if they ordered far enough in advance, they could choose when to pick it up.
- Rocket Mortgage (previously Quicken Loans) has upended the mortgage industry by enabling consumers to apply for a mortgage in a streamlined manner and without needing to speak to a human. As you can imagine, in order to achieve this, they heavily relied on technology.

What are some best practices when implementing a cloud migration? In the next section, we will help you navigate so that your cloud migration project is successful regardless of how complicated it may be.

Digital transformation tips

There are many ways to implement a digital transformation. Some ways are better than others. In this section, we will cover some of the suggestions we have to shorten the implementation time and to minimize disruption to our existing customer base. Let's look at those tips.

Tip #1 – Ask the right questions

You should not just be asking this:

- How can we do what we are doing faster and better?

You should also be asking this:

- How we change what we are doing to better serve our customers?
- Can we eliminate certain lines of business, departments, or processes?
- What are the desired business outcomes we want to achieve when interfacing with our customers?

Having a precise understanding of your customers' journey and experience is key.

Tip #2 – Get leadership buy-in

Digital transformations have a much better chance to succeed when they are performed from the top down. If there is no buy-in from the CEO and the rest of the C-Suite, cloud adoption is destined to be relegated to a few corners of the enterprise, but has no chance of full adoption. This does not mean that a **Proof of Concept** (**PoC**) cannot be performed in one department to work out the kinks. Once the technology is adopted in that department, the bugs are worked out and tangible business results are delivered, we can roll out this solution to all other departments.

Tip #3 – Clearly delineate goals and objectives

In this day and age, where Agile development is so prevalent, it is not uncommon to pivot and change direction as new requirements are discovered. However, the overall objective of the digital transformation should be crystal clear. Is the objective to merely lift and shift the current workflows into the cloud? Then keep your eye on the prize and ruthlessly concentrate on that goal. Is the digital transformation supporting a merger between two companies? In that case, the completion of the merger of the backend systems and operations of both companies should take precedence over everything else. Whatever the goal is, we need to be laser-focused on completing that objective before taking on other initiatives and transformations.

Tip #4 – Apply an Agile methodology to your digital transformation

Embrace adaptive and agile design. The days of waiting for a couple of years to start seeing results, only to discover that we were climbing the wrong mountain, are over. Many corporations now run with lean budgets and only provide additional resources once milestones have been reached and functionality has been delivered.

Embracing an adaptive design enables transformation advocates to quickly tweak the transformation strategy and deploy staffing and resources where they can have the highest impact.

There needs to be a healthy push and pull between accomplishing the objectives laid out for the digital transformation and the inevitable changes in how the objectives will be met. In the case where some of the objectives change midstream, these changes need to be clearly defined again. Make sure to precisely spell out what is changing, what is new, and what is no longer applicable. There are but a few instances where development and projects are run using a waterfall model and most projects use Agile methodologies to deliver results faster and in an incremental manner, therefore increasing ROI by starting to take advantage of features as soon as they are available instead of waiting for all functionality to be delivered.

Adaptability must be deeply ingrained in the ethos and culture of your digital transformation team members.

Look for singles and not home runs. Home run hitters normally also have a lot of strikeouts. Players that specialize in hitting singles get on base much more often. You should take the same approach in your digital transformation. Instead of attempting a moon shot, it is highly recommended to take smaller steps that produce results. If you can demonstrate value early in your transformation, this will validate your approach and demonstrate to leadership that your approach is working. How much job security do you think you will have if your transformation takes three years and the project falls behind with no tangible results?

Pick the low-hanging fruit and migrate those workloads first. You will be able to provide quick results with this approach and you will learn from the mistakes you make in the process, which will help you when you need to accomplish other more difficult migrations.

Tip #5 – Encourage risk-taking

In other words, fail fast. Obviously, there are only so many times we can fail to deliver results before we are shown the door. But if failing only takes one week and we have a month to deliver results, that affords us the luxury to fail three times before we get it right the fourth time. Therefore, in the first couple of attempts we can attempt to shoot further and achieve more. Ideally, we don't have to completely throw out the work performed in the first few attempts, and hopefully we can reuse what was created in the first phases. But at the very least, we will be able to use the lessons learned from those mistakes.

It's better to disrupt yourself than to have someone do it for you.

Tip #6 – Clear delineation of roles and responsibilities

Fully and clearly delineate roles and responsibilities. Make sure that all team members are aligned on what their responsibilities are and check that there are no gaps in your team. Ideally, you will have a good mix of people with vast experience in cloud migration, digital transformation, and process optimization. Couple that with engineers and analysts that are not billing at an expert rate but can execute the plan laid out by these expert resources.

Current technology in general and AWS in particular is changing at an ever-increasing pace. For that reason, attracting talent with the right skills is an essential yet difficult step to achieve in digital transformations.

Some of the positions that will most likely need to be filled in your journey are as follows:

- Software engineers

- Infrastructure architects

- Cloud computing specialists

- Data analysts and data scientists

- Solution architects

- Security specialists

- Project managers

- Quality assurance testers

- DevOps administrators

- UX designers

- Trainers and documentation specialists

- Business analysts

This is a partial list, and your individual project may require more or fewer people filling these roles. Perhaps not all roles will be required. And in your case, you may need additional roles to those included in this list.

In this section, we learned about best practices and what to do in your cloud migration project. In the next section, we will learn about what you should not do and how to avoid making mistakes.

Digital transformation pitfalls

There are many more ways to fail and not as many ways to succeed. There are, however, common patterns to how digital transformations typically fail. Let's review some of them.

Lack of commitment from the C-Suite

Even in cases when the CEO says they are committed to completely transforming their business, they may still to clearly delineate a vision and the path to success, or fail to provide the necessary resources for the transformation to succeed.

Not having the right team in place

It is difficult to know what you don't know because you don't know it. It may take reading this sentence a couple of times before it can be understood, but the important takeaway is that you should engage people that have performed similar digital transformations to the one you are trying to attempt. Why reinvent the wheel if someone else already invented it?

There are many reputable consulting companies that specialize in cloud migration and digital transformation. Your chance of success increases exponentially if you engage them to assist you with your initiative. They understand what the challenges are, and they can help you avoid the pitfalls.

These resources come may come with a hefty price tag, and engaging them may not always be easy. Many digital transformation initiatives fail because of a failure to engage the people with the right expertise to perform them.

Internal resistance from the ranks

With many of these transformations, there may be an adjustment of personnel. Some new people may join the team, in some cases permanently. Some consulting staff may be brought in on a temporary basis, and some staff may become obsolete and may be needed to be phased out. It is important to consider the friction that these changes will create and deal with them accordingly. When moving workloads to the cloud, some of the on-premises administrators may no longer be required, and we can fully expect that they may be a roadblock to the completion of the migration of these workflows.

Specifically, it is not uncommon for infrastructure and system administrators to be resistant to cloud adoption. They often sense that some of their responsibilities may disappear or change. And in many instances, they are not wrong. Properly communicating the objective, how the migration will occur, and clearly delineating new responsibilities is key to a successful migration.

Going too fast

In order to succeed, you must crawl before you walk and walk before you run. It essential to prove concepts at a smaller scale before scaling them up across the enterprise and before we spend millions of dollars. Taking this route will allow you to make small mistakes and refine the transformation process before implementing it in an enterprise-wide fashion.

Not just for cloud migration, but for any project in general, a highly recommended method is to perform PoC projects before going all in. For example, if you have 100 databases in your organization, it is not a bad idea to migrate only one or a few of them to the cloud instead of doing all of them at the same time.

.nea pig departments, it is also important to
d one department at a time. Once you have
out the new technology across the board. If
oo slow to enable you to keep up with more

ocess and absorb the lessons learned from the
ration and migrate more of them.

ot be in the hands of the company's leadership.
ock to success. In this case, business leaders
at they would be able to change the rules and
ie middle of the game.

in the US. Proving that someone owns
requires recording physical documents in the
signatures. With the advent of blockchain and
already exists that can transform the archaic and
vernments. However, a patchwork of laws at the
ised to record these documents at the county level
istry and implementing this technology.

xperience. Back in 2001, I worked at an online
ig robot that could fill tens of thousands of
nagine, this was an expensive machine costing
any had a restriction in that for medicine
e faxed, and many customers had trouble faxing
dispenser ended up being heavily underutilized.
ited to its demise, but unfortunately, this enterprise

eventually went under.

Finally, we have a more recent example. As of August 2020, there is a current case pending
in California where Uber and Lyft are appealing a law that requires them to reclassify all
the people that are driving for the company from independent contractors to employees.

Both companies have made it clear that they will have to cease operations in California at least temporarily to deal with the new law. They may realize that this regulation is so onerous to the point where they will decide to cease operations permanently in the state. There is also precedent: both Uber and Lyft decided to stop operating in the city of Austin, Texas because they decided new regulations in the city would not allow them to ever turn a profit. More information about this can be found here:

```
https://www.vox.com/the-highlight/2019/9/6/20851575/uber-lyft-
drivers-austin-regulation-rideshare
```

Summary

In this chapter, we learned at a high level how AWS classifies its data centers. We touched upon the layout of the AWS infrastructure.

We then pivoted to understand how we can use this infrastructure to implement a digital transformation program and how to migrate to the cloud. We learned that not all cloud migration programs are created equal and that some companies use their migration to the cloud to implement further change in their organization.

Since processes are going to have to be retested anyway, why not take advantage of this change and implement ways to improve the company's processes and business workflows?

We also covered the drivers for a digital transformation and visited some examples of successful digital transformation. Along with this, we saw some useful tips to ensure the success of your digital transformation, as well as some pitfalls that should be avoided so that your transformation does not fail.

In the next chapter, we begin to learn how you can use AWS to create business solutions that can help you with your digital transformation initiatives.

Section 2: AWS Service Offerings and Use Cases

In this section, you'll learn about some common and popular use cases and the AWS services that can be used to support them.

This part of the book comprises the following chapters:

3
Storage in AWS – Choosing the Right Tool for the Job

Storage is a critical and foundational service for any cloud provider. If this service is not implemented in a durable, available, efficient, low-latency manner, it doesn't matter how many other great services are offered.

File, block, and object storage are at the core of many applications. In *Chapter 5*, *Selecting the Right Database Service*, we will learn about other storage services focused on databases. But, in this chapter, we will focus on basic file and object storage.

In this chapter, we will first look at Amazon EBS, EKS, and S3. We will then look at the difference between block storage and object storage. We will also look at versioning in Amazon S3 and finally, explore Amazon S3 best practices.

In this chapter, we will cover the following topics:

- Understanding Amazon **Elastic Block Storage** (**EBS**)
- Investigating Amazon **Elastic File System** (**EFS**)
- Learning about Amazon **Simple Storage Service** (**S3**)

- Understanding the difference between block storage and object storage
- Versioning in Amazon S3
- Exploring Amazon S3 best practices

Let's learn how all of this can be achieved in AWS.

Understanding Amazon Elastic Block Storage

In simple terms, Amazon **Elastic Block Storage** (**EBS**) is a hard drive for a server in AWS. One advantage of Amazon EBS over many typical hard drives is that you can easily detach it from one server and attach it to another server using software commands. Normally, with other servers outside of AWS, this would require physically detaching the hard drive and physically attaching it to another server.

Additionally, if you use the Amazon **Elastic File Storage** (**EFS**) service, you will be able to attach the hard drive (block storage device) to multiple servers (EC2 instances). This greatly simplifies your maintenance and operations.

When using Amazon EBS, data is persisted. This means that data lives even after the server is shut down. Like with other services, Amazon EBS provides high availability and durability. Amazon provides a guarantee of 99.999% availability.

Amazon EBS should not be confused with the instance store that is available in EC2 instances. EC2 instance stores deliver ephemeral storage for EC2 instances. Some of the use cases for EC2 instance stores are any data that does not need to be persisted, such as the following:

- Caches
- Buffers
- Temporary files
- Temporary variables

If data needs to be stored permanently, the following Amazon EBS options are available.

General-purpose Solid State Devices (SSDs)

General-purpose SSD storage provides a solid balance of cost and performance. It can be applied to a wide array of use cases such as the following:

- Virtual desktops
- Development and staging environments
- Application development

Provisioned IOPS SSD

IOPS stands for input/output operations per second. So, provisioned IOPS means that these operations are provisioned consistently. This type of storage is ideally suited for mission-critical applications such as the following:

- Business applications
- Production databases

Throughput Optimized HDD

Throughput Optimized HDDs offer a good value providing a reasonable cost for workloads that call for high performance and have high throughput requirements. Typical use cases include these:

- Big data applications
- Log processing
- Streaming applications
- Data warehouse applications

Cold HDD

This type of storage is normally used for applications that require to optimize costs with large volumes of data—typically, data that needs to be accessed infrequently.

> **Important note**
>
> This would be a good time to note the following. EC2 instances are virtualized and there isn't a one-to-one relationship between servers and EC2 instances. In the same manner, when you use EBS storage, a single physical storage device is not assigned to you by AWS but, rather, you get a slice of several devices that store the data in a distributed fashion across data centers to increase reliability and availability.

In addition, Amazon **Elastic Block Storage** (**EBS**) volumes are replicated transparently by design. Therefore, it is not necessary to provide extra redundancy by setting up RAID or some other redundancy strategy.

Amazon EBS volumes are by default highly available, durable, and reliable. This redundancy strategy and multiple server replication are built into the base price of Amazon EBS volumes. Amazon EBS volume files are mirrored across more than one server within an **Availability Zone** (**AZ**). This will minimize data loss. For data loss to occur, more than one device will have to fail at the same time. Amazon EBS volumes will also self-heal and bring in additional healthy resources if a disk fails.

Amazon EBS volumes offer at least twenty times more reliability than traditional commodity devices.

Amazon EBS Snapshots

Amazon EBS also provides a feature to easily and automatically create snapshots. The backups of data volumes can be performed incrementally. For example, if you have a device with 100 GB of data, the first day the snapshot is created, the snapshot will have to reflect all 100 GBs. If, the next day, 5 GB of additional data are added, when the next snapshot is taken, EBS is smart enough to realize that it only needs to account for the new data and it can use the previous snapshot in conjunction with the new backup to recreate the full picture. This incremental snapshot strategy will translate into lower storage costs.

Snapshots can be compressed, mirrored, transferred, replicated, and managed across multiple AWS AZs by taking advantage of the Amazon Data Lifecycle Manager.

Amazon EBS snapshots are stored as Amazon S3 objects. Amazon EBS snapshots are accessed using the Amazon EBS API and they cannot be accessed directly by users. Snapshots are stored as **Amazon Machine Images** (**AMIs**) and therefore, they can be leveraged to launch an EC2 instance.

This wraps up what we wanted to say about the Amazon EBS service. Now, let's move on and learn about another important service—Amazon Elastic File Storage.

Investigating Amazon Elastic File System (EFS)

Amazon **Elastic File System** (**EFS**) is not that different from Amazon EBS. Amazon EFS implements an elastic fully-managed **Network File System** (**NFS**) that can be leveraged by other AWS Cloud services and on-premises infrastructure. The main difference is that several EC2 instances can be mounted to an EFS volume at the same time. Amazon EFS provides shared file storage that can elastically adjust on demand to expand or shrink depending on how much space your workloads require. It can grow and shrink as you add and remove files. Other than that, the structure will be like it is with Amazon EBS. Amazon EFS provides a typical file storage system where files can be organized into directories and subdirectories.

Common use cases for EFS volumes are also like EBS volumes. They are often used for the following:

- Hosting content management systems
- Hosting CRM applications that require to be hosted within the AWS data center but need to be managed by the AWS customer

Let's now learn about another storage system in AWS—Amazon **Simple Storage Service** (**S3**).

Learning about Amazon Simple Storage Service (S3)

Soon after Amazon released the EC2 service, it quickly released another service – the Simple Storage Service or S3 for short. It was released on March 14, 2006. After the launch of S3, it also launched many other object storage services to compliment S3. We will analyze many of those services in this chapter.

S3 Standard

Initially, when Amazon launched the S3 service, it was simply called Amazon S3. Amazon now offers a variety of object storage services and they all use the S3 moniker, so Amazon has renamed Amazon S3 to Amazon S3 Standard.

S3 Standard delivers highly performant, available, and durable storage for data that will be accessed frequently. S3 Standard has low latency, high performance, and high scalability. S3 Standard is suited for a long list of use cases, including the following:

- Websites with dynamic content

- Distribution of content

- Cloud services and applications

- Data analytics and processing

- Mobile and gaming applications

These are some of the S3 Standard service features:

- It has low latency and high throughput performance.

- It has 99.999999999% durability. This translates into the equivalent of storing 10,000 files in Amazon S3 and expecting to lose one of these files every 10,000,000 years

- This high durability is achieved because six replicas for each object are stored across multiple **AZ**s, so if one AZ completely goes down, the files will still be saved in other AZs.

- It provides 99.99% availability.

- AWS offers an availability **Service Level Agreement (SLA)**.

- An object can be automatically moved and backed up to other types of S3 storage via S3 Lifecycle management.

- SSL is supported for data in transit and encryption is available by default for data at rest.

Like other AWS services, it can be accessed via the AWS console, using the AWS **Command-Line Interface (CLI)**, or with the AWS SDK. Like with other AWS services, Amazon is one of the largest users of the S3 service and it uses it for its Amazon.com site to support its global e-commerce operations. Amazon S3 can be used to persist many types of objects such as the following:

- Plaintext files

- HTML files

- Backup and snapshots

- Data analytics

- JSON, XML, AVRO, Parquet, and ORC files
- Hybrid cloud storage

That's it for Amazon S3 Standard. Let's now look at another service in the S3 family—Amazon S3 Intelligent-Tiering, and let's learn what makes it intelligent.

Amazon S3 Intelligent-Tiering

The S3 Intelligent-Tiering storage service can reduce expenses by systematically moving files to use the most cost-effective way to store data while having no impact on operations or performance. It can do this by keeping the files in two tiers:

- An optimized tier for frequent access
- An optimized tier for infrequent access that has a lower cost

Amazon S3 constantly scans access patterns of files and transfers files that have not been accessed. If a file has not been accessed for 30 days straight, it is moved to the infrequent access tier. If a file in the infrequent access tier is retrieved, it is again transferred to the frequent access tier.

With the S3 Intelligent-Tiering storage class, the additional cost comes from the monitoring charge. There are no fees for retrieval and there are no additional file transfer fees when objects are transferred between the tiers. S3 Intelligent-Tier is a good solution when we know that data is going to be needed for a long time, but we are uncertain about how often this data is going to be accessed.

S3 services can be enabled in a granular way up to the object level. For example, a given bucket can have one object in it that is using S3 Standard, another using S3 Intelligent-Tiering, one more with S3 Standard-IA, and one with S3 One Zone-IA (we are going to cover these two other services in the next few sections). This is a contrived example, but you get the idea of how flexible it can be.

These are some of the key features of Amazon S3 Intelligent-Tiering:

- It leverages the performance and reliability of S3 Standard.
- Automatically and reliably transfer files between the two tiers depending on usage patterns.
- It delivers 99.999999999%, or so-called *11 9s*, durability across multiple AZs.
- If an entire AZ goes down, it is not a fatal event and files are unaffected.
- It delivers 99.9% availability.

- AWS offers an availability SLA

- SSL is supported for data in transit and encryption is available by default for data at rest.

So, what if we know that the data we are creating and storing will be infrequently accessed? Amazon offers a service ideally suited for that, which will also be cheaper than Amazon S3 Standard.

Amazon S3 Standard-IA

Depending on the use case for your data, this storage class might be the ideal solution for your data storage needs. The data can be accessed at the same speed as S3 Standard but with some tradeoffs on the resiliency of the data.

S3 Standard-IA offers a similar profile to the Standard service but with a lower cost for storage but with a retrieval fee billed per GB. Combining low cost with high performance makes S3 Standard-IA a well-suited option for use cases such as backups, snapshots, and long-term storage and as a file repository for disaster recovery. S3 Lifecycle policies could be used to automatically move files between storage classes without any coding needed.

These are some of the key characteristics of Amazon S3 Standard-IA:

- It has high throughput and low latency.

- It delivers 99.999999999%, or so called *11 9s*, durability across multiple AZs.

- If an entire AZ goes down, it is not a fatal event and files are unaffected.

- It delivers 99.9% availability.

- AWS offers an availability SLA.

- SSL is supported for data in transit and encryption is available by default for data at rest.

So, what about if your data is not that critically important and you are willing to give up some durability in exchange for a cheaper alternative? Amazon has a service that fits that criteria. We'll learn about it in the next section.

Amazon S3 One Zone-IA

A better name for S3 Standard-IA might be *S3 Standard-IA that is not critical*. Like the previous service S3 Standard Infrequent-Access, S3 One Zone-IA can be used for files that need to be retrieved with less frequency but need rapid access. One of the reasons this service is cheaper than S3 Standard is, because instead of storing data in three AZs, S3 One Zone-IA persists data in only
one AZ.

S3 One Zone-IA is a good solution for use cases that don't need the reliability of S3 Standard or S3 Standard-IA and therefore get a cheaper price. The reliability is still high, and it still has duplication, but this duplication is not done across AZs. It's a suitable option for storing files such as backup files and data that can be quickly and easily recreated. It can also be a cost-effective way to store data that has been copied from another AWS Region with S3 Cross-Region Replication.

> **Important note**
> Keep in mind that if an AZ goes down or is destroyed, these files will be unavailable and potentially destroyed as well. So, it should only be used with files that are not mission-critical.

S3 One Zone-IA delivers similar high throughput, durability, and speed of S3 Standard, coupled with an inexpensive retrieval cost.

These are some of the key characteristics of Amazon S3 One Zone-IA:

- There are a similar speed and high throughput as S3 Standard.
- It delivers 99.999999999%, or so-called *11 9s*, durability across multiple AZs.
- If an entire AZ fails, data will be lost if the entire AZ is lost.
- It delivers 99.5% availability (lower than Standard S3, but still quite high).
- AWS offers an availability SLA.
- SSL is supported for data in transit and encryption is available by default for data at rest.

So far, we have looked at services that allow us to access the data immediately. What if we are willing to give up that immediate accessibility in exchange for an even cheaper service? Amazon S3 Glacier fits that bill. We'll learn about it in the next section.

Amazon S3 Glacier

When its known that a file will not be needed immediately, S3 Glacier is a good option. S3 Glacier is a secure, durable class for data archiving. It is significantly cheaper than S3 Standard, but it will take longer to retrieve an S3 Glacier file. Data can be stored on S3 Glacier at a cost that would be competitive with an on-premises solution. Within the S3 Glacier, the options and pricing are flexible. S3 Glacier has three different ways to retrieve data:

- **Expedited retrieval** — Expedited retrievals enables quick access to archived data that needs to be accessed on an urgent basis. For the majority of cases (requests smaller than 250 MB+), expedited retrievals can be performed in about 1 to 5 minutes.

- **Standard retrieval** — Standard retrievals enable access of archived data within several hours. Standard data retrievals normally can be completed within 3 to 5 hours. Standard retrieval is the standard default option for Amazon S3 Glacier.

- **Bulk retrieval** — When there is no rush to access data, a bulk retrieval can be performed (at a lower cost). It can be used to retrieve vast amounts of data (even petabyte-size requests) inexpensively. Bulk retrievals typically take between 5 and 12 hours.

Data can be retrieved in as little as a few minutes and as long as a few hours. To use it, files can be uploaded directly to S3 Glacier, or they can be placed there through an S3 Lifecycle policy designed to transfer files between other S3 storage classes.

These are some of the key features of Amazon S3 Glacier:

- It provides slower access to data compared to S3 Standard.

- It delivers 99.999999999%, or so-called *11 9s*, durability across multiple AZs.

- If an AZ goes down, data can be preserved due to the multi-AZ capabilities of the service.

- SSL is supported for data in transit and encryption is available by default for data at rest.

- It's low-cost.

- It has configurable retrieval times from minutes to hours. Pricing will change based on retrieval time.

For data that needs to be preserved but does not need to be accessed immediately and we can wait even longer than a day, Amazon offers yet another option that is even cheaper than standard Glacier. We will learn about that option in the next section.

Amazon S3 Glacier Deep Archive

S3 Glacier Deep Archive is Amazon S3's cheapest option for object storage. It enables long-term storage. It is suited for files that are only going to be retrieved occasionally. It is designed for customers that are required to keep data for 7 years or longer. One of the reasons for this requirement may be to meet a regulatory compliance regulation. Customers that operate in highly regulated environments, such as the financial industry, healthcare industry, and government agencies, often have strict requirements to keep data for a minimum amount of time and in many cases, heavy penalties can accrue if these rules are not properly followed. Other good use cases are backup and disaster recovery. Many customers are using this service instead of magnetic tape systems. S3 Glacier Deep Archive can be used in conjunction with Amazon S3 Glacier, which allows data to be retrieved faster than the Deep Archive service.

These are some of the key features of Amazon S3 Glacier Deep Archive:

- 99.999999999% durability.

- Storage across multiple AZs.

- Lowest cost storage class.

- A good alternative to magnetic tape libraries.

- Data can be retrieved within 12 hours.

In the following, we have a summary of the profile of each storage class and how they compare to each other:

Features	S3 Standard	S3 Intelligent Tiering	S3 Standard-IA	S3 One Zone-IA	S3 Glacier	S3 Glacier Deep Archive
Durability	11 9's	11 9's	11 9's	11 9's	11 9's	11 9's
Availability	99.9	99.9	99.9	99.5%	99.9	99.9
Availability Zones	>=3	>=3	>=3	1	>=3	>=3
Minimum capacity charge per object	N/A	N/A	128KB	128KB	40KB	40KB
Access Latency	milliseconds	milliseconds	milliseconds	milliseconds	1 min - 12 hours	hours
Data Retrieval Fee	none	per GB data retrieved	per GB data retrieved	per GB data retrieved	per GB data retrieved	per GB data retrieved
Type of Storage	Object	Object	Object	Object	Object	Object
SSL Support	Yes	Yes	Yes	Yes	Yes	Yes
Availability SLA	99.9%	99%	99%	99%	99.9%	99%

Figure 3.1 – Summary of storage class features

As we can see from the summary, Amazon has a vast number of offerings for your storage use cases. As we can surmise, depending on how quickly the data needs to be retrieved and how durably it needs to be stored, the costs will vary and allow for savings if high durability and fast retrieval are not required.

Now that we have covered Amazon Elastic Block Storage as well as Amazon S3, we will spend some time understanding the difference between the two services and when it's appropriate to use one versus the other.

Understanding the difference between block storage and object storage

As we saw in the previous sections, Amazon EBS stores data in blocks whereas Amazon S3 stores data as objects. So now that we covered both of these services, the obvious question is which one is better to use. And the obvious answer is—it depends.

Amazon S3 is good for and often used to do the following:

- Host static websites and web pages
- Host web images and videos
- Store petabyte scale amounts of data to perform data analytics on it
- Assisting in mobile applications

Amazon EBS is well suited for the following:

- Support business continuity
- Host big data applications that require high control of the environment using Hadoop, Spark, and similar frameworks
- Enable software testing
- Deployment of databases that need to be managed by the user and not AWS

The following table should also help you to decide what service is best for your use case:

	Performance	Cost	Availability	Storage Limit	File Size Limit
Amazon S3	By default, it supports 100 requests per second and scalable to 300	Average of $0.0235 per GB/month	99.99 % availability	No limit on the number of objects	5TB object limit
Amazon EBS	Provisioned IOPS can deliver 4000 operations per second	Anywhere from $0.025 to $0.100 per GB/month	99.99 % availability	Maximum storage size of 16 TB	File size of up to 16 TB
Amazon EFS	Capable of up to 7000 operations per second	From $0.30 to $0.36 per GB/month	No SLA in force	No limit on system size	File size of up to 52 TB

Figure 3.2 – Choosing the service based on your use case

Hopefully, this section was useful to help you to discern when to use the various storage services that AWS offers. Let's continue learning more about the fundamental service that is Amazon S3.

Versioning in Amazon S3

Amazon S3 has the capability to optionally store different versions of the same object. Have you ever been working on a document for hours and suddenly make a mistake where you delete all of the content in the document, or you make a big mistake and want to go back to a previous version? Many editors such as Microsoft Word offer the ability to undo changes and recover from some of these mistakes. Once you save, close, and open the document again, you may not be able to undo any changes.

What if you have a document where multiple people are making revisions and you want to keep track of who made what changes?

Amazon S3 offers versioning capabilities that can assist with these use cases. So, what is versioning? Simply explained, versioning is the ability to keep incremental copies. For example, if you store a Microsoft Word document in S3, the first version of the document may have 10 pages and the second version has 20 pages. It is easy to view and recover the previous version that only has 10 pages.

As you can imagine, keeping multiple versions of the same document, if there are many changes, can get expensive. This is especially true if you have a high volume of documents. To reduce our costs, we can implement a lifecycle policy where older versions are purged or moved to a cheaper storage option such as Amazon S3 Glacier.

The exact logic of how the lifecycle policy will be implemented will depend on your requirements. But some possibilities are to set up your policy based on document age, the number of versions, or some other criteria.

By the way, lifecycle policies are not limited to just older versions of a document. They can also be used for any kind of document that is persisted in Amazon S3.

So, you are sold on Amazon S3 and have now decided to join the thousands of companies around the world that are building fundamental and mission-critical applications with Amazon S3 as their foundation. Great! Now, let's explore some of the best practices you can implement to take full advantage of the service.

Exploring Amazon S3 best practices

Amazon S3 is one of the simplest services in AWS and at the same time, it is one of the most powerful and scalable services as well. We can easily scale our Amazon S3 applications to be able to process thousands of requests per second while uploading and retrieving files. This scalability can be achieved "out of the box" and without needing to provision any resources or servers.

Some customers in AWS are already leveraging Amazon S3 to host petabyte-scale data lakes and other applications storing billions of objects and performing billions of requests. These applications, with little optimization, can upload and retrieve multiple terabytes of data per second.

Other customers that have low latency requirements have been able to use Amazon S3 and other Amazon file storage services to achieve consistent low latency for small objects. Being able to retrieve this kind of object in 100 to 200 milliseconds is not uncommon.

For bigger objects, it is possible to achieve similar low latency responses for the *first byte* received from these objects. As you can imagine, the retrieval time to receive the complete file for bigger objects is going to be directly proportional to object size.

Time To First Byte (**TTFB**) is a measurement that is often used to gauge the performance of a service or other network resource. TTFB is the length of time taken from the moment a user or client makes a request for an object to the time the first byte of that object is received by the client.

Enhancing Amazon S3 performance

One simple way to enhance performance is to be cognizant of where most of your users are located and where your Amazon S3 bucket is located. Amazon S3 buckets need to be unique globally but files will be stored in a given AWS region. Make sure that when you architect your solution, this is taken into consideration in your design. It will help to reduce the time it takes to transfer files as well as minimize data transfer costs.

One more way to scale Amazon S3 is to scale S3 connections horizontally. Amazon S3 allows you to make as many connections as you wish to any given bucket and access the files thousands of times per second. High scalable performance can be achieved by issuing multiple concurrent requests. You can think of Amazon S3 as a highly distributed system and not just a single endpoint that only has one server to support the workloads.

We mentioned in the previous section that Amazon S3 files can be retrieved with sub-second performance. However, if this level of performance is not enough, and you are looking to achieve single-digit millisecond performance, you can use Amazon CloudFront, Amazon Elemental MediaStore, or Amazon ElastiCache to cache the files in memory or closer to your user base to achieve even higher performance.

Amazon CloudFront

Amazon CloudFront is a **Content Delivery Network (CDN)** that can cache content stored in Amazon S3 and distribute it across disperse geographic regions with thousands of **Points of Presence (PoP)** around the world. Amazon CloudFront enables these objects to be cached close to the people that will be using these resources.

Amazon ElastiCache

Amazon ElastiCache is a managed AWS service that enables you to store objects in memory instead of storing them on disk. Behind the scenes and transparently, Amazon ElastiCache will provision Amazon EC2 instances that will cache objects in the instance's memory. Doing so will reduce latency when retrieving objects by orders of magnitude. Using Amazon ElastiCache does require subtly changing application logic.

First, when you want certain objects to be cached instead of being stored on disk, you need to specify that ElastiCache should be the storage medium. And when you retrieve objects, you should check the cache in ElastiCache to see whether the object that you are trying to retrieve has been cached and, if they haven't, only then check Amazon S3 to get the uncached object.

Amazon Elemental MediaStore

It is sometimes hard to keep up with the amount and variety of services that AWS offers. If your application has video files, Amazon Elemental MediaStore may be the right service for you to leverage.

Amazon Elemental MediaStore enables you to cache and distribute video and media files and to develop workflows around these files. The service also has APIs designed specifically to support video. If you require high performance and low latency with the delivery of video, Amazon Elemental MediaStore is most likely the appropriate solution.

Amazon S3 Transfer Acceleration

Yet another way to achieve single-digit millisecond responses is to use Amazon S3 Transfer Acceleration. This AWS service uses CloudFront edge locations to accelerate data transport over long distances. Amazon S3 Transfer Acceleration is ideally suited to transfer a large amount of data (gigabytes or terabytes) that needs to be transferred across AWS Regions.

You should consider using Amazon S3 Transfer Acceleration in the following cases:

- Application requirements call for the need to upload files to a central location for many places around the globe.

- There is a need to transfer hundreds of gigabytes or terabytes worth of data regularly across AWS regions.

- The available bandwidth is not being fully utilized and leveraged when uploading to Amazon S3.

The benefits of Amazon S3 Transfer Acceleration are as follows:

- It will allow you to transfer files faster and more consistently over long distances.

- It can reduce network variability usage.

- It can shorten the distance traveled to upload files to S3.

- It will enable you to maximize bandwidth utilization.

One highly important consideration when using Amazon S3 is ensuring that the data stored is accessible only by parties that need to access the data. Everyone else should be locked out. Let's learn about the capabilities that AWS offers to assist in data protection and data security.

Protecting your data in Amazon S3

Amazon makes it extremely easy to provision an Amazon S3 bucket and quickly allows you to distribute the data around the world by simply providing a URL pointing to files in the bucket. The good news is that this is so easy to do. The bad news is that this is so easy to do.

There have been many documented cases of sensitive data left lying around in publicly accessible endpoints in S3 and other people being able to access this data. "Leaky" Amazon S3 buckets are a perfect example of how the shared responsibility security model works when using AWS. AWS provides an amazing array of security services and protocols, but if they are not used correctly, data can still be exposed, and breaches can occur.

Following are a couple of instances of the most egregious leaks:

- *Leaky Buckets: 10 Worst Amazon S3 Breaches*: `https://businessinsights.bitdefender.com/worst-amazon-breaches`

- *LA County Non-Profit Leaks 3.5 Million PII Via Misconfigured Amazon S3*: `https://www.trendmicro.com/vinfo/us/security/news/virtualization-and-cloud/la-county-non-profit-leaks-3-5-million-pii-via-misconfigured-amazon-s3`

So, it goes without saying: make sure to configure your Amazon S3 buckets and object security with the least privilege all of the time.

The good news is that as easy as it is to make the bucket public and leave it open to the world, it is almost as simple to lock it down and restrict access only to the required individual and services.

Some of the features that Amazon S3 provides to restrict access to the correct users are as follows.

Blocking Amazon S3 public access to buckets and objects whenever possible

Leveraging Amazon S3 block public access, Amazon S3 bucket administrators can configure a way to control access in a centralized manner and limit public access to Amazon S3 buckets and objects. This feature can be used to deny public access regardless of how objects and buckets are created in Amazon S3.

Avoiding wildcards in policy files

Policy files allow a powerful syntax where you can use a wildcard character (*) to specify policies. Even though wildcards are allowed, they should be avoided whenever possible and instead, names should be spelled out explicitly to name resources, principals, and others.

The same wild card rule of thumb applies to Amazon S3 bucket **Access Control Lists (ACLs)**. ACLs are files that can be used to deliver read, write, or full access to users and if wildcards are used, it can potentially leave the bucket open to the world.

Leveraging the ListBuckets API

The ListBuckets API can be used to scan Amazon S3 buckets. The `GetBucketAcl`, `GetBucketWebsite`, and `GetBucketPolicy` commands can be used to monitor whether buckets are compliant and whether the access controls, policies, and configuration are properly set up to only allow access to authorized personnel.

Leveraging AWS Trusted Advisor to inspect Amazon S3

Another way to verify your security configuration is to deploy a continuous monitoring system using **s3-bucket-public-read-prohibited** and **s3-bucket-public-write-prohibited** and manage the configuration using AWS Config Rules.

Enabling AWS Config

AWS Config is a service that can be used to monitor and evaluate the way resources are configured in your AWS setup. AWS Config continuously audits the environment to ensure that it complies with preestablished desired configurations. If a configuration deviates from the desired standards, alerts can be generated, and warnings can be issued. As you can imagine, it doesn't apply to just Amazon S3 but all AWS services.

AWS greatly simplifies monitoring of your environment, enhances troubleshooting, and ensures that established standards are followed.

Implementing S3 Object Lock to secure resources

S3 Object Lock allows the storage of objects with a **Write Once Read Many** (**WORM**) model. S3 Object Lock assists in the prevention of the accidental or nefarious deletion of important information. For example, S3 Object Lock can be used to ensure the integrity of AWS CloudTrail logs.

Implementing data at rest encryption

AWS offers a couple of methods to encrypt data at rest in Amazon S3:

- **Using Server-Side Encryption** – Server-side encryption is performed right before the object is saved to disk and the object is decrypted when a request comes in to retrieve it. Server-side encryption uses a key that is stored in an alternative place and using a different storage method than the method used to store the data. The available server-side encryption methods in Amazon S3 are as follows:

  a. Server-side encryption using keys managed by Amazon S3 (SSE-S3)

  b. Server-side encryption using customer-managed keys that are kept in the AWS Key Management Service (SSE-KMS)

  c. Server-side encryption using keys brought in by the customer (SSE-C)

- **Using Client-Side Encryption** – Data stored in Amazon S3 can also be encrypted on the client side and then uploaded to the cloud and stored in Amazon S3. With this method, the complete encryption process is managed by the customer and you are in full control of the encryption keys. Similarly, as with server-side encryption, using client-side encryption reduces the risk of losing the data by storing the encryption key in a different place and using a different storage method than what is used to store the data. Amazon S3 delivers a variety of client-side encryption alternatives.

Enabling data in transit encryption

Amazon S3 supports HTTPS (TLS) to assist in the prevention of attacks to nefariously access or modify the traffic between your users and the Amazon S3 buckets. It is highly recommended to also modify your Amazon S3 bucket policies to only permit encrypted connections that use the HTTPS (TLS) protocol.

It is also recommended to implement in AWS Config a rule that enables continuous monitoring controls making use of **s3-bucket-ssl-requests-only**.

Turning on Amazon S3 server access logging

By default, access is not logged. This ensures that you are not charged for the storage space these logs will take. However, it's fairly easy to turn on logging. These logs will give you a detailed record of any traffic that occurs in Amazon S3. These access logs will help determine who accessed your buckets and when they were accessed. This will help not only from a security perspective but also to determine traffic patterns and help you to control your costs.

Considering the use of Amazon Macie with Amazon S3

Amazon Macie leverages the power of machine learning to automatically ensure that sensitive information is not mishandled when using Amazon S3. Amazon Macie can locate and discern sensitive data in Amazon S3. Macie can recognize **Personally Identifiable Information (PII)**, intellectual property, and similar sensitive information. Amazon Macie has instrumentation panels, reports, and warnings that can show how data is being used.

Implementing monitoring leveraging AWS monitoring services

Monitoring is a critical component of any computing solution. AWS provides a variety of services to consistently and reliably monitor Amazon S3. As an example, CloudWatch provides a variety of metrics for Amazon S3 such as the number of put, get, and delete requests.

Using VPC endpoints to access Amazon S3 whenever possible

Using **Virtual Private Cloud (VPC)** endpoints with Amazon S3 enables the use of Amazon S3 without traversing the internet and minimizing risk. A VPC endpoint for Amazon S3 is an artifact within an Amazon VPC that only allows connections from Amazon S3. To allow access from a given Amazon VPC endpoint, an Amazon S3 bucket policy can be used.

VPC endpoints for Amazon S3 use two methods to control access to your Amazon S3 data:

- Controlling the requests made to access a given VPC endpoint
- Controlling the VPCs or VPC endpoints that can make requests to a given S3 bucket by taking advantage of S3 bucket policies

Data exfiltration can be prevented by leveraging a VPC without an internet gateway.

To learn more, please check the following link: `https://docs.aws.amazon.com/AmazonS3/latest/dev/example-bucket-policies-vpc-endpoint.html`.

Leveraging Amazon S3 cross-region replication

By default, Amazon S3 persists data in more than one AZ, but there may be other reasons that require you to provide an even higher level of redundancy. For example, storing the data in different continents. **Cross-Region Replication** (**CRR**) the storage of data across AWS Regions to satisfy those types of requirements. CRR enables automatic, asynchronous replication of objects across AWS Regions in multiple buckets.

In this last section, we learned about some of the best practices that are recommended when implementing Amazon S3 as part of any solution, including how to achieve the best performance, how to minimize sticker shock at the end of the month with your monthly charges by monitoring usage, and how to ensure that only "need to know" users access data in your Amazon S3 buckets.

Summary

In this chapter, we reviewed some of the different options that are provided for storing files. Files make up one of the most valuable assets an enterprise has. These files could store a secret recipe, an important algorithm, client information, and other information that, if it ended up in the wrong hands, could prove catastrophic. For this reason, it is extremely critical that, wherever these files are stored, only the people that should have access to them, can. Similarly, it is of the utmost importance that these folks can access this information whenever they need it so these files should always be available, and some files are so critical that, if they were lost, it could prove fatal to the enterprise.

AWS offers a wide array of services to support the storage of files. Regardless of the AWS service you select for file storage, they all offer features that provide a high degree of security, availability, and durability. Depending on the criticality of your data, you can architect your solution to increase the level of security, availability, and durability. In this chapter, we reviewed many of the options available to increase these variables.

In addition, we went over many best practices that should be used when creating solutions with AWS services regardless of the level of sensitivity of your data.

In the next chapter, we will learn how to harness the power of the cloud to create powerful applications and we will do a deep dive into another important AWS service—Amazon EC2.

4

Harnessing the Power of Cloud Computing

In this chapter, we explore another aspect of the cloud that makes it so powerful. In some senses, the ethereal concept of the cloud boils down to a data center that is managed by a third party. Why is it that there is such a massive shift by companies now to embrace the cloud? By the end of this chapter, you will be armed with the answer to that question, and you will have the necessary ammunition to explain to skeptics why the cloud is so powerful and why it represents a paradigm shift in computing.

We will be covering some of the basic compute services available in AWS, as well as how these services came to be. In addition, we will learn the differences between **Software as a Service (SaaS)**, **Platform as a Service (PaaS)**, and **Infrastructure as a Service (IaaS)**. We will also cover how AWS handles the fundamental services of computing and storage.

In this chapter, we will cover the following topics:

- A brief introduction to cloud computing
- Comparing PaaS, IaaS, and SaaS
- Understanding IaaS

- Understanding PaaS

- Understanding SaaS

- Selection by use case of PaaS, IaaS, or SaaS

- Learning about **Elastic Cloud Computing** (**EC2**)

- Reviewing Amazon EC2 best practices

- Learning about S3 and other storage services

Brief introduction to cloud computing

The first large-scale electronic general-purpose computer was the **Electronic Numerical Integrator and Computer** (**ENIAC**), and it was built between 1943 and 1945. Its design was proposed by the physicist *John Mauchly*. Until it was disabled in 1955, the ENIAC and the engineering team supporting it most likely performed more calculations than had been performed in the history of humanity until that point. As momentous as that achievement was, we have certainly come a long way since then.

The term **paradigm shift** was first introduced in 1962 by the American science philosopher *Thomas Kuhn* in his influential book *The Structure of Scientific Revolutions*. Kuhn defines a paradigm as the formal theories, classic experiments, and trusted methods of scientific research and thought. Kuhn posited that scientists, as a matter of course, accept the predominant paradigm but continuously challenge it by questioning it, constantly refining theories, and creating experiments to validate it. Sometimes the paradigm eventually becomes inadequate to represent the observed behavior through experimentation. When this happens, a paradigm shift occurs, and a new theory or methodology replaces the old ways. Kuhn, in his book, walks us through the example of how the geocentric solar system model was eventually replaced by the heliocentric model because the evidence became overwhelming supporting the latter.

Similarly, in computing, we have observed a few situations where the accepted way of doing things was replaced by a better and more efficient method. A couple of tectonic shifts have occurred since the ENIAC days. Determining which one have been the most relevant is a subjective exercise, but in our view, these are the most important:

- The creation of the first electronic computers, starting with ENIAC

- The advent of mainframes: An ENIAC in every company's backroom

- The PC revolution: A mainframe in everyone's desk

- The emergence of the internet: PCs being connected

- The cloud tsunami: Turning computing into a utility service

As mentioned, this list is by no means final. You can easily argue that there have been other shifts. Does IoT belong on the list? What about blockchain? I don't think we are quite there yet, but I think the next paradigm shift will be the pervasive implementation of artificial intelligence. Also, not all these paradigm shifts have resulted in killing the previous paradigm. Many corporations trust their mission-critical operations to mainframes, PCs are still around, and the internet has a synergistic relationship with the cloud. Let's focus now on the last *paradigm shift* since that is the topic of this chapter.

What exactly is cloud computing? It is a term often thrown around by many people, some of whom don't really understand it and they are just trying to make a sale. Having your infrastructure in the cloud does not mean you have your servers up in the sky. Let's try to define it most plainly. Essentially, **cloud computing** is the outsourcing of a company's hardware and software infrastructure to a third party. Enterprises, instead of having their own data center, borrow someone else's data center. This has many advantages:

- Economies of scale associated with buying in bulk.

- You only pay for the time you use the equipment in increments of minutes.

- Arguably one of the most important benefits is the ability to scale up, out, down, and in.

When using cloud computing, you are not buying the equipment; you are leasing it. Granted, equipment leasing has been around for a long time, but not at the speed that cloud computing provides. With cloud computing, it is possible to start a resource within minutes, use it for a few hours, minutes, or even seconds, and then shut it down. You will only pay for the time you used it. Furthermore, with the advent of *serverless* computing, such as AWS Lambda services, we don't even need to provision servers and we can just call a Lambda function and pay by the function call. Let's have one example to drive the point home: the latest P3 instances available for use with the AWS Sagemaker Machine Learning service can be used for less than $5.00 per hour (2020 pricing). This might sound like a high price to pay to rent one computer, but a few years ago we would have had to pay millions of dollars for a super-computer with similar capabilities. And importantly, after a model is trained, the instance can be shut down and the inference engine can be deployed into more appropriate hardware. The idea of being able to *scale out* and, just as importantly, to *scale in* is often referred to as **elasticity** or **elastic computing**. This concept allows companies to treat their computing resources as just another utility bill and only pay for what they need at any given moment in time.

Next, we will learn about terms that are commonly used to specify how much of your infrastructure will live in the cloud versus how much will stay on-premises.

Comparing PaaS, IaaS, and SaaS

There are many ways to classify cloud services. In this section, we will cover a common classification. Cloud services can be categorized as follows:

- **Infrastructure as a Service (IaaS)**
- **Platform as a Service (PaaS)**
- **Software as a Service (SaaS)**

As the names indicate, each model provides a service at a different level of the stack.

Each of these solutions has its advantages and disadvantages. It is essential to fully understand these tradeoffs in order to select the best option for your organization:

On Premise	IaaS	PaaS	SaaS
Application	Application	Application	Application
Data	Data	Data	Data
Runtime	Runtime	Runtime	Runtime
Middleware	Middleware	Middleware	Middleware
Operating System	Operating System	Operating System	Operating System
Virtualization	Virtualization	Virtualization	Virtualization
Servers	Servers	Servers	Servers
Storage	Storage	Storage	Storage
Networking	Networking	Networking	Networking
		Self Managed	AWS Managed

Figure 4.1 – Cloud service classification

As you can see in the preceding image, the amount of services managed by yourself or AWS is what determines how the stack will be classified. On one extreme we have an on-premises environment, where all the infrastructure is located in your own data center. On the other extreme, we have a SaaS architecture, where all the infrastructure is located on the cloud and off your premises. In the following sections, we will explore the advantages and disadvantages of using each one of them as well as examples of services that fall under each one of these classifications.

Understanding IaaS

Cloud infrastructure services, also known as **IaaS**, comprise highly flexible, fault-tolerant compute and storage resources. IaaS provides access and full management and monitoring of compute, storage, networking, and other miscellaneous services. IaaS enables enterprises to use resources on an *as needed* basis, so they don't need to purchase the equipment.

IaaS leverages virtualization technology. AWS allows you to quickly provision hardware through the AWS console, using the **Command-Line Interface** (**CLI**) or using an API, among other methods. By using an IaaS platform, a business can provision a whole host of resources and functionality that they have with their current infrastructure without the headache of physically maintaining it. From a client perspective, they might not even be aware that the backend services are being provided by an IaaS platform instead of being a company-owned data center.

As we saw in *Figure 4.1*, when using the IaaS solution, we are responsible for managing more aspects of the stack such as applications, runtime, operating systems, middleware, and data. However, in these cases, AWS will manage servers, hard drives, networking, virtualization, databases, and file storage.

We will now cover the advantages and disadvantages of IaaS services, and will also look at some IaaS use cases, and finally, we will see some examples of IaaS offerings.

Advantages of IaaS

These are the advantages of using the IaaS model:

- It offers the most flexibility of all the cloud models.
- Provisioning of compute, storage, and networking resources can be done quickly.
- Resources can be used for a few minutes, hours, or days.
- More thorough control of the infrastructure.
- Highly scalable and fault-tolerant.

Disadvantages of IaaS

Many of the disadvantages that apply to the SaaS and PaaS solutions – such as issues with data encryption and security, vendor lock-in, potential cost overruns, and configuration issues – are also applicable to the IaaS model. More specifically, the disadvantages of IaaS include the following:

- **Security**: In this case, customers have much more control over the stack, and for this reason, it is extremely critical that they have a comprehensive plan in place for security. Since customers are managing applications, data, middleware, and the operating system, there are possible security threats, for example, if certain ports are left open and an intruder guesses which ports are open. Attacks from insiders with unauthorized access and system vulnerabilities can leave data exposed between the backend servers and VMs from nefarious sources.

- **Legacy systems**: While customers can migrate legacy applications into AWS, the older hardware may not be able to provide the needed functionality to secure the legacy applications. Modifications to the older applications may be needed, potentially creating new security issues unless the application is thoroughly tested for new security vulnerabilities.

- **Training costs**: As with any new technology, training may be needed for the customer's staff to get familiar with the new infrastructure. The customer is ultimately still responsible for securing their data and their resources, computer backups, and business continuity. Without this training, it may be difficult to secure the necessary staff to support and maintain the new infrastructure.

Use cases for IaaS

Like with SaaS and PaaS, IaaS is best suited to certain scenarios. It is most suitable when enterprises want to have more control over their infrastructure. Some of the most common instances when an IaaS is used are as follows:

- Backups and snapshots
- Disaster recovery
- Web hosting
- Software development environments
- Data analytics

Examples of AWS IaaS services

These are a few of the IaaS services offered in AWS:

- **Elastic Cloud Compute** (**EC2**): One of the most popular services in AWS. EC2 is basically a fancy word for a server on the cloud.

- **Elastic Block Storage** (**EBS**): In short, Amazon EBS is block-level storage. You can think of it as a hard drive on the cloud.

Let's now look at examples of non-AWS IaaS computing and storage services.

Examples of non-AWS IaaS computing and storage services

Here is a list of other popular services from other competing cloud providers that offer similar services to those offered by AWS:

- **Azure Virtual Machines**: Azure Virtual Machines is Microsoft's answer to EC2, providing similar functionality.

- **Google Compute Engine**: Google Compute Engine is a direct competitor to Amazon EC2.

In the next section, we will cover another common paradigm that is used in cloud deployments, PaaS.

Understanding PaaS

Defining a SaaS service is easy. If everything is managed by AWS, it's a SaaS service. The same applies to a definition of an on-premises service. If you are managing everything on your infrastructure, it's clear you have an on-premises service. As you start going up and down the stack and start taking over the management of some of the components or start offloading some of the management, the line starts getting fuzzy. We'll still try to provide you with a definition for PaaS.

An initial definition could be this: any application where you are responsible for the maintenance of some of the software and some of the configuration data. More formally, **Platform as a Service (PaaS)** is a type of cloud computing service that supplies an environment to enable its users to develop, run, and manage data and applications without worrying about the complexity associated with provisioning, configuring, and maintaining the infrastructure normally required to create applications, including the servers, storage, and networking equipment.

In some ways, PaaS is like SaaS, but instead of providing services to end users that do not need to be technically savvy to use the software, PaaS delivers a platform for developers to potentially use the PaaS service to develop SaaS solutions.

PaaS enables developers to design and create applications while operating at a very high level of abstraction and focusing mostly on business rules and user requirements. These applications, sometimes called middleware, if developed appropriately can be highly scalable and highly available.

Like SaaS, PaaS takes advantage of virtualization technology. Resources can be started or shut down depending on demand. Additionally, AWS offers a wide selection of services to support the design, development, testing, and deployment of PaaS applications.

Let's now look into the advantages and disadvantages of PaaS, some use cases for PaaS, and as well as some examples of services that are considered PaaS services.

Advantages of PaaS

It doesn't matter if you are a three-person start-up or a well-established multinational, using PaaS provides many benefits:

- Cost-effective and continuous development, testing, and deployment of applications
- High availability
- Scalability
- Straightforward customization and configuration of an application
- Reduction in development effort and maintenance
- Security policies simplification and automation

AWS also offers a variety of tools to simplify the migration from an on-premises model to a PaaS model.

Disadvantages of PaaS

PaaS solutions have some limitations as well:

- **Integrations**: Having multiple parties responsible for the technology stack creates some complexity in how integrations need to be performed when developing applications. This becomes particularly problematic when there are legacy services that are on-premises and that are not scheduled to be moved to the cloud in the near future. One of the reasons enterprises like to minimize the number of technology vendors is to not allow these vendors to be able to point fingers at each other when something goes wrong. When something invariably goes wrong, enterprises know exactly who they have to contact in order for the problem to be fixed.

- **Data security**: When running applications using a PaaS solution, by definition the data will reside in a third-party environment. This poses concerns and risks. There might be regulatory requirements as well that need to be met to store data in a third-party environment. Customers might have policies that limit or prohibit the storage of data *off-site*. As an example, China recently passed regulations that require **Personally Identifiable Information** (**PII**) that is generated in China to not leave China. More specifically, if you capture your customer's email on your site and your site is available in China, the servers that store the email must reside in China and that email cannot leave the country. Using a PaaS approach to comply with this regulation requires standing up full-fledged infrastructure mimicking your existing infrastructure in other locations.

- **Vendor lock-in**: Vendor lock-in is not as tight as it is with a SaaS solution. However, migrating from AWS to other vendors (if that is desired) will still not be a simple exercise, and it will have a hefty price tag attached to the effort. The more AWS services your firm uses, the more committed you become to the platform and the more difficult it becomes to wean yourself off the platform if you ever decide to go with a different vendor. Using PaaS implies that you are only leveraging part of the AWS stack of services to fulfill your needs. Therefore, while it won't be a trivial exercise to migrate out of AWS, it will not be as difficult as if you were using the SaaS model, in which you are even more reliant on AWS.

- **Runtime issues**: PaaS solutions in AWS may not support the language and framework that your application may require. For example, if you need an old version of a Java runtime, you might not be able to use it because it may no longer be supported.

- **Legacy systems customizations**: Existing legacy applications and services might be difficult to integrate with AWS. Instead, complex customization and configuration might need to be done for legacy applications for them to properly integrate with the PaaS service. The result might yield a non-trivial implementation that may minimize the value provided by your PaaS solution. As an example, many corporations to this day rely on mainframes for at least some of their needs. If they wanted to move these mainframe applications to the cloud, they would have to rewrite the applications to not require a mainframe since mainframes are not one of the types of hardware that AWS or most typical cloud providers support.

- **Operational limitation**: Even though you have control of some of the layers in the PaaS stack, there are still other layers that are controlled and maintained by AWS. If the AWS layers need to be customized, you have little or no control over these optimizations. For example, if you are required to use a certain operating system but your PaaS provider does not support it then you are stuck with choosing one from the list of available operating systems. For example, AWS does not offer macOS X as one of the supported operating systems.

PaaS use cases

PaaS can be beneficial, and one could argue critical, to the success of today's enterprises. Take a company such as Uber (which is an AWS customer). It is not uncommon for traffic to their app to go up by 50% to 100% during certain holidays. Accordingly, Uber needs more servers during the holidays than other days. If they had an on-premises environment, they would have no choice but to *bite the bullet* and buy servers for the worst-case scenario when they have the highest traffic. But because they operate in a cloud environment, they can spin up more resources when they have usage spikes and they can bring those instances down when site traffic goes down, and they don't need as many compute resources.

Here, we review some examples of PaaS use cases:

- **Business Process Management** (**BPM**): Many enterprises use PaaS to enable BPM platforms in conjunction with other cloud services. BPM software can interoperate with other IT services. These combinations of services enable process management, implementation of business rules, and high-level business functionality.

- **Business Analytics/Intelligence** (**BI**): BI tools delivered via PaaS enable enterprises to visualize and analyze their data, allowing them to find customer patterns and business insights. This enables them to make better business decisions and more accurately predict customer demand, optimize pricing, and determine which products are their best sellers.

- **Internet of Things (IoT)**: IoT is a key driver for PaaS solution adoption and will likely be even more important in the coming years. We have probably only scratched the surface when it comes to IoT applications enabled by a PaaS layer.

- **Communications**: PaaS is often used as a delivery mechanism for communication applications. Voice, chat, video, and messaging can easily be adding by combining and leveraging PaaS platforms.

- **Databases**: A PaaS layer can deliver persistence services. A PaaS database layer can reduce the need for system administrators by providing a fully managed, scalable, and secure environment. We will visit the topic more deeply in a later chapter, but AWS offers a variety of traditional and NoSQL database offerings.

- **API management and development**: A common use case for PaaS is to develop, test, manage, and secure APIs and microservices.

- **Master Data Management (MDM)**: MDM came about from the need of businesses to improve the quality, homogeneity, and consistency of their critical data assets. Some examples of this critical data are customer data, product data, asset data, and vendor data.

MDM is used to define and manage these critical data. Additionally, it provides a single point of reference or a *single source of truth* for this data.

An MDM tool supports an enterprise's MDM. The tool is used to support MDM. MDM tools can identify and remove duplicates, assist with data standardization, and enforcing rules to get rid of incorrect records. Data inconsistencies start when the business starts getting bigger, and business units and product lines start segmenting, creating different business processes, and using different business tools to serve customers. This inevitably creates duplicate and heterogeneous data. The redundancy of the data is compounded by traversing different departments throughout the sales life cycle. Account and product data is often entered redundantly in various systems across the organization and, almost inevitably, these double entries will not be identical.

For example, your marketing department and your finance department may both store customer data in two distinct repositories. Invariably, if both systems are maintained and updated separately, the data will get out of sync. You may have "John D. Smith, 123 Main St." in one place and "Johnny Smith, 123 Main Street" in the other. As it turns out, this is the same person but because there are slight differences, it may be considered two different customers, creating all sorts of problems.

MDM enables methods for ingesting, consolidating, comparing, aggregating, verifying, storing, and routing essential data across the enterprise while ensuring a common understanding, consistency, accuracy, and quality control of this data.

PaaS platforms have proven to be a boon for the development of MDM applications, enabling them to process data more quickly and more efficiently.

Using PaaS is beneficial, sometimes even critical, in many applications. PaaS can streamline a workflow when several parties are simultaneously working on the same task. PaaS is particularly beneficial when customized applications need to be created. PaaS can reduce development and administration costs.

Examples of AWS PaaS services

Here are some examples of the most popular PaaS offerings in the AWS ecosystem:

- **AWS Elastic Beanstalk**: Beanstalk is a simple service that enables the deployment of web applications in a variety of programming languages and can scale up and down automatically.

- **Amazon RDS**: Amazon RDS is another good example of a PaaS. Amazon offers a variety of databases, such as MySQL, Postgres, and Oracle. When using Amazon RDS to use these databases, we can focus on writing our applications against them and let Amazon handle the underlying management of the database engine.

- **AWS Lambda**: Lambda is another quite simple and fully managed service that can easily scale to handle thousands of requests per second. It requires almost no configuration and removes the worry of having to provision your own hardware. More specifically, AWS Lambda is also referred to as a **Function as a Service (FaaS)**.

- **Amazon Elastic Kubernetes Service** (**Amazon EKS**): Amazon EKS is a fully managed service that enables running Kubernetes on the cloud without needing to install Kubernetes or deploy your own servers.

AWS does not have a lock on PaaS. Let's look at some of the services offered by competitors.

Examples of non-AWS PaaS

Here are some examples of PaaS services that are not in the AWS ecosystem:

- **Azure App Service**: Azure App Service is a managed PaaS that can integrate Azure Websites, BizTalk, and mobile services all in one service.

- **Heroku**: Heroku is another PaaS offering. Heroku can also be used to deploy, manage, and scale applications. You can think of Heroku as an alternative to Elastic Beanstalk.

- **Force.com**: Force.com, offered by Salesforce, is yet another PaaS. It can be used to develop and deploy applications and websites. Applications can be created using a cloud **integrated development environment** (**IDE**).

- **Google App Engine**: This is Google's implementation of a PaaS. Like the others, it is fully managed. It supports a wide variety of programming languages, including Java, PHP, Node.js, Python, C#, .Net, Ruby, and Go.

- **Google Kubernetes Engine**: Similar to Amazon EKS, the Google Kubernetes Engine allows you to run Kubernetes without the need to install and maintain the Kubernetes software.

- **OpenShift**: OpenShift is a RedHat offering (now part of IBM). It is another PaaS offering that allows its users to develop and deploy applications with minimal or no infrastructure maintenance.

This concludes the PaaS section. Let's now learn about the next possible scenario – **Software as a Service** (**SaaS**).

Understanding SaaS

SaaS, or *cloud application services*, are services where most of the heavy lifting is done by the cloud provider (in this case, AWS). In this case, you will not have to install software or worry about the operating system or software patches. Your focus will be on customizing the business logic of our application and to support your users. Most SaaS will only need browser access or, in the case of IoT applications, as most of the computation will be done on the cloud side.

In terms of software installation, SaaS gets rid of the need for your staff to visit individuals' devices. AWS is fully responsible for any issues that might arise on the server, middleware, operating system, and storage levels.

Let's now analyze the characteristics that make up SaaS, the advantages and disadvantages of using a SaaS deployment, and some SaaS examples.

Characteristics of SaaS

These are the clues that will help determine if a service is a SaaS:

- It is managed by the vendor (such as AWS).

- It is hosted on a third-party server.

- It can be accessed over the internet.

- AWS is responsible for the infrastructure, operating system, and software patches and updates.

Advantages of SaaS

SaaS has several advantages:

- Reducing the time, money, and effort spent on repetitive tasks

- Shifting the responsibility for installing, patching, configuring, and upgrading software across the service to a third party

- Allowing you to focus on the tasks that require more personalized attention, such as providing customer service to your user base

A SaaS solution allows you to get up and running efficiently. This option, versus the other two solutions we'll analyze, requires the least effort. Using this option allows companies big and small to quickly launch services and to get a project finished on time.

Disadvantages of SaaS

SaaS solutions have some limitations as well:

- **Interoperability**: Interoperability with other services may not be straightforward. For example, if you need integration with an on-premises application, it may be more complicated to perform this integration. Most likely your on-premises installation does not use the same software and technologies that exist in AWS, and that complicates the integration. The reason for this is because your on-premises environment is a hodgepodge of technology from different vendors, which makes it difficult to integrate. In contrast, before you spin up your first service, AWS goes to great lengths and performs rigorous testing to ensure that services interoperate and integrate smoothly.

- **Vendor lock-in**: This is an issue with PaaS and IaaS as well but the further up you go on the stack, the more you are committed to a vendor, in this case, AWS. To some degree, this has always been an issue with almost any technology. Vendors have always had to straddle the line between offering a standard environment that can be ported to other vendors' environments and offering proprietary offerings. A simple example is databases. Oracle and SQL Server are both databases, and they both support the SQL standard, but they also offer extensions to their databases that are not SQL compliant. In an ideal world for them, a vendor wants to offer a product that is easy to convert to but hard to migrate out of.

- **Customization**: The convenience of having AWS manage many things for you comes at a price. Opportunities for customization in a SaaS solution will not be as great as with other services that are further down in the stack. For example, an on-premises solution that offers full control of all levels in the stack will allow full customization. In your on-premises environment, if there is a requirement to use a particular version of Linux with a certain security patch, you simply install the patch. In contrast, if you are using AWS Lambda as your deployment environment, it is not possible to install a certain version of Linux. In fact, with AWS Lambda, which operating system is being used under the covers is transparent to you.

- **Lack of control**: If your organization requires that you only use a certain approved version of an operating system, this may not be appropriate. For example, there might be a regulatory requirement that necessitates detailed testing approval of the underlying operating systems and if the version is changed, a retest and approval are required. In this case, SaaS will most likely not be an acceptable solution. In a SaaS environment, you have non-deterministic latency issues. In other words, it is hard to control how long your processes are going to take.

- **Limited features**: If the SaaS solution you are using does not offer a feature you require, you might not be able to use that feature unless the SaaS vendor provides that feature in the future.

Examples of AWS SaaS solutions

Some of the solutions that AWS offers that could be classified as SaaS solutions are as follows:

- **Amazon WorkMail**: This allows users of the service to access email functionality, update their contacts, and manage calendars using any client application, such as Microsoft Outlook, Apple iOS, or Android email applications. Any email application that supports the IMAP protocol can be used. WorkMail is also directly accessible via a web browser.

- **Amazon WorkSpaces**: This provides system administrators the ability to provide virtual Microsoft Windows or Linux **Virtual Desktop Infrastructure** (**VDIs**) for their users. It obviates the need to purchase, procure, and deploy hardware and eliminates the need to install the software. Administrators can add or remove users as the organization changes. Users can access their VDIs from a wide variety of supported devices and web browsers. With Amazon Workspaces, you no longer have to visit every machine to install commonly used software such as Microsoft Office and other security software. Amazon Workspaces enables virtual environments for your users where this software is already installed, and all they need is access to a browser.

- **Amazon QuickSight**: This is a business intelligence and analytics service that is used to create charts, visualizations, perform ad hoc analysis, and obtain business insights. It seamlessly integrates with other AWS services to automatically discover AWS data sources.

- **Amazon Chime**: Similar to Slack and Zoom, Amazon Chime can be used for online meetings, video conferencing and calls, online chat, and sharing content.

Examples of third-party SaaS solutions

Also, many third-party vendors, including some that offer their services on the AWS Marketplace, are SaaS solutions. There are many examples, but here are a few that decided to build their SaaS offerings on AWS:

- **Splunk**: A software platform that enables search, aggregation, analysis, and visualizations of machine-generated data collected from disparate sources such as websites, mobile apps, sensors, IoT devices, and so forth.

- **Sendbird**: A chat solution specializing in real-time chat and messaging development for mobile apps and websites. It provides client-side SDKs in various languages, a user-friendly dashboard, and moderation tools.

- **Twilio**: A company that offers a wide variety of ways to securely communicate with customers, including email, SMS, fax, voice, chat, and video. Whenever you get an SMS to prove your identity when you log into your bank account, there is a decent chance that Twilio was involved in the process.

Now that we have gone over SaaS, PaaS, and IaaS in great detail, let's spend some time looking at when it's appropriate to use each one of them.

Selection by use case of SaaS, PaaS, or IaaS

Each model that we reviewed, including the on-premises model, has advantages and disadvantages. The one you should choose depends on your specific business requirements, what features are needed, and the developers and testers that comprise your team. You might need a fully *out of the box* solution and *time to market* might be a more important consideration than price. Or perhaps you have regulatory constraints that force you to have complete control of the environment. AWS offers a lot of assurances regarding their **Service Level Agreements (SLAs)**, as well as compliance certifications. The more levels in the stack you decide to manage, most likely the more effort you will have to exert to verify that your systems are compliant with the different regulations.

In general, one good rule of thumb is to let AWS take over the management of your resources whenever possible, and you only take over the responsibility whenever it is necessary. As an example, could you imagine trying to implement the functionality that Amazon Elastic Load Balancing or the Elastic Kubernetes Service provides? Now that we have a comprehensive understanding of the classification we covered in the previous sections, we will learn about some of the fundamental services that underpin these models.

There are two main reasons why not to use SaaS and instead use IaaS or PaaS:

- The use case in question requires a certain type of database or software that is not supported by the AWS SaaS solutions. For example, you may need to use an old version of Oracle that is no longer supported by Amazon RDS.

- The total cost of ownership of running an application using PaaS or IaaS is significantly lower than with the SaaS model. A specific example may be AWS Athena versus using Presto directly. With the current cost structure, some cloud users have found deploying Presto more cost-effective than using AWS Athena. This may change as AWS continuously changes its pricing model. It's important to note that these cost calculations should be carried out using all relevant costs, including staffing and support costs, not just software costs.

Let's now delve deeper into some of the services that AWS offers. We will start with a basic but powerful offering. Even though it is not immediately apparent, the EC2 service that we will cover in the next section underpins many other AWS services.

Learning about Amazon EC2

Amazon **Elastic Cloud Computing** (**EC2**) is a fancy name for a server. Amazon has not invented a brand-new type of computer. At the end of the day, all the fancy nomenclature that is used by AWS and other cloud vendors boils down to a bunch of servers, storage, and networking equipment housed in a data center.

Their secret sauce is as follows:

- Standardizing the management, security, and growth of this infrastructure

- Quickly meeting the client demand for their services in minutes and not months

- Taking full advantage of virtualization technologies and being able to slice one computer to act like many computers

Many of their main competitors offer the ability to spin up resources quickly as well, but there are still some data center vendors that require users to go through a long cycle, so it can be weeks or months before you can start using the provisioned resources, and it could take just as long to decommission these resources. When you are using AWS, though, you can shut off access to resources with the same speed and agility as when you requested and started the resources, with an accompanying reduction in the billing for these resources.

EC2 was developed first and foremost to be used in Amazon's internal infrastructure. It was the idea of Chris Pinkham. He was head of Amazon's worldwide infrastructure from around 2003.

Amazon released a limited beta test of EC2 to the public on August 25, 2006, providing limited trial access. In October 2007, Amazon expanded its offerings by adding two new types of instance (Large and Extra-Large). And in May 2008, two additional instance types were added to the service (High-CPU Medium and High-CPU Extra Large).

EC2 today is arguably the most successful technology product in history; however, it didn't start perfectly. Even though EC2 launched in 2006, it wasn't until November 2010 that Amazon started using Amazon EC2 to power its own retail website.

Amazon EC2 is probably the most important and critical service on the AWS cloud-computing platform. Even though it is not immediately apparent and there are no clues to this, all other compute services on the AWS platform run on the EC2 service. It makes sense: EC2 instances are nothing but compute resources, and why wouldn't Amazon leverage this foundational service to provide compute power to all its other services that require compute? Additionally, if you are trying to create something using AWS and no other service offers the functionality that you desire, you will likely be able to use EC2 as the foundation for your project. You can think of the EC2 service as a computer of almost any size and capability that you can turn on or off at any point and stop being charged when you shut it down.

> **Important note**
> If you do have a use case in which you will be starting and stopping the EC2 service, you will want to ensure that the persistence storage used is independent of the EC2 instance, such as AWS **Simple Storage Service** (**S3**), which enables permanent object storage at a low price and with a high degree of availability and durability. EC2 instances by default offer storage, but this storage is ephemeral, and anything stored in ephemeral storage will be lost immediately when the EC2 instance is shut down.

We briefly mentioned that EC2 allows a wide variety of computer sizes and capabilities. Let's revisit that idea and see how many choices are available. Amazon EC2 delivers a large variety of instance types. Each type addresses different needs, and they are optimized to fit that use case. Instance types are defined by a combination of their memory, CPU, storage, and networking capabilities. Each different type can provide the sweet spot for your individual use case. Each EC2 instance type that Amazon provides comes in different instance sizes, which allows you to match the right instance size with your target workload.

At this point, let's note that **Google Cloud Platform** (**GCP**) allows you to customize the selection of CPU and choose how much RAM memory can be allocated when you are spinning up compute instances. This is something that, as of the writing of this book, is not possible to customize on AWS.

As better CPU cores and memory chips are becoming available, AWS continually improves its EC2 offerings to take advantage of these new components. The Amazon EC2 service is constantly improving. Staying on top of the constant changes can be quite challenging.

For example, when the T instance types came out they were called T1, but now that better components are available, the top-of-the-line T instance types that are available are the T3 instances types.

To see the full list of instance types offered by AWS, see the *EC2 instance types* subsection.

In general terms, the EC2 instance types and their classifications have remained largely unchanged, but the models and sizes within each type continue to evolve. What used to be the *top shelf* offering last year might just be a middle offering this year due to improvements to the underlying component. Depending on budgetary constraints and workload needs, different models and sizes might offer the optimal solution for your project.

AWS offers many different types of EC2 instances. Each one is meant to tackle specific types of computing problems. Let's review and take a look at the instance types that are available.

EC2 instance types

As of April 2020, these are the instance types that Amazon offers:

- General Purpose (A1, M5, T3)
- Compute Optimized (C5)
- Accelerated Computing (P3, G3, F1)

- Memory Optimized (R5, X1, Memory-optimized)
- Storage Optimized (H1, D2, I3)

Let's look at each of them in detail.

General Purpose (A1, M5, T3)

T3s are an AWS workhorse instance. The T3 family of instance types is the most popular type among the general-purpose compute instances. These instance types deliver a balance between compute, memory, and networking resources. If you are new to AWS, T3 instances are probably your best choice. General-purpose instances provide a balance between cost and functionality. The main distinction within this class is between instances that offer fixed versus burstable performance.

T3 uses Intel chips, and T3a uses AMD chips. Both of them offer burstable performance. Burstable performance is used when we have uneven workloads that require an occasional boost. To scale up compute quickly, this burst in capacity can be used.

These bursts of power are not free — you get an allotment of CPU credits. When the CPU is not running at maximum capacity, CPU credits are earned. When there is a need for a boost or burst, the credits are used.

Here's an example to explain the concept of burstable credits better. If you have a T2.medium instance up and running, Amazon gives a baseline allotment of 40% usage for the virtual CPU and enables the instance to earn burstable credits at a rate of 24 credits per hour. Each credit allows the CPU to run at 100% utilization for one minute. This credit allotment is shared across the two cores. CPU credits can be used to keep a base level of performance – the base level of performance is not awarded in addition to the credits earned. This translates into being able to maintain a CPU load of 20% on each of the 2 cores in the T2.medium instance (the 2 cores running at 20% are aggregated to make the 40% baseline allotment). If the credit allotment is exceeded, this will result in an extra charge to your bill but it will still enable you to process requests and handle traffic. If you consistently find yourself paying for burstable traffic, it is probably an indication that it is time to add more instances to your architecture or move your application to a more powerful instance.

Amazon EC2 A1 instances offer good value for the amount of functionality supplied. They are often used in scale-out workloads as they are well suited for this type of job. A1 instances use an ARM chip. Therefore, this type is more suitable for ARM development and for application development that runs open source languages such as Java, Ruby, and Python.

M5 instances are similar to T3 instances. They are also general-purpose instances. They deliver a good balance between compute, memory, and network resources. M5 instances use Intel Xeon processors and are best suited for x86 architecture development.

These instance types are commonly used to run the following:

- Web servers
- Microservices
- Development environments
- Uneven workloads
- Distributed data stores
- A workload that requires equal parts of compute and memory
- Code repositories
- CRM and ERP software

Let's continue our journey through the different instance types offered by AWS.

Compute Optimized (C5)

C5 instance types are ideal for compute-intensive applications. They deliver cost-effective high performance. C5 instances are a good fit for applications that require raw compute power. C5 instances use Intel Xeon Platinum processors. Benchmarks exist that show they can run 25% faster than the previous family of C4 instance types.

These instance types are popularly used in the following:

- Scientific modeling
- Low latency web services
- Video encoding
- High-performance computing
- High traffic web servers
- Multiplayer gaming servers

Let's learn about another popular instance type – the Accelerated Computing family of instances.

Accelerated Computing (P3, G3, F1)

These instances can have additional hardware (GPUs, FPGAs) that delivers massively parallel processing to execute tasks such as graphics processing. These instances have hardware accelerators that enable them to evaluate functions, such as floating-point number calculations, graphics, modeling, and complex pattern matching, very efficiently.

P3 instances can deliver high performance with up to 8 NVIDIA V100 Tensor Core GPUs and up to 100 Gbps of networking throughput. P3 instances can reduce machine learning training dramatically, in some cases from days to minutes.

G4 instances are cost effective and versatile GPU instances that enable the deployment of graphics-intensive programs and machine learning modeling. G4 instances are optimized for machine learning workloads that use NVIDIA libraries. Graphics applications leveraging G4 instances can get a 1.8X boost in graphics performance and a 2X boost in their video transcoding capability compared to the previous generation of the Amazon G3 family of instances. The NVIDIA T4 GPU is often used for graphics applications and 3D modeling. This instance type supports the latest graphics APIs:

- DirectX 12
- OpenCL 2.2
- CUDA 10.1
- OpenGL 4.6
- Microsoft DXR

F1 instances rely on FPGAs for the delivery of custom hardware accelerations. A **Field-Programmable Gate Array** (**FPGA**) is an **Integrated Circuit** (**IC**) that is customizable in the field for a specific purpose. A regular CPU is *burned* at the factory and cannot be changed once it leaves the factory floor. An example of the is the Intel Pentium chip. Intel manufactures millions of these chips, all of them exactly the same. FPGAs are *field-programmable*, meaning they can be changed by the end user after they leave the factory. FPGAs can be customized for individual needs and burned by the customer.

These instance types are often used for the following:

- Artificial intelligence/machine learning
- High-performance computing applications
- Big data analytics
- Genomics research
- Data compression

- Image processing
- Network security
- Search

The next instance type family we will learn about is memory-optimized instances.

Memory-optimized (R5, X1, Memory-optimized)

These are optimized for memory-intensive applications. These instances can deliver fast performance by allowing to load large complete datasets into memory for processing and transformation.

R5 uses the Intel chip and R5a uses the AMD chip. These instances are best suited for memory-intensive applications. The R5 and R5a instance types use the AWS Nitro System. This optimization lowers the cost compared to other competitors.

X1 and **X1e** instances deliver a high ratio of memory to compute. The X1e type delivers the highest memory to compute ratio of all EC2 instance types.

High Memory instances deliver the greatest amount of available RAM, providing up to 12 TB of memory per server. Like the X1/X1e instances, High Memory instances are best suited for production environments of petabyte-scale databases.

It is frequently the case that these instance types are used for the following:

- Real-time data analytics
- In-memory databases
- High-performance databases
- In-memory caches
- ERP applications
- Hadoop or Spark workloads

Storage-optimized (H1, D2, I3)

These instances are best suited for workloads that need massive storage, in particular, sequential read-writes like log analysis.

The **H1** and **D2** instance types form part of the dense storage family of servers that can supply sequential reads and writes with petabyte-scale datasets. H1 and D2 instances deliver storage on HDDs. H1 instances can supply up to 16 TB and D2 can supply up to 48 TB.

I3 instances provide SSD storage up to 16 GB while supplying lower latency than HDD-based storage.

These instance types are frequently used in these cases:

- NoSQL databases such as MongoDB, Cassandra, and Redis
- In-memory databases such as MemSQL and Aerospike
- Data warehouses
- Scale-out transactional databases
- Elasticsearch
- BI and analytics workloads

The following image shows a summary of the current EC2 family instance types and their main characteristics:

	General Purpose		Compute Optimized	Memory Purpose		Accelerate the Computing	Storage Optimized		
Type	T3, A1	MS	CS	RS	XI	P3, G3, F1	H1	I3	D2, I3
Description	Burstable Changing workloads	Balanced consistent workloads	High ratio compute to memory	In-memory DBs	In-memory apps	Graphic processing AI/ML	Balanced of compute and memory HDD backed	Balanced of compute and memory HDD backed	Highest disk ratio

Figure 4.2 – Instance type families and their characteristics

It is very likely that Amazon will continue to enhance its EC2 service by offering new instance types and enhancing the current ones.

> **Important note**
> To find the most up-to-date information on Amazon EC2 instance types, visit this link: `https://aws.amazon.com/ec2/instance-types/`.

Amazon Machine Images

Even though there are so many EC2 instances types to choose from, the number of instance types pales in comparison with the number of **Amazon Machine Images** (**AMIs**) available. An AMI contains the information needed to start an instance. An AMI needs to be specified when launching an instance.

The chosen AMI will determine characteristics of the EC2 instance, such as the following:

- **Operating system**: The currently supported operating systems are as follows:

  a. AWS Linux

  b. Ubuntu

  c. Debian

  d. Red Hat

  e. Oracle Linux

  f. CentOS

  g. SUSE Linux

  h. Debian

  i. Windows Server

- **Architecture**: The architecture that will be used:

  a. 32-bit

  b. 64-bit

- **Launch permissions**: The launch permissions will determine when and where the AMI can be used:

  a. Public: All AWS accounts can launch this AMI.

  b. Explicit: Only specific AWS accounts can launch the AMI.

  c. Implicit: Implicit launch permission is given to launch the AMI.

- **Root device storage**: Another option that can be specified when choosing an AMI is how the data in the root device is persisted. The options include the following:

  a. Amazon EBS store: Uses an Amazon EBS volume launched using an Amazon EBS snapshot as its source

  b. Instance store: Uses an instance store volume launched from a template store in S3

Multiple instances can be launched from a single AMI. This is useful when multiple instances need to be launched with the same configuration. It does not matter if you need one instance or a thousand instances. They can be launched with the same amount of effort, by clicking a few buttons.

An AMI comprises the following:

- An EBS snapshot, or a template (in the case of a instance-backed AMI) for the root volume for the instance. For example, an operating system, an application, or an application server.

- Launch permissions can be used to control the AWS accounts that will be allowed to use the AMI to generate new instances.

- A block device mapping specifying which volumes need to be attached to the instance when it is started.

AWS enables running thousands of AMIs. Some of them are AMIs created by AWS, some are AMIs created by the AWS community, and some of them are offerings by third-party vendors.

We have learned about the incredibly vast number of options that are available when creating and launching Amazon EC2 instances. Now let's explore the best practices in order to best utilize the Amazon EC2 service.

Reviewing Amazon EC2 best practices

How you use and configure EC2 is going depend on your use case. But some general EC2 best practices will ensure the security, reliability, durability, and availability of your applications and data. Let's delve into the recommended practices on how to handle security, storage, backup management, and so on.

Security

Like with almost any AWS service, it's possible to manage the access and security of your EC2 instances, taking advantage of identity federation, policies, and IAM. You can create credential management policies and procedures to create, rotate, distribute, and revoke AWS access credentials.

Like with any other service, you should assign the least privilege possible to all your users and roles. As they say in the military, your users should be on a *need to know* basis.

One advantage or disadvantage of using EC2 directly is that you are fully in charge of managing the operating system changes. For that reason, make sure that you are regularly maintaining and securing the operating system as well as all the applications running on your instance.

Storage

One advantage of using EC2 instances is the fact that when you shut down the instance, you will stop getting charged. The reason that AWS can afford to do this is the fact that once you shut the instance down, they then reassign the resource to someone else. But what does this mean for any data that you had stored in the instance? The answer lies in understanding the difference between instance stores and EBS backed instances.

When you launch an EC2 instance, by default it will have an instance store. This store has high performance. However, anything that is persisted in the instance store will be lost when you shut down the instance.

> **Important note**
>
> If you want data to persist after you shut down the instance, you will need to ensure that you include an EBS volume when you create the instance (or add it later) or store the data in an S3 bucket. If you store the data in the instance store that is attached by default to the EC2 instance, it will be lost the next time the instance is shut down.

EBS volumes are mountable storage drives. They normally deliver lower speed and performance than instance stores but have the advantage that the data will persist when you shut down the instance.

It is also recommended to use one EBS volume for the operating system and another EBS volume for data.

If you insist on using the instance store for persistence purposes, make sure there is a plan in place to store the data in a cluster of EC2 instances with a replication strategy in place to duplicate the data across the nodes (for example, using Hadoop or Spark to handle this replication)

Resource management

When you launch an EC2 instance, AWS can include instance metadata and custom resource tags. These tags can be used to classify and group your AWS resources. Instance metadata is data that is specified for an instance that can then be used to customize, label, and maintain the instance. Instance metadata can be classified into topics such as the following:

- The name of the host
- Events
- Security groups

- Billing tags
- Department or organizational unit tags

The following diagram illustrates the basics of tagging your EC2 instances:

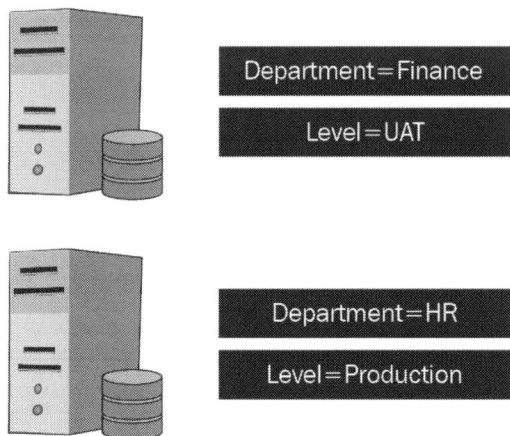

Figure 4.3 – EC2 instance tags

In this example, two tags are assigned to each one of the instances—one tag is given the key **Department** and another is given the key **Level**.

Tags are a powerful yet simple way to classify EC2 instances. They can help in development, code testing, environment management, and billing. Every tag also has a corresponding value.

Limit management

By default, AWS sets limits for a variety of parameters for Amazon EC2 (as well as for other services). If you are planning to use Amazon EC2 in production environments, you should get intimately familiar with those limits. If you know the limits, you will be able to plan when to ask for a limit increase before it becomes critical. Increasing the limits involves contacting the AWS team. It may take a few hours or a few days to get a response. These limits might change but as of April 2020, these are some of the default limits for an AWS account:

- 20 instances per region
- 5 Elastic IPs per region (including unassigned addresses)

Keep in mind that these are soft limits and they can be increased by contacting AWS.

Backup, snapshots, and recovery

It is critically important to have a periodic backup schedule for all EBS volumes. These backups can be performed with EBS snapshots. You can also build your own AMI using an existing instance and persisting the current configuration. This AMI can be used as a template to launch future instances.

To increase application and data availability and durability, it is also important to have a strategy to deploy critical application components across multiple Availability Zones and copy the application data across these Availability Zones.

Make sure that your application architecture can handle failovers. One of the simplest solutions is to manually attach an Elastic IP address or a network interface to a backup instance. Once you have the solution in place, it is highly recommended to test the setup by manually shutting down the primary server. This should failover the traffic over to the backup instance and traffic should be handled with little or no disruption.

In addition to compute services such as EC2, another fundamental service on the cloud is storage. In the next section, we will analyze the various storage services that AWS offers, starting with Amazon S3.

Learning about Amazon storage services

Soon after Amazon released the EC2 service, it quickly released another service – the **Simple Storage Service**, or **S3** for short. It was released on March 14, 2006. After the launch of S3, Amazon also launched many other object storage services to complement S3. We will analyze many of those services in this chapter.

S3 Standard

Initially, when Amazon launched the S3 service, it was simply called Amazon S3. Amazon now offers a variety of object storage services and they all use the S3 moniker, so Amazon has renamed S3 to S3 Standard.

S3 Standard delivers availability, durability, and performance for object storage for any data that will be accessed frequently. S3 Standard has low latency, high performance, and high throughput and is suitable for a long list of use cases, including the following:

- Websites with dynamic content
- Distribution of content
- Cloud applications

- Data analytics and processing
- Mobile and gaming applications

These are some of the S3 Standard service features:

- Low latency and high throughput performance
- 99.9999999999% (11 9's) durability. This translates to the equivalent of storing 10,000 files in Amazon S3 and expecting to lose one of these files every 10,000,000 years.
- This high durability is achieved because 6 replicas for each object are stored across multiple **Availability Zones (AZs)** so if one AZ completely goes down, the files will still be saved in other AZs.
- Provides 99.99% availability.
- AWS offers an availability **Service Level Agreement (SLA)**.
- An object can be automatically moved and backed up to other types of S3 storage via S3 Lifecycle management.
- SSL is supported for data in transit and encryption is available by default for data at rest.

Like other AWS services, it can be accessed via the AWS console, using the AWS CLI, or with the AWS SDK. Like with other AWS services, Amazon is one of the largest users of the S3 service and it uses it to run its global e-commerce operations. S3 can be used to store many types of objects, such as the following:

- Plain text files
- HTML files
- Backup and snapshots
- Data analytics
- JSON, XML, AVRO, Parquet, and ORC files
- Hybrid cloud storage

That's it for Amazon S3 Standard. Let's now look at another service in the S3 family – S3 Intelligent-Tiering – and let's learn what makes it intelligent.

S3 Intelligent-Tiering

The **S3 Intelligent-Tiering** storage service can reduce expenses by systematically moving files to use the most cost-effective way to store data while having no impact on operations or performance. It does this by keeping the files in two tiers:

- An optimized tier for frequent access

- An optimized tier for infrequent access that has a lower cost

S3 constantly scans access patterns of files and transfers files that have not been accessed. If a file has not been accessed for 30 days straight, it is moved to the infrequent access tier. If a file in the infrequent access tier is retrieved, it is transferred to the frequent access tier.

With the S3 Intelligent-Tiering storage class, the additional cost comes from the monitoring charge. There are no fees for retrieval and there are no additional file transfer fees when objects are transferred between the tiers. S3 Intelligent-Tier is a good solution when we know that data is going to be needed for a long time, but we are uncertain about how often this data is going to be accessed. S3 services can be enabled in a granular way up to the object level. For example, a given bucket can have one object in it that is using S3 Standard, another using S3 Intelligent-Tiering, one more with S3 Standard-IA, and one with S3 One Zone-IA. This is a contrived example, but you get the idea of how flexible it can be.

These are some of the key features of S3 Intelligent-Tiering:

- It uses the performance and reliability of S3 Standard.

- It automatically and reliably transfers files between the two tiers depending on usage patterns.

- It delivers 99.999999999% (or 11 9's) durability across multiple AZs.

- If an entire AZ goes down, it is not a fatal event and files are unaffected.

- It delivers 99.9% availability.

- AWS offers an availability SLA.

- SSL is supported for data in transit and encryption is available by default for data at rest.

So, what if we know that the data we are creating and storing will only need to be accessed infrequently? Amazon offers a service ideally suited for that, which is cheaper than S3 Standard.

S3 Standard-Infrequent Access

Depending on the use case for your data, this storage class might be the ideal solution for your data storage needs. The data can be accessed at the same speed as S3 Standard but with some tradeoffs regarding the resilience of the data.

S3 Standard-IA offers a similar profile to the Standard service but with a lower cost for storage but with a retrieval fee per GB. Combining low cost with high performance makes S3 Standard-IA a good option for use cases such as backups, snapshots, long-term storage, and as a file repository for disaster recovery. S3 Lifecycle policies can be used to automatically move files between storage classes without any coding needed.

These are some of the key features of S3 Standard-Infrequent Access:

- High throughput and low latency.

- Delivers 99.999999999% (or 11 9's) durability across multiple AZs.

- If an entire AZ goes down, it is not a fatal event and files are unaffected.

- Delivers 99.9% availability.

- AWS offers an availability SLA.

- SSL is supported for data in transit and encryption is available by default for data at rest.

So, what if your data is not critically important and you are willing to give up some durability in exchange for a cheaper alternative? Amazon has a service that fits those criteria. We'll learn about it in the next section.

S3 One Zone-Infrequent Access

A better name for **S3 Standard-Infrequent Access** might be *S3 Standard-Infrequent Access and not that critical*. Like the previous service, S3 Standard-Infrequent Access, **S3 One Zone-Infrequent Access (S3 One Zone-IA)** can be used for files that need to be retrieved with less frequency but need rapid access on occasion. One of the reasons this service is cheaper than S3 Standard is because instead of storing data in three **AZs**, S3 One Zone-IA stores data in only one AZ.

S3 One Zone-IA is a good solution for use cases that don't need the reliability of S3 Standard or S3 Standard-IA, and it is therefore cheaper. The reliability is still high, and it still has duplication, but this duplication is not done across AZs. It's a suitable option for storing files such as backup files and data that can be quickly and easily recreated. It can also be a cost-effective way to store data that has been copied from another AWS Region with S3 Cross-Region Replication.

S3 One Zone-IA delivers similar high throughput, durability, and low latency as S3 Standard, coupled with a low retrieval cost.

These are some of the key features of S3 One Zone-IA:

- Same low latency and high throughput as S3 Standard.
- It delivers 99.999999999% (or 11 9's) durability across multiple AZs.
- If an entire AZ fails, data will be lost if the entire AZ is lost.
- It delivers 99.5% availability (lower than Standard S3, but still quite high).
- AWS offers an availability SLA.
- SSL is supported for data in transit and encryption is available by default for data at rest.

So far, we have looked at services that allow us to access the data immediately. What if we are willing to give up that immediate accessibility in exchange for an even cheaper service? Amazon S3 Glacier fits that bill. We'll learn about it in the next section.

S3 Glacier

When it's known that a file will not be needed immediately, **S3 Glacier** is a good option. S3 Glacier is a secure, durable class for data archiving. It is significantly cheaper than S3 Standard, but it takes longer to retrieve an S3 Glacier file. Data can be stored on S3 Glacier at a cost that will be competitive with an on-premises solution. Within S3 Glacier, the options and pricing are flexible. S3 Glacier has three different ways to retrieve data:

- **Expedited retrieval**: Expedited retrieval enables quick access to archived data that needs to be accessed on an urgent basis. For the majority of cases (requests smaller than 250 MB), expedited retrieval can be performed in about 1 to 5 minutes.
- **Standard retrieval**: Standard retrieval enables access to archived data within several hours. Standard data retrieval normally can be completed within 3 to 5 hours. Standard retrieval is the standard option.

- **Bulk retrieval**: When there is no rush to access data, bulk retrieval can be performed (at a lower cost). It can be used to retrieve vast amounts of data (even petabyte-size requests) inexpensively. Bulk retrieval typically takes between 5 and 12 hours.

Data can be retrieved in as little as a few minutes and as long as a few hours. To use it, files can be uploaded directly to S3 Glacier, or they can be placed there through an S3 Lifecycle policy, which is designed to transfer files between other S3 storage classes.

These are some of the key features of S3 Glacier:

- Slower access to data than S3 Standard.
- It delivers 99.999999999% (or 11 9's) durability across multiple AZs.
- If an entire AZ goes down, data will be lost if the entire AZ is lost.
- SSL is supported for data in transit and encryption is available by default for data at rest.
- Low-cost.
- Configurable retrieval times from minutes to hours. Pricing will change based on retrieval time.

For data that needs to be preserved but does not need to be accessed immediately, even longer than a day, Amazon offers yet another option that is even cheaper than Glacier. We will learn about that option in the next section.

S3 Glacier Deep Archive

S3 Glacier Deep Archive is S3's cheapest option for object storage. It supports long-term storage, retention, and preservation. It is suitable for files that are only going to be retrieved occasionally. It is designed for customers that are required to keep data for 7 years or longer. One of the reasons for this requirement may be to meet a regulatory compliance regulation. Customers that operate in highly regulated environments, such as the financial industry, the healthcare industry, and government agencies could make use of this service. Other good use cases are backup and disaster recovery. Many customers use this service instead of magnetic tape systems. S3 Glacier Deep Archive can be used in conjunction with S3 Glacier, which allows data to be retrieved faster than the Deep Archive service.

These are some of the key features of S3 Glacier Deep Archive:

- 99.999999999% durability.

- Storage across multiple AZs.

- Lowest cost storage class.

- A good alternative to magnetic tape libraries.

- Data can be retrieved within 12 hours.

Here is a summary of the profiles of each storage class and how they compare to each other:

Features	S3 Standard	S3 Intelligent Tiering	S3 Standard-IA	S3 One Zone-IA	S3 Glacier	S3 Glacier Deep Archive
Durability	11 9's	11 9's	11 9's	11 9's	11 9's	11 9's
Availability	99.9	99.9	99.9	99.5%	99.9	99.9
Availability Zones	>=3	>=3	>=3	1	>=3	>=3
Minimum capacity charge per object	N/A	N/A	128KB	128KB	40KB	40KB
Access Latency	milliseconds	milliseconds	milliseconds	milliseconds	1 min - 12 hours	hours
Data Retrieval Fee	none	per GB data retrieved	per GB data retrieved	per GB data retrieved	per GB data retrieved	per GB data retrieved
Type of Storage	Object	Object	Object	Object	Object	Object
SSL Support	Yes	Yes	Yes	Yes	Yes	Yes
Availability SLA	99.9%	99%	99%	99%	99.9%	99%

Figure 4.4 – Summary of storage class features

As we can see, Amazon has a vast number of offerings for your storage use cases. Depending on how quickly the data needs to be retrieved and how durably it needs to be stored, the costs will vary, and savings can be made if high durability and fast retrieval are not required.

Summary

In this chapter, we reviewed a classification that is commonly used to differentiate the various services available on cloud platforms: **Software as a Service (SaaS)**, **Platform as a Service (PaaS)**, and **Infrastructure as a Service (IaaS)**.

We also learned about a few of the most fundamental services available in AWS. These services are the foundation for the rest of the services offered in AWS. For example, a service such as Amazon SageMaker or Amazon DynamoDB under the hood relies on core services such as EC2 and S3. One way to look at this is if you look purely at the traffic and usage volume, AWS's biggest customer is AWS. However, AWS doesn't charge other AWS departments for its service usage in the same way it charges its regular customers. So, the EC2 group in AWS is not getting rich from the SageMaker team.

Hopefully, after reading this chapter you are now able to decide when it's best to use the compute and storage services covered in this chapter.

In the next chapter, we will get knee-deep into another set of fundamental services in AWS that are the workhorse of many successful start-ups and multinationals alike, and that is the wonderful world of databases.

5

Selecting the Right Database Service

In this chapter, we will review the plethora of database services available in AWS. With so many choices at our disposal, it is easy to get analysis paralysis. So, in this chapter, we will first lay a foundation of how the databases and their use cases can be classified, and then use these classifications to help us pick the right service for our particular use case and our individual circumstances. In this chapter, we will help you navigate the variety of options and give you the confidence that you are using the right tool for the job.

In this chapter, we will cover the following topics:

- A brief history of databases
- Classifying databases using different methods
- Introducing different types of databases
- Choosing the right tool for the job

A brief history of databases

Relational databases have been around for over 50 years. The first database was created by Edgar F. Codd in 1970. The main feature of a relational database is that data is arranged in rows and columns, and rows in tables are associated with other rows in other tables by using the column values in each row as relationship keys. Another important feature of relational databases is that they normally use **Structured Query Language** (**SQL**) to access, insert, update, and delete records. SQL was created by IBM researchers Raymond Boyce and Donald Chamberlin in the 1970s. Relational databases and SQL have served us well for decades.

With the increase in the popularity of the internet in the 1990s, we started hitting scalability limits with relational databases. Additionally, a larger variety of data types started cropping up. RDBMSes were simply not enough anymore. This led to the development of new designs. And with this, we got the fuzzy and confusing term of NoSQL databases. As confusing as the term is, it does convey the idea that it is able to deal with data that is not structured, and it deals with it with more flexibility.

The term NoSQL is attributed to Carlo Strozzi and was apparently first used in 1998 in reference to a relational database that he developed, but didn't use the SQL language. The term was then again used in 2009 by Eric Evans and Johan Oskarsson to describe databases that were not relational.

It is nothing short of amazing what has occurred since then. Hundreds of new offerings have been developed, each trying to solve a different problem. In this environment, it becomes quite difficult to decide what service or product is the best to solve your individual problem. And you must consider not only your current requirements and workloads, but you are also assuming that your choice of database will be able to cover your future requirements and new demand. Let's lay out a few ways to differentiate the offerings and ways that databases can be classified.

Different methods to classify databases

In this section, we will cover a few of the various methods by which databases can be classified. Learning about these classifications will help us understand when it's most appropriate to use them.

Classifying databases by content

Even with all the current offerings, most databases fall into one of these categories:

- Relational databases
- Key-value databases
- Document databases
- Wide column storage databases
- Graph databases

Classifying databases by usage

Broadly speaking, two operations can be performed with a database:

- Ingest data (or write data into the database)
- Retrieve data (or read data from the database)

These two operations will always be present. On the ingestion side, the data will be ingested in two different ways. It will either be data that is replacing existing data (such as an update operation) or it will be brand new data (such as an insert operation). These two operations will always be present. In order to retrieve data, we need to have inserted the data previously. And if we insert data into the database but we never retrieve it, that would make the database useless. But what drives our choice of database is not the fact that these two operations are present but rather the following:

- How often will the data be retrieved?
- How fast should it be accessed?
- Will the data be updated often, or will it be mostly new data?
- How often will the data be ingested?
- How fast does ingestion need to be?
- Will the ingested data be sent in batches or in real time?
- How many users will be consuming the data?
- How many simultaneous processes will there be for ingestion?

The answers to these questions will drive the decision of what database technology to use. For many years now, two technologies are the standards to address these questions. The main question that needs to be answered is *Is it more important for the database to perform during data ingestion or during data retrieval?*

- **Online Transaction Processing Systems (OLTP)**: OLTP databases' main characteristics are the fact that they process a large number of transactions (such as inserts and updates). The focus in OLTP systems is placed on fast ingestion and modification of data while maintaining data integrity normally in a multi-user environment and less emphasis on the retrieval of the data. OLAP performance is normally measured by the number of transactions executed in a given time period (usually seconds). Data is normally stored using a schema that has been normalized usually using **3rd normal form** (**3NF**). Before moving on, let's quickly discuss 3NF. 3NF is a state that a relational database schema design can possess. When a table is using 3NF it will reduce the data duplication, minimize data anomalies, guarantee referential integrity, and increase data management. 3NF was first specified in 1971 by *Edgar F. Codd*, the inventor of the relational model for database management.

  A database relation (for example, a database table) meets the 3NF standard if each of the tables' columns only depends on the table's primary key.

  Let's look at an example of a table that fails to meet 3NF. Let's say you have a table that contains a list of employees. This table, in addition to other columns, contains the employee's supervisor's name as well as the supervisor's phone number. A supervisor can certainly have more than one employee under their supervision, so both the supervisor name and the supervisor phone number will be repeated for employees working under the same supervisor.

  In order to resolve this issue, we could add a supervisor table and put the supervisor name and phone number in the supervisor table and remove the phone number from the employee table.

- **On-line Analytical Processing Systems (OLAP)**: Conversely, OLAP databases do not process many transactions. Once data is ingested, it is normally not modified. It is not uncommon for OLTP systems to be the source systems for OLAP systems. Data retrieval is often performed using some sort of query language (often using the **Structured Query Language** (**SQL**)). Queries in an OLAP environment are often complex and involve subqueries as well as aggregations. In the context of OLAP systems, the performance of queries is the relevant measure. An OLAP database normally contains historical data that has been aggregated and stored in multi-dimensional schemas (normally using the star schema).

For example, a bank might handle millions of transactions a day storing deposit, withdrawal, and other banking data. The initial transactions will probably be stored using an OLTP system. At the end of the day, the data might be copied over to an OLAP system to run reporting based on the transactions for the day and, once it's aggregated, for longer reporting periods.

The following table shows a comparison between OLTP and OLAP:

	OLTP	OLAP
Focus	Insertion and modification of data.	Retrieval and analysis of data.
Data	OLTP data is normally the source of truth and original data.	OLAP systems are fed by OLTP systems.
Transaction	OLTP has short transactions. Usually a combination of updates and inserts.	OLAP has long transactions. Usually just inserts.
Time	Low processing time of transactions.	High processing time of transactions.
Queries	Simpler queries.	Complex queries.
Normalization	Usually normalized (3NF).	Usually not normalized.
Integrity	Important. Normally ACID.	Not as important. BASE can be used.

Figure 5.1 – Comparison between OLTP systems and OLAP systems

In the next section, we will classify databases based on transaction database consistency.

Classifying databases by transaction data consistency

Transaction data consistency in the context of databases refers to the requirement that any database transaction can change data only in allowed ways. Data written to the database will be validated against a set of rules and constraints and all these checks must always be passed before the data is made available to other users. Currently, there are two popular data consistency models. We'll discuss these models in the following subsections.

ACID data consistency model

The ACID model came way before the BASE model, which we will describe next. If performance was not a consideration, using the ACID model would always be the right choice. BASE only came into the picture because the ACID model was not able to scale in many instances, especially with internet applications that serve a worldwide client base. When database sizes were measured in megabytes, we could have stringent requirements that enforced strict consistency. Nowadays, since storage has become exponentially cheaper, databases can be much bigger, often measured in terabytes and even petabytes. For this reason, making databases ACID compliant for storage reasons is much less prevalent. The ACID model guarantees the following:

- **Atomicity**: In order for an operation to be considered atomic, it should ensure that transactions within the operation either succeed or fail. If one of the transactions fails, all operations should fail and be rolled back. Could you imagine what would happen if you went to the ATM and the machine gave you money, but it didn't deduct it from your account?

- **Consistency**: After each transaction is completed, the database is structurally sound and consistent.

- **Isolation**: Transactions are isolated from one another and don't contend with each other. Access to data from multiple users is moderated to avoid contention. Isolation guarantees that two transactions cannot occur simultaneously.

- **Durability**: After a transaction is completed, any changes a transaction makes should be durable and permanent even if there is a failure such as a power failure.

BASE data consistency model

ACID was taken as the law of the land for many years, but with the advent of bigger scale projects and implementations, a new model emerged. In many instances, the ACID model is more pessimistic than required, and it's *too safe* at the expense of scalability and performance.

In most NoSQL databases, the ACID model is not used, and these databases have loosened some of the ACID requirements, such as data freshness, immediate consistency, and accuracy, in order to gain other benefits, such as scale, speed, and resilience. One notable exception for a NoSQL database that uses the ACID model is the .NET-based RavenDB database.

The acronym BASE can be broken down as follows – **Basic Availability**, **Soft-state**, **Eventual consistency**. Let's explore what this means further:

- **Basic availability**: The data is available for the majority of the time (but not necessarily all the time). The BASE model places importance on availability, without guaranteeing consistency of data replication when writing a record.

- **Soft-state**: The database doesn't have to be write consistent, and different replicas don't always have to be mutually consistent. Take, for example, a system that reports sales figures in real time to multiple destinations and also uses multiple copies of the sales figures to provide fault tolerance. As sales come in and get written into the system, different readers may read a different copy of the sales figures. Some of them may be updated with the new numbers and some of them may be a few milliseconds behind and not have the latest updates. In this case, the readers are going to have different results, but if they run the query again soon after, they probably would get the new figures. In a system like this, not having the latest and greatest numbers may not be the end of the world and may be good enough. The trade-off between getting the results fast versus being completely up to date may be acceptable.

- **Eventual consistency**: The stored data exhibits consistency eventually and maybe not until the data is retrieved at a later point.

The BASE model requirements are looser than ACID model ones and a direct one-for-one relationship does not exist between ACID and BASE.

The BASE consistency model is used mainly in aggregate databases (including wide-column databases), key-value databases, and document databases.

Classifying databases by use case

Databases can be used in a wide variety of projects and these projects can be classified in many ways. In our professional consulting practice, we have found it quite useful to divide the use cases using the following classifications.

Cloud-native projects

When building projects natively in the cloud, there are two kinds of projects:

- **Green-field projects**: These are projects that have not been implemented yet and will be developed in the cloud from the ground up.

- **Existing cloud projects**: These are projects that have already started and now need to be enhanced, and new features and functionality need to be implemented, but they were born in the cloud.

Migration projects

Another common use case for cloud projects is cloud migration projects. These are projects that have already been developed on hardware that was not in the cloud and now needs to be migrated to the cloud:

- **Lift and shift projects**: Projects where there is a mandate to migrate an application to the cloud with minimal changes to the functionality AND to the components.

- **Rip the band-aid projects**: Projects with applications to be migrated to the cloud with minimal changes to the functionality, and it's okay to make changes to the underlying components to take advantage of cloud-centric features to better architect the application.

Introducing different types of databases

In this section, we will cover the different types of database that are on offer. Let's start by taking a look at relational databases.

Relational databases

As we are discovering in this chapter, there are many offerings in the database space, but relational databases have served us well for many years without needing any other type of database. For any project that does not store millions of records, a relational database is still probably the best, cheapest, and most efficient option. So, let's analyze the different relational options that AWS offers us.

Amazon Relational Database Service (Amazon RDS)

Given what we said in the previous section, it is not surprising that Amazon has a robust lineup of relational database offerings. They all fall under the umbrella of Amazon RDS. It is certainly possible to install your own database into an EC2 instance and manage it yourself. Unless you have an extremely good reason to do so, though, it may be a terrible idea and, instead, you should consider using one of the many flavors of Amazon RDS. Using Amazon RDS will shift all the infrastructure management responsibility to Amazon. Amazon will automatically handle upgrading the software version, patching, and failover for you. Being a control freak is not a good enough reason to install your own database. Also, when you run the numbers, you might think that running your own instance might be cheaper, but if you take into account all the costs, including system administration costs, you will most likely be better off and save money using Amazon RDS. A good reason to install your own database instead of using RDS is if you have to use a particular database vendor that is not provided by RDS. Another reason may be that there is a regulation that requires you have complete control of the management of the database.

Amazon RDS's flavors fall into three broad categories:

- **Community** (Postgres, MySQL, MariaDB): As it does with many other open source tools, Amazon offers RDS with three different open source offerings. This is a good option for development environments, low usage deployments, defined workloads, and non-critical applications that can afford some downtime.

- **Aurora** (Postgres, MySQL): As you can see, Postgres and MySQL are here, as they are in the community editions. Is this a typo? No, delivering these applications within the Aurora *wrapper* can add many benefits to a community deployment. Some of these are as follows:

  a) Automatic allocation of storage space in 10 GB increments up to 64 TBs

  b) Fivefold performance increase over the vanilla MySQL version

  c) Automatic six-way replication across availability zones to improve availability and fault tolerance

  Amazon started offering the MySQL version of the service in 2014, and it added the Postgres version in 2017.

- **Commercial** (Oracle, SQLServer): The bad blood between Oracle and Amazon is no secret. Internally, Amazon has an initiative to get rid of Oracle in any of its internal projects. Amazon, however, realizes that many customers still run Oracle workloads and for that reason they offer RDS with an Oracle flavor (and a Microsoft SQL Server flavor). Here, you will get all the benefits of a fully managed service. Keep in mind that, bundled in the cost of the usage of this service, there is going to be a licensing cost associated with using this service, which otherwise might not be present if you use a community edition.

Document and key-value databases

Document and key-value databases are close cousins. Both types of database rely heavily on keys that point to a value. The main difference between them is that in a document database, the value stored (the document) will be **transparent** to the database and therefore can be indexed to assist with retrieval. In the case of a key-value database, the value is **opaque** and will not be scannable, indexed, or visible until the value is retrieved by specifying the key. Retrieving a value without using the key would require a full scan of the table. Content is stored as the value. To retrieve the content, you query using the unique key, and that enables accessing the value. Let's delve deeper into these two types of database.

Document databases

In the case of a document database, records contain structured or semi-structured values. This structured or semi-structured data value is called a document. It normally is stored using **Extensible Markup Language (XML)**, **JavaScript Object Notation (JSON)**, or **Binary JavaScript Object Notation (BSON)** format types.

What are document databases good for?

- Content management systems
- E-commerce applications
- Analytics
- Blogging applications

When are they not appropriate?

- Requirements for complex queries or table joins
- OLTP applications

Key-value databases

Key-value databases are the simpletons of the NoSQL world. They are quite easy to use. There are three simple API operations:

- Retrieve the value for a key.
- Insert or update a value using a key reference.
- Delete a value using the key reference.

The values are normally **Binary Large OBjects** (**BLOBs**). Data stores keep the value without regard for the content. Data in key-value database records is accessed using the key (in rare instances, they might be accessed using other filters or using a full table scan). Therefore, performance is high and scalable. The biggest strength of key-value databases is always their biggest weakness. Data access is quick because we use the key to access the data, but operations such as full table scans and filtering are either not supported or are a secondary consideration. Most often, key-value stores use the hash table pattern to store the keys. No column-type relationships exist, which keeps the implementation details simple.

What are key-value databases good for?

- Storing user profiles
- Tracking user sessions and preferences
- Persisting shopping cart data
- Developing mobile applications
- Creating web applications
- Gaming
- Ad tech
- IoT applications

When are they not appropriate?

- Queries using specific data values to filter records
- Queries using relationships between data values
- Operations using multiple unique keys
- Requirements to update values frequently

Examples of document and key-value databases

Examples of document NoSQL databases are as follows:

- Apache CouchDB
- Amazon DocumentDB
- MongoDB
- Elasticsearch

Examples of key-value databases are Redis and MemcacheDB.

There is one database that can be used both as a key-value and document database:
Dynamo DB.

Dynamo DB

Amazon DynamoDB, like other document and key-value stores, can achieve single-digit millisecond performance when retrieving values using a key. If a use case requires even faster access, such as microsecond latency, **DynamoDB Accelerator** (**DAX**) can be used. DAX supports a fully managed in-memory cache.

Some of DynamoDB benefits are as follows:

- Fully managed
- Supports multi-region deployment
- Multi-master deployment
- Fine-grained identity and access control
- Seamless integration with IAM security
- In-memory caching for fast retrieval
- Supports ACID transactions
- Encrypts all data by default

Some DynamoDB implementations have been configured to support over 10 trillion requests per day with bursts of 20 million requests per second.

Wide-column store databases

Wide-column databases can sometimes be referred to as column family databases. A wide-column database is a NoSQL database that can store petabyte-scale amounts of data. Its architecture relies on persistent, sparse matrix, multi-dimensional mapping using a tabular format. Wide-column databases are not normally relational.

When is it a good idea to use wide-column databases?

- Sensor logs and IoT information
- Geo-location data
- User preferences
- Reporting
- Time-series data
- Logging applications
- Many inserts, not many updates
- Low latency requirements

When are wide wide-column databases not a good fit? They are good when the use case calls for ad-hoc queries:

- Heavy requirement for joins
- High level aggregations
- Requirements change frequently
- OLTP uses cases

Amazon Managed Apache Cassandra Service (Amazon MCS, or Amazon Keyspaces)

Apache Cassandra is probably the most popular wide-column store implementation on the market today. Its architecture allows deployments without single points of failure. It can be deployed across clusters and across data centers (or to use Amazon's term, "availability centers"). Amazon MCS is a fully managed service that allows users to deploy Cassandra workloads.

As Amazon does with other open source projects, they have wrapped Cassandra around a managed service, turning it into a serverless service that scales up and down depending on demand. Servers are automatically spun up or brought down and, as such, users are only charged for the servers Cassandra is using at any one time. Since it's managed by AWS, users of the service never have to provision, patch, or manage servers, and they don't have to install, configure, or tune software. Cassandra in AWS can be configured to support thousands of user requests per second.

Also, when using Amazon Keyspaces, Cassandra tables are encrypted by default and replicated across data centers to increase redundancy and provide high availability. It is not unheard of to tune Cassandra in AWS to enable single-digit millisecond performance.

We mentioned that Cassandra is a NoSQL database and, as expected, it doesn't support SQL. The lingua franca for Cassandra is the **Cassandra Query Language** (**CQL**). The quickest method to interact with Apache Cassandra is using the CQL shell, which is called **cqlsh**. With cqlsh you can create tables, insert data into the tables, and access the data via queries, among other operations.

Amazon Keyspaces supports the Cassandra CQL API (version 3.11). Because of this, current code and drivers developed in Cassandra will work without changing the code. Using Amazon MCS instead of just Apache Cassandra is as easy as modifying your database endpoint to point to an Amazon MCS service table.

Indexing and search services

If a tree falls in a forest and no-one is around to hear it, does it make a sound? If content is ingested but it is not accessible, is it useful? Content that cannot be found is useless. There are a variety of popular tools available to enable enterprise search, such as Solr and Elasticsearch. These tools help folks across an enterprise find information regardless of the source type and format. These tools have connectors that allow you to crawl and index disparate sources such as databases, filesystems, and LDAP directories.

An important consideration with these search tools, as is always the case with enterprise applications, is security.

We need to ensure that only authorized users can access specific content across the enterprise, especially if this content is sensitive financial information or **Personal Identifying Information** (**PII**).

Enterprise search allows authorized users to locate information relevant to their work. In order to facilitate this, the data is normally crawled and indexed beforehand.

For search to be useful, it must be relevant. You have no doubt been frustrated with some corporate search tools that provide the result you want but you had to go to page 4 to find what you were looking for. Facilitating relevance requires a combination of powerful tools and processing:

- Careful curation from data stewards.

- Artificial intelligence enhancements, data classification, and optimization.

- A feedback mechanism that allows users to voice their displeasure when they don't find what they are looking for or demonstrate their elation when they do. A rating system that allows users to provide this feedback can then be used to make subsequent searches even better.

Some of the techniques used to facilitate search are as follows:

- Meta-tagging

- Categorization

- Use of taxonomies

- Use of filtering facets

- Auto-summarization

Search can sometimes be more of an art than a science. Consider the case where even the users themselves don't know what they are looking for when they begin the search and only as they start getting results, they realize that they were looking for something different than what they thought. A well-designed search system will enable the user to perform the dance required to better craft their question and find what they are really looking for.

Additionally, content is not static, so a well-architected search system should be designed to be able to get notifications when data changes occur so that this new data can be crawled and indexed. In the next section, we will explore the specific services that AWS offers for enterprise search.

Amazon Elasticsearch

Elasticsearch by itself (without AWS) offers simple REST-based APIs, a simple HTTP interface, and uses schema-free JSON documents. Users can get up and running building mission-critical, fault-tolerant applications in no time.

Amazon does with many popular open source tools. Elasticsearch is no exception, and Amazon has wrapped this popular search tool as an AWS managed service, simplifying its maintenance and making it easy to scale up or down. The open source version of Elasticsearch is maintained by a for-profit company called Elastic. Even though Elasticsearch is open source, both AWS and Elastic.co need to make money to keep the lights on. So how do they monetize the technology? In the case of AWS, the answer is easy. The use of the software Elasticsearch is free, but you pay for computer time and storage necessary to support your deployment. In the case of Elastic.co, they do offer some features for their product that are paid features, as well as providing consulting services.

Elasticsearch was released by the Dutch company Elastic N.V. in 2010. Elasticsearch has a RESTful interface, which makes it easy to integrate with other services. Its distributed engine for search and analytics uses the old workhorse of Apache Lucene as its foundation. Elasticsearch is arguably the most popular search engine. The combination of Logstash, Kibana, and Elasticsearch is often referred as the ELK stack. Kibana is an open source visualization tool that can be used to build interactive dashboards. Logstash is a server-side data processing pipeline that can ingest content from a multitude of sources simultaneously. In turn, Logstash can then transform the data and then distribute it for consumption.

Elasticsearch provides a custom Query Domain Specific Language that allows the creation of powerful and expressive queries. Some of the features of the language are as follows:

- Queries can be expressed using JSON format
- Support for nested queries
- Weighted queries by using conditions or filters to boost a document rating using the value of certain pre-defined fields
- Likes (similar to Facebook)

Some of the use cases for Elasticsearch are as follows:

- Full-text search
- JSON document storage and indexing
- Log analytics
- Security intelligence
- Business analytics

Elasticsearch can store the original document and create a reference to a document in the service's index. With this index, the document can be retrieved with sub-second performance with the help of the Elasticsearch API.

The Amazon Elasticsearch service is fully managed service, which means a lot fewer headaches and less effort because tasks such as software patching, hardware provisioning, database backups, recovery from failure, and monitoring are managed by AWS.

Amazon Kendra

Amazon Kendra is an enterprise search service fully managed by Amazon that uses machine learning to power it. Amazon Kendra enables users of the service to quickly add search capabilities to applications so their end users can discover information stored in disparate data stores and across the enterprise. The content can be structured, semi-structured, and unstructured.

Here are some unstructured examples:

- HTML
- MS Office Word
- PowerPoint
- PDF

These are some semi-structured examples:

- Excel files
- NoSQL databases such as Amazon DynamoDB and Amazon Neptune

These are some structured examples:

- SQL Server
- Amazon Redshift
- Amazon Aurora

Kendra offers connectors for a wide variety of data sources. Some of the supported data sources are as follows:

- Filesystems
- Websites
- Box
- DropBox
- Salesforce
- SharePoint

- Relational databases
- Amazon S3

Have you noticed when you use Google, sometimes you get the answer without hitting *Enter* to submit your query? The result actually comes up in the dropdown. Similar functionality can be found when you use Amazon Kendra. When you type a question, Kendra uses machine learning to ascertain the context and returns the most relevant results. The answer could be a full document or simply a string containing the answer. With a question such as *What is the last day for open enrollment in 2020?*, Kendra will scan to the relevant source and return an exact answer such as *February 15*. Kendra provides samples to allow developers to get up and running quickly. What's more, many of Kendra's features can be used without writing code.

Assuming the data has been entered in the repositories, Kendra can answer questions such as trivia questions (who, what, when, where)

- Who is Apple's CEO?
- When is the US presidential election in 2020?
- When is Singles Day in China in 2021?

These questions will need fact-based answers that may be returned in with a single word or phrase.

Kendra can also answer descriptive questions:

- How do I install my Amazon Echo?
- How do I apply for low income housing in New Jersey?

In this case, the answer will be a sentence, passage, or an entire document.

We could also submit keyword searches that are just a few words by themselves:

- Orange
- American Pie

Here, the intent and scope are not that clear, and Kendra will return relevant documents that contain these keywords or documents that have words that Kendra thinks are relevant to the original keywords.

Kendra can be started in the AWS console, and this method provides the easiest way to get up and running:

- Kendra can be used with unstructured and semi-structured documents. An example may be emails in an Amazon S3 bucket.

- Immediately upon ingestion, Kendra can be used. For example, a query can be performed directly in the console.

- Kendra can be implemented and configured by typing just a few lines of code.

In addition, Kendra has been trained with domain-specific data for areas:

- Technology

- Biotech

- Insurance

- Oil and gas

- Financial services

- Legal services

- Media and entertainment

- Travel and hospitality

- Human resources

- Contemporary news

- Telecommunications

- Mining

- Restaurants

- Automotive

The functionality and performance of Kendra can be extended by injecting customized and personalized synonym lists. Files can be uploaded with specific terminology and Kendra will use these synonyms to enrich user searches.

Kendra provides two methods for index updates:

- A job can be invoked and data sources can be synchronized regularly at using a predefined schedule.

- New connectors can be built that will send data to Kendra from a set of given data sources using an ETL job or an application. Doing so greatly reduces the development life cycle.

Amazon Kendra's machine learning models are regularly retrained and tuned by analyzing and incorporating end-user search patterns and feedback. Improvements to a customer's models are not shared with other customers.

In-memory databases

Gone are the days when we measured a computer's **random-access memory** (**RAM**) in kilobytes. In fact, an internet rumor that refuses to die is that the visionary Bill Gates once said: "*640 KB ought to be enough for anyone*". Gates himself disputes having ever said that but, regardless, no one would make that argument today. In fact, Amazon provides EC2 High Memory Instances that, as of, March 2020 can provide up to 24 terabytes of RAM. In addition, AWS offers **solid state drives** (**SSDs**), which blur the line between primary memory and secondary memory by greatly increasing the speed at which secondary memory can be accessed. Given that, access to ridiculous amounts of primary storage has been greatly increased; a new breed of databases has emerged that take advantage of this ginormous space.

In-memory databases, or **IMDBs** for short are databases that, most of the time, store the entirety of data in main memory. Contrast this with databases that use a machine's RAM for optimization but do not store all the data at the same time in primary memory and instead rely on disk storage. IMDBs generally have better performance than disk-optimized databases because disk access is normally slower than direct memory access. In-memory operations are simpler and can be performed using fewer CPU cycles. In-memory data access obviates seek time when querying the data, which enables faster and more consistent performance than using long-term storage. To get an idea of the difference in performance, in-memory operations are usually measured in nanoseconds, whereas operations that require disk access are usually measured in milliseconds. So, in-memory operations are usually about a million times faster than operations needing disk access.

ElastiCache

Memcached and Redis are two quite popular implementations of IMDBs developed by the open source community. Amazon offers a service for each one of these. As we have seen throughout the book, these two open source tools are not the exception to this model. AWS uses this model with many popular open source tools. They take the tool and create a service container providing resiliency, scalability, and ease-of-maintenance by turning it into an AWS managed service.

Amazon ElastiCache enables users of the service to configure, run, and scale an IMDB and to build data-intensive applications. In-memory data storage boosts applications' performance by retrieving data directly from memory.

Redis versus Memcached

Since ElastiCache offer two flavors of in-memory databases, the obvious question is which one is better? From our research, the answer right now appears to be Redis, unless you are already a heavy user of Memcached. If your shop already has made a commitment to Memcached, it is likely not worth it to port to Redis. But for new projects, the better option is Redis. This could change in the future, but as of this writing Redis continues to gain supporters. Here is a comparison of the features and capabilities of the two:

	Memcached	Redis
Sub-millisecond latency	Yes	Yes
Developer ease of use	Yes	Yes
Data partitioning	Yes	Yes
Support for a broad set of programming languages	Yes	Yes
Advanced data structures	N/A	Yes
Multithreaded architecture	Yes	N/A
Snapshots	N/A	Yes
Replication	N/A	Yes
Transactions	N/A	Yes
Pub/Sub	N/A	Yes
Lua scripting	N/A	Yes
Geospatial support	N/A	Yes

Figure 5.2 – Comparison of Redis and Memcached

Graph databases

Graph databases are data stores that treat relationships between records as first-class citizens. In traditional databases, relationships are often an afterthought. In the case of relational databases, relationships are implicit and manifest themselves as foreign key relationships. In graph databases, relationships are explicit, significant, and optimized. Using graph database language, relationships are called edges.

In some aspects, graph databases are similar to NoSQL databases. They are also schemaless. For certain use cases, they offer much better data retrieval performance than traditional databases. As you can imagine, graph databases are particularly suited for use cases that place heavy importance on relationships among entities.

Accessing data nodes and edges in a graph database is highly efficient. It normally can occur in constant time. With graph databases, it is not uncommon to be able to traverse millions of edges per second.

Regardless of how many nodes there are in a dataset, graph databases can handle nodes with many edges. In order to traverse a graph database, you only need a pattern and an initial node. Graph databases can easily navigate the neighboring edges and nodes around an initial starting node, while caching and aggregating data from the visited nodes and edges. As an example of a pattern and a starting point, you might have a database that contains ancestry information. In this case, the starting point might be you and the pattern might be parent. So, in this case, the query would return the names of both of your parents.

- **Nodes**: Nodes are elements or entities in a graph. They contain a series of properties, attributes, or key-value pairs. Nodes can be given tags, which constitute roles in the domain. Node labels can be employed to assign metadata (such as indices or constraints) to the nodes.

- **Edges**: Edges supply directed, named, and semantically significant connections between two nodes. An example is shown in the following figure. An edge has a direction, a type, a start node, and an end node. Like a node, an edge can also have properties. In some situations, an edge can have quantitative properties, such as a weight, cost, and strength. Due to the efficient way an edge is stored, two nodes can share edges regardless of the quantity or type without a performance penalty. Edges have a direction, but edges can be traversed efficiently in both directions:

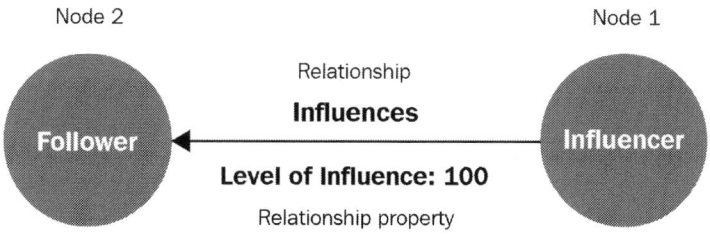

Figure 5.3 – Example of a relationship

Now let's look at Amazon Neptune, which is Amazon's graph database service.

Amazon Neptune

Amazon Neptune is a petabyte-scale graph database engine that is highly performant. It provides native support for encryption. It can store billions of relationships for millions of nodes and can support queries with millisecond latency. Amazon Neptune offers full support for these graph models:

- Property graphs
- W3C's **Resource Description Framework (RDF)**

The following query languages are supported:

- Apache TinkerPop Gremlin
- SPARQL

Amazon Neptune can be configured with high availability using the following:

- Continuous backups using Amazon S3
- Point-in-time recovery
- Read replicas
- Replication across Availability Zones

Neptune is fully managed, which means that AWS handles these tasks for you:

- Hardware provisioning
- Software patching
- Software setup

- Software configuration
- Database backups

From the content provided in this section, hopefully you now feel empowered to determine when graph databases are an appropriate solution. In short, if relationships are central to your use case, you should consider a graph database for your project.

Time-series databases

A **time series database** (**TSDB**) is a database specifically designed and optimized to store events. What is an event, you ask? It is an action that happens at a specific point in time. With events, it's not only important to track *what* happened but it is just as to important to track *when* it happened. The unit of measure to use for the time depends on the use case. For some applications, it might be enough to keep what day the event happened. But for other applications, it might be required to keep track of the time down to the millisecond. Some examples of projects that might benefit from a TSDB are as follows:

- Performance monitoring
- Networking and infrastructure applications
- Adtech and click stream processing
- Sensor data from IoT applications
- Event-driven applications
- Financial applications
- Log analysis
- Industrial telemetry data for equipment maintenance
- Other analytics projects

A TSDB is optimized to measure changes over time. Time series values can be quite different from other data types and require different optimization techniques.

Common operations in a TSDB are as follows:

- Millions of inserts from disparate sources potentially per second
- Summarization of data for downstream analytics
- Access to individual events

Do you feel comfortable about when you should use TSDBs? If you need to store events, to track logs or trades, or if the time and date when something happened take center stage, then a TSDB is probably a good solution to your problem.

Amazon Timestream

First, start with the fact that Amazon Timestream as of March 2020 is still not generally available. In order to work with it, you need to sign up for a preview version. The preview request needs to be approved by Amazon; it might take a few days, a few weeks, or a few months to get access, and you might not get approved. Second, Amazon releases many of its services first as a preview to some of its customers in order to work out the kinks, bugs, and issues. So, the fact that it is still not **generally available** (**GA** in Amazon lingo) may indicate that Amazon does not yet feel comfortable enough with this service. Having gone through this caveat, let's dive into the service.

Amazon Timestream is a scalable and fully managed TSDB. Amazon Timestream can persist and analyze billions of transactions per minute at about 1/10 of the cost of RDBMS equivalents. IoT devices and smart industrial machines are becoming more popular by the day. These kinds of applications generate events that need to be tracked and measured, sometimes with real-time requirements. TSDBs are ideally suited for storing and processing IoT data. Time-series data has the following properties (that might not be present with other data types):

- The order in which the events occur may be important.

- Data is only inserted, it is not updated.

- Queries have a time interval component in their filters.

RDBMSes can store this data, but they are not optimized to process, store, and analyze this type of data. Amazon Timestream was purpose built exclusively for this type of data, and therefore is much more efficient.

As the time-series data comes in, Amazon Timestream has an adaptive query processing engine that can make heads or tails of by inferring data location and data format. Amazon Timestream has features that can automate query rollups, retention, tiering, and data compression. Like many other Amazon services, Timestream is serverless, so it can automatically scale up or down depending on how much data is coming into the streams. Also, because it's serverless and fully managed, tasks such as provisioning, operating system patching, configuration, backups, and tiering are not the responsibility of the DevOps team, allowing them to focus on more important tasks.

Ledger databases

A **ledger database** (**LDB**) is database that delivers a cryptographically verifiable, immutable, and transparent transaction log orchestrated by a central authority:

- **LDB immutability**: Imagine you deposit $1,000 in your bank. You see on your phone that the deposit was carried out, and it now shows a balance of $1,000. Then imagine you check it again tomorrow and now it says $500. You would not be too pleased, would you? The bank needs to ensure that the transaction was immutable, and no one can change it after the fact. In other words, only inserts are allowed, and updates cannot be performed. This assures that transactions cannot be changed once they are persisted.

- **LDB transparency**: In this context, transparency refers to the ability to be able to track changes to the data over time. The LDB should be able to keep an audit log. This audit log at a minimum should include who changed data, when the data was changed, and what the value of the data was before it was changed.

- **LDB cryptographic verifiability**: How can we ensure that our transaction will be immutable? Even though the database might not support update operations, what's stopping someone from using a backdoor and updating the record? If we use cryptography when the transaction is recorded, the entire transaction data is hashed. In simple terms, the string of data that forms the transaction is whittled down into a smaller string of characters that is unique. Whenever the transaction is hashed, it needs to match that string. In the ledger, the hash comprises the transaction data, and it also appends the hash of the previous transaction. By doing this, we ensure that the entire chain of transactions is valid. If someone tried to enter another transaction in between, it would invalidate the hash and it would be detected that the foreign transaction was added via an unauthorized method.

The prototypical use case for LDBs are bank account transactions. If we use an LDB for this use case, the ledger records all credits and debits related to the bank account. It can then be followed from a point in history, allowing us to calculate the current account balance. With immutability and cryptographic verification, we are assured that the ledger cannot be deleted or modified. With other methods, such as RDBMSes, all transactions could potentially be changed or erased.

Quantum Ledger

Amazon **Quantum Ledger** (**QLDB**), like many other Amazon offerings, is a fully managed service. It delivers an immutable, transparent, and cryptographically verifiable ledger managed by a central trusted authority. Amazon QLDB keeps track of application value changes and manages a comprehensive and verifiable log of any change to the database.

Historically, ledgers have been used to maintain a record of financial activities. Ledgers can keep track of the history of transactions that need high availability and reliability. Some examples that need this level of reliability are as follows:

- Financial credits and debits

- Verifying the data lineage of a financial transaction

- Tracking the location history of inventory in a supply chain network

Amazon QLDB offers a variety of blockchain services such as anonymous data sharing and smart contracts while still using a centrally trusted transaction log.

Online Analytics Processing (OLAP) and business intelligence databases

OLAP systems usually exists and are normally compared to **online transaction processing** (**OLTP**) applications. OLTP systems are very often the source data for OLAP systems. Look back at *Figure 5.1* in this chapter to find a comparison chart between OLTP and OLAP databases. Like it does with many other emerging and popular trends, Amazon has a strong entry for OLAP databases – Amazon Redshift.

Redshift

Amazon Redshift is another service that is fully managed by Amazon. It is a petabyte-scale data warehouse capable of offering highly performant storage and analysis. Redshift is a column-oriented data store that can connect to other SQL clients and **business intelligence** (**BI**) tools. This data can then be accessed by users in real time. Redshift has its roots in PostgreSQL 8. Redshift can deliver sub-second performance, assuming a well-architected schema.

Each Amazon Redshift instance can be configured as a cluster. Each cluster has its own engine and has at least one database.

Redshift can be used to build BI applications. It is not unusual for Redshift instances to grow to hundreds of terabytes, and in some cases petabytes, worth of data.

Choosing the right tool for the job

In the previous sections, we learned how to classify databases, and we learned about the different services that AWS provides. Now comes the hard part: deciding which service is the right one for our particular use case. As technologists, we often fall in love with the latest shiny new object we have learned about, and because we have a hammer, everything looks like a nail. Firstly, we should spend a significant amount of time clearly articulating the business problem we are trying to solve. Often, your client will have a set of requirements and, based on your experience, you know they want or need something else. The problem statement should be carved and shaped to its most precise and simple level. Once you get signoff or agreement from all parties involved, only then is it time to start thinking about what the right tool for the job is.

Some of the questions the requirements should answer are as follows:

- How many users are expected?

- How many transactions per day will occur?

- How many records need to be stored?

- Will there be more writes or reads?

- How will the data need to be accessed (only by primary key, or by filtering, or some other way)?

Why are these questions important? SQL has served us well for several decades now, it is pervasive, and it has a lot of mindshare. So, why would we use anything else? The answer is performance. In instances where there is a lot of data and it needs to be accessed quickly, NoSQL databases might be a better solution. SQL vendors realize this, and they are constantly trying to improve their offerings to better compete with NoSQL, including adopting techniques from the NoSQL world. For example, Aurora is a SQL service and it now offers Aurora Serverless, taking a page out of the NoSQL playbook.

Another reason NoSQL has traditionally been a better option is that it offers a cost-effective alternative to file cold storage and applications that have occasional batch access requirements.

As services get better, the line between NoSQL and SQL databases keep on blurring, making the decision about what service to use more and more difficult. Depending on your project, you might want to draw up a **Proof of Concept** (**POC**) using a couple of options to determine which option performs better and fits your needs better.

Another reason to choose SQL or NoSQL might be the feature offered by NoSQL to create schema-less databases. Creating databases without a schema allows for fast prototyping and flexibility. However, tread carefully. Not having a schema might come at a high price. Allowing users to enter records without the benefit of a schema may lead to inconsistent data, which becomes too variable and creates more problems than it solves. Just because we can create databases without a schema in a NoSQL environment, we should not forgo validation checks before creating a record. If possible, a validation scheme should be implemented even when using a NoSQL option.

It is true that going schema-less increases implementation agility during the data ingestion phase. However, it increases complexity during the data access phase. Readers of the data will not know the context of the state of the data.

To drive the point home, let's think of two libraries. One has a card catalog, and everything is organized and labeled used the Dewey Decimal System. The other library is just a pile of books scattered across the building. Which library would you rather use?

Summary

In this chapter, we reviewed many of the database options available in AWS. We started by revisiting a brief history of databases. We then explored how databases can be classified, and then we explored the different types of databases and when it's appropriate to use each one. Finally, we delved into the difficult task of deciding which is the right database service for individual projects. Amazon offers so many database services that it truly makes it a challenge to decide what service to use in individual cases. But that's where you come in, and hopefully you feel much more empowered after reading this chapter.

Finally, we discussed how to decide on the right database for individual projects and the considerations to make this choice a success.

In the next chapter, we will learn about the services that AWS offers to optimize your network, as well as best practices for content delivery.

6
Amazon Athena – Combining the Simplicity of Files with the Power of SQL

In *Chapter 3*, *Storage in AWS – Choosing the Right Tool for the Job*, we covered many of the file and object storage services offered by AWS. In *Chapter 5*, *Selecting the Right Database Service*, we covered many of the AWS database services. What if there was a way to combine the simplicity and cost-effectiveness of files with the power of SQL? In fact, such a way exists in AWS, and it's called Amazon Athena.

Don't assume that because this service exists, we now don't need to use databases for some use cases. In this chapter, in addition to learning about the details and mechanics of Amazon Athena, we will also learn about when it makes sense to use Amazon Athena and when an AWS database service is more appropriate.

In this chapter, once we have introduced Amazon Athena, we will learn more about Amazon Athena workgroups. We will also review Amazon Athena's APIs toward the end of the chapter.

In this chapter, we will cover the followings topics:

- Introduction to Amazon Athena
- Deep diving into Amazon Athena
- Understanding how Amazon Athena works
- Using Amazon Athena Federated Query
- Learning about Amazon Athena workgroups
- Reviewing Amazon Athena's APIs
- Understanding when Amazon Athena is an appropriate solution

Introduction to Amazon Athena

Water, water everywhere, and not a drop to drink… This may be the feeling you get in today's enterprise environments. We are producing data at an exponential rate, but it is sometimes difficult to find a way to analyze this data and gain insights from it. Some of the data that we are generating at a prodigious rate is of the following types:

- Application logging
- Clickstream data
- Surveillance video
- Smart and IoT devices
- Commercial transactions

Often, this data is captured without analysis or is at least not analyzed to the fullest extent. Analyzing this data properly can translate into the following:

- Increased sales
- Cross-selling opportunities
- Lower operational and hardware infrastructure costs
- Avoiding downtime and errors before they occur
- Serving customer bases more efficiently

Previously, one stumbling block to analyzing this data was the fact that much of this information resides in flat files, and in order to analyze them, we had to ingest these files into a database to be able to perform analytics. Amazon Athena allows you to analyze these files in situ without having to go through an **Extract, Transform, Load (ETL)** process.

The idea behind Amazon Athena is simple. It treats any file like a database table and allows you to run `select` statement queries. Additionally, as of September 20, 2019, Amazon Athena also now supports `insert` statements for some file formats (JSON, ORC, Parquet, and text files). However, Amazon Athena is not meant to be used as an operational data store and it does not support `update` statements.

The advantages of queries being run in situ go beyond simplicity. By being able to run queries directly on a file without first performing ETL on them or loading them into a database, you can greatly increase processing speeds as well as lowering costs.

Amazon Athena enables you to run standard SQL queries to analyze and explore Amazon S3 objects. Amazon Athena is serverless. In other words, there are no servers to manage.

Amazon Athena is extremely simple to use. All you need to do is this:

1. Identify the object you want to query in Amazon S3.
2. Define the schema for the object.
3. Query the object with standard SQL.

Depending on the size and format of the file, query results can take a few seconds. As we will see later, there are a few optimizations that can be made to reduce query time as files get bigger.

Amazon Athena can be integrated with the AWS Glue Data Catalog. Doing so enables the creation of a unified metadata repository across services. We will learn more about this in *Chapter 7, AWS Glue – Extracting, Transforming, and Loading Data in AWS the Simple Way*. But for now, let's point out that AWS Glue can crawl data sources, discovering schemas and populating the AWS Glue Data Catalog with any changes that have occurred since the last crawl, including new tables, modifications to existing tables, and new partition definitions, while maintaining schema versioning.

Let's get even deeper into the power and features of Amazon Athena and how it integrates with other AWS services.

Deep diving into Amazon Athena

As mentioned previously, Amazon Athena is quite flexible and can handle simple and complex database queries using standard SQL. It supports joins and arrays. It can use a wide variety of file formats, including these:

- CSV
- JSON
- ORC
- Avro
- Parquet

It also supports other formats, but these are the most common. In some cases, the files that you are using have already been created, and you may have little flexibility regarding the format of these files. But for the cases where you can specify the file format, it's important to understand the advantages and disadvantages of these formats. In other cases, it may even make sense to convert the files to another format before using Amazon Athena. Let's take a quick look at each of these formats and understand when it makes sense to use each of them.

CSV files

A **Comma-Separated Value** (**CSV**) file is a file where each value is delineated by a comma separator and each record or row is delineated by a return character. Keep in mind that the separator does not necessarily have to be a comma. Other common delimiters are tabs and the pipe character (|).

JSON files

JavaScript Object Notation (**JSON**) is an open-standard file format. One of its advantages is that it's somewhat simple to read, particularly when it's indented and formatted. It's basically a replacement for the **Extensible Markup Language** (**XML**) file format, which, while similar, is more difficult to read. It consists of a series of potentially nested attribute-value pairs.

JSON is a language-agnostic data format. It was originally used with JavaScript, but quite a few programming languages now provide native support for it or provide libraries to create and parse JSON-formatted data.

> **Important note**
> The first two formats that we mentioned are not compressed and are not optimized to be used with Athena or speed up queries. The rest of the formats that we are going to analyze are all optimized for fast retrieval and querying when used with Amazon Athena and other file-querying technologies.

ORC files

The **Optimized Row Columnar** (**ORC**) file format provides a practical method to store files. It was originally designed under the Apache Hive and Hadoop project and it was created to overcome issues and limitations that other file formats had. ORC files provide better performance when compared to uncompressed formats for reading, writing, and processing data.

Apache Avro files

Apache Avro is an open source file format that can be used to serialize data. It was originally designed for the Apache Hadoop project.

Apache Avro persists data using JSON format, allowing users of files to easily read them and interpret them. However, the data is persisted in binary format, which has efficient and compact storage. An Avro file can use markers that are used to divide big datasets into smaller files to simplify parallel processing. Some consumer services have a code generator that processes the file schema to generate code that enables accessing the file. Apache Avro doesn't need to do this, making it suitable for scripting languages.

An essential Avro characteristic is its support for dynamic data schemas – data schemas that can be modified over time. Avro can process schema changes such as empty fields, new fields, and modified fields. Because of this, old scripts can process new data and new scripts can process old data. Avro has APIs for the following, among others:

- Python
- Go
- Ruby
- Java
- C
- C++

Avro-formatted data can flow from one program to another even if the programs are written in different languages.

Apache Parquet files

Just because we are listing Parquet files at the end, don't assume they are to be ignored. Parquet is an immensely popular format to use in combination with Amazon Athena.

Apache Parquet is another quite popular open source file format. Apache Parquet has an efficient and performant design. It stores file contents in a flat columnar storage format. Contrast this method of storage with the row-based approach used by comma- and tab-delimited files such as CSV and TSV.

Parquet is powered by an elegant assembly and shredding algorithm that is more efficient than simply flattening nested namespaces. Apache Parquet is well suited to operating on complex data at scale by using efficient data compression. This method is ideal for queries that require reading a few columns from a table with many columns. Apache Parquet can easily locate and scan only those columns, significantly reducing the amount of traffic required to retrieve data.

Columnar storage in general and Apache Parquet in particular delivers higher efficiency than a row-based approach such as CSV. While performing reads, a columnar storage method will skip over non-relevant columns and rows efficiently. Aggregation queries using this approach take less time than row-oriented databases. This results in lower billing and higher performance for data access.

Apache Parquet supports complex nested data structures. Parquet files are ideal for queries retrieving large amounts of data and can handle files that contain gigabytes of data without much difficulty.

Apache Parquet is built to support a variety of encoding and compression algorithms. Parquet is well suited to situations where columns have similar data types. This can make accessing and scanning files quite efficient. Apache Parquet works with a variety of codes, enabling the compression of files in a variety of ways.

In addition to Amazon Athena, Apache Parquet works with other serverless technologies such as Google BigQuery, Google Dataproc, and Amazon Redshift Spectrum.

Understanding how Amazon Athena works

Amazon Athena originally was intended to work with data stored in Amazon S3. As we will see in a later section in this chapter, it can now work with other source types as well.

This feature of Amazon Athena is a game-changer. You can now combine disparate data sources just as easily as if they all had the same format. This enables you to join a JSON file with a CSV file or a DynamoDB table with an Amazon Redshift table.

Previously, if you wanted to combine this data, it would require performing this combination programmatically, which would invariably translate into a long development cycle and more than likely not scale well when using large datasets.

Now all you have to do is write a SQL query that combines the two data sources. Due to the underlying technology used, this technique will scale well, even when querying terabytes' and petabytes' worth of data.

Data scientists and data analysts will be able to work at a speed that would have been impossible just a few years ago.

Under the hood, Amazon Athena leverages Presto. *Presto* is an open source SQL query engine.

It also leverages Apache Hive to create, drop, and alter tables and partitions. It is quite simple to write Hive-compliant **Data Definition Language** (**DDL**) and ANSI SQL statements using the Amazon Athena query editor in the AWS console.

Queries in Amazon Athena can be quite complex and can use joins, window functions, and complex datatypes. Amazon Athena is a good way to implement a schema-on-read strategy. A schema-on-read strategy enables you to project a schema onto existing data during query execution. Doing this eliminates the need to load or transform the data before it is queried, and instead it can be queried wherever it lives.

Presto, also known as PrestoDB, is an open source, distributed SQL query engine with a design that can support, in a scalable fashion, queries on files and other kinds of data sources. Some of the sources that are supported are listed here:

- Amazon S3
- **Hadoop Distributed File System** (**HDFS**)
- MongoDB
- Cassandra

It also supports traditional relational databases, such as these:

- MySQL
- Microsoft SQL Server
- Amazon Redshift
- PostgreSQL
- Teradata

It can handle petabyte-sized files. Presto can access data in situ, without the need to copy the data. Queries can execute in parallel in memory (without having access to secondary storage) and return results in seconds.

Presto was first initiated as an internal project at Facebook, built on top of large Hadoop/HDFS-based clusters. Before launching Presto, Facebook was using Apache Hive, which is also a Facebook creation, which brought the simplicity of SQL to Hadoop environments. Hive had a major impact on the adoption Hadoop ecosystem. It enabled the simplification of complex Java MapReduce jobs into simple SQL-like queries, while still allowing the execution of jobs at scale. One thing to note, at this point, is that it wasn't optimized to provide fast execution for interactive queries.

Facebook started the creation of Presto in 2012. It was started by the Facebook Data Infrastructure group. The rest of Facebook started using Presto in 2013. And in November 2013, Facebook released Presto to the rest of the world under the Apache Software License and published it on GitHub. To date, Facebook continues to make many contributions to the Presto project.

Presto is a distributed system that can use **Massively Parallel Processing** (**MPP**). It runs with one coordinator node that distributes work to multiple worker nodes. A user can invoke a SQL query, which is then transmitted to the coordinator, which in turn uses the execution engine to compile, plan, and schedule a query plan and send it down to the worker nodes. Presto supports the following:

- Complex queries
- Aggregations
- Left outer joins, right outer joins, and inner joins
- Sub-queries
- Distinct counts
- Window functions
- Approximate percentiles

Once the query has been parsed, Presto can distribute the execution across a set of worker nodes. Execution normally happens in memory. New worker nodes can be added, which will result in additional parallelism, which in turn will result in getting results faster.

Presto can be extended to many data source types. It can be extended to support these data sources by building pluggable connectors. Even though Presto is relatively young, it already offers many connectors, including some for non-relational data sources such as HDFS, Amazon S3, MongoDB, Cassandra, and HBase, as well as relational data sources such as Microsoft SQL Server, MySQL, Oracle, PostgreSQL, Amazon Redshift, and Teradata. Data can be queried where it lives, without having to migrate it to a special analytics zone.

One thing to note is that Presto is not a storage method. Presto is a substitute for a storage mechanism. It is a complement to storage systems and when used together with a persistence system, it can be used to solve a wide swath of business use cases. Presto can be deployed on any Hadoop implementation and is bundled with Amazon EMR.

Initially, Amazon Athena only leveraged Presto to access Amazon S3 files, but Amazon is now offering a preview of what they call Amazon Athena Federated Query. We will learn more about it in the next section.

Using Amazon Athena Federated Query

Unless your organization is special, you are storing data in a wide variety of storage types and you are often selecting the storage type on a "fit for purpose" basis. In other words, you are selecting graph databases when they make sense, relational databases when it's appropriate, and S3 object storage or Hadoop HDFS when it makes the most sense. As an example, if you are building a social network application, Amazon Neptune (which is a graph database) may be the best choice. Or, if you are building an application that requires a flexible schema, Amazon Dynamo DB may be a solid choice. AWS offers many different types of persistence solutions, such as these:

- Relational database services
- Key-value database services
- Document database services
- In-memory database services
- Search database services
- Graph database services
- Time-series database services
- Ledger databases database services
- Plain object data stores (such as Amazon S3)

The reason it offers all these kinds of persistence storage systems is to accommodate the different needs that different services can have. Sometimes, corporations have mandates to only use a certain database or certain file storage, but even in such cases, there will probably be "fit for purpose" choices for different cases (a graph database, a NoSQL database, file storage, and more). As a design principle, this pattern is recommended and encouraged. It's about following the principle of "choose the right tool for a particular job."

However, this plethora of choices pose a problem. As the number of different types of storage increases, running analytics and building applications across these data sources becomes more and more challenging. Overcoming this challenge is exactly what Amazon Athena Federated Query can help alleviate.

Amazon Athena Federated Query empowers data scientists, data analysts, and application engineers to run SQL queries across a wide swath of data stores regardless of the data source type and regardless of whether the type is supported by Amazon Athena.

Before Amazon Athena Federated Query or any other way to run federated queries, we had to execute a variety of queries across systems and then merge, filter, and assemble the results once the individual queries were run.

Constructing these data pipelines to process data across data sources creates bottlenecks and requires developing customized solutions that can validate the consistency and accuracy of the data. Also, when source systems are changed, the data pipelines must also be changed. Using query federation in Athena reduces these complexities by enabling users to run queries that retrieve data in situ no matter where it resides. Users can use standard SQL statements to merge data across disparate data sources in a performant manner. Users can also schedule SQL queries to retrieve data and store the results in Amazon S3.

It goes without saying that this is a complicated and slow way to put together results.

Amazon Athena Federated Query allows you to execute a single SQL query across data stores, greatly simplifying your code while at the same time getting those results a lot faster, thanks to a series of optimizations provided by Amazon Athena Federated Query.

The following diagram illustrates how Amazon Athena can be leveraged against a variety of data source types (it only shows some of the data source types supported):

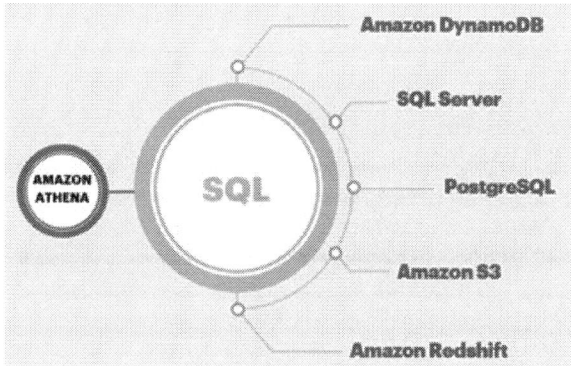

Figure 6.1 – Illustrative example of the data sources types supported by Amazon Athena

As we can see from the preceding figure, Amazon Athena Federated Query can handle a variety of disparate data sources and enables users to combine and join them with ease.

Data source connectors

Executing a SQL query against a new data source can be done simply by adding the data source to the Amazon Athena registry. Amazon Athena has open source connectors. There are also community or marketplace connectors built by third parties. An example of an interesting company that provides such connectors is *Dremio*. You can learn more about it here: https://www.dremio.com/.

Lastly, AWS provides the ability to write your own custom connectors if there isn't a suitable one.

The connector performs the following functions:

- Manages metadata information
- Determines the parts of a data source that are required to be scanned, accessed, and filtered
- Manages query optimization and query parallelism

Connectors are composed of two AWS Lambda functions. One Lambda function handles the metadata and the other function handles record access, the processing, and the reading of the actual data.

Amazon Athena queries can be highly efficient. When a query executes using a federated data source, Amazon Athena can execute the processing of the metadata and data Lambda functions in parallel. The AWS Lambda threads can process different slices of the data at the same time and provide results in seconds, even for gigabyte and terabyte results sets, unless something is not correctly optimized. Additionally, different queries will run independently of each other, making the whole process extremely scalable.

Amazon Athena can do this for any data source type that has an Amazon Athena data source connector available. These connectors run on AWS Lambda. AWS provides data source connectors for the following:

- Amazon DocumentDB
- Amazon DynamoDB
- Amazon Redshift
- Any JDBC-compliant **Relational Database Management System** (**RDBMS**) (such as MySQL, PostgreSQL, and Oracle)
- Apache HBase
- AWS CloudWatch Metrics
- Amazon CloudWatch Logs

These connectors can be used to run federated standard SQL queries spanning multiple data sources, all inside of the Amazon Athena console or within your code.

When a query is sent for processing with a given data source, Amazon Athena launches the connector associated with that data source. At that point, Amazon Athena can uniformly parse the query, identify the table that will be read, manage parallelism and optimization, and push down filter predicates.

Another function that the connector can perform is to restrict access to certain data elements based on a user's profile. The format used by Amazon Athena's connectors to provide results is Apache Arrow. This allows connectors to be written in languages such as Java, Python, C, and C++. Since connectors run using AWS Lambda, the connectors can retrieve data from other data sources in other AWS environments, other cloud providers, or on-premises locations.

In addition, if a connector is not available for a data source type, a customized connector can be built using the Query Federation SDK to enable Amazon Athena to access these data sources. Even these new connectors will run on AWS Lambda, so queries executed with these new connectors will also leverage Amazon Athena's serverless architecture and scale smoothly as demand increases.

The Amazon Athena Query Federation SDK expands on the advantage of federated querying beyond the "out of the box" connectors that come with AWS. By writing a hundred lines of code or less, you can create connectors to custom data sources and enable the rest of your organization to use this custom data. Once a new connector is registered, Amazon Athena can use the new connector to access databases, schemas, tables, and columns in this data source.

Let's now learn about another powerful Athena feature – Amazon Athena workgroups.

Learning about Amazon Athena workgroups

Another new feature that comes with Amazon Athena is the concept of workgroups. Workgroups enable administrators to give different groups of users different access to databases, tables, and other Athena resources. It also enables you to establish limits on how much data a query or the whole workgroup can access, as well as providing the ability to track costs. Since workgroups act like any other resource in AWS, resource-level identity-based policies can be set up to control access given to individual workgroups.

Workgroups can be integrated with SNS and CloudWatch as well. If query metrics are turned on, these metrics can be published to CloudWatch. Additionally, alarms can be created for certain workgroup users if their usage goes above a pre-established threshold.

By default, Amazon Athena queries run in the default primary workgroup. AWS administrators can add new workgroups and then run separate workloads in each workgroup. A common use case is to use workgroups to enable the separation of audiences, such as users who are going to running ad hoc queries and users that are going to be running pre-canned reports.

Each workgroup can then be associated with a specific location. Any queries associated with an individual workgroup will have their results stored in the assigned location. Following this paradigm ensures that only users that should be able to access certain data can access that data. Another way to restrict access is to apply different encryption keys to the different output files depending on the workgroup.

A task that workgroups greatly simplifies is the onboarding of new users. You can override the client-side settings and apply a predefined configuration for all the queries that are executed in a workgroup. Users within a workgroup do not have to configure where their queries will be stored or specify encryption keys for the S3 buckets. Instead, the values defined at the workgroup level will be used as a default.

Also, each workgroup keeps a separate history of all executed queries and any queries that have been saved, making troubleshooting easier.

Reviewing Amazon Athena's APIs

One of the features that make Amazon Athena so powerful is the fact that it uses SQL as the access language. You can connect to Amazon Athena using a JDBC driver. JDBC driver technology has been around for decades and is the gold standard when it comes to accessing SQL data sources. With Amazon Athena, any set of files stored in Amazon S3 becomes a de facto database.

Additionally, with Amazon Athena Federated Query, you can use the same SQL language to combine disparate data sources and perform joins between heterogeneous repositories, for example, a join between an Oracle table and a JSON file stored in an S3 bucket. The fact that these tables are not of the same type will be transparent to Amazon Athena users and they will all look the same to them in the AWS Glue Data Catalog, which Amazon Athena uses.

Optimizing Amazon Athena

As with any SQL operation, there are steps you can take to optimize the performance of your queries and inserts. As is the case with traditional databases, optimizing your data access performance usually comes at the expense of data ingestion and vice versa. Let's look at some tips that you can use to increase and optimize performance.

Optimization of data partitions

One way to improve performance is to break up files into smaller files called partitions. A common partition scheme is to break up a file by using a divider that occurs with some regularity in data. Some examples follow:

- Country
- Region
- Date
- Product

Partitions operate as virtual columns and assist in reducing the amount of data that needs to be read for each query. Partitions are normally defined at the time a table or file is created.

Amazon Athena can use Apache Hive partitions. Hive partitions use this name convention:

```
s3://BucketName/TablePath/<PARTITION_COLUMN_
NAME>=<VALUE>/<PARTITION_COLUMN_NAME>=<VALUE>/
```

When this format is used, the MSCK REPAIR command can be used to add additional partitions automatically.

Partitions are not restricted to a single column. Multiple columns can be used to partition data. Or, you can divide a single field to create a hierarchy of partitions. For example, it is not uncommon to divide a date into three pieces and partition the data using the year, the month, and the day.

An example of partitions using this scheme may look like this:

```
s3://a-simple-examples/data/parquet/year=2000/month=1/day=1/
s3://a-simple-examples/data/parquet/year=2000/month=2/day=1/
s3://a-simple-examples/data/parquet/year=2000/month=3/day=1/
s3://a-simple-examples/data/parquet/year=2000/month=4/day=1/
```

So, which column would be the best to use to partition files and what are some other best practices? Consider the following:

Any column that is normally used to filter data is probably a good partition candidate.

Don't over-partition. If the number of partitions is too high, it increases the retrieval overhead. If the partitions are too small, this obviates any benefit accrued by partitioning the data.

It is also important to partition in a smart way and try to choose a value that is eventually distributed as your partition key. For example, if your data involves election ballots, it may initially seem a good idea to use as your partition the candidates in the election. But what if one or two candidates take most of the votes? Your partitions will be heavily skewed toward those candidates and performance will suffer.

Data bucketing

Another scheme to partition data is to use buckets within a single partition. When using bucketing, a column or multiple columns are used to group rows together and "bucket" or categorize them. The best columns to use for bucketing are columns that will be often used to filter the data. So, when queries use these columns as filters, not as much data will need to be scanned and read when performing these queries.

Another characteristic that makes a column a good candidate for bucketing is high cardinality. In other words, you want to use columns that have a large amount of unique values. So, primary key columns are ideal bucketing columns.

Amazon Athena makes it simple to specify which columns will be bucketed during table creation by using the CLUSTERED BY clause. An example of a table creation statement using this clause follows:

```
CREATE EXTERNAL TABLE employee (
id string,
name string,
salary double,
address string,
timestamp bigint)
PARTITIONED BY (
timestamp string,
department string)
CLUSTERED BY (
id,
timestamp)
INTO 50 BUCKETS
```

As of September 2020, Amazon Athena does not offer support for partitions where the number of partitions does not match the number of buckets.

File compression

Intuitively, queries can be sped up by using compression. When files are compressed, not as much data needs to be read and the decompression overhead is not high enough to negate its benefits. Also, when going across the wire, a smaller file will take less time to get through the network than a bigger file. Finally, faster reads and faster transmission over the network will result in less spending, which, when you multiple by hundreds and thousands of queries, will result in real savings over time.

Compression offers the highest benefits when files are of a certain size. The optimal file size is around 200 MB – 1 GB. Having smaller files translates into multiple files being able to be processed simultaneously, taking advantage of the parallelism available with Amazon Athena. If there is only one file, only one reader can be used on the file while other readers sit idle.

One simple way to achieve compression is to utilize Apache Parquet or Apache ORC format. Files in these formats can be easily split, and these formats are compressed by default. To further improve performance, there are two compression formats that are often combined with Parquet and ORC. These compression formats are *Gzip* and *Bzip2*. The following chart shows how these compression formats compare with other popular compression algorithms:

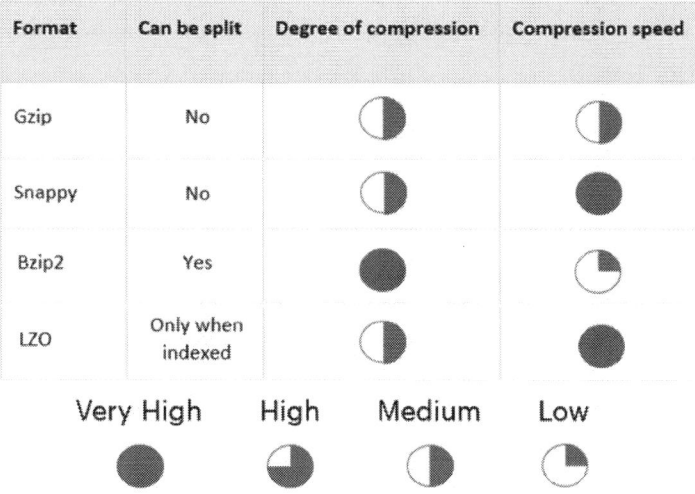

Figure 6.2 – Compression formats

Each format offers different advantages. As we can see in the figure, **Gzip** and **Snappy** files cannot be split. **Bzip2** can be split. **LZO** can only be split in special cases. Bzip2 provides the highest level of compression and LZO and Snappy provide the fastest compression speed.

Let's continue learning about other ways to optimize Amazon Athena. Another thing to do is to ensure that the size of the files that are used is optimal.

File size optimization

As we have seen in quite a few examples in this book, one of the game-changer characteristics of the cloud is its elasticity. This elasticity enables us to run queries in parallel easily and efficiently. File formats that allow file splitting assist in this parallelization process. If files are too big or are not split, too many readers will be idle, and parallelization will not occur. On the flip side, files that are too small (generally in the range of 128 MB or less) will incur additional overhead with the following operations, to name a few:

- Opening files
- Listing directories
- Reading file object metadata
- Reading file headers
- Reading compression dictionaries

So, just as it's a good idea to split bigger files to increase parallelism, it is recommended to consolidate smaller files. Amazon EMR has a utility called **S3DistCP**. It can be used to merge smaller files into larger ones. S3DistCP can also be used to transfer large files in an efficient manner from HDFS to Amazon S3 and vice versa, as well as from one S3 bucket to another.

Columnar data store generation optimization

As mentioned in a previous tip in this section, Apache Parquet and Apache ORC are popular columnar data store formats. The formats efficiently compress data by leveraging the following:

- Columnar-wise compression scheme
- Datatype-based compression
- Predicate pushdown
- File splitting

A way to further optimize compression is to fine-tune the block size or stripe size of the files. Having bigger block and stripe sizes enables us to store more rows per block. The default Apache Parquet block size is 120 MB, and the default Apache ORC stripe size is 64 MB. For tables with a high number of columns, a larger block size is recommended. This ensures that each column size has a reasonable size that still enables efficient sequential I/O.

When datasets are 10 GB or less, using the default compression algorithm that comes with Parquet and ORC is enough to have decent performance, but for datasets bigger than that, it's not a bad idea to use other compression algorithms with Parquet and ORC such as Gzip.

Yet another parameter that can be customized is the type of compression algorithm used on the storage data blocks. The Parquet format by default uses Snappy, but it also supports these other formats:

- Gzip
- LZO
- No compression

The ORC format uses Zlib compression by default, but it also supports the following:

- Snappy
- No compression

The recommended way to choose a compression algorithm is to use the provided default algorithm. If the performance is good enough for your use case, no further optimization is needed. If it's not, try the other supported formats to see if they deliver better results.

Column selection

An obvious way to reduce network traffic is to ensure that only the required columns are included in each query. Therefore, it is not a recommended practice to use the following syntax unless your application requires that every single column in a table be used. And even if that's true today, it may not be true tomorrow. If additional columns are later added to the table schema, they may not be required for existing queries. Take this, for instance:

```
select * from table
```

Instead of that, use this:

```
select column1, column2, column3 from table
```

By explicitly naming columns instead of using the star operator, we reduce the number of columns that get passed back and therefore lower the number of bytes that need to be pushed across the wire.

Let's now learn about yet another way to optimize our use of Amazon Athena. Next, we will explore the concept of predicate pushdown.

Predicate pushdown

The core concept behind predicate pushdown (also referred to as predicate filtering) is that specific sections of a SQL query (a predicate) can be "pushed down" to the location where the data exists. Performing this optimization can help reduce (often drastically) the time it takes a query to respond by filtering out results earlier in the process. In some cases, predicate pushdown is achieved by filtering data in situ before transferring it over the network or loading it into memory.

The ORC and the Parquet formats support predicate pushdown. These formats have data blocks representing column values. In each block, statistics are stored for the data held in the block. Two examples of the statistics stored are the minimum and the maximum value. When a query is run, these statistics are read before the rest of the block and depending on the statistics, it is determined whether the complete block should be read.

In order to take maximum advantage of predicate pushdown, it is recommended to identify the column that will be used the most when executing queries and before writing to disk, sort by that column. Let's look at a quick example to drive the point home.

File 1	File 2	File 3
Stats: Min=1; Max 3	Stats: Min=4; Max 6	Stats: Min=7; Max 9
Value	Value	Value
1	4	7
2	5	8
3	6	9

Figure 6.3 – Predicate pushdown example

In the preceding example, there are three files. As you can tell, the data is already sorted using the value stored in the column labeled **Value**. Let's say we want to run the following query:

```
select * from Table where Value = 5
```

As mentioned before, we can look at the statistics first and observe that the first file's maximum value is 3, so we can skip that file. On the second file, we see that our key (Value = 5) falls within the range of values in the file. We would then read this file. Since the maximum value on the second file is greater than the value of our key, we don't need to read any more files after reading the second file.

ORDER BY clause optimization

Due to the nature of how sorting works, when we invoke a query that contains an **ORDER BY** clause, it needs to be handled by a single worker thread. This can cause query slowdown and even failure. When using the ORDER BY clause, it is recommended, if the business case allows it, to use the **LIMIT** clause to reduce the number of rows returned and to limit the amount of work that needs to be performed by the worker thread.

Join optimization

Tables joins can be an expensive operation. Whenever possible, they should be avoided. In some cases, it makes sense to "pre-join" tables and merge two tables into a single table to improve performance when queries are executed at a later point.

That is not always possible or efficient. Another way to optimize joins is to make sure that larger tables are always on the left side of `join` (and the smaller tables on the right-hand side). When Amazon Athena runs a query that has a `join` clause, the right-hand side tables are delegated to worker nodes, which in turn bring these tables into memory, and the table on the left is then streamed to perform the join. Using this approach, a smaller amount of memory will be used and the query performs better.

And now, yet another optimization will be explored by optimizing `group by` clauses.

group by clause optimization

The best practice when a `group by` clause is present is to arrange the columns according to the highest cardinality. For example, if you have a dataset that contains zip code and gender, it is recommended to write the query like this:

```
select zipcode, gender, count(*) from dataset group by zipcode,
gender
```

This way is not recommended:

```
select zipcode, gender, count(*) from dataset group by zipcode,
gender
```

This is because it is more likely that the zip code will have a higher cardinality (there will be more unique values) in that column.

Additionally, this is not always possible, but when there is a `group by` clause present, it is recommended to minimize the number of columns in the `select` clause.

Approximate function use

Amazon Athena has a series of approximation functions. As an example, there is an approximation function for the `DISTINCT()` function. If you don't need an exact count, you can instead use `APPROX_DISTINCT()`, which may not return the exact number of distinct values for a column in a given table, but it will give a good approximation for many use cases.

For example, you should not use this query:

```
select DISTINCT(last_name) from employee
```

Instead, you should use this query:

```
select APPROX_DISTINCT(last_name) from employee
```

This may be suitable for a given use case if an exact count is not required. This concludes the optimizations section for Amazon Athena. It is by no means a comprehensive list, but rather it is a list of the most common and practical optimization techniques that can be used to quickly gain efficiencies and increase query performance.

Summary

In most of the other chapters in this book, we covered more than one service. In this chapter, we focused exclusively on one service – Amazon Athena. As we discovered, Amazon Athena is a simple yet powerful service that can "convert" any file into a database by allowing us to query and update the contents of that file by using the ubiquitous SQL syntax.

We then learned how we can add some governance to the process by learning about Amazon Athena workgroups and how they can help you to control access to files by adding a level of security to the process.

Finally, as we have been learning throughout the book, there is not a single AWS service (or any other tool or product, for that matter) that is a silver bullet to solve all problems. Amazon Athena is no different, so we learned in the last sections of this chapter about some scenarios where Amazon Athena is an appropriate solution and we learned about other use cases where other AWS services such as Amazon RDS may be a more appropriate tool for the job.

In the next chapter, we will learn strategies for how to simplify data ingestion into data repositories and how to transform data so that it can be more easily consumed by end users and other services. We will learn about an important AWS service that was created exactly for this purpose – AWS Glue.

7

AWS Glue – Extracting, Transforming, and Loading Data the Simple Way

In this chapter, we will deep dive into this service. First, we will learn about the basics of AWS Glue. We will then look at AWS Glue crawlers. Afterward, we will look at the AWS Glue Data Catalog. Finally, we will look at some AWS Glue best practices. Let's roll up our sleeves and get to it.

In this chapter, we will cover the following topics:

- Why is AWS Glue a cornerstone service?

- Introduction to AWS Glue

- Cataloging with the AWS Glue Data Catalog

- Crawling with AWS Glue crawlers
- AWS Glue best practices

Why is AWS Glue a cornerstone service?

Traditionally, the most important resources that a business has are its human and financial capital. However, in the last few decades, more and more businesses have come to the realization that another resource may be just as important. It's only been in the last few years that they have come to understand that another commodity that is just as valuable, if not more valuable, is its data capital.

Data has taken a special place at the center of some of today's most successful enterprises. For this reason, business leaders have concluded that in order to survive in today's business climate they must collect, process, transform, distill, and safeguard their data like they do their other traditional business capital.

Businesses that have made this realization have been able to transform and reinvent their value propositions. Data-driven businesses will be able to increase their profitability and efficiency, reduce costs, deliver new products and services, better serve their customers, stay in compliance with regulatory requirements, and ultimately, thrive. Unfortunately, as we have seen many examples of in recent years, companies that don't make this transition will not be able to survive.

An important part of being a data-driven enterprise is the ability to ingest, process, transform, and analyze this data. AWS Glue is a foundational service at the heart of the AWS offering and we will dedicate the rest of this chapter to this service.

With the introduction of Apache Spark, enterprises can process petabytes' worth of data daily. Being able to process this amount of data opens the door to making data an enterprise's most valuable asset. Processing this data at this scale allows enterprises to literally create new industries and markets. Some examples of business activities that have benefited greatly from this massive data processing are as follows:

- Personalized marketing
- Drug discovery
- Anomaly detection (such as fraud detection)
- Real-time log and clickstream processing

AWS has created a service that leverages Apache Spark and takes it to the next level. The name of that service is AWS Glue.

Introduction to AWS Glue

What is AWS Glue? AWS Glue is a fully managed service that is used to extract data from data sources, ingest the data into other AWS services such as Amazon S3, and transform this data so that it can then be used by consuming services or users. It is not meant to be used for small batches and files. Under the hood, AWS Glue uses Apache Spark, running it in a serverless environment. It can process terabyte- and petabyte-scale workloads, but it comes with some overhead and that's the reason why it should only be used for big data projects.

Another important feature of AWS Glue is that it can handle disparate sources such as SQL and NoSQL databases – not just Amazon S3 files.

As we mentioned in the introduction, it is hard to overestimate the value of data in the current environment. Regardless of the industry, properly harnessing and leveraging data is critical to be able to compete today. AWS Glue and its underlying Apache Spark engine function as cornerstone technologies in many enterprises to process the vast amounts of data generated.

As is the case with quite a few other AWS services, AWS Glue leverages a popular open source technology (in this case, Apache Spark) and places wrappers around it to supercharge the technology even further.

Let's look at a simple but powerful example of this. The traditional way to set up Apache Spark is to set up a cluster of powerful machines. Depending on how much data is going to be ingested and how many transformations need to be performed, it is not uncommon to have Spark clusters with dozens and sometimes even hundreds of nodes. As you can imagine, a dedicated infrastructure setup like this can be extremely expensive.

Using AWS Glue, we can create a similarly powerful cluster of machines that are spun up when demand requires it, but importantly, the cluster can be spun down as and when demand wanes. If there is no work to be processed, the cluster can be completely shut down and the compute costs then go down to zero. By making costs variable and not having to pay for idle machines, the amount of use cases that can be handled by AWS Glue versus a traditional Apache Spark cluster increases exponentially. Projects that would have been prohibitively expensive before now become economically feasible.

Here is a list of common use cases that leverage AWS Glue:

- The population of data lakes, data warehouses, and lake houses
- Event-driven ETL pipelines
- The creation and cleansing of datasets for machine learning

To achieve its intended purpose as an **Extract, Transform, and Load** (**ETL**) service, AWS Glue has a series of components. These are as follows:

- The AWS Glue console
- The AWS Glue Data Catalog
- AWS Glue classifiers
- AWS Glue crawlers
- AWS Glue code generators

Let's pay a visit to the major ones.

Operating the AWS Glue console

The AWS Glue console is used to create, configure, orchestrate, and develop ingestion workflows. The AWS Glue console interacts with other components in AWS Glue by calling APIs to update the AWS Glue Data Catalog and to run AWS Glue jobs. These jobs can be run to accomplish the following kind of actions:

- **Definition of AWS Glue objects such as connections, jobs, crawlers, and tables** – The console can be used to create a variety of AWS Glue objects. We will learn more about crawlers in an upcoming section. A table in AWS Glue is simply a file after it has been processed by AWS Glue. Once processed, the file can act as a SQL table and SQL commands can be run against it. As is the case with any kind of SQL database, we will need to create a connection to connect to the table. All these objects can be created in the AWS Glue console.

- **Crawler scheduling** – AWS Glue crawlers, which we will learn about shortly, have to be scheduled. This scheduling is another action that can be performed in the AWS Console.

- **Scheduling of job triggers** – The scheduling of job triggers that will perform ETL code can also be implemented in AWS Glue.

- **Filtering of AWS Glue objects** – In the simplest AWS Glue implementations, it may be easy to locate different objects by simply browsing through the objects listed. Once things start getting a little complicated, we will need to have the ability to filter these objects by name, date created, and so on. This filtering can be performed in the AWS Glue console.

- **Transformation script editing** – Lastly, one more task that can be accomplished in the AWS Glue console is the creation and maintenance of ETL scripts.

Cataloging with AWS Glue Data Catalog

The AWS Glue Data Catalog is a persistent metadata repository. It is another service managed by AWS that enables the storage, annotation, and publishing of metadata. Under the hood, the AWS Glue Data Catalog operates similarly to an Apache Hive metastore.

There is only one AWS Glue Data Catalog per AWS Region. By having only one repository per Region, different services can persist and access the extracted metadata. It is important to make a clear distinction between the metadata and the actual data in each dataset. Often, the data itself is sensitive data that cannot be shared unless such authority is granted directly. But in many cases, it's okay to share the metadata for a given dataset. For example, if a file contains social security numbers, names, addresses, and phone numbers, only a select group of individuals may need access to the actual data. But it is okay to disseminate to a wider audience the fact that this file contains social security numbers, names, addresses, and more.

AWS **Identity and Access Management** (**IAM**) policies can be created to give access permission to AWS Glue Data Catalog datasets. These policies can be used to manage access by a variety of groups. Certain groups may be allowed to publish data, others may be allowed to access the metadata, and others still may be given access to the actual data. Using IAM policies, it is possible to give detailed and granular access to the appropriate parties at the required level.

Another feature of the AWS Glue Data Catalog is its schema version history. Version history will be kept about each ingestion and each Data Catalog update so that these changes can be monitored and audited over time.

The Data Catalog also delivers audit and governance functionality. It can track when schema changes are performed and when data is accessed. This allows auditors to determine when and by whom changes are performed.

The catalog can be changed using **Data Definition Language** (**DDL**) statements or using the AWS Management Console. Any schemas that are created are automatically persisted until they are explicitly removed. These files can in turn be accessed using Amazon Athena. Amazon Athena leverages a schema-on-read methodology that enables table definitions to be applied to files in Amazon S3 during query execution, instead of happening during file ingestion. This minimizes additional file writes and data transformation. Additionally, these table definitions created by AWS Glue can be deleted and the underlying files will still persist in Amazon S3.

Crawling with AWS Glue crawlers

AWS Glue crawlers are used to scan files, extract the file metadata, and populate the AWS Glue Data Catalog with this metadata information. Once the files have been crawled, users will be able to access the contents of the files while treating these files as SQL tables. An AWS Glue crawler can scan multiple file locations simultaneously. Once these files have been scanned and the tables are available, they can then be used in other jobs and the data contained can be transformed and ingested into other downstream processes.

We already had the opportunity to learn about Amazon Athena in the previous chapter, *Chapter 6, Amazon Athena – Combining the Simplicity of Files with the Power of SQL*. We learned in that chapter that AWS Athena allows you to treat a file as a database table and you can run queries against that file. But how does Amazon Athena know about the structure of the file to be able to run those queries? One way is to create a `table` from that file and provide details about that file when executing the `create table` statement. This statement is going to be a little more verbose than your typical `create table` statement because, in addition to the table structure, it needs to specify how the data will be loaded and provide the file structure or layout of the file as part of the DDL statement.

Here is an example:

```
CREATE EXTERNAL TABLE IF NOT EXISTS s3_source (
    insert_date DATE,
    time STRING,
    state INT,
    referrer STRING,
    file_loc STRING,
    file_size INT,
    source_ip STRING,
    source_host STRING,
    source_uri STRING,
    source_method STRING,
```

```
    operating_system STRING,
    client_browser STRING,
    client_browser_version STRING
    ) ROW FORMAT SERDE 'org.apache.hadoop.hive.serde2.RegexSerDe'
    WITH SERDEPROPERTIES (
    "input.regex" = "^(?!#)([^ ]+)\\s+([^ ]+)\\s+([^ ]+)\\s+([^
]+)\\s+([^ ]+)\\s+([^ ]+)\\s+([^ ]+)\\s+([^ ]+)\\s+([^ ]+)\\
s+([^ ]+)\\s+[^\(]+[\(]([^\;]+).*\%20([^\/]+)[\/](.*)$"
    ) LOCATION 's3://athena-us-east1/cf/csv/';
```

As you can see in this example, much of it looks like a typical `create table` statement. However, we can also see at the end of it a section that tells us how the file should be treated. After all, we are doing more than simply creating a table, but also populating the table with the contents of the file.

Amazon Athena then takes this definition and adds it to a managed Data Catalog and persists this definition with other tables and database definitions previously defined about other Amazon S3 files. This Data Catalog can be internal to Amazon Athena or you can also leverage the AWS Glue Data Catalog to store these definitions.

> **Important note**
> Whenever possible, it is highly recommended to use the AWS Glue Data Catalog instead of the internal Amazon Athena Data Catalog.

Regardless of which catalog is used there, only one catalog will exist per AWS Region. The catalog can be modified leveraging DDL statements or using the AWS console. Their definitions can also be explicitly removed. Amazon Athena utilizes the so-called *schema-on-read* pattern. This simply translates into the schema and table definitions being applied as the query is executed, and not before. A traditional database uses the opposite pattern, the so-called *schema-on-write* pattern. In that case, the schema is applied to the data during the creation of the table and the schema can only be modified if the table is physically modified.

Each of these approaches has its advantages and disadvantages. Schema-on-write queries will most likely be more performant but making changes to the schema will require some heavy lifting. Schema-on-read queries will have some performance overhead but if changes need to be made to the schema, it will not be as difficult because changes to the schema do not require any physical changes to the underlying data.

Another more efficient way to populate the Data Catalog is to use an AWS Glue crawler. A crawler can go through data sources including Amazon S3 files and databases and extract the metadata for this data and use it to populate the AWS Glue Data Catalog. AWS Glue crawlers are extremely scalable and can crawl multiple data sources simultaneously. Once the AWS Glue Data Catalog is populated, it can be fed into other processes to perform ETL tasks.

Out of the box, AWS provides crawlers for many data source types. A few of them are listed as follows:

- **Amazon Simple Storage Service (Amazon S3)**

- Amazon DynamoDB

- MariaDB

- Amazon Aurora

- Microsoft SQL Server

- MySQL

- PostgreSQL

- Oracle

- MongoDB

- Amazon DocumentDB (with MongoDB compatibility)

In addition to discovering the schema information for new data sources, it can also discover changes that have occurred in data sources that it previously ingested and it will update the Data Catalog with the new metadata.

There is one important consideration when it comes to security with this architecture. Regardless of which AWS or third-party services are used to access tables from the AWS Glue Data Catalog, any restrictions placed on the underlying S3 files will still persist. If a user tries to access a resource using SQL commands from one of the tables in the AWS Data Catalog and they don't have access to the underlying table, they will not be able to view the contents of that table.

> **Important note**
> One important limitation to note is that while AWS Glue crawlers can discover schema information and extract metadata from individual files and tables, it does not discover relationships between the data sources.

Categorizing with AWS Glue classifiers

As data is crawled from the various data sources, its metadata will be extracted and the Data Catalog will be populated. Additionally, it can also be classified by AWS Glue classifiers. Classifiers recognize the format of the data and persist this information. Classifiers also assign a certainty score depending on how sure they are about the format of the data.

AWS Glue comes with a set of out-of-the-box classifiers and also provides the ability to create custom classifiers. During the classifier invocation, AWS Glue will run the custom classifiers first, using the sequence specified in the crawler configuration. If the custom classifier cannot determine the format of a given data source, AWS Glue will then run the built-in classifiers to see if they can determine the format.

Lastly, it is important to note that, in addition to providing a format, a classifier will return a certainty score with a value between 0.0 and 1.0. A score of 1.0 indicates that the classifier has 100% certainty about the format of the data.

As you can imagine, some of the built-in classifiers can recognize some of the most common file formats, including the following:

- Apache Avro
- Apache ORC
- Apache Parquet
- JSON
- Binary JSON
- XML
- **Comma-Separated Values (CSV)**
- **Tab-Separated Values (TSV)**

Generating code with AWS Glue code generators

AWS Glue automatically generates highly scalable Python or Scala ETL code to ingest and transform data. The resulting code is optimized for distributed computing. The choice of language between Python and Scala is up to you, based on your coding preferences. Once the code is generated it can be customized and edited using the AWS Glue Studio. The AWS Glue Studio is an editor that allows developers to create quite of bit of functionality using a drag-and-drop job editor. However, for proficient developers, editing the code directly is also possible.

If you want to customize the generated code, AWS Glue has development endpoints that enable developers to make changes to the code. It can then be tested and debugged. AWS Glue provides the ability to create custom readers, writers, and transformations. Code created with these endpoints can be incorporated into code pipelines, then versioned and managed in code repositories like any other code.

Once the code is developed it can be triggered as an AWS Glue job. These jobs can be triggered in a variety of ways:

- **On a schedule** – For example, every day of the week at 9 a.m. or once a week on Tuesday at 3 p.m
- **By manual intervention** – When the user actually kicks off the job via either the Console or the AWS CLI
- **Event triggers** – Based on a triggering event such as a file loading or a row in a database being inserted

Often, these jobs will have dependencies on each other. AWS Glue provides orchestration capabilities to cobble together the ETL dependencies as well as handling retry logic in case a job fails. The execution of all these jobs is tracked by Amazon CloudWatch, which will enable users to monitor these jobs. Alerts can be created and received for various actions including a job completion or a job failure.

> **Important note**
>
> It is also possible to integrate AWS Glue jobs with other orchestration tools such as Apache Airflow and Control-M. You can learn more about **Apache Airflow** at `https://airflow.apache.org/`.
>
> More information about **Control-M** can be found at `https://www.bmc.com/it-solutions/control-m.html`.

AWS Glue serverless streaming ETL

You may be too young to remember, but back in the day if you went to a store and tried paying with a credit card, they had these massive books where the checkout person had to look up your card number to determine if you card was fraudulent. Not only did this method slow down the checkout process, but as you can imagine, by the time fraudulent cards were added to the book, it could have been used many times over to purchase thousands of dollars' worth of merchandise.

As technology improved, this process got quicker to the point where these records became automated and were being updated on a nightly basis. But fraud has always been a cat-and-mouse game. Criminals got smart and made sure to use stolen cards faster to still be able to profit from their crime.

The ideal solution is to be able to report and disseminate the theft of the card in real time. This presents some formidable technological challenges, but technologies like AWS Glue do support streaming processing support.

Streaming ETL jobs can be created in AWS Glue to continuously process files from streaming services such as Amazon Kinesis and Amazon MSK. These jobs can process, clean, and transform the data almost instantaneously. This data then becomes available to data analysts and data scientists so that they can run their models and analysis on the data. Other common use cases for AWS Glue streaming ETL jobs are as follows:

- Processing IoT event streams

- Consuming clickstreams and other web activities

- Analyzing application logs

AWS Glue streaming ETL jobs can be incorporated into data pipelines to enrich and aggregate data, join batch and streaming sources, as well as running analytics and machine learning models. All this can be done at scale, enabling the processing of hundreds of thousands of transactions per second.

So far in this chapter, we have learned about the basics of AWS Glue. We also learned about the components that make up AWS Glue and make it the juggernaut that it is. In the next section, we will put it all together and explain how the various components work together to provide a powerful combination and deliver one of the most popular services in the AWS ecosystem.

Putting it all together

Now that we have learned about all the major components in AWS Glue, let's look at how all the pieces fit together. The following diagram illustrates this:

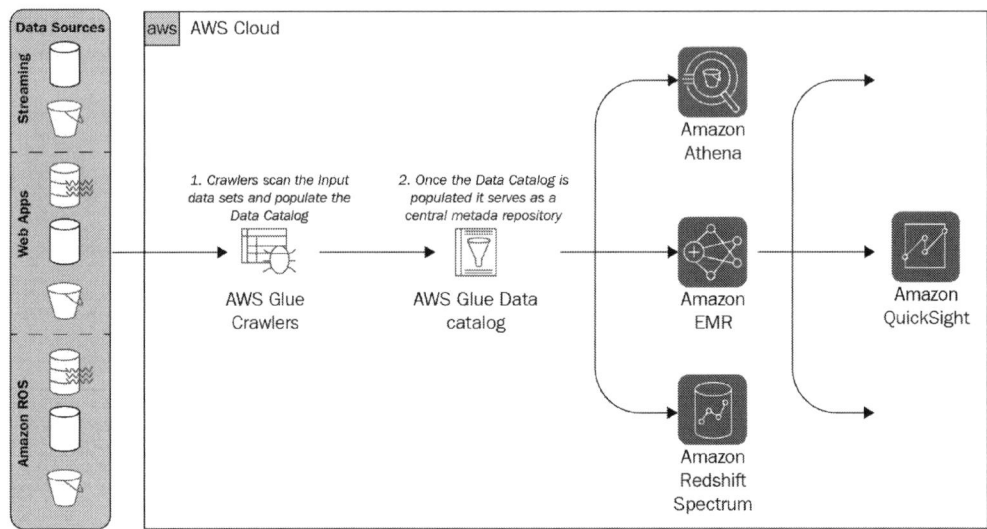

Figure 7.1 – AWS Glue typical workflow steps

In the preceding diagram, we see can the various steps that can take place when AWS Glue runs. The steps are explained in the following points:

1. The first step is for the crawlers to scan these sources and extract metadata from them.

2. This metadata can then be used to seed the AWS Glue Data Catalog.

3. In turn, this metadata can be used by other AWS services such as Amazon Athena, Amazon Redshift Spectrum, and Amazon EMR. These services can be used to write queries against the ingested data using the metadata from the AWS Glue Data Catalog to build these queries.

4. Finally, the results of these queries can be used for visualizations in other AWS services including Amazon QuickSight and Amazon SageMaker.

A wide variety of data sources can be ingested with AWS Glue, such as Amazon S3 objects, Amazon RDS records, or web application data via APIs.

Hopefully, the discussion in these sections has given you a good taste of the basics of AWS Glue and its importance in the AWS ecosystem. Hopefully, you are also now convinced that data and the insights that can be derived from processing and distilling it are critical in today's enterprises.

We will now spend some time learning about some of the best ways to implement AWS Glue in your environment.

AWS Glue best practices

As we have done with many of the other services covered in the book, we will now provide some recommendations on how to best architect the configuration of your AWS Glue jobs.

Amazon Athena, under the hood, uses the open source software Presto to process **Data Manipulation Language** (**DML**) statements and Apache Hive to process DDL statements. An example of a DML statement is a `select` statement and an example of a DDL statement is a `create table` statement.

Similarly, under the hood, AWS Glue runs its ETL jobs using Apache Spark.

Knowing that these are the underlying technologies used under the hood by these AWS services will enable you to better leverage and optimize your use of Amazon Athena and AWS Glue.

Choosing the right worker type

AWS Glue can execute with one of three different worker types. Worker types are also known as **Data Processing Units** (**DPUs**).

Each type has different advantages and disadvantages, and they should be chosen based on the use case that we have on hand.

Worker types or DPUs come in these configurations:

- **Standard** – The standard worker comes with 16 GB memory, 4 vCPUs for compute capacity, and 50 GB of attached EBS storage with two Spark executors.

- **G.1X** – G.1X worker types have 16 GB of memory, use 4 vCPUs, and come with 64 GB of attached EBS storage and only one Spark executor.

- **G.2X** – The G.2X worker types have 32 GB of memory, use 8 vCPUs, and come with 128 GB of attached EBS storage and only one Spark executor.

AWS Glue's serverless architecture takes advantage of Spark's compute parallelism and can scale in a horizontal manner regardless of the type of worker.

If a certain workload is more memory intensive, AWS Glue jobs that can benefit from vertical scaling should use the G1.X or G2.X worker types.

Optimizing file splitting

AWS Glue automatically splits files when processing common traditional file formats such as CSV and JSON, as well as some of the more modern formats, including AVRO and Parquet, by using something called AWS Glue DynamicFrames.

> **Important note**
>
> To learn more about DynamicFrames, you can visit `https://aws.`
> `amazon.com/blogs/big-data/work-with-partitioned-`
> `data-in-aws-glue/`.

A "file split" is a section in a file that an AWS Glue worker can process independently. Out of the box, file splitting can be performed on line-delimited native formats. This enables the parallel execution of Apache Spark jobs on AWS Glue spanning multiple nodes. AWS Glue jobs can be optimized to handle files that have a file size between hundreds of megabytes and a couple of gigabytes by leveraging horizontal scaling and attaching more AWS Glue workers.

File splitting can also increase performance with block-based compression formats. Each compression block can be read on a file split boundary, and can then be processed independently and simultaneously with other files. Compression formats that don't support splitting, such as `gzip`, do not achieve performance gains from file splitting. To achieve horizontal scalability with compression formats or files that can't be split, the inputs should use several medium-sized files.

Split files can be accessed using Amazon S3, deserialized into an AWS Glue DynamicFrame partition, and handled by an Apache Spark task. The size of a deserialized partition can be much larger than a typical disk block file split size of 64 MB, such as for highly compressed formats that can be split like Parquet, or larger files that use compression formats such as `gzip` that cannot be split. Normally, a deserialized partition is not brought into memory, and is only assembled as required using Apache Spark's lazy transformation evaluation. For this reason, there is no memory pressure on AWS Glue tasks.

However, when a partition is explicitly cached in memory or when it spills onto disk, it can return **out-of-memory (OOM)** or out-of-disk exceptions. AWS Glue can handle these use cases with AWS Glue worker types that use DPU instances that can be vertically scaled.

Exceeding Yarn's memory overhead allocation

Apache Yarn is the resource manager that is used under the hood by Apache Spark and AWS Glue. **Yarn** stands for **Yet Another Resource Negotiator**. Yarn oversees allocating resources when Spark is running and handling applications workloads. On top of handling memory allocation for each executor running jobs, Yarn also oversees the allocation of additional memory assigned to the JVM and metadata that needs to be loaded for the JVM to run correctly. By default, this overhead is allocated 10% of the total executor memory. Operations that require a lot of memory, such as table joins or dataset processing with skewed distribution, may require additional overhead and may throw an error. If you know that your application is going to be memory intensive, it is recommended to allocate additional overheard memory from the start to avoid these types of errors.

Another way to avoid these OOM issues is to use AWS Glue's vertical scaling feature. Using workers that have been assigned more memory and disk space can help to avoid this problem.

Lastly, using the dashboard provided by AWS Glue with job metrics can assist in the debugging and resolution of these OOM issues. For memory-intensive jobs, such as on large datasets with significant skew, use the G1.X and G2.X worker types.

For more information about how to debug these types of issues, visit `https://docs. aws.amazon.com/glue/latest/dg/monitor-profile-debug-oom- abnormalities.html`.

Leveraging the Apache Spark UI

Another useful tool in the Spark arsenal is the Apache Spark UI. Spark UI can used to inspect, monitor, and optimize AWS Glue ETL jobs. It allows you to visualize the jobs by providing **Directed Acyclic Graphs (DAGs)** of the job's execution. It can also be used to identify demanding stages and large shuffles, and to analyze query plans. The UI will enable you to quickly identify the bottlenecks in your Spark jobs and enable you to make adjustments to increase performance and remove those bottlenecks.

More information about the Spark UI can be found at `https://docs.aws.amazon. com/glue/latest/dg/monitor-spark-ui.html`.

Processing many small files

It is not uncommon for AWS Glue to routinely handle thousands and even millions of files. For use cases where Amazon Kinesis Firehose is involved, this would be more the norm than the exception. In these situations, it is possible for the Apache Spark driver to run out of memory while reading these files.

Apache Spark version 2.2 can handle about 600,000 files on a standard worker type. To increase the number of files that a worker can handle, AWS provides an option to process these files in larger batches. One way to do this is to use a G1.X worker to read the files instead of a standard worker.

Another way is to reduce the number of files that are processed at one time. This can be achieved by taking advantage of AWS Glue file groupings. Doing so reduces the chance of getting OOM exceptions. To enable file grouping, the `groupFiles` and `groupSize` parameters need to be configured. Here is a sample call that set those parameters:

```
dyf = glueContext.create_dynamic_frame_from_options("s3",
    {'paths': ["s3://path-to-files/"],
    'recurse':True,
    'groupFiles': 'inPartition',
    'groupSize': '2084236'},
    format="json")
```

The purpose of this command is to create a dynamic frame that can then be fed into other ETL jobs for processing. The `paths` parameter determines the S3 folder that contains the files that will be used to create the frame. The `recurse` parameter indicates whether subdirectories in this folder should be included for processing.

The `groupFiles` parameter can be configured to group files in an S3 partition within a folder or across Amazon S3 partitions. In many instances, grouping in each partition is enough to bring down the number of parallel Spark tasks and reduce the amount of memory being used by the Spark tasks.

In a battery of tests, ETL jobs configured using this grouping parameter proved to be about 7 times faster than other jobs without this configuration when handling over 300,000 files spanning across over a hundred Amazon S3 partitions. A significant portion of time is spent with Apache Spark building in-memory indices while listing Amazon S3 files and scheduling many short-running tasks to handle these files. When grouping is enabled, AWS Glue should be able to handle over one million files at one time using the standard AWS Glue worker types.

Tuning the `groupSize` parameter can have a significant impact in the number of files that can be processed at any one time, which in turn translates into how many files can be produced. Properly tuning this parameter can result in achieving significant task parallelism, while not properly configuring can result in the cluster being underutilized and having many of the workers sitting idle.

By default, when the number of files exceeds about 50,000, AWS Glue will automatically enable grouping. AWS Glue can figure out an appropriate value for the `groupSize` parameter and sets it accordingly to minimize the amount of excessive parallelism.

Data partitioning and predicate pushdown

Partitioning files is an important technique used to split datasets so that these files can be accessed quickly and efficiently. Picking a good key to split files is critical to gaining these efficiencies. As an example, a dataset may be divided and organized into folders using the ingestion date as the key. In this case, you may have a series of subfolders organized by year, month, and day.

Here is an example of what a directory using this name scheme could look like:

```
s3://employees/year=2020/month=01/day=01/
```

Partitioning the data in such a way enables predicate pushdown. Predicate pushdown is a fancy way of saying that by partitioning the data, we don't need to read all the directories and files to get the results we need when we have a query with a filter on it.

Predicate pushdown uses filter criteria using partition columns. With predicate pushdown, the data is not read into memory first and then filtered. Instead, because the data is presorted, we know what files meet the criteria being sought, and only those files are brought into memory and the rest of the files are simply skipped.

For example, imagine you have a query like this:

```
select * from employees where year = 2019
```

Here, `year` is the partition and `2019` is the filter criteria. In this case, the file we had as an example previously would be skipped.

Using pruning can deliver massive performance boosts and greatly reduced response times. Performance can be improved even more by providing even more filters in the selection criteria, which will result in eliminating additional partitions.

Partitioning data while writing to Amazon S3

The last task during processing is to persist the transformed output in Amazon S3. Once this is done, other services such as Amazon Athena can be used for their retrieval. By default, when a DynamicFrame is persisted, it is not partitioned. The results are persisted in a single output path. Until recently, it was only possible to partition a DynamicFrame by converting it into a Spark SQL DataFrame before it was persisted. However, native partitioning using a keys sequence can be used to write out DynamicFrame.

This can be accomplished by setting the partitionKeys parameter during sink creation. As an example, the following code can be used to output a dataset:

```
%spark
glueContext.getSinkWithFormat(
    connectionType = "s3",
    options = JsonOptions(Map("path" -> "$output_path",
"partitionKeys" -> Seq("process_year"))),
    format = "parquet").writeDynamicFrame(employees)
```

This method creates a DataSink that persists data to an output destination. This destination can be repositories on Amazon S3, Amazon RDS, and so on. This method allows setting the data format that should be used when persisting the data.

In this case, $output_path is the output directory in Amazon S3. The partitionKeys parameter specifies the column that will be used as a partition when writing the data to Amazon S3.

When the data is written out, the process_year column is removed from the dataset and is instead used to help form the directory structure. Here is how the directory could look if we listed it out:

```
PRE year=2020
PRE year=2019
PRE year=2018
PRE year=2017
PRE year=2016
```

So, what are some good columns to use when selecting partition keys? There are mainly two criteria that should drive this selection:

- Use columns that have a low (but not extremely low) cardinality. For example, a person's name, a phone number, or an email would not be good candidates. Conversely, a column that only has one or two values is also not a good candidate.

- Use columns that are expected to be used often and will be used as filters.

As an example, if your dataset contains log data, using dates and partitioning them by year, month, and day is often a good strategy. The cardinality should be just right. We should have plenty of results for each day of the logs and using predicate pushdown would result in only retrieving files for individual days.

There is another benefit to properly partitioning files, in addition to improving query performance. A proper partition also minimizes costly Apache Spark shuffle transformations for downstream ETL jobs.

Having to repartition a dataset by calling the `repartition` or `coalesce` functions quite frequently leads to workers having to shuffle data. This can have a negative impact on the time it takes to run ETL jobs and will most likely require more memory. By contrast, writing data from the start into Amazon S3 using Apache Hive partitions does not require the data to be shuffled and it can be sorted locally within a worker node.

This concludes the best practices that we recommend using to best deploy AWS Glue. This list by no means is comprehensive and only scratches the surface. Deploying AWS Glue at scale is not trivial and architects can build a career purely by mastering this powerful and fundamental service.

Summary

In this chapter, we introduced one of the most important services in the AWS stack – AWS Glue. We also learned about the high-level components that comprise AWS Glue such as the AWS Glue console, the AWS Glue Data Catalog, AWS Glue crawlers, and AWS Glue code generators. We then learned how everything is connected and how it can be used. Finally, we spent some time learning about recommended best practices when architecting and implementing AWS Glue.

In this chapter, we reviewed how we can choose the right worker type when launching an AWS Glue job. We learned how to optimize our file size during file splitting. We saw what can cause Yarn to run out of memory and what can be done to avoid this problem. We learned how the Apache Spark UI can be leveraged for troubleshooting. We were presented with definitions of data partitioning and predicate pushdown, and why they're important, along with other best practices and techniques.

In the next chapter, we will learn how to best implement your applications so that they are secure and compliant.

8
Best Practices for Application Security, Identity, and Compliance

In the past, a common refrain from companies was that they were hesitant to move to the cloud because they believed the cloud was not secure. A big part of this pushback was that companies didn't understand what the cloud was or what its capabilities were. It is true that it is possible to have security vulnerabilities even if you are using cloud infrastructure. However, as we will see in this chapter, AWS provides a comprehensive catalog of services that will enable you to create extremely secure sites and applications.

It is imperative when creating applications and implementing workflows, to consider security from the start of your design and not as an afterthought. First, we will explain why security is important in any system – not just in the cloud. Next, we will learn how AWS in general and AWS IAM in particular can help us to design and build robust and secure cloud applications. Also, as we will see in this chapter, AWS provides a veritable cornucopia of other security services.

In this chapter, we will cover the following topics:

- Understanding the importance of security, identity, and compliance on AWS

- Getting familiar with Identity and Access Management

- Managing resources, permissions, and identities using IAM

- Learning about other AWS security services

Understanding the importance of security, identity, and compliance on AWS

As is the case with any computer system, ensuring that it's secure and that only authorized users access the system is of paramount importance. Additionally, making sure that the system is compliant with corporate policies and government regulations is also critical.

AWS offers a plethora of security services to assist with these requirements. In this chapter, we will do a review of these services.

AWS is used both by the smallest of start-ups and fortune 500 companies. If there is a security incident on a website maintained by one individual out of their mom's closet, they might lose their livelihood and it might be catastrophic to them. But the damage may only be a few thousand dollars and that individual may be able to recover after a few months, perhaps by creating a brand new website with new branding.

For multinational enterprises such as *Yahoo* and *Experian*, which have had security breaches in recent years, monetary and reputational damage could be of a higher magnitude. So, the stakes are much higher.

In the case of Yahoo, it had what are to this day the two largest data breaches in history. In 2016, Yahoo reported two hacker attacks. Even though these breaches were reported in 2016, they happened in previous years. The first breach likely occurred in 2014 and it impacted over 500 million users. The second incident was reported later in 2016, but occurred around August 2013. This second breach impacted all 3 billion Yahoo users. Some of the data that was taken includes usernames, phone numbers, emails, security questions and answers, birth dates, and passwords.

Here is an example of the monetary damage suffered by Yahoo and its shareholders. This breach was disclosed after Verizon made an offer to buy Yahoo in 2016 for about $4.8 billion. As a result of the disclosure of the breach, a discount of $350 million was negotiated for the transaction to go through. The deal closed in June 2017.

You can find out more details about the Yahoo breach here: `https://www.nytimes.com/2016/09/23/technology/yahoo-hackers.html` and here: `https://www.nytimes.com/2016/12/14/technology/yahoo-hack.html`.

In the case of Experian, the attack happened in 2017. In this instance, the private data of about 165 million users in the US, Britain, and Canada was stolen. The breadth of the breach makes it one of the largest instances of identity theft. Equifax decided to quickly settle and, among other concessions, it offered its users a monetary settlement and free credit monitoring.

In both cases, the monetary damage was significant, but it pales in comparison to the reputational damage. And that is much harder to calculate. How much business did Experian and Yahoo not get as a result of a lack of trust from their users? We'll never know exactly but most likely it's multiple times the explicit monetary damage.

These two cases are just a few instances of the many security incidents that have been reported in the press in recent years. Who knows how many others have gone unnoticed or unreported? If you weren't already, hopefully, this has scared you straight to being hypersensitive about application security. Security should be incorporated at the beginning of your application design and not as an afterthought.

Fortunately, AWS provides a broad set of security offerings that can assist in ensuring your application is secure and that your application data is safe. Notice that we used the word *assist*. Just because you are using AWS, it does not mean that your applications will be instantly secure.

A quick example of how easy it is to leave your data exposed: There is nothing in AWS barring you from creating a bucket in AWS that is both unencrypted and public. You may get some warnings asking you if you are certain that you want to proceed, but it won't disallow it. You could then put a client file in that bucket that may contain emails, passwords, names, addresses, and so on. This combination would immediately make this data accessible to anyone in the world with an internet connection (including any bad guys).

Even though you may have not published the URL for the bucket, don't assume that it is secure. Bad actors know these mistakes happen sometimes and they are constantly sending requests to random AWS S3 buckets, trying to guess if they were created unsecured and exposed. And occasionally, they get lucky and hit pay dirt.

In the following section, we will learn more about what security AWS provides without involving the user and what services and tools AWS provides to its users to keep their systems secure.

Understanding the shared responsibility model

AWS uses what they call the **shared responsibility model**. This means that the responsibility for keeping applications secure falls both on AWS and its users. However, the lines of responsibility are quite clear. AWS is solely responsible for some aspects (for example, physical data center security) and users are solely responsible for other aspects (for example, making sure that Amazon S3 buckets that will contain sensitive information are private, accessible to only authorized users, and encrypted).

This model enables AWS to reduce the burden of securing some of the components needed to create applications while enabling users to still customize the applications to suit their clients' needs and budgets.

In some cases, depending on the service chosen, some responsibilities may fall on AWS or on the AWS user. For example, if you use Amazon RDS to stand up an instance of MySQL, the patching of the database and the underlying operating system would be performed by AWS.

If you instead decide to install MySQL directly into an Amazon EC2 instance, you will still be able to use the MySQL functionality. But in this case, the responsibility to patch the operating system and the database would fall on you.

One quick note, if your use case requires you to deploy MySQL manually into an EC2 instance, another option rather than deploying it yourself and risking the database not being deployed properly and securely is to work with an AWS Consulting Partner. AWS has a list of trusted consulting partners that they recommend and that can assist AWS customers. AWS ranks these partners by the level of service that they are able to provide. They have changed the ranking names in the past, but as of December 2020, the rankings are as follows:

- Select partner
- Advanced partner
- Premier partner

Where Premier partner is the highest level. The current list of consulting partners can be found here: `https://partners.amazonaws.com/`.

Deciding whether to use managed services versus deploying applications yourself is an important decision. Both approaches have advantages and disadvantages and the decision to use one or another method would be dictated by your business needs. For example, using Amazon RDS will require less maintenance since the patching is performed by AWS but your organization may require you to keep complete control of what changes happen to the software (perhaps because of regulatory reasons), in which case using the approach to install MySQL on your own would make more sense.

One common refrain heard to distinguish which components are the responsibility of AWS and which are the responsibility of the customer is as follows:

- AWS is responsible for the security **OF** the cloud.

- The AWS customer is responsible for security **IN** the cloud.

The following diagram illustrates the separation of duties:

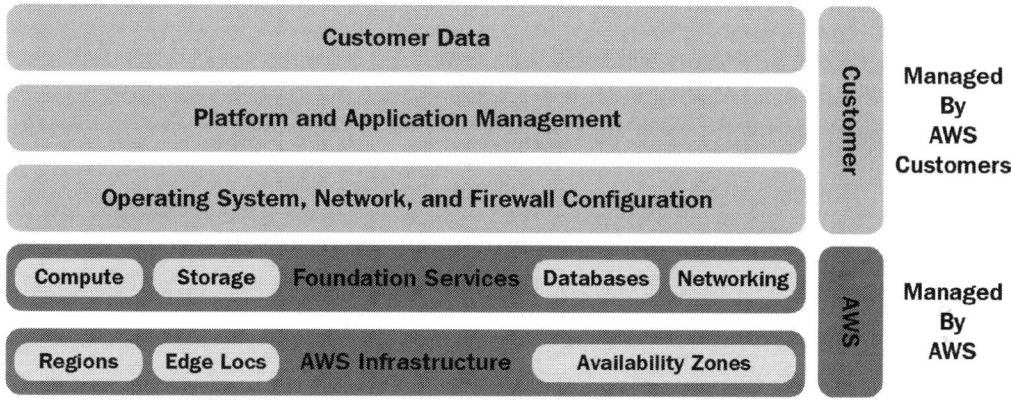

Figure 8.1 – Shared responsibility model

The preceding figure shows in broad strokes how the responsibilities are broken down. For example, it clearly shows that infrastructure elements such as Regions, Edge Locations, and Availability Zones are the responsibility of AWS. This includes the physical security of the data centers. You may have a better chance of getting into the Pentagon than getting into an AWS data center. Also, you may have passed an AWS data center and may have not noticed. AWS data centers are always unmarked buildings. And customer data is clearly the customer's responsibility. When it comes to customer data, the encryption of the data is also the customer's responsibility.

These areas of responsibility can be fuzzy depending on how a certain functionality is implemented. We see in the chart that databases fall under the purview of AWS but as we saw above, it is possible for the customer to install a database, in which case, they would be responsible for the management of it. Similarly, the chart shows operating systems, the network, and firewall configuration to be the responsibility of the customer. But in some cases, for example, when using AWS Lambda, the management of these items is the responsibility of AWS. Some other examples of managed services where this level of security is handled by AWS and not by the customer are as follows:

- Amazon RDS

- Amazon DynamoDB

- Amazon S3

- Amazon EMR

- AWS Glue

Another way to understand how security in AWS works is by using the analogy of locks and doors. AWS provides you with the doors and the locks to secure your applications and your data, but you can still leave the door open and not secure the lock and leave the contents of your home exposed to the world.

For example, Amazon RDS is a managed service and AWS does much of the heavy lifting to make a database secure, but you can still publish the credentials to access your Amazon RDS instance in GitHub, and let anyone that gets access to these credentials access your database.

Getting familiar with Identity and Access Management

Perhaps the most fundamental and important service in AWS is **Identity and Access Management (IAM)**, which can secure every single other software service offered by AWS. IAM is used to create and manage AWS users. These users can be aggregated into groups. Permissions against AWS services and resources can also be managed with AWS IAM and permissions can be given directly to users or by assigning permissions to groups that users belong to.

More specifically, AWS IAM can be used to do the following:

- **Manage users and their access permissions**:

    - Users can be created in IAM.

    - Users can be assigned individual security credentials (passwords, access keys, and multi-factor authentication capabilities).

    - Users can be assigned temporary security credentials to give them access to AWS services and resources.

    - Users can be given different permissions to determine which actions they can perform.

- **Manage IAM roles and role permissions**:

    - Roles can be created in IAM.

    - Permissions can be managed in IAM to determine which actions can be performed by a user, an entity, or an AWS service.

    - AWS services can be enabled to assume a role.

    - Entities can be assigned to assume roles.

- **Manage federated users and federated user permissions**: Identity federation can be enabled to enable users, groups, and roles to access resources such as the AWS Management Console, AWS APIs, and other resources. This can occur without creating an individual IAM user for each identity.

In the next section, we will learn how to manage resources, permissions, and identities by taking advantage of the IAM service.

Managing resources, permissions, and identities using IAM

To understand AWS IAM, we must first understand how authentication and identity management works. Users, groups, roles, permissions, and policies are fundamental concepts that need to be fully understood in order to grasp how resources are secured using AWS IAM. In the following sections, we'll define those terms.

Users

An IAM user is an individual that needs to access, interact with, and potentially modify data and AWS resources. Users can interact in one of three ways:

- AWS Console
- The AWS **Command Line Interface (CLI)**
- AWS API

Other than the root user, when a new user is set up, no implicit permissions or credentials are given, and that new user will not be able to access any resources until permission is explicitly assigned.

Groups

An IAM group, put simply, is a collection of users. Putting users into groups facilitates permission management. Having users combined into groups gives a system administrator a more efficient way to administer permissions. Users that have similar profiles are grouped together. They could be grouped together based on similar characteristics and on having similar needs, such as the following:

- Job function or role
- Department
- Persona

Then, permissions for users that belong to one group can be managed all at once through the group.

Roles

In IAM, a role is an object definition that can be used to configure a set of permissions assigned to that role. The role can then be assigned to other entities such as a user. A role is not directly connected to a person or a service. Rather, the role can be assumed by an entity that is given the role. Role credentials are always only temporary and rotated on a schedule defined by the AWS **Session Token Service (STS)**. It is best practice to use roles whenever possible instead of granting permissions directly to a user or group.

Furthermore, roles enable you to grant multi-account access to users, services, and applications. It is possible to assign a role even to users that are not part of your organization. Obviously, this has to be done in a judicious manner, but the flexibility is there if required. If you have been around technology for a little while, the idea of users and groups should not be new. However, IAM roles may require a little more explanation. Let's continue discussing them in the next section.

IAM roles play a fundamental task in the security access landscape. By assigning permissions to a role instead of directly to a user or group, roles facilitate and simplify system administration and allow these permissions to be given only temporarily.

Policies

A policy is a named document with a set of rules that specify what actions can be performed. Each policy laid out in the document gives a set of permissions. These policies can then be assigned to the IAM entities covered previously—users, groups, and roles. The syntax for AWS policy documents comes in two flavors:

- JSON
- YAML

Policies can be defined in the two following ways:

- **Managed policies**: When policies are defined as managed policies, they are created as standalone policies, and therefore they can then be attached to multiple entities. Out of the box, AWS provides a set of predefined managed policies that can be used in many use cases. Managed policies can be combined to deliver additional access to roles, users, or groups. Finally, AWS users can define and customize their own managed policies.

- **Inline policies**: Inline policies are created within the definition of an IAM entity and therefore can only be assigned to the entity they are attached to. They do not have their own **Amazon Resource Name** (**ARN**). Since inline policies are related to a specific entity, they are not reusable.

It is best practice to use managed policies whenever possible and use inline policies only when there is a good reason to do so.

Permissions

Permissions are lists of actions that can be taken on AWS resources. When a user or group is created, initially they have no permissions. One or more policies can be attached to the new user or group to enable access to resources.

When creating policies, it a good idea to abide by the principle of least privilege. In simple terms, this means that entities should be given a high enough level of access to perform assigned tasks but nothing more. For example, if an Amazon EC2 instance is created and we know that it will only be accessed by five users with five different IPs, we should whitelist those IPs and only give them access instead of opening the Amazon EC2 instance to the whole world.

AWS provides a policy simulator. This policy simulator can be used to test new policies that you may create and ensure they have the correct syntax. You can learn more here:

```
https://docs.aws.amazon.com/IAM/latest/UserGuide/access_
policies_testing-policies.html
```

Permissions can be assigned to AWS users, groups, and roles via policies. These permissions can be given with policies in one of two ways:

- **Identity-based policies**: In this case, the policies are attached to users, groups, or roles.

- **Resource-based policies**: In this case, the policies are attached to AWS resources such as Amazon S3 buckets, Amazon EC2 instances, AWS Lambda, and so on.

Hopefully, the concepts of users, groups, roles, permissions, and policies are a bit clearer now. IAM is far from the only security service that AWS offers. In the next section, we will learn about some of the other services that AWS offers to make your applications more secure and robust.

Learning about other AWS security services

AWS offers many other security services and comprehensive coverage of each one of them would be a book by itself. We will just quickly cover them and describe them in this section.

AWS Organizations

AWS Organizations is a service that can be used to manage multiple AWS accounts in a consolidated manner. It provides a centralized location where you can see all your organization's bills and manage all your AWS accounts from one place. By having this central location, it becomes much easier to establish, manage, and enforce your organization's security policies. Having this central control ensures that security administrators and auditors can perform their jobs more efficiently and with more confidence.

These are the most important and relevant concepts when working with the AWS Organizations service:

- **Organization**: The overarching owner that will control all AWS accounts.

- **Root account**: The owner account for all other AWS accounts. Only one root account can exist across the organization. The root account needs to be created when the organization is created.

- **Organizational unit**: A grouping of underlying AWS accounts and/or other organizational units. An organizational unit can be the parent of other organizational units and so on. This enables the potential creation of a hierarchy of organizational units that resembles a family tree. See the following diagram for more clarity.

- **AWS account**: A traditional AWS account that manages AWS resources and services. AWS accounts reside under an organizational unit or under the root account.

- **Service Control Policy (SCP)**: A service control policy specifies the services and permissions for users and roles. An SCP can be associated with an AWS account or with an organizational unit.

The following figure illustrates how these components interact with each other:

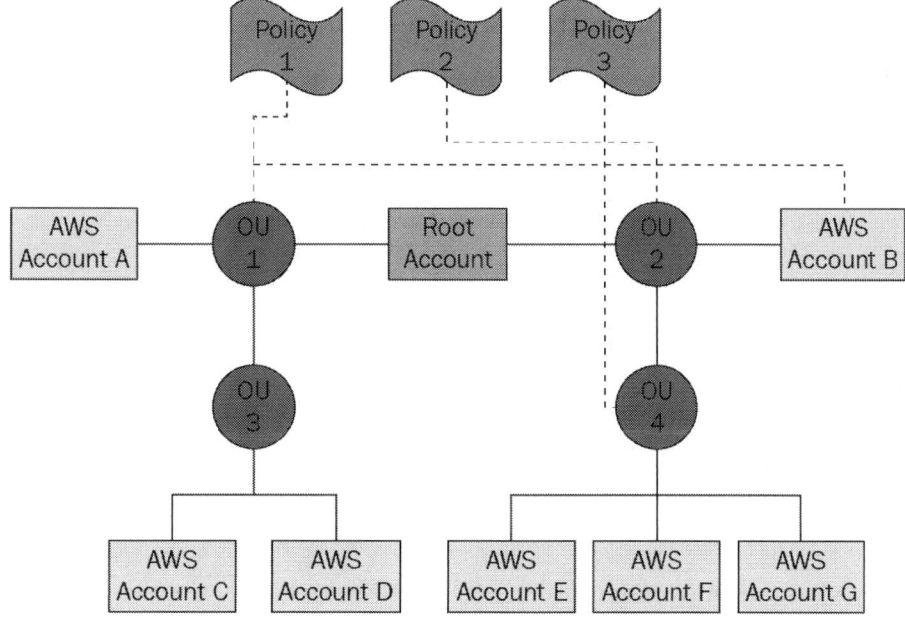

Figure 8.2 – Sample organizational unit hierarchy

As we can see in the figure, **Policy 1** is associated with **Organizational Unit** (OU) 1 and with **AWS Account B**. **Policy 1** is also applied to all children of **OU 1** (**OU 3**, **AWS Account C**, and **AWS Account D**). Since **Policy 1** is associated with **AWS Account B** directly, it overrides **Policy 2**, which is associated with **OU 2** and all its children except for **AWS Account B**. **Policy 3** is associated with **OU 4** and all its children (**AWS Accounts E, F**, and **G**).

Without AWS Organizations, all these policies would have to be repeated individually for each account. Every time there was a change to a policy, it would have to be changed individually in each account. This old approach had a high likelihood of policies that were supposed to be identical getting out of sync.

AWS Control Tower

If you have a simple AWS setup with a few servers and only one AWS account, then you don't need AWS Control Tower. But if you are part of an environment that has hundreds or thousands of resources and multiple AWS accounts and teams, then you will want to learn about and leverage AWS Control Tower. AWS Control Tower simplifies the administration, governance, and security setup of a multi-account environment.

AWS Control Tower enables you to set up company-wide policies and apply them across multiple AWS accounts. Without AWS Control Tower, you would have to apply the individual files to each account, opening the possibility of having inconsistencies in your accounts.

Amazon GuardDuty

Amazon GuardDuty is an AWS service that can be used to detect threats, malicious behavior, and activity from unauthorized actors. It provides protection to all other AWS resources and your enterprise's data. Applications getting more traffic is normally good news because it normally means more business. But with additional traffic comes more work to track and monitor additional logs and activity.

Amazon GuardDuty enables and simplifies the monitoring of this activity. Amazon GuardDuty leverages machine learning and advanced anomaly detection to compile, process, and prioritize potential malicious activity. GuardDuty can analyze billions of events in real time across a variety of AWS real-time and near-real-time streams such as AWS CloudTrail logs, Amazon VPC Flow Logs, and DNS logs.

However, keep in mind that Amazon GuardDuty doesn't do anything with the analysis. It is an Intrusion Detection System and not an **Intrusion Prevention System** (**IPS**). If you need enforcement for malicious IPs, you will need a third-party solution such as Aviatrix GuardDuty Enforcement.

AWS Shield

AWS Shield is an AWS managed **Distributed Denial of Service (DDoS)** protection service used to protect systems and data. AWS Shield delivers automatic attack detection and resolution that can keep your application running or at least reduce the amount of downtime. Since AWS Shield Standard comes with all AWS accounts, you normally have to contact AWS support to assist you if you suffer a DDoS attack. AWS Shield comes in two flavors:

- **AWS Shield Standard**: Provided at no additional charge to all AWS customers
- **AWS Shield Advanced**: Provides a higher level of protection but at an additional cost

AWS Shield Standard can protect against and handle the more common types of attacks. The more common DDoS attacks happen at the network and transport layer. AWS Shield Standard can help you protect Amazon CloudFront and Amazon Route 53 against (Layer 3 and 4) attacks.

AWS Shield Advanced provides higher protection for more services. AWS Shield can be used to defend against attacks targeting the following:

- Amazon EC2 instances
- **Elastic Load Balancing (ELB)**
- Amazon CloudFront
- AWS Global Accelerator
- Amazon Route 53

To get this level of protection, you will need to subscribe to AWS Shield Advanced (and pay an additional fee). AWS Shield Advanced not only protects against network and transport layer attacks, it delivers additional monitoring and resolution, protecting against large and sophisticated DDoS attacks, providing real-time reporting when attacks occur. It integrates with AWS **Web Application Firewall (WAF)** (which we will learn more about in the next section). As an additional feature, AWS Shield Advanced provides 24-hour support from AWS **DDoS Response Team (DRT)**. Finally, with AWS Shield Advanced, AWS will cover any charges your account incurs for certain services that can be attributed to an attack.

AWS Web Application Firewall

AWS WAF, as the name implies, is a firewall for your web applications. It can be used to create a layer of protection around your web applications and RESTful APIs. It guards against the most well-known web exploits. AWS WAF can be used to control network traffic. This traffic is controlled by creating rules. These rules can target well-known exploits such as SQL injection or cross-site scripting. Furthermore, these rules can be customized to filter transactions that meet user-defined patterns. To get a jump start, AWS WAF has Managed Rules, which simplifies management. These rules can be managed by AWS, and AWS Marketplace Sellers also offer preconfigured rules. AWS and Marketplace rules are constantly modified as new threats are identified. AWS WAF also provides an API to assist in the development, deployment, and maintenance of these security rules.

AWS WAF can be deployed on the following:

- Amazon CloudFront
- Application Load Balancer
- Origin servers running on EC2
- Amazon API Gateway
- AWS AppSync

AWS WAF pricing depends on the number of rules that are deployed and the number of requests that applications receive.

AWS Firewall Manager

AWS Firewall Manager makes setting up firewalls simple. It enables users to administer firewall rules in a central dashboard. This can be achieved even across multiple AWS accounts and applications.

Cloud environments are dynamic. This can create maintenance headaches as new applications come online. AWS Firewall Manager simplifies the process of provisioning new applications and ensuring they are compliant with an enterprise's security policies by enabling users to manage firewall settings from one location.

If new security rules need to be created or if existing rules need to be modified, they can also be changed only once. Some of the services in AWS that can benefit from AWS Firewall Manager are the following:

- Application Load Balancer
- API Gateways

- Amazon CloudFront distributions

- Amazon EC2

One drawback of AWS Firewall Manager is that it requires the use of AWS Organizations, which may be cost-prohibitive in some instances. This provides the ability to add AWS WAF rules, AWS Shield Advanced protection, security groups, and AWS Network Firewall rules to VPCs across accounts and resources using a centralized dashboard.

Amazon Cloud Directory

Amazon Cloud Directory is a fully managed service that provides the ability to create directories. These directories are hierarchical trees that can store data across different dimensions. Amazon Cloud Directory can be used in the development of quite a few applications, including the following:

- Organizational charts

- Device registries

- Policy hierarchies

Traditional directory services such as **Active Directory Lightweight Directory Services (AD LDS)** and other **Lightweight Directory Application Protocol (LDAP)** directories only allow a single hierarchy; Amazon Cloud Directory provides the ability to generate hierarchical directories spanning more than one dimension.

Amazon Cloud Directory can scale to millions and even hundreds of millions of objects. It has a dynamic and extensible schema that can integrate with other AWS services and custom applications. Like many other AWS services, it can also be accessed via the AWS CLI and it provides an API to the most popular programming languages.

Amazon Inspector

Amazon Inspector is a service that automatically checks application compliance against certain predefined policies and is used to increase compliance. Amazon Inspector can identify vulnerabilities, exposure, and deviations from predefined best practices. Once the assessment has been completed, the service generates a comprehensive report of security flaws and issues sorted by severity level. These findings can then be used to close these security gaps.

Amazon Inspector security assessments enable users to look for unauthorized network accessibility for Amazon EC2 instances. It can find vulnerabilities on EC2 instances. Amazon Inspector assessments are available as pre-defined rule components that can map to security best practices and vulnerability definitions. Some samples of predefined rules are as follows:

- Someone trying to access EC2 instances from outside your network
- If someone turns on remote root login
- Identify software and operating system versions that are due for patching

These rules are constantly monitored and enhanced by the AWS security team.

Amazon Macie

Amazon Macie is another fully managed security service. It can be used to protect your data and its privacy. It leverages **artificial intelligence** (**AI**) and **machine learning** (**ML**) to find and protect sensitive data in AWS environments.

In today's enterprises, data comes in at ever-increasing speed. Handling those growing volumes of data creates scalability issues. With more data, complexity and expenses increase. Amazon Macie enables the automation of sensitive data discovery. Since it leverages machine learning, it can scale and can handle petabyte-sized datasets. Macie creates a list of Amazon S3 buckets in a user's account and it can flag which ones are not unencrypted, which ones can be accessed publicly, and buckets that are being shared with other AWS accounts that are not defined in AWS Organizations.

Amazon Macie uses machine learning and pattern matching on these buckets. Amazon Macie can be configured to identify sensitive data such as personally identifiable information and deliver alerts to a predefined user base. Once these alerts and issues are generated, they can be easily sorted and filtered in the AWS Management Console. They can then be sent to Amazon EventBridge. It can then be integrated with other AWS services using workflow or event management systems. It can also be used together with other AWS services.

An example is AWS Step Functions. AWS Step Functions can leverage automated remediation actions. This can assist with the compliance of rules and regulations, such as the **Health Insurance Portability and Accountability Act** (**HIPAA**) and **General Data Privacy Regulation** (**GDPR**).

AWS Artifact Reports

AWS Artifact Reports is a simple service that delivers a centralized repository to store, manage, and access a variety of compliance reports from third-party auditors who have audited and certified that a given standard or regulation is met by the AWS infrastructure or by a given service. These rules, standards, and regulations may be global, regional, or industry-specific. As these rules and regulations change, AWS is constantly engaging third parties to ensure that compliance is up to date.

The AWS Artifact Agreements service provides the ability to access, approve, terminate, and manage agreements with AWS. It can be used to manage one AWS account or, leveraging AWS Organizations, you can manage multiple AWS accounts.

Some of the types of reports that can be managed with AWS Artifact are as follows:

- **Service Organization Control** (**SOC**) reports
- **Payment Card Industry** (**PCI**) reports
- Certifications from accreditation agencies around the world
- Industry-specific compliance reports
- Compliance reports about AWS security controls
- **Business Associate Addendums** (**BAAs**)
- **Nondisclosure Agreements** (**NDAs**)

AWS Certificate Manager

AWS Certificate Manager is another security service. It can be used to create, maintain, and deploy public and private **Secure Sockets Layer/Transport Layer Security** (**SSL/TLS**) certificates that can then be added to other AWS services and other applications. SSL/TLS certificates can secure network communications by enabling encryption. They can also be used to authenticate a website's identity in public and private networks. AWS Certificate Manager streamlines and automates the management process for certificate management.

AWS Certificate Manager can be used to provision and renew a certificate and install it on another AWS service such as **Elastic Load Balancers** (**ELBs**), Amazon CloudFront, and APIs on API Gateway. It can also be used to create private certificates for internal applications. These certificates can then be centrally managed. When you provision public and private certificates using AWS Certificate Manager, there is no charge. The cost is bundled with the cost of spinning up the underlying resources (like an EC2 instance). When you use AWS Certificate Manager Private Certificate Authority, there is a monthly charge for the use of the private Certificate Authority and for the private certificates that are issued.

AWS CloudHSM

AWS makes encrypting data at rest quite simple if you use encryption keys provided by AWS. However, in some instances, this solution may not be appropriate for certain use cases that may require you to provide your own keys.

Using your own keys for encryption is slightly more complicated but doable. For that, AWS provides a service called AWS CloudHSM.

AWS CloudHSM is a **hardware security module** (**HSM**) that empowers users to generate their own encryption keys. CloudHSM provides the ability to create encryption keys using FIPS 140-2 Level 3 validated HSMs. AWS CloudHSM can be integrated with other AWS services via well-defined industry-standard APIs. Some of the APIs supported are as follows:

- PKCS#11
- Microsoft **CryptoNG** (**CNG**) libraries
- **Java Cryptography Extensions** (**JCEs**)

AWS CloudHSM complies with many security standards. It is also possible to export the generated keys to a wide variety of third-party HSMs. Like many of the other security services we have learned about in this section, AWS CloudHSM is fully managed by AWS, enabling you to focus on your applications and not the administration of your key management service. Some of the tasks that AWS handles when using this service are as follows:

- Provisioning the required hardware to run the service
- Applying software patching
- Making sure the service is highly available
- Performing backups

CloudHSM has a serverless architecture that allows users to seamlessly and effortlessly scale.

AWS Directory Service

Microsoft Active Directory (AD) has been a popular choice for user and role management for decades, which, in computer years, is a long time. Given this popularity, AWS offers a fully managed implementation of Microsoft Active Directory. AWS Directory Service for Microsoft AD, also known as **AWS Managed Microsoft Active Directory**, allows AWS services that require directory services to integrate with Microsoft Active Directory. AWS Managed Microsoft AD uses the actual Microsoft AD. It does not need to stay in sync because it does not copy the contents of existing ADs to the cloud. For this reason, the standard Microsoft AD administration tools can be used, and you can leverage the built-in AD capabilities, such as group policies and single sign-on. Using AWS Managed Microsoft AD, you can integrate Amazon EC2 and Amazon RDS for SQL Server instances with Microsoft AD.

AWS Key Management Service

AWS **Key Management Service (KMS)** is a fundamental AWS security service. AWS KMS can be used to assist in the management of encryption of data at rest. KMS provides the ability to create and manage cryptographic keys. It can also be used to manage which users, services, and applications have access to them. AWS KMS is a secure and fault-tolerant service. It has a set of hardware security modules. These modules are compliant with the **Federal Information Processing Standard** 140-2 (**FIPS** 140-2). AWS KMS integrates with AWS CloudTrail so that it is simple to see who has used the keys and when.

AWS Secrets Manager

AWS Secrets Manager is a security service that can be used to protect secrets. These secrets may be strings such as passwords that can be used to access services, applications, and IT resources. AWS Secrets Manager facilitates the rotation, management, and retrieval of API keys, database credentials, passwords, and other secrets. These secrets can be retrieved using the Secrets Manager APIs. By using AWS Secrets Manager, the need to store passwords clearly in plain text files is obviated. Some of the services that can integrate with AWS Secrets Manager are as follows:

- Amazon RDS

- Amazon Redshift

- Amazon DynamoDB

- Amazon Neptune

- Amazon DocumentDB

AWS Secrets Manager can be customized to support additional types of secrets. Some examples of use cases are the following:

- API keys
- OAuth authentication tokens

Another feature of AWS Secrets Manager is that it allows secrets to be rotated periodically without impacting applications that are using them for password management and other uses.

AWS Single Sign-On

Being able to sign on to multiple enterprise applications using a user's network login ID has been a pervasive way to manage application access for a while now.

With AWS **Single Sign-On** (**SSO**), this functionality can be implemented without too much effort and it can also be centrally managed even in a multi-account AWS environment. AWS SSO can be used to manage user access and user permissions for multiple AWS accounts in one central place leveraging AWS Organizations. AWS SSO can be used to configure and maintain all account permissions automatically. It does not need additional configuration for each individual account. User permissions can be assigned using roles. Some of the applications that can be seamlessly integrated with AWS SSO are the following:

- Salesforce
- SAP
- Dropbox
- Box
- Office 365

To manage user identities, AWS SSO provides an identity store, or it can connect with an existing identity store. Some of the supported identity stores are the following:

- Microsoft Active Directory
- **Azure Active Directory** (**Azure AD**)
- Okta Universal Directory

Any activity that occurs when using AWS SSO will be recorded using AWS CloudTrail.

AWS Security Hub

AWS Security Hub provides a central location to see security alerts and security posture over multiple AWS accounts. AWS Security Hub provides tools such as the following:

- Firewalls

- Endpoint protection

- Vulnerability and compliance scanners

When these tools are not centralized, you may be required to deal with many alerts across different consoles. But AWS Security Hub delivers a centralized service to view, organize, prioritize, and manage these security alerts across multiple AWS services and accounts.

Some of the services that can work with AWS Security Hub are the following:

- Amazon Inspector

- AWS IAM Access Analyzer

- Amazon GuardDuty

- Amazon Macie

- AWS Firewall Manager

- Other AWS Marketplace third-party services

AWS Security Hub also provides the ability to act on security findings and investigate using Amazon Detective or Amazon CloudWatch Events rules and integrate these alerts with ticketing systems, chat apps, and incident management services.

Summary

In this chapter, we laid the groundwork to enable you to understand how security is implemented in AWS. As we saw in the chapter, a fundamental pillar of this is the shared responsibility model. We saw how some components of security are the responsibility of AWS and some parts are the responsibility of the customer. We then looked at the most basic and fundamental security service in AWS – AWS IAM. We reviewed concepts such as users, groups, permissions, roles, and policies and how they are connected to each other. Finally, in the last section of the chapter, we learned about other security services and how they can make your cloud environment even more secure.

Hopefully, after completing this chapter, you feel more confident about how AWS can be leveraged to write world-class applications offering the highest levels of security.

This concludes Section 2. In Section 3, starting with *Chapter 9, Serverless and Container Patterns*, we will learn about microservices, container patterns, and serverless technologies available in AWS.

Section 3: Applying Architectural Patterns and Reference Architectures

In this section, you'll understand the AWS cloud architectural patterns and how they can be applied to a variety of use cases.

This part of the book comprises the following chapters:

- *Chapter 9, Serverless and Container Patterns*
- *Chapter 10, Microservice and Event-Driven Architectures*
- *Chapter 11, Domain-Driven Design*
- *Chapter 12, Data Lake Patterns – Integrating Your Data across the Enterprise*
- *Chapter 13, Availability, Reliability, and Scalability Patterns*

9
Serverless and Container Patterns

In this chapter and this section of the book, we will learn about a variety of patterns that are commonly used by many of the top technology companies in the world, including Netflix, Microsoft, Amazon, Uber, eBay, and PayPal. These companies have survived and thrived by adopting cloud technologies and the design patterns that are popular on the cloud. It is hard to imagine how these companies could exist in their present form if the capabilities delivered by the cloud did not exist. In addition, the patterns, services, and tools presented in this chapter make the cloud that much more powerful.

In this chapter, we will first present the concept of containerization. We will then move on to learn about two popular tools – Docker and Kubernetes. Toward the end of the chapter, we will also cover AWS Batch and its components, along with its best practices.

In this chapter, we will cover the following topics:

- Understanding containerization
- Virtual machines and virtualization
- Containers versus VMs
- Learning about Docker
- Learning about Kubernetes

- Learning about AWS Fargate
- Learning about AWS Batch

Let's get started.

Understanding containerization

It's almost 6 o'clock and it's getting close to dinner time. You are getting hungry. And you feel like cooking some juicy steaks. Time to fire up the grill. But think about everything that's going to be required:

- Steaks
- Grill
- Matches
- Charcoal or gas
- Condiments
- Tongs

So, it's more than just steaks.

Some companies specialize in bundling all the necessary elements to facilitate this process and you can just buy everything in a package. A similar analogy would be if you went to a restaurant. The cook handles all of the elements listed here for you and all you have to do is eat.

It's the same with software. Installing something like a website is much more than just installing your code. It might require the following:

- An operating system
- A database
- A web server
- An app server
- Configuration files
- Seeding data for the database
- Underlying hardware

In the same way that the restaurant chef handles everything for you, container technology can help to create a standalone bundle that can take care of everything related to a deployment and simplify your life. Containers enable you to wrap all the necessary components in one convenient little package and deploy them all in one step. Containers are standardized packages of software that include all dependencies, enabling applications to run smoothly, uniformly, and reliably regardless of how many times they are deployed. Container images are lightweight, independent, standalone, and executable software bundles that include all that is needed to run an application:

- Source code
- Runtime executable
- System tools
- System libraries and JAR files
- Configuration settings

Containerization is the process of bundling your application into containers and running them in isolation even if there are other similar containers running in the same machine. Let's now look at the advantages of containers.

Advantages of containers

There is a reason that containers are so popular. They have many advantages over non-containerized software deployed on bare metal. Let's analyze the most relevant advantages.

Containers are more efficient

Containers allow us to deploy applications in a more efficient manner for a variety of reasons. Many applications today require a loosely coupled stateless architecture. A **stateless** architecture doesn't store any state within its boundaries. They simply pass requests forward. If state is stored, it is stored outside of the container, such as in a separate database. Architectures like this can be designed to easily scale and handle failures transparently because different requests can be handled independently by different servers. It is a loosely coupled architecture. A **loosely coupled** architecture is one where the individual components in the architecture have little or no knowledge of other components in the system. Containers are ideally suited for this type of application. A good example of this stateless architecture leveraging containers is the Google search engine. As Google users, we are completely unaware of this, but Google is constantly adding armies of stateless servers to handle our search requests. If a server fails, it is quickly replaced by an identical server that takes its place and takes over the load.

Less infrastructure waste

With the low cost and speed associated with bringing instances up and down, resources such as memory can be allocated more aggressively. If we can spin up a server quickly if traffic spikes, and we can run our servers at a higher CPU utilization rate without the risk of overloading our systems. Think of the prototypical web application. More than likely, traffic is variable depending on many factors (such as the time of day, day of the week, and so on). If we use containers, we can spin up new instances whenever traffic increases. For example, think about the website for a stockbroker firm such as Charles Schwab. It would be surprising if their web traffic was not considerably higher during the working week than on the weekends because the market is open Monday through Friday.

Containers are simple

Containers enable isolated, autonomous, and independent platforms without the overhead of an operating system. Developers can redeploy a configuration without having to manage application state across multiple VMs.

Some containers are cross-platform and can be deployed on Mac, Windows, or Linux environments.

Containers can increase productivity

The fast and interactive nature of the deployment of containers can offer fast feedback to accelerate the development cycle. The deployment of containers can be automated, further enhancing productivity. Containers can be started in a repeatable and consistent manner in one instance or multiple instances regardless of the instance type or size.

Using containers to deploy applications can enable you to deploy your application across an array of servers. It doesn't matter if that server array has 10 servers, 100 servers, or 1,000 servers.

Disadvantages of containers

There is always a downside to every technology. There is no silver bullet.

In the case of containers, these are some of the disadvantages.

Container speeds are slightly slower compared with bare-metal servers

A **bare-metal** server is a server that can be used by one user at a time. Before the age of virtualization, there was no other kind of server. There was no way to slice a server and have multiple users on each slice. Multiple users could use a server but without any real separation. **Virtualization** enables us to slice up a server and provide dedicated slices to individual users.

In this case, the user will think they have complete and exclusive use of the server, when in actuality, they are only using a portion of the server. In this case, there is a performance penalty that is paid compared to the bare-metal approach.

The performance for containers has higher overhead constraints compared to bare metal due to the following:

- **Overlay networking**: In order to provide virtualization, an extra network layer needs to be overlaid on top of the operating system. This overlay creates overhead.

- **Interfacing with other containers**: The connections between containers will not be as fast if they existed within the container. This also creates overhead.

- **Connections to the host system**: There are also connections between the containers and the underlying host system. There is also going to be some latency with these connections when compared to intra-process connections.

The overhead is small but if your application requires you to squeeze performance to gain the edge no matter how small, you will want to use bare metal instead of containers. An example of this use case is high-frequency trading platforms, where performance is measured in microseconds.

Ecosystem inconsistencies

Although the popular Docker platform is open source and pervasive, it is not fully compatible with other offerings such as Kubernetes and Red Hat's OpenShift. This is due to the normal push/pull forces between competitors and their desire to grow the market together (by offering compatible and uniform features) while at the same time growing their own market share (by offering proprietary features and extensions).

Graphical applications

Docker was initially created to easily deploy server applications without a graphical interface. Interesting applications have cropped up, such as X11 video forwarding, which enables running a UI application inside of a container; but since this is more of a bolt-on rather than part of the original design, it is a far from perfect solution.

In summary, containers can be great for certain use cases, but they are not a magic bullet for all scenarios. Containers are well suited to running microservices that don't require microsecond performance. Containers can simplify microservice delivery by enabling a packaging mechanism around them.

Let's explore in more depth the topic of VMs and virtualization.

Virtual machines and virtualization

In order to understand VMs and virtualization, let's first look at an analogy. For many of us, one of our goals is to own a house. Can you picture it? Three bedrooms, a beautiful lawn, and a white picket fence, maybe? For some of us, at least for now, that dream may not be achievable, so we must settle to rent an apartment in a big building.

You can think of the beautiful house as a normal standalone server dedicated to serving only one client or one application. The apartment in this case is the virtual machine. The apartment serves its purpose by providing housing with some shared services. It might not be as beautiful and convenient as the house, but it does the job. With the house, if you live alone, you are wasting resources because you can only use one room at a time. Similarly, with a standalone server, especially if you have an application with variable traffic, you will have lulls in your traffic where a lot of the capacity of the machine is wasted.

As you can see from the example, both approaches have advantages and drawbacks, and your choice is going to depend on your use case. From the perspective of virtual machine users, they would be hard-pressed to know whether they are using a dedicated machine or a virtual machine.

Currently, two main types of VMs exist:

- **System Virtual Machines (SVMs)** (also known as full virtualization VMs): SVMs are a physical machine substitute. SVMs provide the underpinnings to fully execute an operating system. They leverage a hypervisor architecture.

- The second type is **hypervisors**. A hypervisor is a software component that can span and run **Virtual Machines (VMs)**. Another name commonly used for hypervisors is **Virtual Machine Monitors (VMMs)**. A hypervisor isolates the operating system and resources from other VMs and facilitates the generation and management of those VMs.

A hypervisor leverages native execution to share and manage hardware resources, providing multiple isolated environments all within the same server. Many of today's hypervisors use hardware-enabled virtualization, hardware that is specifically designed for VM usage.

One important point is that you can have two VMs running alongside each other on the same physical machine and have each one running a different operating system. For example, one could be running Amazon Linux and the other VM could be running Ubuntu.

Now that we have learned about these concepts, let's compare containers and virtual machines.

Containers versus VMs

There is a definite line of distinction between VMs and containers. Containers allow you to isolate applications within an operating system environment. VMs allow you to isolate what appears to the users and represent it as a completely different machine to the user, even with its own operating system.

The following diagram illustrates the difference:

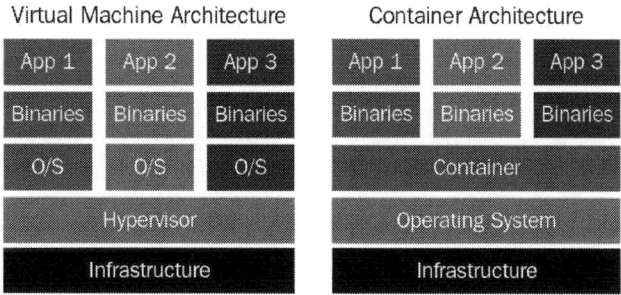

Figure 9.1 – VMs versus containers

As we can see in *Figure 9.1*, in the case of a VM architecture, each virtual slice has its own operating system and all the slices sit on top of the hypervisor. In the case of a container architecture, there is only one operating system installed for each instance. There is only one container engine, but multiple binaries and multiple applications can be installed for each slice.

It's also useful to highlight that in the majority of cases, when you run containers in AWS (and in most cloud environments, for that matter), you will be running these containers on a VM. Therefore, there will be multiple containers running in a VM. In turn, that VM will be running alongside a set of other VMs running in the same hypervisor running on top of a physical machine. The only exception to this rule might be if you pay extra to get a dedicated instance.

In which case, you will be guaranteed that no other VMs will run in your dedicated instance, as shown in the following diagram:

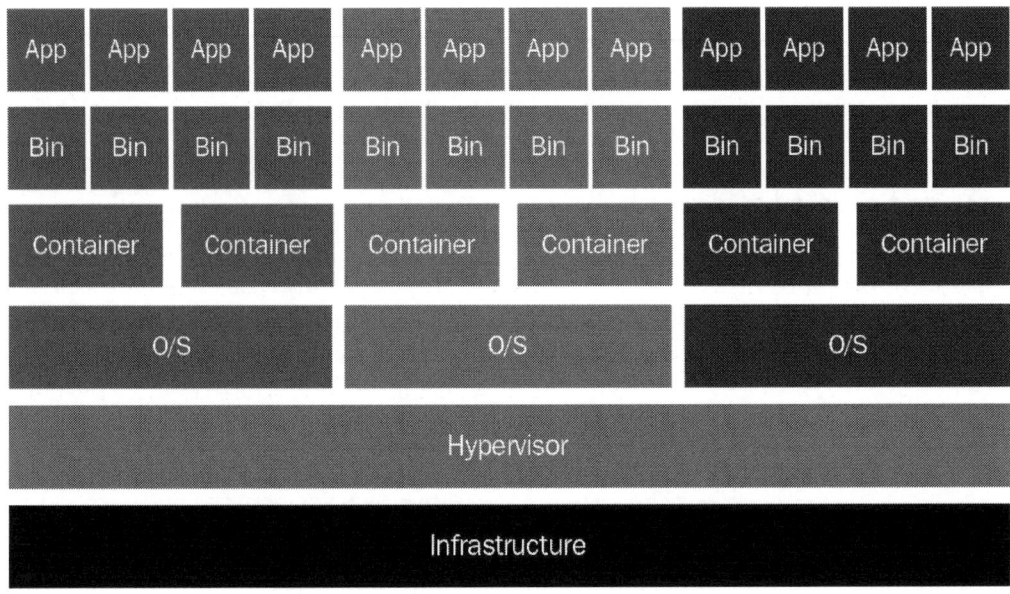

Figure 9.2 – Architecture for AWS virtualization

In the example in *Figure 9.2*, we are running on a single piece of hardware and only one hypervisor. The hypervisor is supporting and enabling three different operating system instances and each of them is supporting two containers each, for a total of six containers.

VMs and hypervisors are transparent to you when using AWS. Whenever you launch an EC2 instance, AWS does a lot of work for you behind the scenes. The EC2 instance appears to you as your own dedicated instance, but in truth, the new instance is just another VM in an army of VMs that AWS launched for other AWS users.

So far, we have learned about the general concepts of containerization and virtualization. In the next sections, we will drill down into more specific topics and learn about actual implementations of these concepts, starting with the popular open source software Docker.

Learning about Docker

It would be a disservice to you, reader, for us to talk about containers and not mention Docker. **Docker** is not the only way to implement containers, but it certainly is a popular container software. Perhaps the most popular one. Docker has almost become synonymous with the term container. Docker, Inc., the maker of the product, follows a freemium model, offering both a free version and a premium version. Docker was released to the public in 2013 at the PyCon Conference and it was open sourced in March 2013.

As container software, Docker can package an application together with all its libraries, configuration files, and dependencies. Docker can be installed in Linux environments as well as on Windows. The virtual containers that Docker enables allow having applications in isolation without affecting any other processes running on the same physical machine.

Docker is often used by both developers and system administrators, making it an essential tool for many DevOps teams. Developers like using it because it allows them to focus on writing code without having to worry about the implementation and deployment details of the system where it will eventually be deployed. They can be assured that the characteristics of the environment will be identical regardless of the physical machine. Developers can also leverage many of the programs and extensions that come bundled with Docker. System administrators use Docker frequently because it gives them flexibility and its light footprint allows them to reduce the number of servers needed to deploy applications at scale.

> **Important note**
> The full Docker documentation, installation instructions, and a download link for the Community edition of Docker can be found here: `https://docs.docker.com/`.

Docker components

Docker does not have a monolithic architecture. It has a set of well-defined components, each of which is in charge of an individual function and is fully dedicated to performing only that function.

The following are the major Docker components. Let's go through them in detail to increase our understanding of Docker.

Dockerfile

Every Docker container needs to have a **Dockerfile**. A Dockerfile is a plain old text file containing a series of instructions that show how the Docker image will be built. Don't worry, we'll cover Docker images in a second.

Some of the instructions that a Dockerfile will contain are the following:

- **Operating system supporting the container**: What is the operating system associated with the container? For example, Windows, Linux, and so on.

- **Environmental variables used**: For example, most deployments require a list of variables. Also, is this a production or test deployment? What department is this deployment for? What department should be billed?

- **Locations of files used**: For example, where are the data files located? Where are the executable files?

- **Network ports used**: For example, what ports are open? Which port is used for HTTP traffic?

Let's now move to the Docker image component.

Docker images

After the Dockerfile has been created, the next step is to create an image. The Docker build utility can take a Dockerfile and create an image. The Docker build utility's purpose is to create *ready-for-deployment* container images. The Dockerfile contains instructions that specify how the Docker image will be built. The **Docker image** is portable across environments and instance types, and that's one of the reasons for Docker's popularity. You can deploy the same image in a Linux environment or a Windows environment, and Docker will handle the details to ensure that the deployment functions correctly in both environments. One recommended best practice is to ensure that any external dependencies specified in the Dockerfile have the version of the dependency explicitly declared. If this is not done, inconsistencies may result even from the same Dockerfile because a different version of a library may be picked up.

Docker run

Docker run is a utility where commands can be issued to launch containers. In this context, a container is an image instance. Containers are designed to be transient and ephemeral. Containers can be restarted, stopped, or started via the Docker run utility. The utility can launch several instances of the same image, and those instances can run simultaneously (in order to support additional traffic). For example, if you have 10 similar instances taking traffic and the traffic increases, you can use the Docker run utility to launch an additional instance.

Docker Hub

When you build a container, you can configure it from scratch, creating your own Dockerfile and configuring it yourself. However, many times, it is not necessary to reinvent the wheel. If you want to leverage the work that others have done already, you can use Docker Hub. **Docker Hub** is a collection of previously created containers where Docker users share their containers. In Docker Hub, you will find Docker images created by Docker and by other vendors who, in some instances, support those containers. Also, other Docker users publish versions of the containers they have created that they have found useful. You can also share your own containers with the public if you choose to do so. However, if you choose, you can also upload containers into a local Docker registry and keep them private and only share them with select groups and individuals.

Docker Engine

Docker Engine is the heart of Docker. When someone says they are using Docker, it is shorthand for saying "Docker Engine." Docker Engine instantiates and runs containers. Docker, the company, offers two versions of Docker Engine: the open source version, dubbed Docker Engine Community Edition, and Docker Engine Enterprise Edition.

Docker launched Docker Engine Enterprise Edition in 2017. However, as with many companies that use the freemium model, the original open source version is still available and maintained. It is now called Docker Engine Community Edition. The Enterprise Edition has added advanced features, such as vulnerability monitoring, cluster management, and image management.

Docker Compose

Docker Compose is another Docker tool that can be used to configure and instantiate multi-container Docker applications. In order to configure it, a YAML file is used. Once the YAML configuration is defined, the service can be started with one command. Some of the advantages of using Docker Compose are as follows:

- More than one isolated environment can be deployed per instance.

- Volume data can be preserved as new containers are instantiated.

- Only containers that have been modified need to be reinstantiated.

- Variables can be passed in via the configuration file.

A common use case for Docker Compose is to set up development, test, and UAT environments all on one host.

Docker Swarm

Docker Swarm groups virtual or physical machines running Docker Engine that have been configured to run as a cluster. Once the machines have been clustered, you can run regular Docker commands, and those commands will be executed on the cluster rather than on an individual service. The controller for a swarm is called the swarm manager. The individual instances in the cluster are referred to as nodes.

The process of managing nodes in a cluster in unison is called **orchestration**.

Operating instances as a cluster or a swarm increases application availability and reliability. Docker swarms consist of multiple worker nodes and at least one manager node. The worker nodes perform the application logic and handle the application traffic, and the manager oversees the management of the worker nodes, thus managing resources efficiently.

In the next section, we will learn about Kubernetes, which is an alternative to Docker Swarm and another way to handle node orchestration.

Learning about Kubernetes

Kubernetes is another open source project that is extremely popular for container deployment. We'll explore this further shortly, but for now, let's say that if Docker is a rail car, Kubernetes is the train conductor, orchestrating things and making sure that all the rail cars reach their destination reliably. Kubernetes is a container orchestration platform used to automate much of the manual work that goes into deploying, managing, and monitoring containerized applications.

A Kubernetes cluster can span AWS availability zones and can even be configured to straddle cloud and on-premises deployments. Kubernetes, as of today, is the undisputed leader for container deployment and orchestration. It is suited to hosting systems that require massive and fast scaling, such as real-time data streaming applications that leverage Apache Kafka.

Kubernetes was originally created at Google. Google is coy about the exact details of how its search service works, but there is no doubt that they use an advanced version of Kubernetes, or something similar, to orchestrate all the containers necessary to support the service. They have said that most of the code at Google runs in containers.

To give you an idea of how reliant Google is on containers and the scale at which they operate, think of this: as of May 2020, Google deploys over 2 billion containers a week.

Google open sourced and contributed the Kubernetes code to the **Cloud Native Computing Foundation** (**CNCF**) in July 2015.

In addition to Google and AWS, Kubernetes has the backing and support of a cadre of big players:

- Microsoft
- IBM
- Intel
- Cisco
- Red Hat

Kubernetes enables the deployment of a container-based infrastructure in production environments. Some of the functionality that Kubernetes enables includes the following:

- The orchestration of containers across multiple hosts and across data centers
- The optimization of hardware utilization and enablement
- The control and automation of application deployments
- The scaling of containerized applications
- Declarative language for service management
- Enhanced application reliability and availability by minimizing single points of failure
- Health checks and self-healing mechanisms, including auto-restart, auto-replication, auto-placement, and auto-scaling

Additionally, Kubernetes leverages a whole ecosystem of ancillary applications and extensions to enhance their orchestrated services. Some examples include these:

- **Registration services**: Atomic Registry, Docker Registry
- **Security**: LDAP, SELinux, RBAC, OAUTH
- **Networking services**: OpenvSwitch and intelligent edge routing
- **Telemetry**: Kibana, Hawkular, and Elastic
- **Automation**: Ansible playbooks

The benefits of Kubernetes are as follows:

- Give teams control over their resource consumption.
- Enable the spread of the workload evenly across the infrastructure.
- Automate load balancing over various instances and availability zones.
- Facilitate the monitoring of resource consumption and resource limits.
- Automate the stopping and starting of instances to keep resource usage at a healthy level.
- Automate deployments in new instances if additional resources are needed to handle the load.
- Effortlessly perform deployments and rollbacks and implement high availability.

Let's now look at the advantages of Kubernetes.

Kubernetes advantages

As more enterprises move more of their workloads to the cloud and leverage containers, Kubernetes keeps on getting more and more popular. Some of the reasons for Kubernetes' popularity are as follows.

Faster development and deployment

Kubernetes facilitates the enablement of self-service **Platform-as-a-Service** (**PaaS**) applications. Kubernetes provides a level of abstraction between the bare metal and your users. Developers can easily request only the resources they require for certain purposes. If more resources are needed to deal with additional traffic, these resources can be added automatically based on the Kubernetes configuration. Instances can easily be added or removed, and these instances can leverage a host of third-party tools in the Kubernetes ecosystem to automate deployment, packaging, delivery, and testing.

Cost efficiency

Kubernetes in particular and container technology in general enable better resource utilization than what is provided just by hypervisors and VMs. Containers are more lightweight and don't need as much compute and memory resources.

Cloud-agnostic deployments

Kubernetes can run on other environments and cloud providers and not just on **Amazon Web Services** (**AWS**). It can also run on the following:

- Microsoft Azure
- **Google Cloud Platform** (**GCP**)
- On-premises

The enables you to migrate workloads from one environment to another without having to modify your applications, and it avoids vendor lock-in. You can also deploy your applications across the cloud platforms or your own environment. In that case, if the whole cloud provider stops delivering functionality, your application still won't go down.

Management by the cloud provider

It is hard to argue that Kubernetes is not the clear leader and standard bearer when it comes to container orchestration. For this reason, all the major cloud providers, not just AWS, offer managed Kubernetes services. Some examples are these:

- Amazon EKS
- Red Hat Openshift
- Azure Kubernetes Service
- Google Cloud Kubernetes Engine
- IBM Cloud Kubernetes Service

These managed services allow you to focus on your customers and the business logic required to serve them, as shown in the following figure:

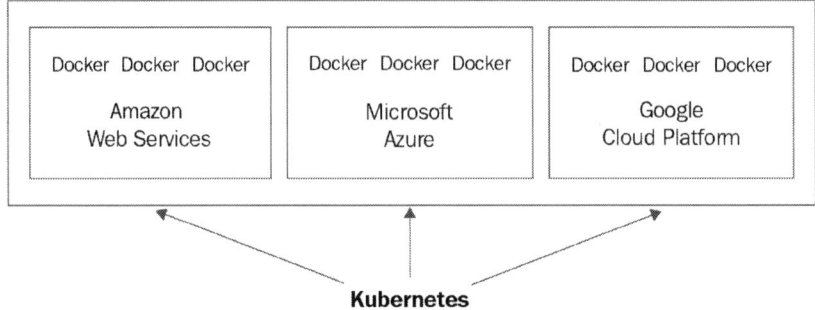

Figure 9.3 – Sample architecture for a multi-cloud Kubernetes deployment

As shown in the figure, as long as there is connectivity, Kubernetes can sit on one cloud provider and orchestrate, manage, and synchronize Docker containers across multiple cloud provider environments. Some of those Docker containers could even sit in an on-premises environment.

Kubernetes versus Docker Swarm

So, at this point, you may be wondering when to use Kubernetes and when it's a good idea to use Docker Swarm. Both can be used in many of the same situations. In general, Kubernetes can usually handle bigger workloads at the expense of higher complexity, whereas Docker Swarm has a smaller learning curve but may not be able to handle highly complex scenarios as well as Kubernetes. Docker Swarm is recommended for speed and when the requirements are simple. Kubernetes is best used when more complex scenarios and bigger production deployments arise.

Amazon Elastic Container Service for Kubernetes (Amazon EKS)

Amazon Elastic Container Service for Kubernetes (**Amazon EKS**) is a service managed by AWS that simplifies running Kubernetes workloads on AWS and does not need to provision and maintain Kubernetes clusters. Amazon EKS is simply a managed wrapper around the Kubernetes kernel. This ensures that existing Kubernetes applications are fully compatible with Amazon EKS.

Amazon EKS facilitates running Kubernetes with effortless availability and scalability. It greatly simplifies restarting containers, setting up containers on VMs, persisting data, and more. Amazon EKS can detect unhealthy masters and can replace them automatically. You never have to worry about Kubernetes version management and upgrades. Amazon EKS handles it transparently. It is extremely simple to control when and if certain clusters are automatically upgraded. If you enable EKS to handle these upgrades, Amazon EKS updates both the masters and nodes.

The combination of AWS with Kubernetes allows you to leverage the performance, scalability, availability, and reliability of the AWS platform. It also offers seamless integration with other AWS services, such as **Application Load Balancers** (**ALBs**) for load balancing, **AWS Identity and Access Management** (**AWS IAM**) for fine-grained security, AWS CloudWatch for monitoring, AWS CloudTrail for logging, and AWS PrivateLink for private network access.

In the following sections, we will explore the various components of Kubernetes.

Managed Kubernetes Control Plane

Amazon EKS provides a system that offer high scalability and availability that can run over multiple AWS **Availability Zones** (**AZs**). It is referred to as the Managed Kubernetes Control Plane. Amazon EKS can handle the availability and scalability of the Kubernetes masters and individual clusters. Amazon EKS automatically instantiates three Kubernetes masters using multiple AZs for fault tolerance. It can also detect if a master is down or corrupted and automatically replace it.

A **Kubernetes master** is a grouping of three processes operating in a node in the Kubernetes cluster. This node is designated as the master node. The name of these three processes are as follows:

- `kube-apiserver`
- `kube-controller-manager`
- `kube-scheduler`

Security

Amazon EKS simplifies the security management of Kubernetes clusters. It offers avant-garde functionality and integration with other AWS services and third-party vendors. Here are some examples of these features:

- **Network policies**: Network policies can be defined to determine what traffic can flow across pods and endpoints in the cluster. Network policies are not meant to be primarily used as a security tool. Their primary function is network traffic management. Nonetheless, these policies can be used to block traffic into certain pods or endpoints. So, they can also operate as a type of firewall. Network policies can be used to lock down a network inside a cluster minimizing potential security risks.

- **Role-Based Access Control** (**RBAC**): RBAC can be used to determine which users have certain permissions through the Kubernetes API. The permissions can be applied within a particular namespace or across multiple namespaces.

- **Pod security policies**: RBAC policies enable access. Pod security policies restrict access. A pod security policy can be used to define policies such as restricting containers to run as root or not allowing a pod to share process ID namespaces with the host.

- **Secrets management**: As is the case in many applications, Kubernetes applications sometimes require to access secrets such as passwords or SSH keys. These secrets can be secured with Kubernetes's secrets management framework.

IAM authentication

Amazon EKS integrates Kubernetes RBAC. RBAC is how Kubernetes controls roles natively across control systems with IAM authentication in collaboration with Heptio. RBAC roles can be assigned to individual IAM entities, facilitating fine-grained control permissions to access Kubernetes masters.

VPC support

Clusters execute in an Amazon VPC, enabling the cluster administrator to leverage VPC security groups and network ACLs. VPCs are fully isolated entities and resources are not shared across customers. This provides a high level of isolation and enables the use of Amazon EKS to provision secure and reliable systems.

Amazon EKS can interoperate with network security services to integrate with the AWS VPC **Container Network Interface** (**CNI**) plugin and provide fine-grained networking policies. This controls access at the microservice level via the Kubernetes API.

PrivateLink support

Amazon EKS supports **PrivateLink** as a method to provide access to Kubernetes masters and the Amazon EKS service. With PrivateLink, the Kubernetes masters and Amazon EKS service API endpoint display as an **Elastic Network Interface** (**ENI**), including a private IP address in the Amazon VPC. This provides access to the Kubernetes masters and the Amazon EKS service from inside the Amazon VPC, without needing to have public IP addresses or have traffic go through the internet.

Automatic version upgrades

Amazon EKS manages patches and version updates for your Kubernetes clusters. Amazon EKS automatically applies Kubernetes patches to your cluster, and you can also granularly control things when and if certain clusters are automatically upgraded to the latest Kubernetes minor version.

Community tools support

Amazon EKS can integrate with many Kubernetes community tools and supports a variety of Kubernetes add-ons. One of these tools is KubeDNS. **KubeDNS** allows users to provision a DNS service for a cluster. Similar to how AWS offers console access and a command-line interface, Kubernetes has a web-based UI and a command-line interface tool called `kubectl`. Both of these tools offer the ability to interface with Kubernetes and provide cluster management.

Logging

Amazon EKS is integrated with Amazon CloudWatch Logs and AWS CloudTrail to support reliable visibility and auditability of the cluster and traffic activity. CloudWatch Logs can be used to view logs from the Kubernetes masters, and CloudTrail can be used to inspect API activity logs to the Amazon EKS service endpoints.

This section completes our coverage of Kubernetes. We now move on to a service offered by AWS that can also be used to manage massive workloads. AWS Batch is geared more toward workloads that can run in batches.

Amazon ECS versus Amazon EKS

So, at this point, a question that you are probably asking yourself is when should you choose Amazon ECS and when is Amazon EKS the right solution.

Both services can use a wide variety of compute environments. Both Amazon ECS and Amazon EKS can be run on the following:

- AWS Fargate

- EC2 instances

- AWS Outposts

- AWS Local Zones

- AWS Wavelength

Both of them can also run side by side and integrate with other services in the AWS service stack. Now let's look at the differences.

Ease of use versus flexibility

Amazon ECS is usually a good option for simple use cases. Amazon ECS provides a quick solution that can host containers at scale. For simple workloads, you can be up and running quickly with Amazon ECS. There aren't that many configuration options, which reduces the time it takes to set up but also limits the configuration options.

For example, if you need a load balancer, an AWS ALB or a **Network Load Balancer** (**NLB**) can be integrated with Amazon ECS.

Amazon ECS is used by AWS to control some of the other AWS services, such as these:

- Amazon SageMaker

- Amazon Polly

- Amazon Lex

- AWS Batch

In contrast, Amazon EKS is a good option because it has a vibrant ecosystem and community, consistent open source APIs, and broad flexibility. It can handle more complex use cases and requirements, but it has a steeper learning curve.

Learning about AWS Fargate

Yet another AWS service that is important to understand when it comes to container management is AWS Fargate.

AWS Fargate is a serverless compute engine for container management that can be used with Amazon ECS and Amazon EKS. AWS Fargate further simplifies the management of these two services and enables users to focus on application development rather than infrastructure management. With AWS Fargate, the provisioning of infrastructure and the management of servers is handled by AWS. The benefits of using AWS Fargate are as follows:

- Obviates the provisioning and management of servers

- Reduces costs by matching resources with workloads

- Enhances security with an application isolation architecture

Why isn't Amazon ECS or Amazon EKS by itself enough, and why would we use AWS Fargate to manage these workloads?

Well, AWS Fargate is not a container management service in itself; it is a method to launch container services.

It simplifies the management of Kubernetes and Docker deployments. Without AWS Fargate, setting up these two services may require a good understanding of how to provision, schedule, and manage masters, minions, pods, services, and containers, as well as knowing how to administer server orchestration. Typically, you would need a skilled DevOps engineer to set this up. AWS Fargate takes the burden away from your engineers and greatly simplifies these deployments. Importantly, you don't have to commit to using AWS Fargate from the start. You can start by using Amazon ECS or Amazon EKS, test them out, and once the process is working, it can then be migrated to use Amazon Fargate.

Amazon ECS and Amazon EKS are only container orchestration services. They enable users to launch EC2 containers in the form of tasks. In this case, a task is one or more EC2 instances that have a Docker container. Each of these EC2 instances can send traffic to other AWS services, such as AWS RDS. A cluster of EC2 instances may be running within an AWS ECS auto-scaling group with predefined scaling rules. For this to happen, the ECS container agent will be constantly polling the ECS API, checking whether new containers need to be launched and whether old containers need to be idled depending on traffic. All this may seem fine and dandy, but there is still a degree of EC2 instance management that needs to happen, which increases complexity.

The orchestration of EC2 instances is no less difficult than orchestrating any other kind of server. Behind the fancy name, an EC2 instance is still a server in a closet somewhere. It still needs to be managed, monitored, secured, and connected to function properly.

These operational issues are not exclusive to AWS EC2 instances; it is something that needs to be managed regardless of the container service being used. To minimize this burden, AWS introduced AWS Fargate, which further abstracts, automates, and facilitates container orchestration.

If AWS EC2 is **Infrastructure as a Service (IaaS)**, then AWS Fargate offers **Containers as a Services (CaaS)**. This means that we do not need to worry about setting up containers. All the details involved in their launching are handled by AWS Fargate, including networking, security, and most importantly, scaling. The details of how this happens are abstracted away. AWS Fargate further simplifies the management of containers in the cloud, while still being able to leverage Amazon ECS and Amazon EKS.

Learning about AWS Batch

One way to classify software development projects is by the latency that the application requires. For example, for a UI application, the latency needs to be under a second in order to keep the application responsive and not frustrate the UI users. Other applications do not require such low latency. For example, if you need to run a complicated report for your boss every day but they said it's okay to wait 24 hours to deliver the report, then you can change the architecture of the application to take advantage of cheaper resources. For the second type of project, where low latency is not a consideration, AWS Batch is a well-suited solution.

AWS Batch enables developers to create efficient solutions for long-running compute jobs. AWS is a managed service that allows you to focus on the business logic required, and AWS handles the scheduling and provisioning of the tasks. AWS Batch enables the execution of Docker images, which in turn contain a helper application. AWS Batch then instantiates another node with the container image and can then fetch an initialization script and execute batch jobs.

AWS Batch can run jobs asynchronously, efficiently, and automatically across multiple instances. AWS synchronizes the execution of multiple tasks, considering any dependencies that may exist between them. AWS Batch can spawn multiple workers for individual tasks in order to massively scale. AWS Batch can simply and effortlessly run even thousands of batch computing jobs.

AWS Batch can dynamically launch the best amount and type of instances. It calculates this optimal configuration based on the expected traffic and resource requirements of the specific batch jobs.

With AWS Batch, AWS fully manages the provisioning, so you are not required to deploy and manage batch resources, enabling you to focus exclusively on the analysis of results and problem solving. AWS Batch can plan, schedule, and execute batch jobs using any of the AWS compute services. An example would be Amazon EC2 Spot Instances.

AWS Batch simplifies the definition and submission of batch jobs to the job queue. AWS Batch determines the location where the jobs will be run, potentially starting extra AWS instances as necessary. AWS Batch tracks the job progress to determine when to launch or stop instances. AWS Batch can also handle jobs that are part of a bigger workload or workflow, by defining dependencies between jobs.

The following is the layout of a typical AWS Batch architecture:

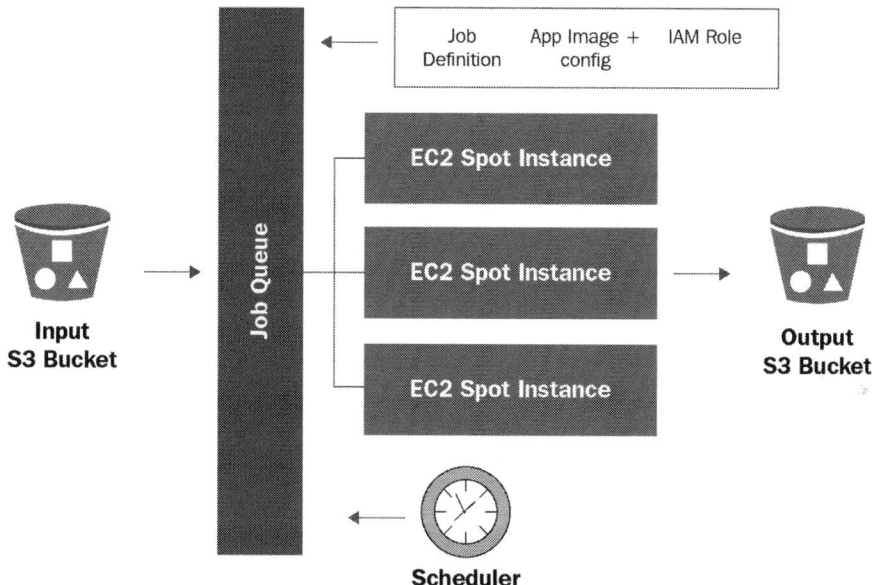

Figure 9.4 – Typical AWS Batch job architecture

The diagram shows how tasks can be dropped in an **Input S3 Bucket**. A **Scheduler** can periodically check the input bucket and place any incoming files into the **Job Queue** if there are any. EC2 Spot Instances can then take tasks off the job queue and perform any necessary actions for the incoming tasks. Once the process is complete, the results can be placed in the output bucket.

AWS Batch components

AWS Batch has these components to handle the tasks.

Jobs

Jobs are a unit of work submitted to AWS Batch, which can be a shell script, an executable, or a Docker container image.

Job definitions

A **job definition** contains a description of the job to be executed. Some of the parameters that a job definition specifies are as follows:

- CPU requirements

- Memory requirements

- IAM roles required to provide AWS Batch with access to other AWS services

- Parameters and environmental variables

- Other information to assist in the submission and execution of a job

Job definitions are pre-defined well before running a job. They can also be saved and published so that they can be used by others.

Job queues

These are lists of work to be completed by your jobs. You can leverage multiple queues with different priority levels.

Compute environment

This entails the compute resources that run your jobs. Environments can be configured to be managed by AWS or by you. Additionally, you can specify the number of instances and type(s) of instances on which your jobs will run. You can specify the instance types, or you can allow AWS to select the right instance type for you.

Lastly, a scheduler controlled by AWS can be used to run jobs that have been sent to the job queues.

The sample project described in the following section defines each of the preceding components (except for the scheduler) for our simple batch job. Our focus is solely on the development of business logic (to complete the batch work) and the configuration of how that work is to be completed; AWS manages the rest.

We have covered the components of AWS Batch. Let's now cover some of the features of AWS Batch.

Features of AWS Batch

Some of the core features of AWS Batch are as follows:

- AWS Batch can modify the time of execution for jobs to times when there is more capacity available or compute time is less expensive.

- AWS Batch minimizes the idling of compute resources by automating resource utilization.

- AWS Batch increases efficiency by optimizing the utilization of AWS services.

- AWS Batch can rank jobs to better align the allocation of resources with business requirements.

We have covered some of the AWS Batch features. Let's now delve into some recommended AWS Batch best practices.

AWS Batch best practices

The most important question to answer before selecting AWS Batch as your solution, and the most important question to answer for any software development project, is this: *"What is the business problem I am trying to solve?"* Answering this is easier said than done. Many times, this question needs to be refined iteratively because what seemed to be an obvious question turns out to be different once we dig deeper. Once, and only once, this question is fully defined and detailed, we can decide what the right tool for the job is.

AWS Batch is well suited to long-running jobs where low latency is not a requirement. If you expect tasks to complete quickly, AWS Lambda or another container technology will probably be better suited for your workload. Cost is an important consideration in most initiatives, but it is not always the most important. Sometimes speed is paramount and sometimes reliability is the most important consideration. For this reason, AWS Batch provides three strategies for how job runs can be optimized.

Spot Capacity Optimized strategy

The purpose of this strategy is to minimize costs. This strategy leverages Spot Instances. At any given moment, there are instances across the AWS ecosystem that are not being used. Instead of remaining idle, AWS gives you the opportunity to bid on these instances and use them at a price you determine. In some cases, you can save as much as 90% on your costs compared to using an on-demand instance.

The drawback is that AWS reserves the right to pull instances at any time with little notice if someone else requests the instance and is willing to pay the on-demand price. For this reason, Spot Instances are well suited to workloads where it is not a critical situation if the instance is pulled out. So, something like a batch processing job is a good use case to take advantage of Spot Instances, especially if it is not vital that the job finishes at a specific time. Combining Spot Instances with EC2 Auto Scaling can be a great strategy. Any time a Spot Instance is pulled from your workload, Auto Scaling can spin up another instance to replace the pulled instance.

Let's look at an example. It's not as profitable as it once was, but let's say that you decide to use AWS Batch to do some Bitcoin mining. In this case, it would definitely be a good idea to use Spot Instances instead of on-demand instances. **Bitcoin mining** requires lowering costs as much as possible in order for it to be profitable. Spot Instances cover this requirement since they are significantly cheaper than on-demand instances. In addition, Bitcoin mining is a batch-oriented process. If a Spot Instance is terminated in the middle of the mining process, it is not a critical failure and the mining process can be restarted once new Spot Instances are instantiated.

It is also recommended to set up your deployment across AZs and across instance types. Spot prices are AZ-specific and instance type-specific. So, if a certain instance type in a certain AZ becomes popular and gets pulled from the Spot Instance pool, other AZs and instance types can take over the load.

Let's explore how AWS Batch takes advantage of Spot Instances. When your workload is about to be launched, AWS Batch picks an instance type from a list of instance types that you previously defined. AWS picks these instances by calculating which instance types have the most spot capacity. AWS does not care if your workload was configured to require a few instances or thousands of instances. Once the workload is launched, AWS Batch monitors and manages the instances to make sure that the requested capacity is met and that the number of instances running at any one time is what is needed to meet your workload needs.

As the workload is running, if demand spikes in a certain AZ and some of the instances are reclaimed, AWS Batch will adjust automatically and fire up instances in a different AZ that has greater availability of instances and is not as busy as the previous one. If for some reason AWS Batch does not find any capacity that meets your spot criteria and is unable to launch new instances, an error will be generated, which can trigger SMS alarms to notify your administrators. For this reason, it is recommended to be open to using as many instance types as possible, even if some of the instances are not ideally suited to your workload.

Best Fit Progressive strategy

AWS Batch provides this strategy for workloads that require a certain level of throughput and time sensitivity while still enabling the workloads to take advantage of Spot Instances.

Let's say you have a workload that is quite compute-intensive, so whenever possible, you want to use the C5 instance types, but you know that M5 instance types would suffice. In this case, it may be best to use the Best Fit Progressive strategy and specify these two instance types in your list of acceptable instance types. As with other strategies, you can specify whether you want to use on-demand instances or Spot Instances. Use on-demand instances if you have high availability and time-sensitive requirements and use Spot Instances when you can afford to wait for the results, which will result in considerable compute service savings.

It can happen that AWS Batch cannot provision the resources necessary to meet your capacity with your preferred instance type. When this happens, AWS Batch starts going down the instance type priority list you specified, looking for the next best instance type. Under normal circumstances, AWS Batch tries to provision different instance sizes within the same family first. If it cannot allocate enough instances in that family to meet the necessary capacity, AWS Batch will then launch instances from a different family. The attempts continue until the required capacity is met or it runs out of available instances from which to select, in which case an error will occur, and it can be captured to notify your administrators.

Best Fit strategy

This used to be the only option available with AWS Batch. Using the **Best Fit** strategy means that AWS will try to use the least amount of instances to run a workload and do so at the lowest cost. The Best Fit strategy is recommended when cost is the most important consideration and you are willing to give up some throughput and availability for it. If the process is configured appropriately, workloads may take longer but they will definitely be completed nonetheless.

With this strategy, if additional instances of an instance type are not available, AWS Batch simply waits for the resources to become available. If enough instances do not become available, no more jobs will execute until the jobs that are executing complete, and only then will the new jobs execute with the newly released resources. The Best Fit strategy can keep costs low but limit scaling.

Spot pricing

Regardless of the execution strategy that you choose to run AWS Batch, you also have the option to set a bid for your Spot Instances as a percentage of the current on-demand price. If you choose this option, AWS Batch will only launch instances that have spot prices lower than the lowest per-unit-hour on-demand instance price. The lower the percentage, the less likely it is that instances will become available. This is an important thing that should be closely monitored to make sure that you balance the need for availability and throughput with your costs. Generally, you want to set this variable as close to 100% as possible and then experiment a little to figure out what the best value is for your particular use case.

This concludes the section on AWS Batch. As discussed, this AWS service is a good choice when you have tasks that do not require sub-second or even sub-minute responses but do require massive amounts of computing power.

Summary

In this chapter, we explored in depth what containers are. We also learned about the different types of container tools that are available. In particular, we investigated Docker. Docker is quite a popular container tool today and it is a foundational piece of software for many successful companies.

We also learned about the orchestration tool Kubernetes and how it interfaces and integrates with Docker. Kubernetes is also quite popular and it helps many companies simplify their DevOps processes.

Then, we looked at how Kubernetes and Docker can work together as well as with other AWS services. These tools were specifically created to host and maintain containers.

We also spent some time going over Amazon EKS and how it works together with Kubernetes.

Lastly, we also learned about AWS Batch, which is another tool that can be used to containerize software applications.

The software and services covered in this chapter will be instrumental in ensuring the success of your next project. The more complex the project, the more important it is that you use the tools covered in this chapter.

In the next chapter, we will learn about the microservices architecture pattern, which builds upon the concepts we learned about in this chapter.

10
Microservice and Event-Driven Architectures

This chapter builds upon the concepts we covered in *Chapter 9, Serverless and Container Patterns*. Now that we have covered the basics of containers and discovered what some of the most popular container implementations are today, we can continue to learn about higher-level concepts that will use containers to create modern, modular, and nimble applications. If your company operates in the cloud, it is very likely that they are taking advantage of the capabilities of the cloud. One architectural pattern that is extremely popular nowadays is the microservice architecture. At the beginning of *Chapter 9, Serverless and Container Patterns*, we mentioned some well-known companies that use containers. We won't repeat the list of companies again, but you can safely assume that these companies leverage containers to implement many microservices across the enterprise.

In this chapter, we will do a deep dive into the ins and outs of this cornerstone pattern. Specifically, we will cover the following topics:

- Understanding microservices

- Microservice architecture patterns

- Benefits of an event-driven architecture

- Disadvantages of an event-driven architecture

- Learning about the microkernel architecture

- Reviewing microservices best practices

Let's get started.

Understanding microservices

Like many ideas that become popular in technology, it is hard to pin down an exact definition of microservices. Different groups start co-opting the term and start providing their own unique twist on their own definition. And the popularity of microservices is hard to ignore. It might be the most common pattern used in new software development today. In addition, the definition has not stayed static and has evolved over time in the last few years.

Given all these caveats, let's try to define what a microservice is:

A **microservice** is a software application that follows an architectural style that structures the application as a service that is loosely coupled, easily deployable, and testable and is organized in a well-defined business domain. A loosely coupled system is one where components have little or no knowledge about other components and there are few or no dependencies between these components.

In addition, a certain consensus has been reached, to some degree, around the concept of microservices.

Some of the defining features that are commonly associated with microservices are the following:

- In the context of a **microservice architecture**, services communicate with each other over a network with the purpose of accomplishing a goal using a technology-agnostic protocol (most often HTTP).

- Services can be deployed independently of each other. The deployment of a new version of one of the services, in theory, should not impact any of the associated services.

- Services are assembled and built around business domains and capabilities.

- Services should be able to be developed using different operating systems, programming languages, data stores, and hardware infrastructure and still be able to communicate with each other because of their common protocol and agreed-upon APIs.

- Services are modular, small, message-based, context-bound, independently assembled and deployed, and decentralized.

- Services are built and released using an automated process – most often a **continuous integration** (**CI**) and **continuous delivery** (**CD**) methodology.

- Services have a well-defined interface and operations. Both consumers and producers of services know exactly what the interfaces are.

- Service interfaces normally stay the same or at least have background compatibility when code is changed. Therefore, clients of these services do not need to make changes when the code in the service is changed.

- Services are maintainable and testable. Often these tests can be fully automated via a CI/CD process.

- Services allow fast, continuous, and reliable delivery and deployment of large and complex projects. They also facilitate organizations to evolve their technology stack.

Microservices are the answer to monolithic architectures that were common in mainframe development. Applications that follow a monolithic architecture are notoriously hard to maintain, tightly coupled, and difficult to understand. Also, microservices aren't simply a layer in a modularized application like was common in early web applications that leveraged the Model/View/Controller MVC pattern. Instead, they are self-contained, fully independent components with business functionality and clearly delineated interfaces. This doesn't mean that, within a microservice, it might not leverage other architectural patterns and have its own individual internal components.

Doug McIlroy is credited with the philosophy surrounding Unix; microservices implement the Unix philosophy of *"Do one thing and do it well"*.

Martin Fowler describes microservices as those services that possess the following features:

- Software that can leverage a CI and CD development process. A small modification in one part of the application does not require the wholesale rebuild and deployment of the system; it only requires rebuilding, deploying, and distributing a small number of components or services.

- Software that follows certain development principles such as fine-grained interfaces.

Microservices fit hand in glove with the cloud and serverless computing. They are ideally suited to be deployed using container technology. In a monolithic deployment, if you need to scale up to handle more traffic, you will have to scale the full application. When using a microservice architecture, only the services that are receiving additional calls need to be scaled. Depending on how the services are deployed and assuming they are deployed in an effective manner, you will only need to scale up or scale out the services that are taking additional traffic and you can leave untouched the servers that have the services that are not in demand.

Microservices have grown in popularity in recent years as organizations are becoming nimbler. Parallelly, more and more organizations have moved to adopt a DevOps and CI/CD culture. Microservices are well-suited for this. Microservice architectures, in some ways, are the answer to monolithic applications. A high-level comparison between the two is shown in the following diagram:

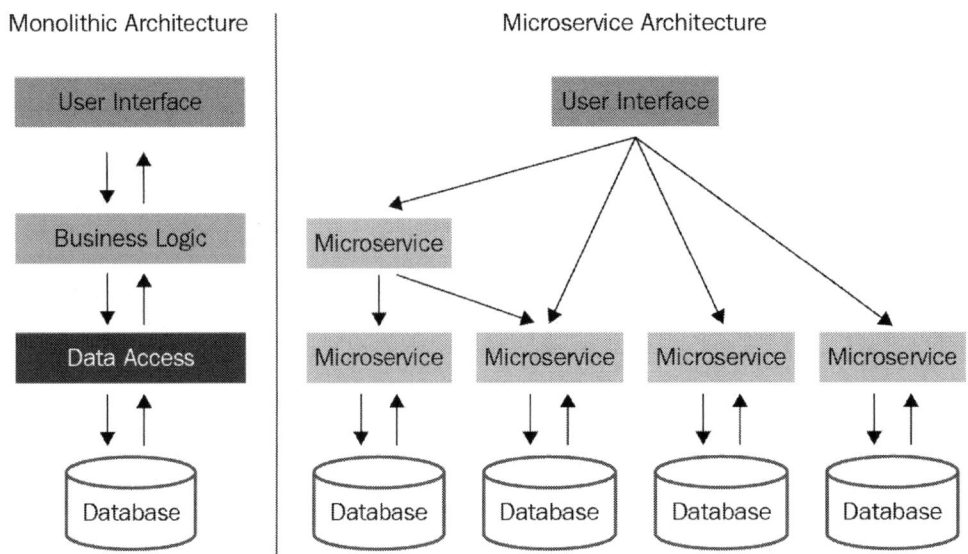

Figure 10.1 – Monolithic versus microservice architectures

In a monolithic architecture, communication occurs across the whole application independent of business boundaries. Initially and for simple applications, this architecture may be appropriate, but complexity increases quickly as the number of business domains that the application handles increases.

In a microservice architecture, the boundaries between services are well-defined according to business domains. This enables applications to scale more smoothly and increases maintainability.

Microservice architecture patterns

In the last section, we covered the fundamentals of microservices. Let's now learn about three popular architecture patterns that are often used when creating microservices.

These patterns are as follows:

- Layered architecture
- Event-driven architecture
- Microkernel architecture

In the next sections, we will describe in detail these three common architectures and we'll go through the advantages and disadvantages of each of them.

Layered architecture

This pattern is quite common in software development. As indicated by the name, in this pattern, the code is implemented in layers. Having this layering enables the implementation of *"separation of concerns"*. This is a fancy way of saying that each layer focuses on doing a few things well and nothing else. Having this separation of concerns allows us to optionally run each of these layers on separate servers and therefore allows us to run each layer on hardware that is optimized for that task.

The topmost layer communicates with users or other systems. The middle layer handles the business logic and routing of requests, and the bottom layer's responsibility is to ensure that data is permanently stored, usually in a database.

Having this separation of concerns or individual duties for each layer allows us to focus on the most important properties for each layer. For example, in the presentation layer, accessibility and usability are going to be important considerations, whereas in the persistence layer, data integrity, performance, and privacy may be more important. Some factors will be important regardless of the layer. An example of a ubiquitous concern is security. By having these concerns separate, it enables teams to not require personnel that are experts in too many technologies. With this pattern, we can hire UI experts for the presentation layer and database administrators for the persistence layer. It also provides a clear delineation of responsibilities. If something breaks, it can often be isolated to a layer, and once it is, you can reach out to the owner of the layer.

From a security standpoint, a layered architecture offers certain advantages over more monolithic architecture. In a layered architecture, we normally only place the presentation layer services in a public VPC and place the rest of the layers in a private VPC. This ensures that only the presentation layer is exposed to the internet, minimizing the attack surface.

If a hacker wanted to use the database in an unauthorized manner, they would have to find a way to penetrate through the presentation layer and the business logic layer to access the persistence layer. This by no means implies that your system is impenetrable. You still want to ensure to use all security best practices and maybe even hire a white hat group to attempt to penetrate your system. An example of an attack that could still happen in this architecture is a SQL injection attack.

Another advantage of having a layered architecture is gaining the ability to swap out a layer without having to make modifications to any of the other layers. For example, you may decide that AngularJS is no longer a good option for the presentation layer and instead you want to start using React. Or you may want to start using Amazon Aurora Postgres instead of Oracle. If your layers were truly independent, you would be able to convert the layers to the new technology without having to make modifications to the other layers.

Here is a sample pattern of what a layered architecture may look like using microservices:

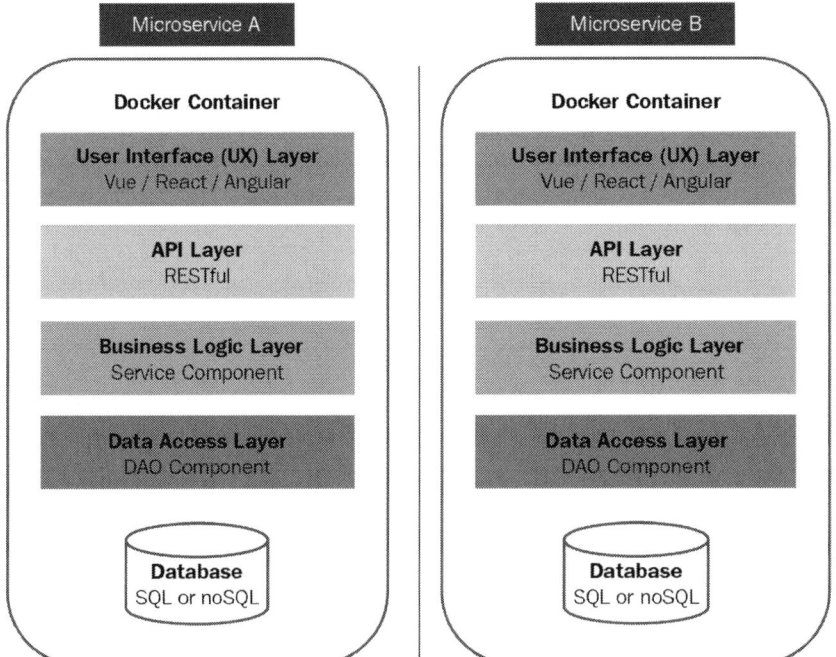

Figure 10.2 – Sample layered microservice architecture

Notice that the architectural pattern repeats across microservices but microservices exist completely independently of each other, including having their own API, business logic, and data store. In this architecture, each layer takes a set of functions and specializes in performing these functions. This is the breakdown of the separation of duties:

User Interface (UX) layer: The user interface layer mostly manages the interface between the user (normally a human) and the rest of the application. There may be some validation performed at this layer, but the main purpose of this layer is the user experience.

API layer: Interfacing through the UX layer may be only one of many ways to communicate with the rest of the application. For example, there may be a way to do a batch upload of data. There may be integration with other applications that have their own UX. The application may be integrated with IoT devices that generated data and don't have an interface. In addition, the application may have a variety of UIs (desktop-based, browser-based, mobile app, and so on). For all these reasons, it's a good idea to have a well-defined API layer that can be used by all these integration points.

Business Logic layer: This layer would contain and execute the business rules of the application. An example would be any calculations that need to be performed. More specifically, in finance, *"Assets minus Liabilities must always equal Equity"*. This would be a rule or a calculation that it would make sense to implement in this layer.

Data Access layer: Most applications require a layer where data can be persisted. This persistence mechanism can take many forms: files, graph databases, traditional RDBMS databases, and so on. In addition, we may use a combination of these storage methods.

Just because you are using a layered approach, it does not mean that your application will be bug-free or easy to maintain. It is not uncommon to create interdependencies among the layers. Let's look at an example.

Example scenario

The presentation layer receives a profile change request from a user to update their email address. This change moves along all the layers without modification until it reaches the persistence layer. Let's assume something went wrong and the email address did not get stored correctly. We now need to troubleshoot the problem, which in this architecture entails verifying all the layers to identify where the issue lies. This means that there is strong coupling among the layers in terms of the APIs being exposed. For this reason, it is important to minimize the number of changes and transformations that are performed on the data in the higher levels unless they're necessary.

Event-driven architecture

Event-Driven Architecture (EDA) is another pattern commonly used when implementing microservices. When the event-driven pattern is used, creating, messaging, processing, and storing events are critical functions of the service. Contrast this with the layered pattern we just visited, which is more of a request/response model and where the user interface takes a more prominent role in the service. Another difference is that layered architecture applications are normally synchronous whereas an EDA relies on the asynchronous nature of queues and events.

More and more applications are being designed using EDA from the ground up. Applications using EDA can be developed using a variety of development stacks and languages. Event-driven architecture is a programming philosophy, not a technology and language. EDA facilitates code decoupling, making applications more robust and flexible. At the center of EDA is the concept of events. Let's spend some time understanding what they are.

Understanding events

To better understand the event-driven pattern, let's first define what an event is. An **event** is a change in state in a system. Examples of changes that could be events are the following:

- A modification of a database
- A runtime error in an application
- A request submitted by a user
- An EC2 instance failing
- A threshold being exceeded
- A sensor in an IoT system recording a temperature of 20 degrees
- A code change that has been checked into a CI/CD pipeline

Hopefully, this list demonstrates that many changes can be an event. But not all changes are events. A change becomes an event when we decide to make it an event. Another way to understand this is, consider this example, October 13 might be just any date on the calendar, and the fact that the date changed from October 12 to October 13 is just a date. But if October 13 happens to be your birth date, then it becomes important and it is now an event. In the next section, we'll discuss two other critical elements in event-driven architecture: the concept of producers and consumers.

Producers and consumers

Events by themselves are useless. If a tree falls in the forest and no one is around to hear it or see it fall, did it really fall? The same question is appropriate for events. Events are worthless if someone is not consuming them, and in order to have events, producers of the events are needed as well. These two actors are two essential components in event-driven architecture. Let's explore them at a deeper level:

Producers: An event producer first detects a change of state and if it's an important change that is being monitored, it generates an event and sends a message out to notify others of the change.

Consumers: Once an event is detected, the message is transmitted to a queue. Importantly, once the event is placed in the queue and the producer forgets about the message, consumers fetch messages from the queue in an asynchronous manner. Once a consumer fetches a message, they may or may not perform an action based on that message. Examples of these actions are as follows:

- Triggering an alarm

- Sending out an email

- Updating a database record

- Opening a door

- Taking a photograph

- Performing a calculation

In essence, almost any process can be a consumer action.

As you can imagine, due to the asynchronous nature of event-driven architecture, it is highly scalable and efficient.

Event-driven architecture is loosely coupled architecture. Producers of events are not aware of who is going to consume their output and consumers of events are not aware who generated the events. Let's now learn about two popular types of models designed around event-driven architecture.

Event-driven architecture models

There are a couple ways to design an event-driven model. One of the main design decisions that needs to be made is whether events need to be processed by only one consumer or by multiple consumers. The first instance is known as the **competing consumers** pattern. The second pattern is most commonly known as the **pub/sub** pattern. EDA can be implemented using these two main patterns. Depending on the use case, one pattern may be a better fit than the other. Let's learn more about these two models.

Event streaming (message queuing model)

In the event streaming model, events are *"popped off"* the queue as soon as one of the consumers processes the message. In this model, the queue receives a message from the producer and the system ensures that the message is processed by one and only one consumer.

Event streaming is well suited for workloads that need to be highly scalable and can be highly variable. Adding capacity is simply a matter of adding more consumers to the queue and we can reduce capacity just as easily by removing some of the consumers (and reducing our bill). In this architecture, it is extremely important that messages are processed by only one consumer. In order to achieve this, as soon as a message is allotted to a consumer, it is removed from the queue. The only time that it will be placed back in the queue is if the consumer of the message fails to process the message and it needs to be reprocessed.

Use cases that are well-suited for this model are those that require that each message be processed only once but the order in which the messages are processed is not necessarily important.

Let's look at a diagram of how an event streaming architecture would be implemented:

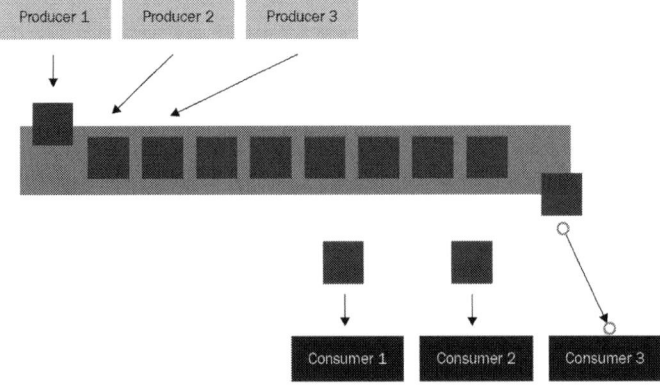

Figure 10.3 – Event streaming model

In the preceding diagram, we have multiple producers generating events and placing them into a single queue (on the left-hand side). We also have multiple consumers consuming events off the queue (on the right-hand side). Once a consumer takes an event from the queue, it gets removed and no other consumer will be able to consume it. The only exception is if there is an error and the consumer is unable to complete the consumption of the event. In this case, we should put some logic in our process to put the unconsumed event back in the queue so that another consumer can process the event.

Let's make this more concrete with a real-life example.

Example scenario

In order to visualize this model, think of the queues that are common in some banks, where you have a single queue that feeds into all the tellers. When a teller becomes available, the first person in the queue goes to that teller for processing and so forth. The customer needs to visit only one teller to handle their transaction. As tellers go on a break or new tellers come in to handle the increased demand, the model can gracefully and transparently handle these changes. In this case, the bank customers are the producers – they are generating events (for example, making a check deposit), and the bank tellers are the consumers – they are processing the events that the customers are creating.

We have explained the event streaming model. Now let's move on and learn about another type of event-driven model – the publish and subscribe model or pub/sub model.

Publish and subscribe model (pub/sub model)

As happens with event streaming, the **publish and subscribe** model (also known as the *"pub-sub"* model) assists in communicating events from producers to consumers. However, unlike event streaming, this model allows several consumers to process the same message. Furthermore, the pub/sub model may guarantee the order in which the messages are received.

As the publishing part of the name indicates, message producers broadcast messages to anyone that is interested in them. You express interest in the message by subscribing to a topic.

The publish and subscribe messaging model is suited for use cases in which more than one consumer needs to receive messages. An example of this is a stock price service. In this case, typically, many market participants are interested in receiving prices in real time on a topic of their choosing (in this case, the topics are the individual tickers). In this case, the order in which the order tickets are received is incredibly important. If two traders put in a purchase to buy a stock for the same price, it is critical that the system process the order that was received first. If it doesn't, the market maker might get in trouble with accusations of front-running trades:

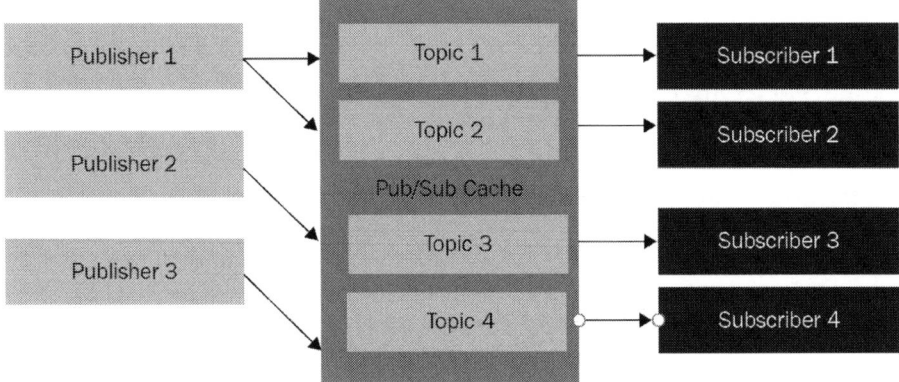

Figure 10.4 – Publish and subscribe model

In this model, many publishers push events into a **pub/sub cache** (or queue). The events can be classified by topic. Subscribers listen to the queue and check for events being placed in it. Whenever events make it to the queue, the consumers notice them and process them accordingly. Unlike the model in the previous section, when a subscriber sees a new event in the queue, it does not pop it off the queue; it leaves it there and other subscribers can also consume it, and perhaps take a completely different action for the same event.

Optionally, the events in the cache can be classified by topic, and subscribers can subscribe only to the topics they are interested in and ignore the rest.

The publish-subscribe model is frequently used with stateful applications. In a stateful application, the order in which the messages are received is important. The order can impact the application state.

Benefits of event-driven architecture

EDA can assist an organization to obtain an edge over its competitors. This edge stems from the benefits that the pub/sub model can provide. Some of the benefits are explained in the following sub-sections.

No more polling

The publish and subscribe model delivers the benefit of real-time events through a *"push"* delivery mechanism. It eliminates the need to constantly be fetching sources to see whether data has changed. If you use a polling mechanism, you will either waste resources by checking for changes when no changes have occurred, or you will delay actions if changes occur when you haven't polled. Using a *"push"* mechanism minimizes the latency of message delivery. Depending on your application, delays in message delivery could translate into a loss of millions of dollars.

Example: Let's say you have a trading application. You want to buy a stock only when a certain price is reached. If you were using polling, you would have to constantly ping every so often to see if the price had changed. This has two problems:

1. Computing resources will have to be used with every ping. This is wasteful.

2. If the price changes in between pings, and then changes again, the trade may not execute even though the target price was reached.

With events, the ping will be generated only once when the target price is reached, greatly increasing the likelihood that the trade will happen.

Dynamic targeting

EDA simplifies the discovery of services and does so in an effortless and natural way, minimizing the number of potential errors. In EDA, there is no need to keep track of data consumers and, instead, interested parties simply subscribe to the topics that are of interest. If there are parties interested in the messages, the messages get consumed by all of them. In the pub/sub model, if there aren't any interested consumers, the message simply gets broadcast without anyone taking any action.

Example: Continuing with our trading application example, let's assume that each stock is a topic. Letting users of the application select what topic/stock interests them, will greatly reduce the number of events generated and therefore will reduce the resource consumption.

Communication simplicity

EDA minimizes code complexity by eliminating direct point-to-point communication between producers and consumers. The number of connections is greatly reduced by having a central queue where producers place their messages and consumers collect messages.

Example: Let's assume that our trading application has 10 stocks and 10 users. If we didn't have an intermediate queue to hold the events, every stock would have to be connected to every user, for a total of 100 connections. But having a queue in the middle would mean that we only have 10 connections from the stocks to the queue and 10 connections from the users to the queue, giving us a total of 20 connections, greatly simplifying the system.

Decoupling and scalability

The publish and subscribe model increases software flexibility. There is no explicit coupling between publishers and subscribers. They all are decoupled and work independently of each other. Having this decoupling promotes the individual development of services, which in turn allows us to deploy and scale these services independently. Functionality changes in one part of the application should not affect the rest of the application so long as design patterns were followed, and code is truly modularized. So long as the agreed-upon APIs stay stable, making a change in the publisher code should not affect the consumer code.

Example: In our trading application, if a new stock ticker is added, users don't need a new connection to the new stock. We simply create a connection from the new stock to the queue and now anybody can listen for events in that new topic. Something similar happens when new users get added. The user just needs to specify which stocks they are interested in. Nothing else needs to be changed in the system. This makes the overall architecture quite scalable.

As we have seen, the advantages of EDA are many. However, no software solution is perfect, and EDA is no exception. Let's now investigate the disadvantages that come with it.

Disadvantages of Event-Driven Architecture

As with other technologies, event-driven architecture also has drawbacks. Some of the drawbacks are explained in the following sub-sections.

Event-driven architectures are not a silver bullet

It is worth noting that, like any other technology, the EDA pattern should not be viewed as a solution that can solve all problems. A problem may not require the added complexity of setting up a message queue. We might only require a "point-to-point" communication channel because we don't foresee having additional producers or consumers. The EDA pattern is quite popular with new IoT applications, but it is not suitable for other use cases. If your application is synchronous in nature and it only requires accessing and updating a database, using EDA may not be necessary and might be overcomplicated. It is important to determine how much interactivity and inter-process communication will be required in our application before recommending EDA as a pattern for a given problem. EDA applications require some effort to maintain and troubleshoot when problems arise (by having to check consumers, producers, and queues) and an individual problem might not warrant their use.

Example: What if our trading application only focused on one stock? In that particular example, we might want to avoid the complexity of creating queues, topics, and so on and keep it simple without using a queue.

When things go wrong

Like any other technology that depends on an underlying infrastructure, it is possible in an EDA implementation for messages to get lost for various reasons, including the failure of hardware components. Dealing with such failures can be difficult to troubleshoot and even more difficult to find a solution to recover from them. These issues stem from the asynchronous nature of the architecture. This property makes the resulting applications massively scalable but with the downside of potentially losing messages. Overcoming this shortcoming can be challenging.

Example: Due to the asynchronous nature of EDA applications, it is not easy to troubleshoot them. In our trading application, we might lose a message due to hard failure. We obviously want to minimize or even eliminate these occurrences. However, trying to replicate the behavior to debug them may be difficult, if not impossible.

Learning about microkernel architecture

The **microkernel architecture** pattern (also sometimes called a plugin architecture pattern) is another useful pattern to implement microservices. It is important to note that it is also used to build other software and not just microservices. The resulting application created using microkernel architecture can be considered a product. A **product** is a fully standalone application that can be distributed and implemented in a simple manner without much configuration or extra scripting. The most famous example of an application or product using this pattern is the Eclipse IDE. However, many enterprises also use this pattern to develop external and internal applications.

Another important feature of the microkernel architecture and the reason it is named as such is that the kernel can be extended by installing plugins in the kernel. The kernel provides the core functionality and the plugins allow users to extend the behavior in the manner they desire (assuming a plugin exists with the functionality they want to include). These plugins provide extensibility while implementing separation of concerns and ensuring that bugs in the kernel stay in the kernel and bugs in the plugins stay in the plugins.

The basic kernel provides the core functionality while enabling extensibility, flexibility, and the isolation of features. The plugins provide additional functionality and close the extensibility loop.

Now that we have learned about some of the most common microservice architectures, let's learn about best practices and when we implement them.

Microservices best practices

As with any technology, the devil is in the details. It is certainly possible to create bad microservices. Let's delve into how some common pitfalls can be avoided and some recommended best practices.

Best practice #1: Decide whether microservices are the right tool

The world's leading technology companies, such as eBay, Facebook, Amazon, Microsoft, Twitter, and PayPal are all heavy users of microservices architecture and rely on it for much of their development. However, it's not a panacea. As technologists, once we get a hammer, everything looks like a nail. Make sure that your particular use case is best suited for this architecture. If it's hard to break down your application into functional domains, a microservice architecture might not be the best choice.

Best practice #2: Clearly define the requirements and design of the microservice

Creating microservices, like other software projects, requires preparation and focus. A sure way for a software project to fail is to start coding without having a clear goal in mind for the function of the software. Requirements should be written down in detail and approved by all stakeholders. Once the requirements are completed, a design should be created using a language and artifacts that are understood by all parties involved, including domain experts.

A clear distinction should be made between business requirements and functions, the services that will be provided, and the microservices that will be implemented to provide the services. Without this delineation, it is likely the microservices will be too big and not fragmented enough and no benefit will be delivered from using a microservice architecture. On the other hand, it is also possible for your design to have too many microservices and for you to over-engineer the solution. If there are too many microservices, the solution will be difficult to maintain, understand, and troubleshoot.

Best practice #3: Leverage Domain-Driven Design (DDD) to create microservices

In *Chapter 11, Domain-Driven Design*, we will learn about the **Domain-Driven Design (DDD)** methodology. We will learn more about it in that chapter but DDD is ideally suited for the development of microservices. DDD is a set of design principles that allow us to define an object-oriented model using concepts and nomenclature that all stakeholders can understand using a unified model language. It allows all participants in the software definition process to fully understand the relevant business domains and deliver better microservices because you can get buy-in and understanding from everyone more quickly.

Best practice #4: Ensure buy-in from all stakeholders

Software development involves many parties in an organization. Developers, architects, testers, domain experts, managers, and decision-makers, among others. In order to ensure the success of your project, you need to make sure to get buy-in from all of them. It is highly recommended that you get approval from all stakeholders at every major milestone – particularly during the business requirement and design phase. In today's Agile culture, the initial requirements and design can often change, and in those instances, it is also important to keep stakeholders updated and in agreement.

Deploying a microservice entails much more than just technology. Getting approval and mindshare from the status quo is key. This cultural transformation can be arduous and expensive. Depending on the team's exposure to this new paradigm, it might take a significant effort, especially if they are accustomed to building their applications in a monolithic manner.

Once you start delivering results and business value, it might be possible to start getting into a cadence and a harmonious state with all team members. And for that reason, it is important to make sure that you start delivering value as soon as possible. A common approach to achieve this is to deliver a **Minimum Viable Product** (**MVP**) that delivers the core functionality to start deriving value and continue building and enhancing the service once the MVP is deployed in production and starts being used.

Best practice #5: Leverage logging and tracing tools

One of the disadvantages of using a microservice architecture is the added burden of logging and tracing many components. In a monolithic application, there is one software component to monitor. In a microservice architecture, each microservice generates its own logging and error messages. With a microservice architecture, software development is simplified while operations become a little more complicated. For this reason, it is important that our services leverage the logging and tracing services that AWS offers, such as AWS CloudWatch and AWS CloudTrail, and that the logging and error messages generated are as uniform as possible. Ideally, all the microservice teams will agree on the logging libraries and standards to increase uniformity. Two products that are quite popular to implement logging are the ELK stack (consisting of Elasticsearch, Logstash, and Kibana) and Splunk.

Best practice #6: Think microservices first

Software development can be a fine art more than a hard science. There are always conflicting forces at play. You want to deliver functionality in production as quickly as possible but at the same time, you want to ensure that your solution endures for many years and is easily maintainable and easily expandable. For this reason, some developers like using a monolithic architecture at the beginning of projects and then try to convert it to a microservice architecture.

If possible, it is best to fight this temptation. The tight coupling that will exist because of the architecture choice will be difficult to untangle once it is embedded. Additionally, once your application is in production, expectations rise because any change you make needs to be thoroughly tested. You want to make sure that any new changes don't break existing functionality. You might think that code refactoring to ease maintenance is a perfectly valid reason to change code in production. But explaining to your boss why the production code broke when you were introducing a change that did not add any new functionality will not be an easy conversation. You may be able to deliver the initial functionality faster using a monolithic architecture, but it will be cumbersome to later convert it to a more modular architecture.

It is recommended to spend some time upfront on correctly designing your microservices' boundaries and do it correctly from the start. If you are using an Agile methodology, there will no doubt be some refactoring of microservices as your architecture evolves and that's okay. But do your best to properly design your boundaries at the beginning.

Best practice #7: Minimize the number of languages and technologies

One of the advantages of the microservice architecture is the ability to create different services using different technology stacks. For example, you could create Service A using Java, the Spring MVC framework, and MariaDB and you could create Service B using Python with a Postgres backend. This is doable because when Service A communicates with Service B, they will communicate through the HTTP protocol and via the RESTful API, without either one caring about the details of the implementation of the other.

Now, just because you can do something, doesn't mean you should do it. It still behooves you to minimize the number of languages used to create microservices. Having a small number or maybe even using just one language will enable you to swap people from one group to another and be able to act more nimbly and be more flexible.

There is a case to be made that one stack might be superior to the other and more suited to implement a particular service, but any time you have to deviate from your company's standard stack, you should make sure that you have a compelling business case to deviate from the standards and increase your technology footprint.

Best practice #8: Leverage RESTful APIs

A key feature of the microservice pattern is to deliver its functionality via a RESTful API. **RESTful APIs** are powerful for various reasons, among them the fact that no client code needs to be deployed in order to start using them, as well as the fact that they can be self-documenting if implemented properly.

Best practice #9: Implement microservice communication asynchronously

Whenever possible, communication between microservices should be asynchronous. One of the tricky parts about designing microservices is deciding the boundaries among the services. Do you offer granular microservices or do you only offer a few services? If you offer many services that perform a few tasks well, there will undoubtedly be more inter-service communication between the services.

In order to perform a task, it may be necessary for Service A to call Service B, which in turn needs to call Service C. If the services are called synchronously, this interdependency can make the application brittle. For example, what happens if Service C is down? Service A won't work and will hopefully return an error. The alternative is for the services to communicate asynchronously. In this case, if Service C is down, Service A will put a request in a queue and Service C will handle the request when it comes back online. Implementing asynchronous communication between services creates more overhead and is more difficult than synchronous communication, but the upfront development cost will be offset by increasing the reliability and scalability of the final solution.

There are many ways to implement asynchronous communication between microservices. Some of them are as follows:

- **Amazon SNS**: SNS is a distributed publish-subscribe service. Messages are pushed to any subscribers when messages are received from the publishers.

- **Amazon SQS**: SQS is a distributed queuing system. With SQS, messages are NOT pushed to the receivers. Receivers pull messages from the queue and once they pull a message, no one else can receive that message. The receiver processes it and the message is removed from the queue.

- **Amazon Kinesis**: Amazon SNS and Amazon SQS are good options with simple use cases. Amazon Kinesis is more appropriate for real-time use cases that need to process terabytes of data per minute.

- **Apache Kafka**, via asynchronous REST (ATOM): Apache Kafka, as well as the rest of the options listed below, is an open source solution. This means that all management and administration needs to be handled by the users and are not managed by AWS like the previous services. On the flip side, because these options are open source, it is possible that they may be cheaper than AWS alternatives. If you select them based on price, make sure to include all soft costs such as administration costs. Apache Kafka supports both a queue and a pub-sub architecture.

- **ActiveMQ**: Apache ActiveMQ is another popular open source messaging tool. It supports a variety of messaging protocols – multi-protocol. It is written in Java but it offers connectivity to C, C++, Python, and .NET among other languages. It supports a variety of standard protocols.

Best practice #10: Implement clear separation between microservice frontends and backends

Even today, many backend developers have an outdated perspective about what it takes to develop UIs and tend to oversimplify the complexities involved in constructing user-friendly frontends. The UI can often be neglected in design sessions. A microservice architecture with fine-grained backend services that have a monolithic frontend can run into trouble in the long run. Picking the hottest SPA tool to develop your frontend is not enough. There are great options out there that can help create sharp-looking frontends. Some of the most popular frontend web development frameworks currently are the following:

- Vue

- React

- Angular

Having a clear separation between backend and frontend development is imperative. The interaction and dependencies between the two should be absolutely minimal, if not completely independent.

As new UIs become more popular or easier to use come online, we should be able to swap out the frontend with minimal interruptions and changes to the backend.

Another reason for having this independence comes about when multiple UIs are required. For example, our application may need a web UI, an Android application, and an Apple iOS application.

Best practice #11: Organize your team around microservices

On a related note to the previous best practice. There might be different teams for individual microservices and it's important to assign ownership of each of these services to individuals in your team. However, hopefully, your team is as cross-functional as possible and team members can jump from one microservice to another if the need arises. In general, there should be a good reason to pull one team member from the development of one service to another, but when this does happen, hopefully, they are able to make the leap and fill the gap.

In addition, the team should have a decent understanding of the overall objectives of the projects as well as knowledge of the project plan for all services. Having a narrow view of only one service could prove fatal to the success of the business if they don't fully understand the business impact that a change in their service could have on other services.

Best practice #12: Provision individual data stores for each individual microservice

Separating your garbage into recyclables and non-recyclables and then watching the garbage man comingle them can be frustrating. The same is true of microservices that have well-defined and architected boundaries and then share the same database. If you use the same database, you create strong coupling between the microservices, which we want to avoid whenever possible. Having a common database will require constant synchronization between the various microservice developers. Transactions will also get more complicated if there is a common database.

Having a separate data store makes services more modular and more reusable. Having one database per microservice does require that any data that needs to be shared between services needs to be passed along with the RESTful calls, but this drawback is not enough to not separate service databases whenever possible.

Ideally, every microservice will have an individual allocation for its data store. Every microservice should be responsible for its own persistence. Data can be reused across services, but it should only be stored once and shared via APIs across the services. Whenever possible, avoid data sharing across microservices. Data sharing leads to service coupling. This coupling negates some of the advantages of the separation of concerns of the microservice architecture, so it should be avoided as much as possible.

Best practice #13: Self-documentation and full documentation

A well-designed RESTful API should be intuitive to use if you choose your domain name and operation names correctly.

Take special care to use labels for your APIs that closely match your business domains. If you do this, you won't need to create endless documents to support your application. However, your documentation should be able to fill the gaps and take over where the intuitiveness of your API ends. One of the most popular tools to create this documentation is a tool called **Swagger**. You can learn more about the Swagger tool here: `https://swagger.io/`.

Best practice #14: Use a DevOps toolset

Another technology that goes hand in hand with microservice development in addition to DDD is the popular **DevOps paradigm**. Having a robust DevOps program in place along with a mature CI/CD pipeline will allow you to quickly and effortlessly develop, test, and maintain your microservices.

A popular combination is to use Jenkins for deployment and Docker as a container service.

Best practice #15: Invest in monitoring

As we learned in the preceding section regarding the disadvantages of microservices, they can be more difficult to monitor and troubleshoot than legacy monolithic architectures. This increased complexity must be accounted for and new monitoring tools that can be adapted to the new microservice architecture need to be used.

Ideally, the monitoring solution offers a central repository for messages and logs regardless of what component of the architecture generated the event.

The monitoring tools should be able to be used for each microservice. And the monitoring system should facilitate root cause analysis. Fortunately, AWS offers a nice selection of monitoring services, including the following:

- Amazon CloudWatch
- Amazon CloudTrail
- Amazon X-Ray

To learn more about these and other monitoring services in AWS, you can visit:

```
https://docs.aws.amazon.com/AWSEC2/latest/UserGuide/
monitoring_ec2.html
```

Best practice #16: Two pizzas should be enough to feed your team

This is a rule popularized by Jeff Bezos. He famously only invites enough people to meetings so that two large pizzas can feed the attendees. Bezos popularized the *two pizza* rule for meetings and project teams to encourage a decentralized, creative working environment and to keep the start-up spirit alive and well.

This rule's goal is to avoid groupthink. *Groupthink* is a phenomenon that occurs when you have large groups and people start going with the consensus instead of feeling comfortable pushing back at what they think are bad ideas. In some ways, it is human nature to be more hesitant to disagree in large groups.

It is not uncommon for members of the group that are lower in the corporate hierarchy to be intimidated by authority figures such as their boss and people with a bigger title. By keeping groups small and encouraging dialog, some of this hesitancy may be overcome and better ideas may be generated.

Bezos' idea to keep meetings and teams small to foster collaboration and productivity can be backed up by science. During his 50 years of studies and research of teams, J. Richard Hackman concluded that four to six is the optimal number of team members for many projects and that teams should never be larger than 10.

According to Hackman, communication issues *"grow exponentially as team size increases."* Perhaps counterintuitively, the larger a team is the more time will be used to communicate, reducing the time that can be used productively to achieve goals.

In the context of microservice development, the *two pizza rule* is also applicable. You don't want your microservice development and deployment teams to be much bigger than a dozen people or so. If you need more staff, you are probably better off splitting the microservice domains so that you can have two teams creating two microservices rather than one huge team creating an incredibly big and complex microservice.

Obviously, there is no hard rule about exactly how many people is too many people, and in some cases, 10 people may be a good number, while in other cases 14 may be more suitable. But at some point, the number becomes too big and unmanageable. For example, having a 100-person monolithic team with no hierarchy or natural division in it most likely would be too unmanageable.

Many of the best practices mentioned don't just apply to microservice development but are also useful in software development in general. Following these practices from the beginning of your project will greatly increase the chances of a successful implementation that is on time and on budget, as well as making sure that these microservices are useful, adaptable, flexible, and easily maintainable.

Best practice #17: Twelve-factor design

A popular methodology that is out there to enhance microservice development is one dubbed *the twelve-factor app*. This methodology accelerates and simplifies software development by making suggestions such as ensuring that you are using a version control tool to keep track of your code. You can learn more about this methodology here:

```
https://12factor.net/
```

This concludes our list of best practices.

Summary

In this chapter, we explored what microservice architecture is exactly. We also analyzed a popular implementation of microservice architecture – event-driven architecture. We drilled down further into two kinds of event-driven architectures, namely, the event streaming model and the publish and subscribe model.

We detailed the benefits of event-driven architecture as well as the disadvantages of using it. One more topic we covered was another common microservice architecture, called the microkernel architecture.

Lastly, we went through recommended best practices in the development of microservices. Hopefully, you can leverage the list of tried and true best practices in your next project and benefit from them.

Using architectures such as event-driven architectures in the modern-day enterprise is no longer an option. If you continue to use legacy patterns, it is a surefire way for your project and your company to fall behind the times and lag behind your competition.

Using a microservice architecture will tend to make your application more scalable, more maintainable, and more relevant.

In the next chapter, we will look at domain-driven design, which is a powerful pattern often used to build microservices.

11
Domain-Driven Design

In today's world, software is used to solve many complicated problems. From meeting worldwide demand for your e-commerce site to enabling a real-time stock trading platform, many companies, big and small, are leveraging **Domain-Driven Design** (**DDD**) to bring their products and services to market in a timely manner. DDD provides a conceptual foundation to solve complex problems and allows designers to modularize their software development and focus more on business concepts rather than the technical details. It is also a powerful methodology that facilitates creative collaboration between technical and domain experts. It enables these groups to iterate over a design to refine it and provides a common language for these parties to communicate effectively and create a conceptual model that can be used to effectively describe domain requirements in detail.

The objective of this chapter is to introduce you to DDD, the microservices that can be created using this pattern, and what the best practices to create microservices in AWS are.

In this chapter, we will cover the following topics:

- Domain-driven design
- Microservices
- Microservices in AWS
- Microservice examples

Domain-driven design

DDD might fall into the shiny object category, as many people see it as the latest trendy pattern. However, DDD builds upon decades of evolutionary software design and engineering wisdom.

To get a better understanding of it, let's have a brief look at how the ideas behind DDD came about.

History of domain-driven design

DDD has its roots in the **Object-Oriented Programming** (**OOP**) concepts pioneered by Alan Key and Ivan Sutherland. The term OOP was coined by Alan Key around 1966 or 1967 while in grad school.

Ivan Sutherland created an application called Sketchpad, which was an early inspiration for OOP. Sutherland started working on this application in 1963. Objects in this early version of an OOP application were primitive data structures that were displayed as images on the screen and started using the concept of inheritance even in those early days. Sketchpad has some similarities with JavaScript's prototypal inheritance.

OOP came about because developers and designers were getting more and more ambitious in trying to tackle harder and harder problems, and procedural languages were not enough. Another seminal development was the creation of a language called **Simula**. Simula is considered the first fully OOP language. It was developed by two Norwegian computer scientists—Ole-Johan Dahl and Kristen Nygaard.

Much development and many projects relied heavily on OOP for a long time. Building upon the advances of OOP, Eric Evans wrote the book *Domain-Driven Design: Tackling Complexity in the Heart of Software* in 2003. In his book, Evans introduced us to DDD, and posited that DDD represents a new, better, and more mature way to develop software building on the evolution of **Object Oriented Analysis and Design (OOAD)**.

Definition of a domain

Now that we have taken a drive down memory lane regarding the history of DDD, let's first nail down what is a domain before we delve into the definition of DDD. According to the Oxford English dictionary, one of the definitions of a domain is "a sphere of knowledge or activity."

Applying this definition to the software realm, domain refers to the subject or topic area that the application will operate in. In application development terms, the domain is the *sphere of knowledge and activity that will be used during application development*.

Another common way that this word is used is to refer to the domain layer or the domain logic. Many developers also refer to this as the business layer or the business logic. The business logic in an application is the rules that apply to the business objects. Let's look at an example of a business rule.

If a bank account holder tries to retrieve a certain amount of money from his bank and his account does not have enough balance to honor the request, the bank should not allow the account holder to retrieve any of the funds (and charge them an *insufficient funds fee*).

Can you spot the potential business objects in this example? Pause for a second before we give you the answer to see if you can figure it out. Two candidates are these:

- Bank account holder
- Bank account

Depending on the application, you might want to not model the holder as a separate object and just rely on the account, but it's going to depend on the operations that need to be performed on the objects. If you decide to merge the account with the holder, this might generate data duplication (for example, you might store the same address twice in the case where a holder has two accounts and only one address). This issue might not be an issue at all in your implementation.

Definition of domain-driven design

As we mentioned earlier, Eric Evans coined the term **domain-driven design**, so who better to ask for a definition than Evans? As it turns out, even for him, the definition has been a moving target, and the definition that he originally gave in his book is no longer his preferred definition. Moreover, defining DDD is not a simple exercise, and Evans defines DDD in multiple ways. This is not necessarily a bad thing—by having multiple definitions, we can cover the term using different lenses. One of Evans's preferred definitions is a set of guiding principles.

Evans said that one way to define DDD is as a set of driving principles:

- Focus on the core domain – "*people get distracted by technology and we want to bring that attention back to the business domain,*" said Evans. Even that whole business domain is too much to focus on, according to him; DDD requires us to focus on the core, the critical, most valuable part.

- Explore models in a creative collaboration with domain practitioners and software practitioners – "*we have to collaborate, not just quiz [business experts] for requirements.*"

- Speak a ubiquitous language in an explicitly bounded context.

The principles of DDD can be distilled to this:

- Place the project's primary focus on core domains.

- Create complex designs based on the domain model.

- There should be collaboration between the technical and domain experts.

- There should be a constant iteration of the conceptual domain model.

Let's analyze these principles in more detail and understand what they mean exactly:

- **Focus on the core domain** – Firstly, this is not new. We should focus on the business domain, the business problem that we are trying to resolve, and not focus initially on the tool that is going to be used to solve the problem. Secondly, we should really narrow down the domain that we are trying to operate on. For example, if we are modeling bank deposit account numbers, we probably should not be trying to model loan and credit card accounts in the same domain. Domains need to be laser-focused as much as possible.

  In addition, not all domains are created equal. Even if the domains seem to describe the same thing, they can be vastly different across enterprises. Giving eBay and Amazon as examples, Eric Evans says it is easy to assume that online auctions would be a core domain for eBay. That would be a mistake. You can buy books on Amazon and eBay, but they have different core domains. Seller ratings are what make eBay effective. From Eric Evans:

  A star rating tells me that lots of people did business with a seller and I trust that. Developing trust between a buyer and a seller is a subdomain of online auctions, and their approach to building trust is part of the core domain of eBay. eBay would not be around today if they didn't get that right.

- **Explore models in creative collaboration** – Creating models that describe the real world is one of the keys to successful software projects. These models should not try to completely replicate the real world, but rather capture the essence of what's important for a given implementation. Let's continue with our banking example. For a financial application, capturing the name of the teller that takes a deposit might be overkill, and would unnecessarily complicate the model. But for an auditing application, who took the deposit might be critical. If a teller is skimming off the top and we don't keep track of this information, the pattern might never be found.

It is also important to continuously question the model and see how it can be improved. New insights might be gained, or the real world might have changed. Think about how far we have come in the development of web applications in the last 20 years. For this reason, it is important to constantly collaborate with domain experts, improve the model, and resolve any emerging domain-related and domain-drift issues.

- **Speak a ubiquitous language** – Having a common language, or a *lingua franca*, is critical to fostering innovation, and it allows to maximize adherence to the DDD philosophy, thereby harvesting maximum benefits. DDD best practices are not static. Innovation continues within the DDD community, especially as it pertains to architectural practices, and one of the keys to the continued progress of DDD is to embrace these innovations. It allows team members from different backgrounds, with different roles and various levels of expertise, to communicate without ambiguity. How often has your spouse or close relative asked for something and you misunderstood the request, doing something different from what they wanted you to do? English in particular, and languages in general, introduce a lot of ambiguity. Reducing or eliminating this ambiguity and having a ubiquitous language is essential to the success of DDD projects, leaving the door open for continued evolution and progression.

These three principles make up the core and foundation of DDD. Everything else emanates from the se principles and extends them.

In his books and lectures, Evans further defines some common terms that are useful when describing and discussing DDD practices:

- **Context** – Where a word appears can make all the difference to its meaning. Statements that apply to a model need context in order to be understood. For example, let's take the word *connection*. If we are using it in the context of a social network, it might refer to how two people are related. If we are using it in the context of a computer network, it might refer to how two computers are physically connected.

- **Context map** – A context map should be simple enough that it can be understood by all stakeholders. Having an individual bounded context creates a new problem in the absence of a global view. Additionally, models are normally not static. The definition of the context of related models may not be completed yet, and their definition might be pending.

To avoid confusion, context bounds should be clearly defined. If these boundaries are fuzzy, different teams may unknowingly make changes to their models that blur the lines with our models or complicate the interconnections between models. Connections between different contexts may bleed into each other.

For this reason, identifying the role each model and their bounded context plays in the project is critical. Implicit models of non-object-oriented subsystems should also be considered. Each bounded context should be explicitly called out and named, and these names should be documented in the ubiquitous language. In the following figure, you can find an example of a context map diagram. Note its simplicity. It should be simple enough that all stakeholders can understand it and communicate using it:

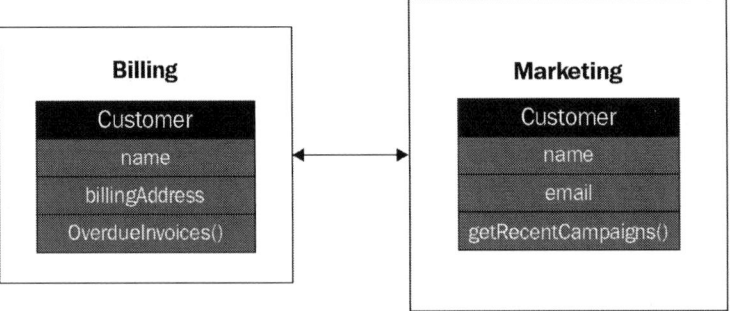

Figure 11.1 – Context map example

- **Domain** – A realm of influence, knowledge, or activity. The topic or area that the technical expert in the project uses to create the design.

- **Model** – A series of abstractions that succinctly but completely describe the important aspects of a domain, and that can be used to perform operations and solve problems in that domain.

- **Bounded context** – A description of boundaries (typically a subsystem within the domain) within which the model is defined and applied. There is a high correlation between project size and project complexity. With the project size, more models will likely be required to describe the domain. When the project size increases, the code bases become larger, more models need to be created, and there is a higher interaction between models, which could translate into more bugs, less reliability, less understanding of the code, and more confusion among team members. In short, more complexity. Therefore, with bigger projects, we need to be more cognizant in defining the context within which a model applies. We need to explicitly set boundaries in terms of team structure and how specific components are used.

Too many cooks spoil the soup. When the various stakeholders are concurrently making changes to the same bounded context, the model can fragment and become corrupted. As the team size increases, problems become bigger and more frequent. There is no perfect model size; it is a continuous calibration. Decomposing the model into smaller map contexts can lead to a loss of valuable integration and coherence.

- **Strategies** – A system should have the least number of parts possible to accurately describe the real world. It should still cover all critical and relevant parts of the real world, but it should not have any extra *fluff*. Strategic design is a group of principles that can preserve the model integrity, refining the domain model, and maintaining multiple models.

- **Entity** – Traditionally in OOP, objects are defined by their attributes, properties, and methods. Entities in DDD are objects that are identified by their consistent thread of continuity.

- **Value object** – Value objects are immutable objects with properties, but no distinct identity.

- **Domain event** – Domain events are objects that are used to record discrete events that have a relation to the model activity. We need to be careful about what events to track. Just as we need to ensure that a model captures the critical components of a domain, we should only track events that add value to the current domain in question.

- **Aggregate** – Aggregates are clusters of entities and values with well-defined boundaries surrounding the grouping. Instead of permitting entities or values to carry out actions on their own, the collective aggregate of entities is allocated to only one aggregate root entity. With this approach, external entities don't have direct access to entities or value objects within the aggregate but instead only have access to the aggregate root entity and use the aggregate to communicate directions to the rest of the group.

- **Service** – Services consist of business logic that cannot be naturally associated to an object. If a functionality must exist in an application, but it cannot be naturally related to an entity, it's best to make it a service. In technology in general, and DDD in particular, the term service is overloaded, and it is used to describe different things depending on the context. Therefore, there is a cloud of confusion surrounding the notion of services and trying to distinguish between application services, domain services, infrastructure services, SOA services, and so on. In all these instances, the use of the term *service* is correctly used; however, its meaning is different and can span all layers of an application. We probably won't resolve this problem here; all we can do is caution you of this pitfall.

- **Repositories** – Repositories in DDD are services that have a common interface to give access to entities and values within an aggregated grouping. The repository must have methods to create, modify, access, and delete (or obsolete) objects within a grouping. By using a repository service to create data queries, you can take out direct references to queries in the business logic and make it cleaner and clearer.

- **Factories** – Factories in DDD encapsulate the logic of creating complex objects and aggregates, hiding the inner workings of object manipulation from users of the factory.

- **Continuous integration** – Independently of DDD, **continuous integration**, **continuous development**, and **continuous testing** (**CI/CD/CT**) is becoming more and more pervasive by the day. Many enterprises today have adopted DevOps and are getting more adept with the usage of CI/CD/CT. DDD highly encourages the use of it. Briefly, CI/CD/CT is the process of having a shared code repository into which code changes are checked in at least once a day, if not more often. Upon check-in of the code, an automated process is triggered, which checks the integrity of the code base, compiles it if applicable, and runs automated unit tests and regression tests. These checks allow us to quickly detect problems that may have been introduced with the new code that was checked in.

This was a long list. Like many methodologies in technology, DDD has its own dialect of terms that need to be thoroughly digested and understood in order for you to become an accomplished practitioner. If you buy the DDD philosophy, make sure that you thoroughly familiarize yourself with the DDD lingo.

Reasons to use domain-driven design

In this section, we will learn the most compelling benefits of DDD and what makes DDD so powerful. These benefits are described in the following list:

- **Greases the wheels of communication** – By putting a premium on agreeing on a common language to describe the domain model, members of the team will be able to communicate much more easily. Business analysts will talk to architects, architects will talk to developers, and developers will talk to testers, all using the same *lingua franca*. Hopefully, the ubiquitous language will not use too many **TLAs** (**three-letter acronyms**). But if it does, they will all be spelled out and described by the ubiquitous language established early on.

- **Increases flexibility** – As we discussed earlier in this chapter, DDD has its origins in and relies on the concepts of object-oriented analysis and design. Most concepts in the domain model will be associated with an object and will therefore be modular and encapsulated. Because of this modularity and encapsulation, the code will be simpler to maintain, code refactoring will be easier to perform, and we will be nimbler when implementing new business requirements whenever they come in. Moreover, using DDD tends to produce loosely coupled architectures and systems that in turn tend to be low maintenance and tend to have a low cost of ownership versus tightly coupled architectures.

- **Emphasis on domain over interface** – DDD places emphasis on building applications around the concepts of the domain by leveraging domain business owners and their expertise. Because of this, DDD can produce applications that closely represent the domain being modeled. Also, the ease of use and the interface might suffer because of the domain emphasis. While a balance is desired, the focus of DDD on domain means that DDD implementations usually deliver a product that resonates well with business users, stakeholders, and project owners.

Challenges with domain-driven design

As is the case with any technology and any design philosophy, DDD is not a magic bullet. Now we will examine the challenges that you might encounter when implementing the DDD methodology in your projects in your organization:

- **Domain expertise** – Your project might have experienced developers and architects who are well versed in the tools being used, but if at least some of your team members don't have domain expertise in the domain being modeled, then the project is destined to fail. If you don't have this domain expertise, it's probably best to not use DDD and perhaps not even start your project until someone on your team acquires this skillset regardless of the methodology used.

- **Iterative development** – Agile development has become a popular methodology. A well-implemented agile program allows companies to deliver value quicker and for less cost. DDD heavily relies on iterative practices such as agile. However, enterprises often struggle to make the transition from the traditional and less flexible waterfall models to the new methodologies.

- **Technical projects** – There is no magic hammer in software development, and DDD is no exception. DDD shines with projects that have a great deal of domain complexity. The more complicated the business logic of your application, the more relevant DDD is. DDD is not well suited for applications that have low domain complexity but a lot of technical complexity. An example of such a project is the development of a new neural network algorithm. Even though the algorithm may later be applied to a variety of domains, the development of the algorithm itself is highly technical and does not require a lot of domain knowledge. DDD emphasis is on the domain experts and encourages developers to lean on them to generate the ubiquitous language and a project domain model. If a project is technically complex, it might be challenging for domain experts to handle this complexity. The solution is to find domain experts that are highly technical, but finding talent that checks all the boxes is easier said than done. In cases like this, DDD might not be the best approach.

A fundamental concept in the implementation of DDD is the idea of microservices. We will explore them in detail in the next section and see how they relate to DDD.

Microservices

A microservice is an architectural pattern that is used to build distributed applications. One of the fundamental features of a microservice is that they break a complex application into simpler independent components or services. Another fundamental feature of a microservice architecture is that it allows each service to scale up or down depending on demand, offers a highly redundant architecture, and provides fault-tolerant mechanisms.

Microservices and serverless technologies

One of the most important reasons that cloud technology is getting mindshare and being implemented at light speed is the concept of elasticity. In the old days, whenever a new project came up, the first task was always to perform a sizing exercise to determine how much infrastructure capacity was going to be needed for the new project. This involved ordering and provisioning computers, hard drives, routers, and other equipment. Depending on the project size, these could be million-dollar decisions that would involve many signatures and approvals and would take months or years to lock down. Invariably, these sizing exercises would result in underprovisioning or overprovisioning the necessary hardware.

Neither option is a pleasant outcome: if we overprovisioned, we ended up with extra capacity that was never used, and if we underprovisioned, we now have a lot of angry customers who would not be able to access our service. While working on the online bill-payment service at a large telecom a few years ago that had their capacity on-premises, it was not uncommon to provision hardware so that servers were at 10% of their CPU utilization. The company put a high premium on the website always being responsive, so they were forced to target this CPU utilization to be able to target the worst-case scenario, when traffic spiked.

This problem completely disappears with many of the services offered by AWS (as well as other cloud providers). **Elastic Load Balancing (ELB),** DynamoDB, and AWS Lambda are some of the few services that are fully managed by AWS, and can scale up and down automatically depending on traffic or many other metrics and thresholds that you define.

It is certainly doable and, in many instances, simple to create microservice architectures to take full advantage of these AWS fully managed services.

Monolithic architecture versus microservices architecture

Another common architecture pattern that started in the age of mainframes and has unfortunately lingered is monolithic architecture. The scientific name for this kind of architecture is *spaghetti code*. With the advent of COBOL, applications have traditionally been built as monolithic beasts. When a monolithic architecture is used to build an application, it is quite difficult to make changes. Whenever a change is made, it is difficult to ascertain what other part of the application are going to be affected. Adding new functionality requires reconfiguring, updating, and testing the entire code base. This translates into costly and cumbersome development cycles that slow down time-to-market. Since changes are so difficult, it is often common to patch the application instead of refactoring, which just exacerbates the problem.

The microservice architectural pattern addresses this particular problem. Services are developed and deployed independently. Microservices enable autoscaling based on traffic volume. Containers and microservices are well suited for deployments that use elastic load balancing because of the highly transient nature of container workloads and the rapid scaling needs. Microservices can quickly ramp up or scale down without impacting other application components.

Advantages of microservices

There are numerous advantages to using the microservice pattern. The most important benefit is simplicity. Applications are simpler to develop, manage, and optimize when we split them into smaller and more manageable components. Maintaining the microservice code is also simpler because each microservice is independent and standalone. We can manage the code base for each service in individual repositories. This even allows us to create each service using a different programming style, a different language, a different type of database, and even a different cloud provider. Some other microservice advantages are shown in the following list:

- **Independent development** — We can assign small teams of developers to each service. These teams can work more efficiently than a larger team (following the Jeff Bezos two-pizza rule).

- **Resiliency** — Due to the high availability and fault tolerance inherent in microservices, an application can still function when individual components break down. AWS allows you to quickly and automatically spin up replacements for any components that fail.

- **Scalability** — If demand increases, meeting the new demand is simple when using a microservice architecture. It can be set up so that new components are launched when traffic comes in, and they can also be automatically shut down when demand diminishes.

- **Life cycle automation** — Individual components in a microservice architecture can be activated in a plug-and-play fashion using CD pipelines. Many enterprises today leverage the DevOps philosophy to assist with this life cycle automation. This results in shorter development life cycles and lower costs.

DDD and microservices

Before we start looking at how DDD and microservices relate to each other, let's first try to define what they are. It is certainly not an easy task to accomplish. Microservices have become a popular way to implement services in the cloud. Because they are so popular, like many other common technology terms, the term microservice has become overloaded and is not easy to define. That's not going to stop us from trying. This is our favorite definition:

Microservices are an architectural and organizational method used to design and develop software where the resulting code is comprised of small independent services that communicate over a well-defined API. Microservices are a quick, agile, and flexible way to provide functionality.

Even Martin Fowler, one of the giants of the software industry, has a hard time pinning the term down. Martin Fowler defines a microservices-based architecture as one possessing the following features:

- Implements a CI/CD development methodology. A code revision in one section of the system requires recompiling and deploying only a minimal number of services.

- Follows principles such as fine-grained interfaces to independent services and business-driven development.

Like anything in software design, microservices are not a magic bullet. But one of their main benefits is that they provide decoupling. Decoupling is the process of organizing software design around business capabilities providing decentralized functionality. They are essentially smart endpoints and dumb pipes ensuring the following. Again, from Martin Fowler:

> *Applications built from microservices aim to be as decoupled and as cohesive as possible – they own their own domain logic [that applies to their part of the business problem], and act more as filters in the classical Unix sense – receiving a request, applying logic as appropriate, and producing a response.*

This quote from Fowler gave us our first clue that microservices and DDD are quite compatible. Both microservices and DDD put a premium on focusing on the business domain while designing systems and a lesser focus on the plumbing and tools used to make the system work.

Communication between microservices

One of the most common methods for microservice communication is via REST using synchronous HTTP(S) calls. This is well suited for many use cases. However, using this request–response pattern creates point-to-point dependencies that in turn create a two-way coupling between the sender and receiver, making maintenance of one component difficult without impacting other components.

Because of this, a common alternative architecture is to use a queue architecture that uses middleware as a backbone for microservice communication to create decoupled, scalable, and highly available systems.

Microservices in AWS

Now that we understand what DDD and microservices are and how important they are in achieving a well-architected framework, let's see how we can use the plethora of AWS services to implement domain-driven designs and microservices. First, let's get this out of the way. Amazon offers a variety of ways to run container services and enable microservices architectures. AWS also offers an array of services that can complement these containers in the creation of microservices. The orchestration services offered are listed in the following screenshot:

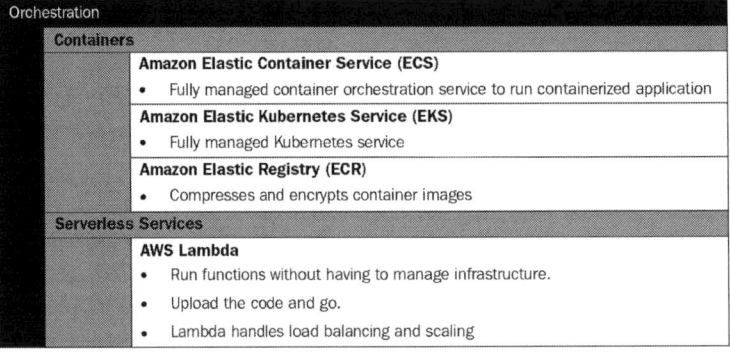

Figure 11.2 – Microservice container services in AWS

The compute services that can used to create microservices are as follows:

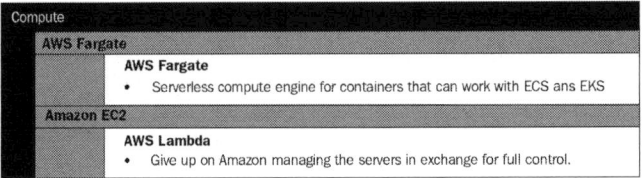

Figure 11.3 – Microservice compute services in AWS

The storage services that can be leveraged to create microservices are listed as follows:

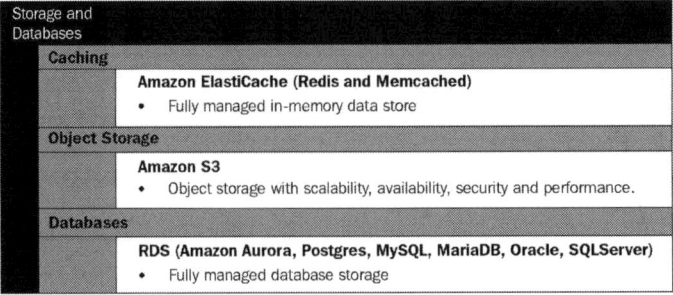

Figure 11.4 – Microservice storage and database services in AWS

The networking services that are normally used to create microservices are as follows:

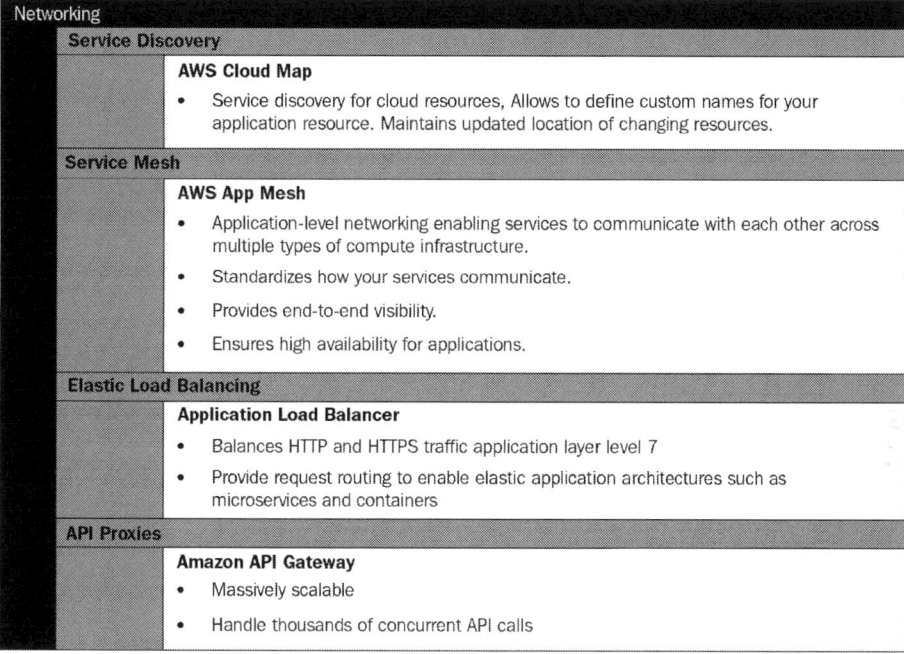

Figure 11.5 – Microservice networking services in AWS

The messaging services that AWS offers to create microservices are as follows:

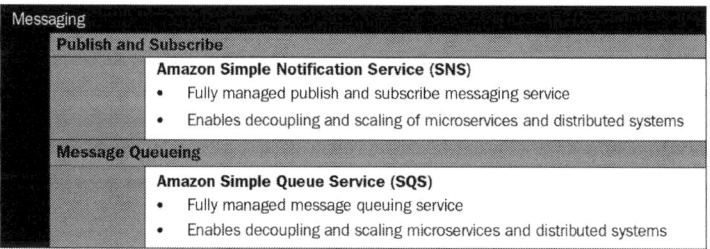

Figure 11.6 – Microservice messaging services in AWS

Here are the AWS logging services at your disposal to create microservices:

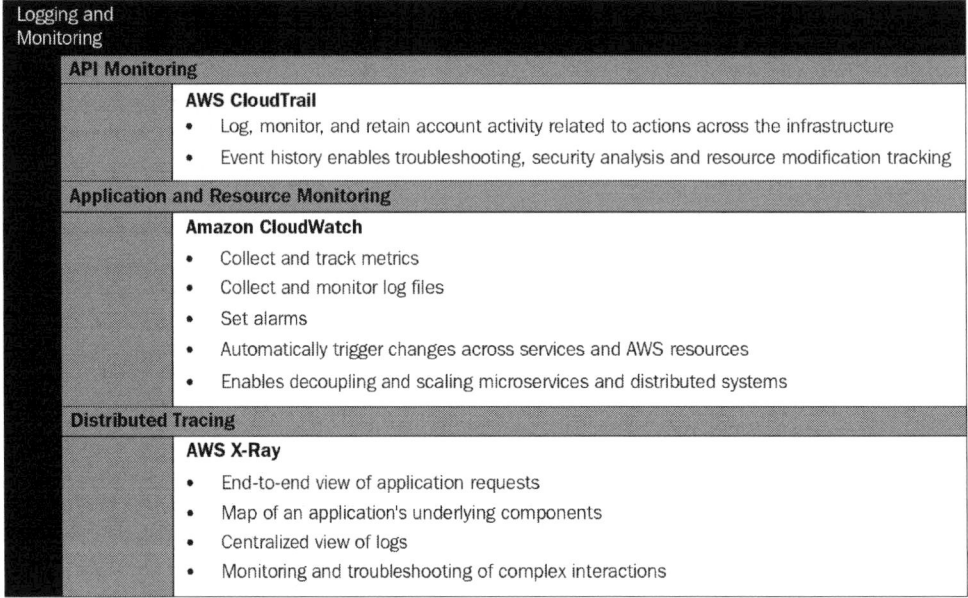

Figure 11.7 – Microservice logging and monitoring services in AWS

To complete the circle, we need to develop these services. The following services can certainly help with that:

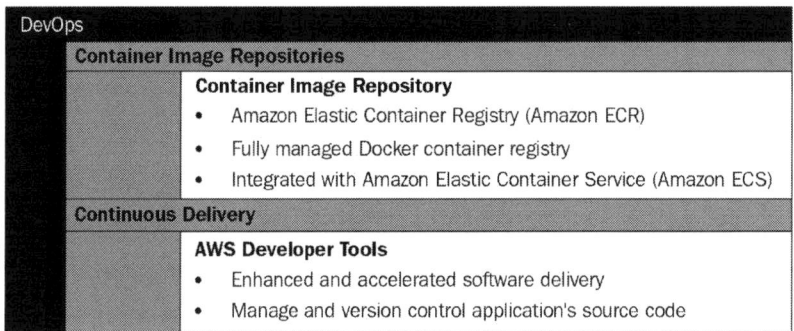

Figure 11.8 – Microservice DevOps services in AWS

In this section, we listed many of the services that can be used to build microservices. In the next section, we will narrow the list down to the fundamental services that can be used to create microservices in AWS.

Fundamental services for creating microservices in AWS

In the last section, we listed a pretty expansive list of services that can be used to create microservices in AWS. I would not call it a comprehensive list. There are probably only a handful of AWS services where you could make the case that they cannot be used as a component to build or assist in building a microservice. For example, even though it is not on the list, in the next section, we will look at how to use Amazon Comprehend to build a text-to-speech microservice. Additionally, you can always use other third-party open source software and proprietary tools to assist in the development of your microservices. However, a few of the services listed earlier are so fundamental to the creation of microservices that they merit a deeper dive to get a better understanding of them.

AWS Lambda

AWS Lambda is a simple yet powerful serverless compute service that allows you to easily deploy code on the cloud. These services can be invoked through an API or they can be triggered in response to certain events (a file being dropped into S3, a row being added to a DynamoDB table, an error occurring and being logged by CloudWatch, and so on). This might be the simplest and yet most powerful service in AWS. One of the holy grails of computing is to be able to treat it as a utility and to make it as easy to use as turning on a light switch. AWS Lambda comes close to this. In order to use it, you write code, you upload it, and then you use it. Like anything else, it's easy to create Lambda services, but it is not easy to create well-architected, efficient Lambda services. The latter takes thoughtful design and upfront effort.

AWS Lambda enables users to create functions in AWS without having to launch any infrastructure. With simple applications, a developer can transmit their code and determine how much memory a function can use. Lambda functions are ephemeral—the code only executes during invocation and resources are released as soon as the function completes. As an example, you could have an AWS Lambda function doing some computation and invoke it only once after you create it. You would be charged for that single invocation and you would never be charged again. Since there isn't a dedicated resource constantly up, there may be some initialization that needs to occur. This is especially true when a function is not executed often.

An AWS Lambda function can be triggered in a variety of ways:

- API Gateway

- DynamoDB events

- S3 events

- ELB target groups

One drawback of AWS Lambda is that it only supports certain languages, runtimes, and versions. As of the publication of this book, the supported languages by AWS Lambda are as follows:

- Node.js (8.10, 10)

- Python (2.7, 3.6, 3.7)

- Ruby (2.5)

- Java (8)

- Go (1.x)

- .NET Core (1.0, 2.1)

Please note that Docker is not listed as one of the supported runtimes. AWS Lambda does not support running Docker containers.

Amazon Elastic Container Service (Amazon ECS)

Like Amazon Elastic Kubernetes Service and AWS Fargate, Amazon ECS is a fully managed, highly scalable, fault-tolerant container management service that can be used to run, stop, and manage Docker containers on a cluster. The cluster runs a serverless infrastructure managed by Amazon. If you desire more control over the deployment, tasks can be hosted on a cluster of **Amazon Elastic Compute Cloud** (**Amazon EC2**) instances that you manage. When doing this, you launch Amazon ECS using the EC2 launch type.

Like other Amazon services, Amazon ECS can be launched, managed, and stopped using three methods:

- API calls

- AWS **Command Line Interface** (**CLI**)

- AWS Console

Amazon ECS can be used to schedule the addition or removal of containers to and from the cluster based on the following factors:

- Workloads and demand
- Isolation policies
- Availability requirements

Amazon ECS can greatly reduce operational costs by obviating the need to operate and maintain your own cluster management and removes the need to manually scale the infrastructure up and down.

Furthermore, another reason that Amazon ECS reduces operational costs is by enabling a consistent deployment, management, scaling, and building experience. At any time, these processes can be automated and homogenized; it will minimize the need to troubleshoot differences across instances and let us focus on building sophisticated microservice applications.

Amazon Elastic Kubernetes Service (Amazon EKS)

Kubernetes is an open source framework with an ever-growing mindshare. Its extensible and portable architecture enables the management of containerized workloads. It offers a powerful declarative configuration of framework features. There is a thriving and growing developer community that has created a wide variety of tools, and many companies have cropped up to help with the deployment and support of Kubernetes deployments.

It was originally developed by Google, and Google released the code base to the open source community in 2014.

Kubernetes v1.0 was released in July 2015 and the mindshare it has gained since then has been truly amazing.

To give you an idea of its popularity, a 2019 **Cloud Native Computing Foundation (CNCF)** survey found that 84 percent of companies are running production environment containers. Of these companies, 78 percent were using Kubernetes to manage those containers.

Amazon Elastic Kubernetes Service (**Amazon EKS**) is a fully managed Kubernetes service. Many of today's biggest companies, as well as nimble start-ups, use Amazon EKS to run their mission-critical applications. Amazon EKS fully leverages the AWS infrastructure to offer a secure, highly reliable, and massively scalable environment.

As it does with many other open source solutions, Amazon unsurprisingly has a service that wraps Kubernetes, bringing in all the Amazon fully managed magic. The full name of this service is Amazon EKS. Some of the advantages of using Amazon EKS over a Kubernetes implementation on EC2 instances are as follows:

- EKS clusters can be launched using AWS Fargate via a serverless deployment. As is detailed in the next section, Fargate obviates the need to maintain infrastructure, and enables resources to be launched, used, and paid for as needed. It also increases application security through component isolation.

- Amazon EKS can easily integrate with other Amazon services, such as Amazon CloudWatch, Auto Scaling groups, AWS **Identity and Access Management (IAM)**, and Amazon **Virtual Private Cloud (VPC)**.

- Amazon EKS can seamlessly integrate with AWS App Mesh and deliver a Kubernetes native experience to enable the consumption of service mesh features and provide monitoring tools, traffic controls, and granular security capabilities. Amazon EKS allows you to create highly scalable and reliable applications by allowing you to deploy them across multiple **Availability Zones (AZs)**.

Amazon EKS can run upstream Kubernetes and has been certified as Kubernetes conformant so that it can take advantage of all third-party tooling available from the Kubernetes ecosystem. This also means that it is not difficult to lift and shift other Kubernetes applications into EKS without code refactoring.

AWS Fargate

AWS Fargate is a compute engine for Amazon ECS that enables you to run Docker containers. It is fully managed, meaning that AWS handles many of the infrastructure details for you. When using AWS Fargate, it is not necessary for you to provision, maintain, or administer clusters of virtual machines to run containers. Your job gets boiled down to focusing on building and designing the business logic of the application instead of having to deal with infrastructure.

AWS Fargate is a service that facilitates running Docker containers without having to worry about managing servers. ECS supports both running containers on EC2 instances and with Fargate.

These Docker containers run as an ECS task. Tasks are managed by services, and services can be deployed using an ELB to process external traffic over HTTP. When using this method of deployment, tasks are persistent—the containers continue running, even if no requests are received. Because the container is always running, no warmup period is needed.

ECS tasks can be configured to run on a regular basis or they can be triggered by a CloudWatch event. This enables the use of ECS tasks for jobs that do not require a persistent Docker container. It makes these kinds of tasks well suited for Fargate.

Amazon ECS has two modes:

- Fargate launch type
- EC2 launch type

Using the Fargate launch type, the application can be deployed in the containers, the memory and CPU requirements can be specified, IAM or networking policies can be defined, and after all this, the application can be then be launched. In this mode, you do not have to worry about container management, and you can focus on your application development and business requirements. This mode eliminates the need for cluster management. It is not necessary to choose instance types and manage cluster scheduling and optimization. Using the Fargate launch type, server scaling is handled by the infrastructure. It is just as easy to launch one server as it is to launch a hundred, and all those servers can be spun down just as quickly and easily as they were brought up while stopping the billing clock.

More granular control and flexibility can be achieved by using the EC2 launch type. The EC2 launch type enables the optimization of instance type choices using traffic volume and patterns to make the choice.

AWS Fargate can be integrated with Amazon ECS. You can do so by doing the following:

1. Define the application requirements.
2. Configure the CPU and memory requirements.
3. Define the IAM and networking policies for the containers.
4. Upload the code bundle to Amazon ECS.

Once deployed, AWS Fargate automatically launches, manages, and shuts down servers.

AWS abstracts the underlying infrastructure, which means that it handles much of the security management for you. This simplifies server management tremendously, but at the cost of giving up control of deployments and not allowing certain customizations.

Whenever possible, it is recommended that you delegate as much of the security responsibilities as possible to the container. Using this approach enables applications to safely run within the user space of the container. Furthermore, this approach simplifies the deployment process.

Perhaps not surprisingly, there are also economic benefits to using managed services such as AWS Fargate. Even though a Fargate instance is normally going to be more expensive than a vanilla EC2 instance, the **Total Cost of Ownership (TCO)** is often going to be lower for most use cases. When building a business case to present to your leadership to allow them to choose a solution, make sure that you include all costs associated with a nonelastic solution or an on-premises solution. Costs like in-house staff can easily be overlooked.

AWS Fargate can potentially reduce costs in the following ways:

- You only get charged for the time in which application traffic is flowing and not for the time that the underlying virtual instances are up and running.

- It can automatically provision the correct number of containers that need to run in order to handle a workload.

It is not uncommon for AWS Fargate deployments to reduce costs by more than 10 percent when compared to EC2/EKS/ECS deployments, and when using TCO metrics, a total saving of 25 percent or higher over a typical container deployment is not uncommon.

Amazon EKS versus Amazon ECS

A question that is often asked is, what service is better? Amazon EKS or Amazon ECS? The answer is going to depend on your particular use case. Let's review the strengths and weaknesses of each while comparing them head to head and you can use this information to apply it to your particular problem. The following diagram gives you a general idea of which is better based on their characteristics:

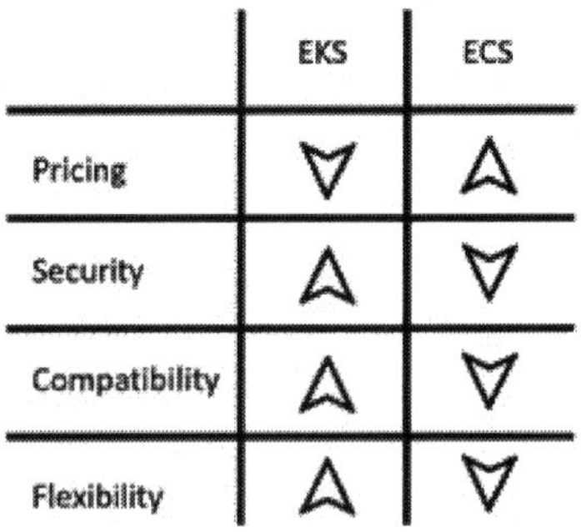

Figure 11.9 – Amazon EKS versus Amazon ECS comparison

Pricing

When deploying Amazon ECS, you only pay for the EC2 instances used by ECS. With Amazon EKS, there is also a charge for the Amazon EKS cluster. When using Amazon EKS clusters, however, you can run several applications in the same cluster.

Security

There actually isn't much difference in terms of security for both services. Both services can be deployed in a secure manner, but there are a few subtle differences. Amazon ECS is tightly integrated with AWS IAM, which enables users to provide granular access to the functionality provided by the containers. Amazon EKS does not provide this integration natively, but it can do with an add-on called KIAM.

Compatibility

Amazon ECS is a proprietary AWS service, whereas Amazon EKS is open source and can also be deployed using other cloud providers, such as Azure and GCP.

Flexibility

Amazon ECS is considered easier to deploy, but that ease of use comes at the price of offering less flexibility and less customization than Amazon EKS.

Microservice examples

In the previous section, we packed a lot of information into a small space. We listed and discussed a lot of AWS services that can be used to build microservices. This might seem overwhelming, and perhaps we confused you. It is important to note that when building your own microservices, many of the services listed will not be used. Your job as an architect is to be able to discern which one is the right tool for your given business requirements. Another important consideration when choosing services is to make sure that the architecture you propose fits with the culture of the company. For example, you might not want to recommend using Java as the programming language for the microservices if the current client is a Microsoft shop—C# might be a better recommendation. Let's try to dial it down and now work on a simple microservice example using DDD.

Using microservices to transform media files

Cross-device and cross-platform support for media files is a good example of a *simple* microservice. A company such as Netflix needs to support any kind of device that a user decides to use to view a video. They could be watching it on their phone, their TV, or their computer. Different devices need different file formats and video screen sizes. Netflix might handle this requirement in one of two ways:

- It could have a copy for each individual format required (eager loading).

- It could keep only one version of the file in a particular format and convert that file to a new format when a request is received from a device that needs the new format (lazy loading).

Both approaches have advantages and disadvantages, and we should choose an option based on the metric that we are trying to optimize. If disk storage is not a concern and load times are considered critical, the first option is preferable. If disk space is at a premium and we can tolerate slow load times sometimes, the second option is better. Since we have multiple formats and multiple screen sizes, storing all combinations can consume a lot of space, and some of these combinations might not ever be used.

For the first option, we only need a lot of space, such as is provided by S3 or CloudFront, but we don't really need any additional services. If we chose the second option, AWS Lambda can assist and automate the solution by allowing us to develop a solution where files are generated on the fly for different platforms and with different file formats.

More precisely, if a user makes a request for a file for a format that isn't available in Amazon S3, the backend process will seamlessly handle the request and generate the file transparently for the user. The user will be unaware that the file was not present and had to be created, except perhaps for a slight delay in the delivery of the file.

This use case is not a made-up case; Netflix must deal with this issue, and Netflix is one of AWS's biggest customers. To give you an idea of the scalability that Netflix requires to handle this use case, consider that Netflix has the following:

- Over 70 billion hours of content in a quarter

- Over 180 million users

- More than 50 formats

Despite all the complexities involved in the scale of such an endeavor, the architecture of our solution is simple. The following figure shows a recommended solution for this use case:

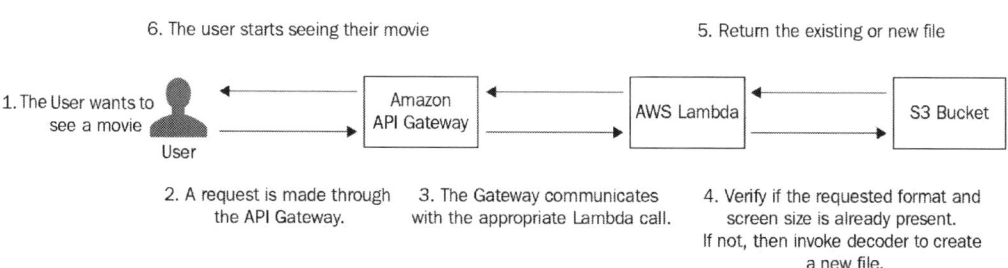

Figure 11.10 – Microservice to transform media files

This architecture is somewhat simplified from how it happens with Netflix. It assumes that the full video file is returned to the user when, in reality, the files are streamed and not delivered all at once. This would work with small files. Hopefully, it gives you an idea of how simple it can be to set up a powerful microservice.

Text-to-speech microservice

Alexa devices are pervasive, and they have entered the mainstream zeitgeist. What might be less obvious is that Alexa relies heavily on a microservice architecture, and you can build your own Alexa application. We are not talking about just building Alexa skills that allow you to add functionality to the Alexa device, but an end-to-end solution.

This is a more complicated use case than our first example, and it involves more AWS services and intercommunication. Hopefully, you can also envision how this can be further enhanced.

In the following figure, you can see the architecture for an application that is used for text-to-MP3-file conversion. Optimally, the application should be able to perform these file conversions asynchronously; once an SNS message is received, the response can return to the client, and therefore files can be processed concurrently.

This approach uses two methods that leverage AWS Lambda along with the API Gateway service to implement a RESTful web service:

- Lambda 1: This function sends a notification specifying that an MP3 file needs to be converted.

- Lambda 2: This function fetches the URL of the MP3 file stored in the S3 bucket.

In the following example shown in the following image, by using the **Amazon Simple Notification Service (Amazon SNS)**, we remove the dependency between consumers and producers. Producers can continue to produce even while consumers are down:

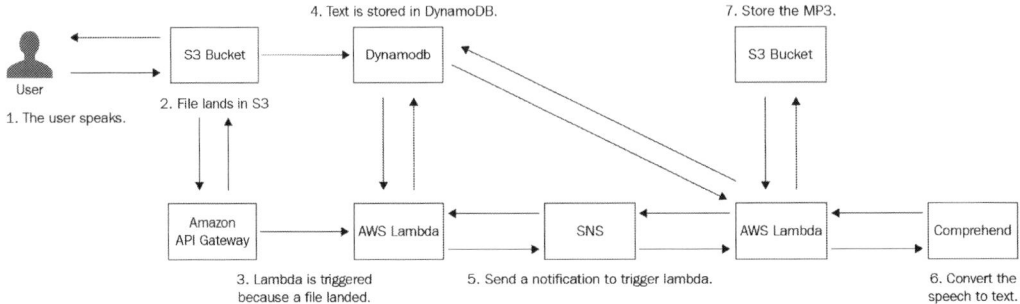

Figure 11.11 – Text-to-speech microservice

Additionally, new users (new consumers of the service) can invoke the service at any time.

Consumers can be decoupled and make requests at any time (batch or real time), and if the process fails, consumers can retry sending their request repeatedly (for example, to train a machine learning model or to produce an analytical report).

Having these features allows each team to have their own domain, as well as their own responsibilities, versioning, SLAs, and choice of tools and services. This point is important. **Enterprise Service Bus services (ESBs)** involved complex logic, orchestration, and transformation. They didn't incorporate this complexity without reason, but because there were business requirements that called for this functionality. These processes were often convoluted because they needed to work for everyone in the organization and they had to be deployed in a centralized manner, and not within the services that should own them. Using a centralized architecture and centralizing the business logic resulted in brittle deployments that were hard to maintain—the opposite of what a modern and agile architecture looks like.

With a microservice architecture, code is not centralized. Everything is federated, meaning that each bounded context owns its own business logic, orchestration, transformation logic, and so forth.

The choice of how each microservice is implemented is going to depend on the skillsets available and on the business requirements. A microservice can be developed to use a protocol such as REST or JMS to mediate the communication. Alternatively, real event streaming can be used by the microservices to utilize all the power of stream processing and to manipulate event data streams.

Summary

In this chapter, we explored what DDD is. We first explored the history of it and how we arrived at this point. We also learned about the most important pattern in DDD, the bounded context pattern. We identified how DDD fits in a cloud-centric architecture and why there is a great synergy between the two, mainly in how DDD and the cloud allow us to focus on business logic and requirements while the DDD methodology and the cloud infrastructure handle many of the technical details. We also examined how DevOps is a common methodology used to design and implement DDD projects.

We also discussed microservices—what they are and how they are useful. We learned about which AWS services can support microservices and more precisely which AWS services are fundamental to the development of microservices such as AWS Lambda, Amazon ECS, Amazon EKS, and AWS Fargate.

Finally, we oversaw a walkthrough of two sample microservices and how they can be implemented using AWS technologies.

In the next chapter, we will explore the data lakes pattern and why it is important in today's enterprises.

12
Data Lake Patterns – Integrating Your Data across the Enterprise

Picture this – you are getting ready to watch television, excited to see your favorite team. You sit down and try to change the channel, only to find out that the remote control is not working. You try to find batteries. You know you have some in the house, but you don't remember where you put them. Panic sets in and you finally give up looking and go to the store to get more batteries.

A similar pattern repeats over and over in today's enterprises. Many companies have the data they need to survive and thrive but have difficulty accessing the data effectively and turning it into actionable and useful information. The reality for many of them is that they have the data they require to run their business and make effective decisions, but they struggle to get that information on a timely basis to the right people.

The **data lake pattern** is an incredibly useful pattern in today's enterprise to overcome this challenge. In this chapter, we will do our best to set you up for success in your data lake journey. In this chapter, we will cover the following:

- The definition of a data lake
- The purpose of a data lake
- Data lake components
- Characteristics of a data lake
- The difficulty of making a data lake work like Google
- Data lake best practices
- Key metrics of a data lake

Definition of a data lake

It's a good time to be alive. We have a tremendous amount of information available at just a few keystrokes (thank you, Google) or a simple voice command (thank you, Alexa).

The data that companies are generating is richer than ever before. The amount they are generating is growing at an exponential rate. Fortunately, the processing power needed to harness this deluge of data is ever increasing and becoming cheaper. Cloud technologies such as AWS allow us to scale data almost instantaneously and in a massive fashion:

Figure 12.1 – The problem with the abundance of information

Do you remember, before the internet, that we thought that the cause of collective stupidity was a lack of information?

Well, it wasn't…

Data is everywhere today. It was always there, but it was too expensive to keep it. With the massive drops in storage costs, enterprises are keeping much of what they were throwing away before. And this is the problem.

Many enterprises are collecting, ingesting, and purchasing vast amounts of data but are struggling to gain insights from it:

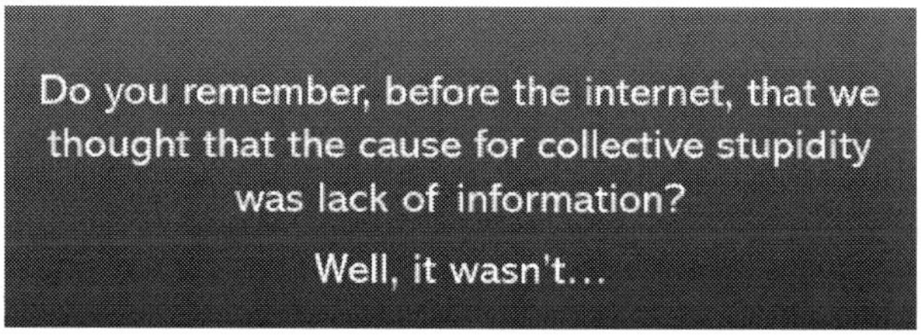

> Do you remember, before the internet, that we thought that the cause for collective stupidity was lack of information?
>
> Well, it wasn't...

Figure 12.2 – The problem of trying to find the right information

The preceding statement might seem harsh, but it highlights a tremendous problem that all enterprises suffer today. Many Fortune 500 companies are generating data faster than they can process it. The maxim *data is the new gold* has a lot of truth to it, but just like gold, data needs to be mined, distributed, polished, and seen. What good is your *gold* if no one is deriving insights from it? With this in mind, how great would it be if we had a tool that would allow us to ask our questions in plain English and we got quick responses to them? We have made great strides toward having such a tool, if the questions are simple. Services such as Alexa come to mind for simple questions. But what if our question is not simple? What if the answer to our question generates another question? What if we want to drill down into the results? What if we want to refine the question? This is where a well-architected data lake can be a great solution.

What is a data lake?

A **data lake** is a centralized data repository that can contain structured, semi-structured, and unstructured data at any scale. Data can be stored in its raw form without any transformations, or some preprocessing can be done before it is consumed. From this repository, data can be extracted and consumed to populate dashboards, perform analytics, and drive machine learning pipelines in order to derive insights and enhance decision making.

Purpose of a data lake

If your company is a bootstrap start-up that has a small client base, you might not need a data lake. However, even the smaller entities that adopt the data lake pattern in their data ingestion and consumption will be nimbler than their competitors. Especially if you already have other systems in place, adopting a data lake will come at a significant cost, so the benefits must clearly outweigh these costs, but in the long run, this might be the difference between crushing your competitors and being thrust into the pile of failed companies.

Some of the benefits of having a data lake are as follows:

- **Increasing operational efficiency**: Finding your data and deriving insights from it becomes easier with a data lake.

- **Making data more available across the organizations and busting silos**: Having a centralized location will enable everyone in the organization to have access to the same data if they are authorized to access it.

- **Lowering transactional costs**: Having the right data at the right time and with minimal effort will invariably result in lower costs.

- **Removing load from operational systems such as mainframes and data warehouses**: Having a dedicated data lake will enable you to optimize it for analytical processing and enable you to optimize your operational systems to focus on its main mission of supporting day-to-day transactions and operations.

The question C-Suite executives are asking is no longer *"Do we need a data lake?"* but rather *"How do we implement a data lake?"* They realize that many of their competitors are doing the same, and studies have shown that organizations are deriving real value from data lakes. An Aberdeen survey saw that enterprises that deploy a data lake in their organization can outperform competitors by 9% in incremental revenue growth. You can find more information on the Aberdeen survey here:

```
https://tinyurl.com/r26c2lg
```

Components of a data lake

A data lake is one of those terms that means different things to different people. We mentioned earlier that a data lake comprises the following:

- Unstructured and structured data

- Raw data and transformed data

- Different data types and data sources

For that reason, there is no perfect way to create a data lake. In general, though, many data lakes are implemented using the following logical components.

Landing or transient data zone

This is a buffer used to temporarily host data as you prepare to permanently move it to the landing data zone defined later.

It contains temporary data, such as a streaming spool, an interim copy, and other non-permanent data before being ingested.

Raw data zone

After quality checks and security transformations have been performed in the transient data zone, the data can be loaded into the raw data zone for permanent storage:

- In the raw zone, files are transferred in their native format, without changing them or associating them with any business logic.

- The only change that will be applied to the raw zone files is tagging to specify the source system.

- All data in the lake should land in the raw zone initially.

- Most users will not have access to the raw zone. Mostly, it will be processes that copy data into the trusted data zone and curate it.

Organized or trusted data zone

This is where the data is placed after it's been checked to comply with all government, industry, and corporate policies. It's also been checked for quality:

- Terminology is standardized in the trusted data zone.

- The trusted data zone serves as the single source of truth across the data lake for users and downstream systems.

- Data stewards associate business terms with the technical metadata and can apply governance to the data.

- No duplicate records should exist in the trusted data zone.

- Normally users only have read access in the trusted data zone.

Curated or refined data zone

In this zone, data goes through more transformation steps. Files may be converted to a common format to facilitate access, and data quality checks are performed. The purpose of this process is to prepare the data to be in a format that can be more easily consumed and analyzed:

- Transformed data is stored in this zone.

- Data in this zone can be bucketed into topics, categories, and ontologies.

- Refined data could be used by a broad audience but is not yet fully approved for public consumption across the organization. In other words, users beyond specific security groups may not be allowed to access refined data since it has not yet been validated by all the necessary approvers.

Sandboxes

Sandboxes are an integral part of the data lake because they allow data scientists, analysts, and other users to manipulate, twist, and turn data to suit their individual use cases. Sandboxes are a play area where analysts can make data changes without affecting other users:

- Authorized users can transfer data from other zones to their own personal sandbox zone.

- Data in a personal private zone can be transformed, morphed, and filtered for private use without affecting the original data source:

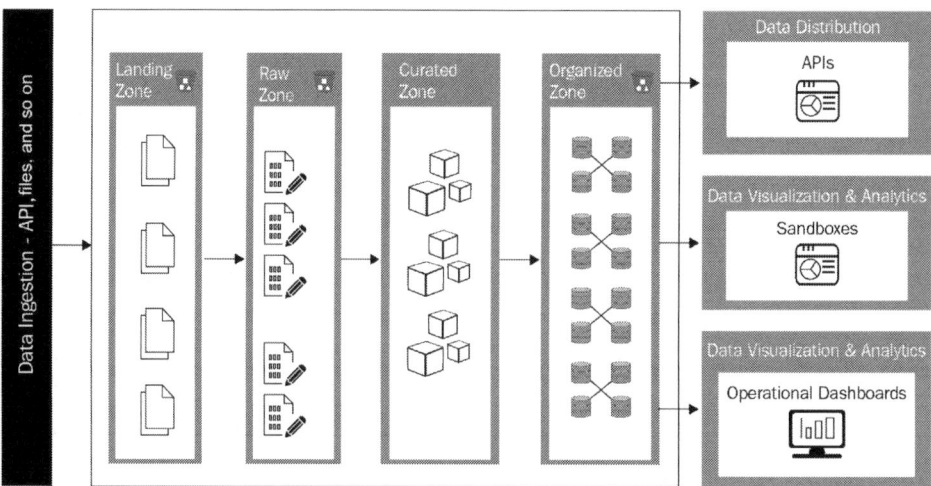

Figure 12.3 – The different components of a data lake

These zones and their names should not be taken as dogma. Plenty of folks use other labels for these zones, and they might use more zones or fewer zones. But these zones capture the general idea of what is required for a well-architected data lake.

An analogy that will help you understand how the various zones in a data lake work is that of how gold is mined, distributed, and sold. Gold is a scarce resource, and it is often found in small quantities combined with a lot of other materials that have no value to the people mining it.

When it's mined in industrial quantities, you have excavators dumping dirt into a truck or a conveyor belt (this is the ingestion step in the landing zone and raw zone).

This dirt then goes through a cleansing process (analogous to the data quality step in the curated zone).

The gold is set aside, turned into ingots or bars, and transported for further processing (like in the curation in the organized zone).

Finally, these gold bars may be melted down and turned into jewelry or industrial parts so that individuals can use them for different purposes (this is analogous to individual user sandboxes).

Characteristics of a data lake

Another important thing to analyze when setting up data lakes is the characteristics of the data lake. As we will see in a later section, these characteristics can be measured and help us gauge the success or failure of a data lake:

- **Size**: This is the "volume" in the often-mentioned three Vs of big data (volume, variety, velocity) – how big is the lake?

- **Governability**: How easy is it to verify and certify the data in your lake?

- **Quality**: What is the quality of the data contained in the lake? Are some records and files invalid? Are there duplicates? Can you determine the source and lineage of the data in the lake?

- **Usage**: How many visitors, sources, and downstream systems does the lake have? How easy is it to populate and access the data in the lake?

- **Variety**: Does the data that the lake holds have many types? Are there many types of data sources that feed the lake? Can the data in the lake be extracted in different ways and formats, such as files, Amazon S3, HDFS, traditional databases, NoSQL, and so on?

- **Speed**: How quickly can you populate and access the lake?

- **Stakeholder and customer satisfaction**: Users, downstream systems, and source systems are the data lake customers. We recommend periodically probing the data lake customers in a formal and measurable fashion – for example, with a survey – to get feedback on levels of satisfaction or dissatisfaction.

- **Security**: Is the lake properly secured? Can only users with the proper access obtain data in the lake? Is data encrypted? Is **Personally Identifiable Information** (**PII**) properly masked for people without access?

Google – the gold standard

When working with clients during a data lake engagement, a common request from them is, "*Just make it work like Google.*" It's not an unreasonable request. Google is one of the most successful, most pervasive, and most intuitive projects in the history of computing. Additionally, the Google index doesn't contain only one company's data. It contains most of the data on the internet. Being able to properly index a small fraction of that data for one client should be a walk in the park, right?

According to Internet Live Stats (see the following link), on average, every second, Google undertakes more than 40,000 search queries. This equates to over 3.5 billion searches per day and 1.2 trillion searches per year. The word *google* has now become a verb. As a scientist, I am not a big believer in the paranormal, but even I get scared sometimes when I type a few letters in the Google search bar and it seems to read my mind regarding what I want to search.

If you are curious, you can look up almost in real time how many searches are completed over a certain period of time by Google users here:

```
https://www.internetlivestats.com/google-search-statistics/
```

Google has set high expectations for search applications. A fair assumption is that if the Google index can contain more than 50 trillion pages and can process 200 billion searches each month, taking care of a few million pages for a client should be a simple problem. In this section, we'll analyze why this seemingly simple assumption is not quite accurate, and why performing search in the enterprise is a different problem with added complexity. Once we understand the complexities, we will review architectural patterns and best practices that can assist in dealing with these additional dimensions.

Data and metadata curation

Google employs an army of people that toil every day to improve Google's search results, but the size of this army pales when you compare with the throngs of bloggers and marketers outside of Google that are burning the midnight oil to continuously tweak and improve their websites, trying to be the lucky site that shows up on the first page of Google's results for a given keyword. For example, can you imagine the amount of brainpower that goes into trying to hit the first page when someone does a search for the keyword *"cars"*?

Web masters continuously add new content and perform **Search Engine Optimization** (**SEO**) on the most relevant pages on their websites to keep the Google index gods happy. In the old days, there were ways to sometimes *"trick"* Google and make changes to a web page that made it appear as a top result, even if it didn't really deserve to be there. For example, a trick that used to be used was *keyword stuffing*. **Keyword stuffing** is the practice of repeating a certain term or related terms in order to maximize your position on Google results. Nowadays, the only way and the recommended way to make it to the top of Google's search results is to write good-quality content relevant to the keyword that you are trying to target.

Web content homogeneity

Another difference between Google content and enterprise content is the type of documents that exist on the web versus the type of documents that exist in the enterprise. Conservatively, the web contains 50 trillion pages. Also, conservatively, around 200 billion searches are performed every month. However, most pages are HTML pages, with the occasional PDF document, and there are only a few other pages of other types.

This homogeneity is normally absent when you are talking about enterprise documents. HTML, in this case, is just one of many possible types that you will encounter in the enterprise. *Figure 14.4* shows some of the data source types that are common in the enterprise:

Infrastructure	Social Networking	Ticket Tracking
File systems	Atlassian Confluence	ServiceNow
Web crawlers	Jive	TeamForge
FTP	IBM Connections	RightNow
AWS S3	SocialCast	JIRA
Mongo DB	Yammer	Collibra
Social Media	**Big Data**	**ERP**
Twitter	HDFS Connector	SalesForce
Facebook	Kafka Connector	MS-Exchange
Instagram	Kinesis Connector	SAP
Snapchat	HBase Connector	LotusNotes

Figure 12.4 – Sample data source types for a data lake

There are products in the marketplace that can handle a variety of these feeds but not without a significant effort to configure and customize the ingestion of these sources.

Enhancing document relevance based on document relationships

Google's relevancy algorithm gives a heavy weighting to the relationships between web pages. If a given page is referenced heavily by other web pages on the internet, Google considers this page to be important. This is not dissimilar to the case with a commonly referenced research paper. The more a paper is referenced, the more likely it is that the paper had something important to say on the topic it covers. In internet parlance, the page is said to have *"inbound links."* Google calls the importance of a page based on the number of inbound links a page's **PageRank**. Enterprise assets normally are not going to have as many explicit relationships as an internet web page. And in many cases, they won't have any relationships, so implementing something like a PageRank in the context of the enterprise is difficult. We need to find a proxy metric in order to implement something similar. One metric that will be available is the number of times a document is found, opened, and read. In addition, like Yelp, a ranking mechanism can be used. A ranking system might allow users of a search application to assign a score to a document, letting other users know whether they found the document useful.

Veracity and validity of data

As powerful and useful as the internet is, many of us are still using it to find internet videos or to support our confirmation bias regarding our political beliefs and prove to our Facebook friends that they are wrong. A question that we might have that can be easily found on the internet is *What is the seating capacity of Wembley Stadium?* The first link that we find might have the seating capacity before the stadium was renovated. The fact that the answer is stale and not quite accurate is not life or death. It might just mean that I lose a friendly wager with a friend. In a corporate situation, getting the answer right could be the difference between keeping your job and an embarrassing article in the New York Times. For example, if your boss asks you to prepare the numbers for the quarterly report, you better make sure that you are using the latest and most accurate data. A small mistake could turn into a costly overrun.

Related to veracity and validity is the concept of versioning and expiration. Certain documents and data will have different versions, and for some use cases, we need to make sure that users are always presented with the most up-to-date version. In some other cases, earlier versions may suffice. Yet in some cases, it may be important that different versions are compatible with the use case at hand. An example of this may be a machine learning model that was trained with a certain time series; and if it is fed a different version of the dataset, the results are different and inconsistent.

Locating documents across the enterprise using faceted search

Faceted search enables end users to find resources using categorical metadata that has been previously assigned to the resource. A **facet** is an attribute/value pair. Here are some examples of attributes that could be used as facets for the domain of cell phones:

- **Price**: Under $400, $400 to $600, $600 to $800, over $800

- **Brand**: HTC, Apple, Samsung, Sony, Motorola

- **Operating system**: Android, iOS, Blackberry OS

- **Generation**: 3G, 4G, 5G

By using faceted search, summary information can be retrieved to assist in the search process. It allows users to *drill down* into the initial results and further refine the search. Many e-commerce sites provide a faceted search feature. In this case, a shopper can use faceted search filters to narrow down the list of products to those that are more interesting.

Faceted search is a popular feature that exists in many search offerings. Faceted search enables users to quickly locate information. These searches can comprise the following:

- Fact retrieval searches

- More complicated exploratory searches

- Discovery-oriented searches suited to problem-solving

When you combine faceted search with keyword search, it creates a powerful combination. In fact, you would be hard-pressed to find an enterprise search solution that does not offer faceted search as part of the solution.

That's not to say that correctly implementing faceted search in an application is simple. You must consider complex taxonomies, content types, security issues, available real estate, and user interface requirements.

Some of the most popular enterprise search solutions are as follows:

- Coveo

- Sinequa

- Microsoft Search

- Lucidworks

- Amazon CloudSearch

These tools provide advanced implementations of faceted search. As an example, when you use Coveo, you can use their drag and drop interface to quickly enable faceted search in your implementation with a few clicks and without coding. With Amazon CloudSearch, enabling faceted search is simply a matter of adding extra JSON tags to the search query.

Hopefully, it is starting to become clear how difficult it is to *"make it work like Google"* when implementing enterprise search solutions.

Security

While executing a search query in Google, individual user permissions are not an issue. There is no need for anyone to identify themselves for security reasons. Everyone is entitled to view all documents.

Now let's turn our attention to the enterprise. In many cases, security is critical. There are critical documents and resources in this environment that should only be accessed and/or modified by only a limited group of people. This necessitates having tight security controls around these resources to ensure that only authorized personnel can view and change them.

Maturity

There are a few distinct phases that need to be carefully considered and calibrated to successfully implement a search solution:

- Search tool and technologies' installation and configuration

- Identifying the corpus population (identify the data that will be searched)

- Data curation (adding links, tags, and other relevant information to facilitate and speed up finding relevant documents)

The first phase is usually the one that requires the least effort. The last phase normally requires the most effort and is the most important to get right to ensure that search results are relevant. After the first and second phases are complete, an end user will be able to perform searches and obtain search results, but these results won't be appropriately ranked by relevance. Only after the last phase is done will the results be ranked by relevance. Compared to any project that you might be starting today, Google has a 20-year lead on you with their data curation. Imagine for a second that every web site out there was brand new. It would take Google some time to determine which sites were the most relevant to each given set of keywords. More importantly, we mentioned that a big part of Google's secret sauce is PageRank, which relies heavily on links between sites. The time that it would take Google to index this brand new internet would pale in comparison with the time that it would take the rest of the internet to create the inbound links that Google runs on. Search result relevancy was the most important factor that allowed Google to win the search wars against the Yahoos and AltaVistas of the world.

Data lake best practices

So far, in this section, we have spent our time discussing why it is so challenging to implement enterprise search to the same level of effectiveness as internet search engines such as Google. The rest of this section will discuss ways to overcome or mitigate these challenges. In addition, we will analyze best practices to improve the usability of your data lake implementation that will empower users to get their work done more efficiently and allow them to find what they need more quickly.

Machine learning

As we mentioned in the *Google – the gold standard* section, there is usually no real financial motivation for data stewards and curators in many organizations to optimize documents to make them easier to find. If you have a website, your livelihood depends on web surfers being able to find your site, engage, and take certain actions (such as reading your content, buying your product, watching your videos, and so on). In the enterprise, document creators and curators will most likely get their yearly salary regardless of how many times their content is accessed. To assist with this conundrum, AWS offers Amazon Kendra. **Amazon Kendra** is a service that enables more relevant search results by using artificial intelligence to analyze user behavior, watching user navigation patterns to understand what resources should be given more importance when it comes to a given keyword and a given user. Here are some examples of machine learning's use in this field:

- **Classification**: Machine learning research in classification has made great strides and can be quite useful and effective. Classification is a great example of where machines can complement and enhance human productivity. A common way to use machine learning classification is to let the machine learning algorithm take a first pass at the data and classify items for which the algorithm has a high level of confidence (say, 80%). Depending on how much fuzziness there is in the data, many of the samples in the dataset might get classified by the algorithm. After the algorithm is done with the classification, we can then use human curators to classify the data that the algorithm could not classify.

- **Recommendation engines**: Another common machine learning algorithm that is used in the context of search is the recommendation engine. Recommendation engines can suggest other documents or resources that a user might be interested in based on their previous search behavior. Perhaps the most famous example of a recommendation engine is the one used by Netflix. Netflix uses this technology to recommend new movies to its users based on their previous movie choices.

Natural language processing and natural language understanding

Natural Language Understanding (**NLU**) can make search applications much more robust. By using NLU, search queries can become much *smarter*. For example, by using NLU, a search tool will know that when you are looking for the word *"cow,"* it might be a good idea to also return results that include the word *"cattle."* Additionally, by using NLU technology, the tool may be smart enough to know that when you are searching for the word *"bat,"* you are referring to a baseball bat (and not the animal) because you had recently searched for the word "baseball."

Entity extraction

Entity extraction is a machine learning technique. It is used to identify and classify key elements in a text and to bucket some of the elements of the text into pre-defined categories. It can be used to transform unstructured data into structured data. Entity extraction can automatically generate tags for a document, making the document more accessible. Once these tags are generated, they can be used as part of a faceted search or as a keyword. Many search technologies and vendors offer support for entity extraction embedded in the services. Some of these services have become quite sophisticated and go well beyond generic terms. Many of these tools support industry-specific terminology.

Security

Obviously, security is always a critical consideration when implementing search projects across the enterprise. AWS realized this early on. Like many other services in the AWS stack, many of AWS offerings in the search space integrate seamlessly and easily with the **AWS Identity and Access Management** (**AWS IAM**) service. Having this integration does not mean that we can just push a button and our search solution will be guaranteed to be secure. Similar to other integrations with IAM, we still have to make sure that our IAM policies match our business security policies, that we have robust security in place to ensure that sensitive data can only be accessed by authorized users, and that these security settings can only be changed by our company's system administrators.

The silo mentality

Depending on your company culture, and regardless of how good your technology stack is, you might have a mindset roadblock among your ranks, where departments within the enterprise still have a tribe mentality and refuse to disseminate information outside of their domain. For this reason, when implementing your data lake, it is critical to ensure that this mentality does not persist in the new environment. Establishing a well-architected enterprise data lake can go a long way toward breaking down these silos.

Data governance

One of the biggest challenges when implementing a data lake is the ability to fully trust the veracity, source, and lineage of the current data.

For the data in a lake to provide value, it is not enough to just dump data into the lake. Raw data will not be valuable if it does not have structure and a connection to the business and is not cleansed and deduplicated. If there isn't data governance built for the lake, users would be hard-pressed to trust the data in the lake. Ungoverned data that does not possess data lineage is a lot less useful and trustworthy than data that possesses these qualities. Ungoverned data increases regulatory and privacy compliance risks. Analysis and transformation of data that is initially incorrect and incomplete will result in data that is incorrect and incomplete, and most likely any insights derived from this data will be inaccurate.

In order to fully trust and track the data in the lake, we will provide context to the data by instituting policy-driven processes to enable the classification and identification of the ingested data.

We will put a data governance program in place for the data lake and leverage any existing data governance programs. Wherever possible, we will use existing data governance frameworks and councils to govern the data lake.

The enormous volume and variability of data in today's organizations complicates the tagging and enrichment of data with the data's origin, format, lineage, organization, classification, and ownership information. Most data is fluid and dynamic, and performing exploratory data analysis to understand it is often essential to determine its quality and significance. Data governance provides a systematic structure to gain an understanding of and confidence in your data assets.

To set a foundation, let's agree on a definition of data governance.

Data governance is the process that organizations use to make sure that the data used throughout the organization is of high quality, can be sourced, and can therefore be trusted. If the data's veracity can be trusted, it can be used to guide decisions and gain insights.

Data governance is imperative, and yet many enterprises do not value it highly. The only thing worse than data that you know is inaccurate is data that you think is accurate even though it's inaccurate.

Here are a few business benefits of data lake governance:

- Data governance enables the identification of data ownership, which aids in understanding who has the answers if you have questions about the data. For example, were these numbers here produced by the CFO or an external agency? Did the CFO approve them?

- Data governance facilitates the adoption of data definitions and standards that help to relate technical metadata to business terms. For example, we may have these technical metadata terms (`f_name`, `first_name`, and `fn`), but they all refer to the standardized business term *"First Name"* and have been associated via a data governance process.

- Data governance aids in the remediation processes that need to be done for data by providing workflows and escalation procedures to report inaccuracies in data. For example, a data governance tool with workflows in it may be implemented to provide this escalation process. Has this quarter's inventory been performed, validated, and approved by the appropriate parties?

- Data governance allows us to make assessments of the data's usability for a given business domain, which minimizes the likelihood of errors and inconsistencies when creating reports and deriving insights. For example, how clean is the list of email addresses we received? If the quality is low, we can still use them, knowing that we are going to get many bounce-backs.

- Data governance enables the lockdown of sensitive data, and it helps you to implement controls on the authorized users of the data. This minimizes the possibility of data theft and the theft of trade secrets. For example, for any sensitive data, we should always implement a "need to know" policy and lock down access as much as possible.

Relevant metadata

Next, let's list some of the metadata that is tracked by many successful implementations and that we might want to track in our own implementation:

- **ACL**: Access list for the resource (allow or in rare cases deny). For example, Joe, Mary, and Bill can access the inventory data. Bill can also modify the data. No one else has access.

- **Owner**: The responsible party for this resource. For example, Bill is the owner of the inventory data.

- **Date created**: The date the resource was created. For example, the inventory data was last updated on 12/20/2020.

- **Data source and lineage**: The origin and lineage path for the resource. In most cases, the lineage metadata should be included as part of the ingestion process in an automated manner. In the rare cases where metadata is not included during ingestion, the lineage metadata information may be added manually. An example of when this might be when files are brought into the data lake outside of the normal ingestion process. Users should be able to easily determine where data came from and how it got to its current state. The provenance of a certain data point should be recorded so that its lineage can be tracked.

- **Job name**: The name of the job that ingested and/or transformed the file.

- **Data quality**: For some of the data in the lake, data quality metrics will be applied to the data after the data is loaded, and the data quality score will be recorded in the metadata. The data in the lake is not always perfectly clean, but there should be a mechanism to determine the quality of the data. This context will add transparency and confidence for the data in the lake. Users will confidently derive insights and create reports from the data lake with the assurance that the underlying data is trustworthy. For example, the metadata may be that a list of emails had a 7% bounce rate the last time it was used.

- **Format type**: With some file formats, it is not immediately apparent what the format of the file is. Having this information in the metadata can be useful in some instances. For example, types may include JSON, XML, Parquet, Avro, and so on.

- **File structure**: In the case of JSON, XML, and similar semi-structured formats, a reference to a metadata definition can be useful.

- **Approval and certification**: Once a file has been validated by either automated and manual processes, the associated metadata indicating this approval and certification will be appended to the metadata. Has the data been approved and/or certified by the appropriate parties? Datasets should never be moved to the trusted data zone until this certification has been achieved. For example, inventory numbers may be approved by the finance department.

- **Business term mappings**: Any technical metadata items, such as tables and columns, always have a corresponding business term associated with them. For example, a table cryptically called `SFDC_ACCTS` could have an associated corresponding business term for it, such as `Authorized Accounts`. This business term data doesn't necessarily have to be embedded in the metadata. We could just pass a reference to the location of the definition for the business term in the enterprise business glossary.

- **PII, General Data Protection Regulation (GDPR), confidential, restricted, and other flags and labels**: Sometimes we will be able to determine whether data contains PII depending on where the data landed, but to further increase compliance, data should be tagged with the appropriate sensitivity labels.

- **Physical structure, redundancy checks, and job validation**: Data associated with the validation of the data. For example, this could be the number of columns, number of rows, and so on.

- **Data business purpose and reason**: A requirement to add data to a lake is that the data should be at least potentially useful. Minimum requirements should be laid out to ingest data into the lake, and the purpose of the data or a reference to the purpose can be added to the metadata.

- **Data domain and meaning**: It is not always apparent what business terms and domains are associated with data. It is useful to have this available.

There are a variety of ways that data governance metadata can be tracked. The recommended approaches are as follows:

- S3 metadata

- S3 tags

- An enhanced data catalog or vendor to maintain this information

Now that we have gone over some of the best practices to implement a data lake, let's now review some ways to measure the success of your data lake implementation.

Key metrics in a data lake

More so now than ever, digital transformation projects have tight deadlines and are forced to continue to do more with fewer resources. It is vital to quickly demonstrate added value and results. As we will see in later chapters, AWS offers many services to assist in the creation of an enterprise data lake. However, the tooling needed to measure the success of enterprise data lake implementations is still somewhat lacking.

A successful data lake implementation can serve a corporation well for years. A key to this success and longevity is being able to effectively communicate whether the implementation is adding value or not. However, most metrics for an enterprise data lake are not binary and are more granular than just saying that a project is *green* or *red*.

Metrics to gauge the success of your data lake

A list of metrics that can be used to gauge the success of your data lake follows. It is not meant to be a comprehensive list but rather a starting point to generate the metrics applicable to your implementation:

- **Size**: You may want to track two measurements: **total lake size** and **trusted zone size**. The total lake size itself might not be significant or provide any value. The lake could be full of useless data or valuable data. However, this number has a direct effect on your billing costs. One way to keep this number in check and reduce your costs is to set up an archival or purge policy. Your documents could be moved to long-term storage such as Amazon S3 Glacier, or they could be permanently deleted. Amazon S3 provides a convenient way to purge files by using life cycle policies.

   For the trusted zone size, the bigger the number, the better. It is a measure of how much *clean data* exists in the lake. You can dump enormous amounts of data into the raw data zone. If it's never transformed, cleaned, and governed, it is useless.

- **Governability**: This might be a difficult characteristic to measure but it's an important one. Not all data must be governed. The critical data needs to be identified and a governance layer should be added on top of it. There are many opportunities to track governability. The criticality of data is key to establishing an efficient data governance program. Data on the annual financial report for the company is just a little more important than data on the times that the ping pong club meets every week. Data that is deemed critical to track is dubbed a **Critical Data Element** (**CDE**). One way to ensure effective governability is to designate CDEs and relate them at the dataset level to the data in the lake. You can then track what percentage of CDEs are matched and resolved at the column level. Another way is to track the number of approved CDEs against the total CDEs. One final method is to track the number of modifications made to CDEs after the CDEs have already been approved.

- **Quality**: Data quality does not need to be perfect. It just needs to be good enough for the domain.

   For example, if you are using a dataset to generate this quarter's financial report, the numbers being used better be accurate.

   If the use case is trying to determine who should receive a marketing email, the data still must be fairly clean. However, if some of the emails are invalid, it's not going to be a huge issue.

- **Usage**: Borrowing a term from the internet, you might want to track the number of page requests, the number of visits, and the number of visitors to your data lake in general. Also, track the individual components of the lake.

  Tracking these metrics gives you one indication of where to focus your efforts. If a certain section of the data lake is not getting much traffic, you might want to consider rendering it obsolete.

  AWS provides a convenient way to track your usage metrics by using SQL queries directly against AWS CloudTrail using Amazon Athena.

- **Variety**: Measure the variety of a couple of components of the data lake.

  Ideally, the data lake should be able to ingest a wide variety of input types: RDBMS databases, NoSQL databases such as DynamoDB, CRM application data, JSON, XML, emails, logs, and so on.

  Even though the input data might be of many different types, you might want to homogenize the data in the lake as much as possible into one format and one storage type; for example, you may decide to standardize on the Apache Parquet format or JSON or XML for all data stored in your Amazon S3 buckets. This allows users of the data lake to access it in a standard way.

  Complete uniformity might not be achievable or even desired. For example, it doesn't make sense to convert unstructured data into Parquet. Use this metric as a loose guideline and not a strict policy.

- **Speed**: There are two useful measurements to use when it comes to speed. The first is how long it takes to update the trusted data zone from the moment you start the ingestion process. Second, how long does it take for users to access the data?

  In both cases, it is not required to squeeze every possible millisecond from the process. It just needs to be good enough. For example, if the nightly window to populate the data lake is 4 hours and the process is taking 2 hours, that might be acceptable.

  However, if you know that your input data will double what it usually is, you will want to start finding ways to speed up the process since you will be hitting the limit.

  Similarly, if user queries are taking a few seconds and they are using the queries to populate reports, the performance might be acceptable. The time that it takes to optimize the queries further might be better spent on other priorities.

- **Customer satisfaction**: Other than security, this might be one of the most important metrics to continuously track.

  We are all at the mercy of our customers. In this case, the customers are our data lake users. If you don't have users in your lake or your users are unhappy, don't be surprised if your data lake initiative withers on the vine and eventually dies.

  You can track customer satisfaction in a variety of ways, ranging from the informal to the strict and formal. The most informal way is to periodically ask your project sponsor for a temperature reading.

  To formalize this metric, we recommend a formal survey of the data lake users. You can multiply those opinions by the level of usage from each of the survey participants. If the lake gets a bad grade from a few sporadic users and great grades from hardcore users, it probably means that your data lake implementation might have a steep learning curve. However, when users get familiar with it, they can be hyper-productive.

- **Security**: Compromising on your security metrics is normally not an option. It is paramount to ensure that the data lake is secure and users have access only to their data.

  Having only a few breaches in the lake is not acceptable. Even one breach might mean that critical data in the lake is compromised and can be used for nefarious purposes by competitors or other parties.

  One more security-related issue is the topic of sensitive and PII data storage. Storing PII data incorrectly can carry big penalties for a company's reputation as well as its bottom lines via fines and lost business. To minimize this risk, AWS offers Amazon Macie, which can automatically scan your data lake to locate and flag errant PII in your repositories.

  However, even with security metrics, there might be instances where good enough is acceptable. For example, banks and credit card issuers have a certain level of credit card fraud that they find acceptable. Completely eliminating credit card fraud might be a laudable goal but it might not be achievable.

Summary

In this chapter, we explored what a data lake is and how a data lake can help a large-scale organization. We also looked at the components and characteristics of a successful data lake. Additionally, we looked at the ultimate data lake (Google) and why it's difficult to replicate its functionality. On the flip side, we explored what can be done to optimize the architecture of a data lake. Finally, we delved into the different metrics that can be tracked in order to keep control of your data lake.

In the next chapter, we will learn about a variety of patterns that facilitate the creation of resilient applications and systems by learning about availability, reliability, and scalability patterns.

13
Availability, Reliability, and Scalability Patterns

In *Chapter 4, Harnessing the Power of Cloud Computing*, we saw how some characteristics of the cloud, such as elasticity, make the cloud so powerful. Having the ability to start instances on demand when they are needed and shut them down as soon as the demand subsides makes the cloud cost-effective and powerful. Because of the elasticity of the cloud, we can programmatically implement systems that are highly available, offer high reliability, and that can be automatically scaled up and down quickly.

In this chapter, we will explore in depth the concepts of availability, reliability, and scalability and why understanding them in depth is critical to the success of all your projects. We will also learn which AWS services can be used to make your applications highly available, fault-tolerant, and massively scalable. By the end of this chapter, you will have the confidence to choose the right service for your individual use cases and to talk confidently to your peers about how you should architect your designs.

In this chapter, we will cover the following topics:

- Availability in cloud computing
- Reliability in cloud computing
- Scalability in cloud computing
- Architectures to provide high availability, reliability, and scalability
- **Recovery Point Objective (RPO) and Recovery Time Objective (RTO)**
- Chaos engineering
- Scaling in and scaling out versus scaling up and scaling down
- Availability in AWS
- **Elastic Load Balancing (ELB)**

Availability in cloud computing

Intuitively and generically, the word *"availability"* conveys that something is available or can be used. In order to be used, it needs to be up and running and in a functional condition. For example, if your car is in the driveway, it is working and is ready to be used, it meets some of the conditions of availability. However, in order to meet the technical definition of *"availability"*, it also needs to be turned on. A server that is otherwise working properly but is shut down is not going to be of much help to run your website.

It does not matter if your computing environment is on your own premises or if you are using the cloud – availability is paramount and critical to your business. A **system's availability** is the amount of time over a period of time that the system and its components are available.

If a component of the system goes down and you can only perform certain functions, the system is said to be partially available. If a component in the system goes down, but the full functionality is still available to the system's users then the system is still fully available. In fact, in order to minimize downtime and to provide high availability, a well-architected system will eliminate (or at least minimize) single points of failure. Additionally, the system should be resilient enough to automatically identify when any resource in the system fails and automatically with an equivalent resource. For example, if you are running a Hadoop cluster with 20 nodes and one of the nodes fails, a recommended setup is to immediately and automatically replace the failed node with another well-functioning cluster.

The only way that this can be achieved on a pure *"on-prem"* solution is to have excess capacity servers sitting ready to replace any failing nodes. However, in most cases, the only way that this can be achieved is by purchasing additional servers that potentially may never be used. As the saying goes, *it's better to have and not need, than to need and not have.* The potential price that could be paid if we don't have these resources when needed could be orders of magnitude greater than the price of the hardware depending on how critical the system is to your business operations.

Cloud services like AWS completely eliminate this problem by allowing you to start up resources and services automatically and immediately when you need them and only get charged when you actually start using these newly launched resources.

In mathematical terms, the formula for availability is simple:

$$\text{Availability} = \frac{\text{Uptime}}{(\text{Uptime} + \text{Downtime})}$$

For example, let's say you're trying to calculate the availability of a production system in your company. That asset ran for 732 hours in a single month. The system had 4 hours of unplanned downtime because of a disk failure, and 8 hours of downtime for weekly maintenance. So, a total of 12 hours of downtime.

Using the preceding formula, we can calculate the following:

Availability = 732 / (732 + 12)

Availability = 732 / 744

Availability = 0.9838

Availability = 98.38%

When you have a single point of contact that will bring the system down, availability is a function of two parameters:

- On average, how often will the component fail or have to be taken offline?
- On average, how quickly can we restore the component?

Let's look at a quick fun fact: Availability was an issue even in the days of the ENIAC computer in 1945. ENIAC used common octal-base radio tubes of the day (basically vacuum tubes). It was not uncommon for several tubes to burn out on a given day. This translated into ENIAC being available only 50% of the time. Special high-reliability tubes became available in 1948, somewhat increasing reliability. The majority of the failures occurred during the startup and shutdown phases. As the tubes and cathodes started warming up or cooled, the tubes were under higher thermal stress and therefore were more fragile. Eventually, engineers working on ENIAC were able to reduce tube failures to a rate of about one tube failing every two days. In 1954, the ENIAC broke a record for its operation with a continuous period of operation of 116 hours—close to five days. Could you imagine if your laptop had this track record?

Now that we have covered the concept of availability, let's move on to the next important concept to be covered in this chapter – the concept of reliability.

Reliability in cloud computing

Let's get an intuitive understanding of *"reliability"* first, as we did in the previous section. A resource is said to have *"reliability"* if it often works when we try to use it. You will be hard-pressed to find an example of anything that is perfectly reliable. Even the most well-manufactured computer components have a degree of *"unreliability"*. To continue with the car analogy, if you go to your garage and you can usually start your car and drive it away, then it is said to have high *"reliability"*. Conversely, if you can't trust your car to start (maybe because it has an old battery), it is said to have low *"reliability"*.

Reliability and availability are sometimes erroneously used interchangeably. As we saw with the car analogy, they are related but they are not the same and don't have the exact same meaning. The terms have different objectives and can have different costs to maintain certain levels of service.

Reliability is the measurement of how long a resource performs its intended function. And availability is the measurement of how long a resource is in operation as a percentage of the total time it was in operation and not in operation (see the formula for availability listed on the previous page for a better understanding). As an example, a machine may be available 90% of the time but have a reliability of 75%.

Understanding the difference between reliability and availability – as well as their relationship – will help you create better-architected systems.

Reliability is the probability of a resource or application meeting a certain performance standard and continuing to perform for a certain period of time. Reliability is leveraged to gain an understanding of how long the service will be up and running in the context of various real-life conditions. As an example, an application should be available with an uptime of 99.99 %, however, penetration by a cyber-attack may cause a major outage beyond what is normally expected. As a result, the application may be down for a prolonged period of time – hours, days, or even weeks.

The reliability of an application can be difficult to measure. There are a couple of methods to measure reliability. One of them is to measure the probability of failure of the application components that may have an effect on the availability of the whole application.

More formally, we can calculate the **Mean Time Between Failures** (**MTBF**):

$$MTBF = \frac{(\text{total elapsed time} - \text{sum of downtime})}{\text{number of failures}}$$

MTBF represents the time elapsed between component failures in a system. In the same manner, **Mean Time To Repair** (**MTTR**) may be measured as a metric representing the time it takes to repair a failed system component. Making sure that the application is repaired in a timely manner is important to meet service level agreements. There are other metrics that can be used to track reliability, such as the fault tolerance levels of the application. The greater the fault tolerance of a given component, the lower the susceptibility of the whole application to being disrupted in a real-world scenario.

Reliability was the second critical concept to understand in this chapter. Let's move on to the next section where we will learn about another important concept – the concept of scalability.

Scalability in cloud computing

How do you define *"scalability"* in an intuitive manner? A resource is said to possess *"scalability"* if it can handle a variety of different tasks that you may throw at it. Let's continue working with our car analogy. Let's say that you had to deliver a package using your car. If the package fits and you can perform the task, then you can confidently say that your vehicle was able to scale to handle the task at hand. What if you need to haul groceries? What if your neighbor needs to haul a mattress? If your car happens to be a pickup truck, you might be able to complete the task and the truck can scale to handle the task. But as you can see, the *"scalability"* of your car is about to hit its limit.

In the context of computer science, *"scalability"* can be used in two ways:

- The ability of an application to continue to properly function when the volume of users and/or transactions it handles increases. The increased volume is typically handled by using bigger and more powerful resources or adding more similar resources. Good examples in this context are the many successful worldwide internet companies, such as Netflix and Twitter.

- A system that can not only function well when it rescales but actually take full advantage of the new scale. For example, a program is said to be scalable if it can be reinstalled on an operating system with a bigger footprint and can take full advantage of the more robust operating system, achieving greater performance, processing transactions faster, and handling more users.

Scalability can be tracked over multiple dimensions, for example:

- **Administrative scalability** – Increasing the number of users of the system

- **Functional scalability** – Adding new functionality without altering or disrupting existing functionality

- **Heterogeneous scalability** – Adding disparate components and services from a variety of vendors

- **Load scalability** – Expanding capacity to accommodate more traffic and/or transactions

- **Generation scalability** – Scaling by installing new versions of software and hardware

- **Geographic scalability** – Maintaining existing functionality and existing SLAs while expanding the user base to a larger geographic region

Now that we understand the three important concepts of availability, reliability, and scalability, let's understand how we can put them to work to create powerful architectures in the cloud. Specifically, we will learn how the cloud can effectively provide ubiquitous systems that provide high availability, high reliability, scalability, and elasticity with little effort.

Architectures to provide high availability, reliability, and scalability

We have come a long way in terms of making our systems more reliable, scalable, and available. It wasn't that long ago that we didn't think anything of saving precious photographs and documents on our PC hard drives, assuming that they were going to be able to store this data indefinitely. In reality, even though PC components have decent reliability, they will eventually fail. It's the nature of hardware with moving parts such as disk drives.

Since then, great advances have been made to increase the reliability of individual components, however, the real increase in reliability comes from redundantly storing information on multiple devices as well as in different locations. Doing so increases reliability exponentially.

For example, the S3 Standard service stores files redundantly with at least 6 copies and in at least 3 data centers. If a copy is corrupted, the S3 storage system automatically detects the failure, makes a replica of the file using one of the remaining uncorrupted copies, and just like that the number of copies for a file remains constant. So, in order for S3 to lose a file, all six replicas would need to fail simultaneously. The likelihood of this happening naturally is extremely rare.

The concept of copying data across resources to increase reliability and availability is known as **redundancy**. Redundancy is easy to implement with copies of files and objects. It is a much more difficult problem to implement with databases. The reason it's hard is that replicating state across machines is hard.

It is also important to note that in the database context, redundancy has two meanings. One being *"bad"* redundancy and the other being *"good"* redundancy. Many of the database services that AWS offers provide *"good"* redundancy out of the box. Some of these services can easily and automatically replicate data for you. For example, Amazon DynamoDB automatically replicates data as it is inserted or updated. Another example is the capability that the Amazon RDS system has to easily create read replicas. These processes are completely transparent to the user of the service and the administrators and are guaranteed to be eventually consistent.

Examples of *"bad"* redundancy are unnecessarily denormalized database tables or manual copies of files. Using these methods to create redundancy will most likely lead to inconsistent data, inaccuracies, and erroneous analysis of your data.

In the next three subsections, we will learn about three different types of application architectures:

- Active architecture
- Active/passive architecture
- Sharding architecture

Each one has different advantages and disadvantages. Let's learn about each one of them in more detail.

Active architecture

In this architecture, there is only one storage resource with a single point of failure. An architecture like this can be described as an active architecture. If your hard drive fails, you are out of luck. This name might not seem entirely intuitive. You can imagine this architecture as a circus performer working without a net. If something fails, there is no backup recovery plan.

The following diagram illustrates the architecture. We have only one **Active Node** and if any hardware failure occurs with the node, the whole system fails:

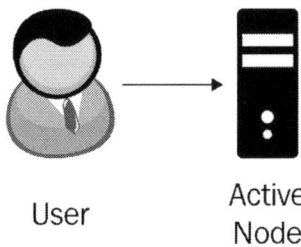

Figure 13.1 – Active architecture

Let's now look at the active/passive architecture in the next section.

Active/passive architecture

The next logical evolution to implement a more available architecture is to have a simple backup. Instead of having just one resource, a simple solution is to let a primary server (the active node) handle reads and writes and synchronize its state on a secondary server (the passive node). This is known as an active/passive architecture.

As we can see in the following diagram, the system is composed of two resources. During normal operation, users communicate with the **Active Node** and any changes to the **Active Node** get replicated to the **Passive Node**:

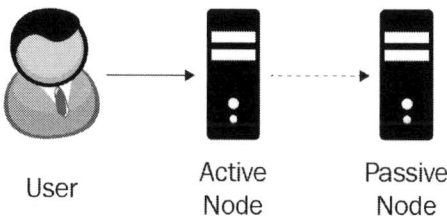

Figure 13.2 – Active/passive architecture

An active/passive architecture improves availability by having a fresh copy of all your critical data. As we can see in the following diagram, if the active node fails, you can manually or automatically redirect the traffic to the passive node. In which case, the passive node becomes the active node and then you can take the necessary steps to fix or replace the failed node. There will be a period of time when you are replacing the failed node, and the whole system can fail if the new active node fails before you can replace the failed node. The following diagram illustrates this process:

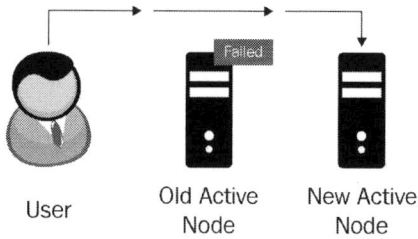

Figure 13.3 – Active/passive architecture with a down active node

The first generations of the active/passive architectures used a synchronous process for transactions. Transactions were not committed until the passive node acknowledged that it had processed the writes. This clearly was not a suitable solution. If the passive node went down, it became a bottleneck in the architecture. This architecture can actually decrease the reliability of the system because now two components can fail, bringing the whole system down.

To improve availability, later generations of this architecture used asynchronous replication.

Asynchronous replication is a store and forward method to back up data. Asynchronous replication stores data in primary storage first (in a synchronous manner). After this, it sends a request to write the data in a secondary storage location but without waiting for this second write to finish. This approach speeds up the storage process. If the write to the second location fails, the process will keep on trying multiple times until it succeeds. It doesn't matter if it takes a couple of tries because the requester is not waiting for the process to finish.

While the high-level architecture looks quite similar, it can now handle failures in the active node or the passive node while continuing to process transactions.

The drawbacks of this architecture are as follows:

- The system will still fail if both nodes fail during similar timeframes.

- Any data that was not replicated to the passive node when the active node went down will be lost.

- Since the passive node is used just for backup purposes, the performance and throughput of the system are limited by the capacity of the active node, and the capacity of the passive node is wasted because it is not handling any user traffic.

As applications became more complex and they started handling worldwide internet traffic, and user expectations grew to have *"always on"* availability, the active/passive architecture was not able to scale to handle these new demands and new architecture was needed.

The next architecture we will learn about avoids some of the shortcomings of the active/passive architecture at the expense of added complexity and additional hardware.

Sharding architecture

Building on the active/passive architecture, engineers developed a new architecture where there are multiple nodes and all nodes participate in handling traffic. With this architecture, the work is divided using a scheme to parcel out the work. One method is to divide the work using a primary key. Let's say a primary key is a number and you have 10 shards. We could set up the process so that any requests that come in with a primary key starting with 1 would be sent to the first shard. If it begins with a 2, it goes to the second shard, and so on. As you may have already guessed, if you use this scheme, you should make sure that your keys are balanced and that there is a fairly even distribution of transactions across all the numbers.

An example of a potentially unbalanced key would be if you have a polling application, your table stores the votes, and your key is the candidates in the election. It is possible that only a few of the candidates will get the majority of of the votes and the data will be unbalanced as shown in the following diagram:

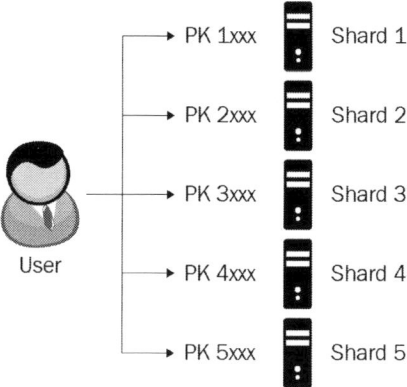

Figure 13.4 – Sharding architecture

Also, as you can imagine, **sharding architecture** increases throughput, increases availability, and reduces the number of system failures. One drawback is that a sharding system can be quite complex to implement. However, there are more than a few services that implement sharding managed by AWS so that you do not need to worry about the sharding implementation details and can focus purely on the business logic of your application.

As we saw in this section and learned about these three common architectures, each has different advantages and disadvantages. Whenever possible, an active architecture should be avoided except for simple projects that are not mission-critical, and for development work. When using an active architecture, we are risking the loss of data. Active architectures are inherently *"single-point-of-failure"* architectures.

Now that we have learned about these architectures and that losing data and having downtime are real possibilities in the real world, let's turn our attention to learning how to measure this downtime and data loss within these systems.

Recovery Point Objective (RPO) and Recovery Time Objective (RTO)

Two critical concepts to measure availability are those of **Recovery Point Objective (RPO)** and **Recovery Time Objective (RTO)**. Fully understanding these two concepts will allow you to choose the best solution for your particular use case, budget, and business requirements.

The concepts of RPO and RTO, in addition to an analysis of the business impact, will provide the foundation to nail down an optimal recommendation for a business continuity plan. The strategy used should ensure that normal business operations resume within an acceptable time frame that meets or exceeds the RPO and RTO for the agreed-upon **Service Level Agreement** (**SLA**).

It would appear that these two concepts are the same or at least quite similar. In the next section, we will delve into the two concepts to fully understand how they differ.

RTO

RTO is the targeted time that can elapse after a problem occurs with a resource and before it again becomes accessible. In other words, it is the amount of time needed to recover and make a service available to maintain business continuity. The time elapsed should not exceed that which is specified in the SLA. This time interval is called **tolerance**.

Example: We have an SLA that specifies that the accounting database cannot be unavailable for more than 60 minutes. If we have an outage and the database is back up and running within 40 minutes, the outage is said to have met the RPO.

Now let's learn about RTO (and how it differs from RTO).

RPO

RPO refers to how old the data that is restored can be. In other words, it is the time elapsed between a data corruption incident and the last time that a backup was taken. This will be closely tied to the architecture that is used as well as how often data is replicated. Any data that is lost that was not saved during this period will be lost and will have to be manually re-entered.

Example: A database with an active/passive architecture is automatically backed up using the passive node every 5 minutes. A component fails in the active node, which causes it to go down. Upon inspection of the data, it is determined that 3 minutes' worth of updates were lost when we lost the active node. Also, reviewing the SLA, we see that we are targeting an RPO of 10 minutes, which means that we are still within an acceptable range as dictated by the SLA.

We have now learned about RTO and RPO. These are objectives – meaning this is what we expect will happen. Two other concepts will now be covered: **Recovery Point Actual (RPA)** and **Recovery Time Actual (RTA)**. They describe what actually happened. In other words, RTO and RPO are estimates of what will happen. RPA and RTA are measurements of what actually occurred.

Recovery Point Actual and Recovery Time Actual

To determine whether you've met your objectives (RPO and RTO), they need to be compared to actual data points. If the actual time (RTA) it takes to recover is longer than the objective (RTO), it means that your SLA was not met and you need to do better. In order to ensure you are ready, a plan must be put in place to test your recovery steps and ensure you meet the objectives. Periodically, it is highly recommended to schedule planned outages to test the plan.

Let's switch our attention to the concept of chaos engineering.

Chaos engineering

Chaos engineering is a methodology devoted to building resilient systems by purposely trying to break them and expose their weaknesses. It is much better to deal with a problem when we are expecting it to happen. A well-thought-out plan needs to be in place to manage failure that can occur in any system. This plan should allow the recovery of the system in a timely manner so that our customers and our leadership can continue to have confidence in our production systems.

A common refrain is that "*we learn more from failure than we learn from success*". Chaos engineering takes this refrain and applies it to computing infrastructure. However, instead of waiting for failure to occur, chaos engineering creates these failure conditions in a controlled manner in order to test the resiliency of our systems.

Systemic weaknesses can take many forms. Here are some examples:

- Insufficient or non-existent fallback mechanisms any time a service fails.

- Retry storms result from an outage and timeout intervals that are not properly tuned.

- Outages from downstream dependencies.

- Cascading failures caused by a single-point-of-failure crash in upstream systems.

You can think of chaos engineering as a series of experiments to continuously test fragility and try to find weaknesses in our systems in order to harden and reinforce them.

The steps that can be taken to implement each one of these experiments are the following:

1. Define what the *"steady state"* of the system looks like. This is a set of metrics for the system that signals what normal behavior should be.

2. Make an assumption (the hypothesis) that this steady state will continue to prevail under *"normal conditions"* (the control group) as well as under *"abnormal conditions"* (the experimental group).

3. Introduce *"chaos"*. Change conditions that mimic real-world events such as a server crash, a hard drive malfunction, severed network connections, system latency, and so forth.

4. Attempt to disprove the hypothesis by observing the differences between the steady state (the control group) and the altered state (the experimental group).

5. Make improvements to the system based on the results observed from running the experiment.

The following diagram illustrates this cycle of steps:

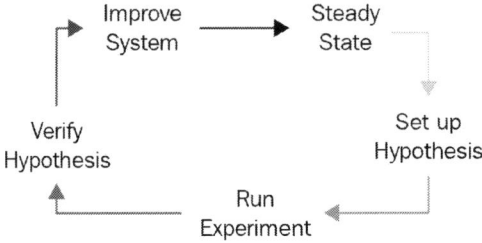

Figure 13.5 – Chaos engineering cycle

If we are unable to disrupt the steady state after introducing chaos (traffic still flows and users are still serviced), this will increase our confidence in the system. Whenever a weakness is found, appropriate measures can be taken to close the gap and eliminate the weakness. But all this happens under controlled conditions and on our own terms rather than in the form of a phone call or a page at 3 A.M. in the morning waking you up in bed. This is the perfect application of the adage, *You learn more from failure than success.*

Whenever we introduce a form of chaos that is unable to break the system, it's proof that our system can handle that chaotic scenario. It is only when an experiment makes the system fail that we realize we have a weakness or vulnerability that needs to be addressed.

Netflix takes chaos engineering to a whole different level with a tool they created called *"Chaos Monkey"*. The purpose of the tool, as the name implies, is to cause havoc. Netflix purposely has this tool deployed in the production environment to randomly terminate instances and containers and find weaknesses in their infrastructure. In addition, Netflix has open-sourced the tool and you can access it and use it in your AWS environment. You can find it here: `https://netflix.github.io/chaosmonkey/`.

In fact, Netflix is quite mature in their chaos engineering and Chaos Monkey is just one component of a whole suite of services appropriately dubbed the *"Simian Army"*.

Some of the additional services that this tool offers are the following:

- **Latency Monkey** – Latency Monkey injects delays into the RESTful client-server communication layer. The purpose of the service is to simulate the degradation of a service. It also provides metrics to determine whether upstream services are affected by these latencies. In addition, by creating delays, it can recreate the failure of a node or the failure of a whole service and determine whether we can survive it.

- **Conformity Monkey** – Conformity Monkey can be used to track down instances that are not conforming to pre-established policies that lay out best practices. The service can automatically shut down instances that don't adhere to these policies. An example would be an instance that is an orphan and does not belong to an **Auto-Scaling Group** (**ASG**). If your production environment expects all instances to belong to an ASG, finding one that doesn't have a parent could be a sign of a rogue instance initiated by a hacker.

- **Doctor Monkey** – Doctor Monkey measures the health of instances by running health checks on them. It also tracks external signs of health such as the CPU load and excessive traffic to detect troubled instances. Once a problem is detected in an instance, the instance is removed from service.

- **Security Monkey** – Security Monkey complements Conformity Monkey. It can locate security flaws and vulnerabilities. An example being a security policy that does not conform to our company policy or an improperly configured AWS security group. Security Monkey, as you can imagine, also terminates offending instances. Another feature of the service is to validate SSL and DRM certificates and send alerts if they are supposed to be renewed soon.

- **10-18 Monkey** – **10-18** Monkey (short for **Localization-Internationalization**, or **l10n-i18n**) can detect configuration issues and runtime issues for resources running throughout the world in any AWS region, which are obviously going to be using a variety of languages and character sets.

- **Chaos Gorilla** – Chaos Gorilla is Chaos Monkey's sibling service. It can simulate the failure of an entire AWS **Availability Zone (AZ)**. It can ensure that services automatically re-balance to utilize other AZs without customer impact.

In the next section, we will learn about the important concepts of scaling up and scaling down, which make up the foundation of cloud elasticity.

Scaling in and scaling out versus scaling up and scaling down

You've worked nights and weekends on your site. D-day has finally come and your site has gone live. It's up and running and people are starting to use it. You come back the next day and even more traffic is hitting. On the third day, you look at the stats and realize that you have a problem – too many people are signing up and using your service. While this is a nice problem to have, you better act fast or the site will start throttling and the user experience will go down or be non-existent. But the question now is how do you scale? Scalability challenges are encountered by IT organizations all over on a daily basis. For many applications, and especially for internet-facing applications, it is difficult to predict demand and traffic. Therefore, it also difficult to predict how much storage capacity, compute power, and bandwidth is going to be needed. So when you reach the limits of your deployment, how do you increase capacity? If the environment is "on-premises", the answer is *very painfully*. Approval from the company leadership will be needed. New hardware will need to be ordered. Delays will be inevitable. In the meantime, the opportunity in the marketplace will likely disappear because your potential customers will bail to competitors that can meet their needs.

If your environment is on the cloud, things become much simpler. You can simply spin up an instance that can handle the new workload. However, questions still remain. Let's visit some of those questions and how to answer them.

New demand can be handled mainly in one of two ways:

- Scaling up (vertical scaling)
- Scaling out (horizontal scaling)

Let's analyze what these two types of scaling entail.

Scaling up or vertical scaling

Scaling up is achieved by getting a bigger boat. For example, all sizes are not available for instance type but these are some of the names of the different-sized instances that AWS offers:

- nano
- micro
- small
- medium
- large
- xlarge
- 2xlarge
- 4xlarge
- Others

So, if you are running a job on a medium instance and the job starts hitting the performance ceiling for that machine size, you can swap your work into a larger machine. As an example, a database may need additional capacity to continue performing at a prescribed level. The new instance would have a better CPU, more memory, more storage, and faster network throughput.

Doing this in a cloud environment is simpler than in an *"on-premises"* environment, but it still requires copying all the data to the new instance, then bringing down the old instance and starting the new instance. We can do this in such a way that availability never suffers and such that the process is transparent. Scaling up can also be achieved using software – for example, by allocating more memory or overclocking the CPU. The concept of *"scaling up"* is not new. Before the cloud arrived, it was just called something different. The scaling up of a resource was done in on-premises data centers for a long time. The difference is that when it happened in this environment, it was called *"buying a new, bigger server to replace the old smaller server"* and doing so could take months, whereas in the cloud it normally just takes a few minutes.

Scaling out or horizontal scaling

Scaling out is another method that can be used to handle more transactions and more traffic. It is normally associated with distributed architectures. There are several methods to scale out, mainly the following:

- Adding infrastructure capacity by adding new instances or nodes on an application-by-application basis

- Adding additional instances independently of the applications

- Scaling out can also be achieved with a software approach by adding more processes, adding more connections, or adding more shards

A loosely coupled distributed architecture enables the scaling of the various components of the architecture independently. As an example, if you have a multi-tier architecture with a web tier, an application tier, and a database tier, you can expand or contract any of these tiers independently of each other.

More specifically, let's say that you had a system comprised of three web servers, three application servers, and one database server. Let's assume now that you get a call from your overnight support staff warning you that calls are taking longer than the service level agreement allows. You have a hunch that you need to add capacity in order to decrease the response time but you don't know where yet. After careful research, you determine that your application servers are running at 95% CPU utilization while the web servers are only using 30% of their CPU. This seems to indicate that the bottleneck exists in the application servers. You decide to add two additional application servers and after doing so, the average CPU utilization in your application servers goes down to 50% and response times greatly improve.

So, in our example, we were able to improve the system by modifying only one type of resource while leaving the other alone because that's where the bottleneck existed. This is a common fix for a multi-tiered architecture where each tier has a well-defined responsibility.

This implies that a series of services can be enabled independently and then cobbled together and synchronized to form a complete solution. Each service is a collection of features and functions that operate independently. This independence facilitates and simplifies the scaling of the complete system.

The following diagram illustrates how we can improve system performance by scaling up, scaling out, or both:

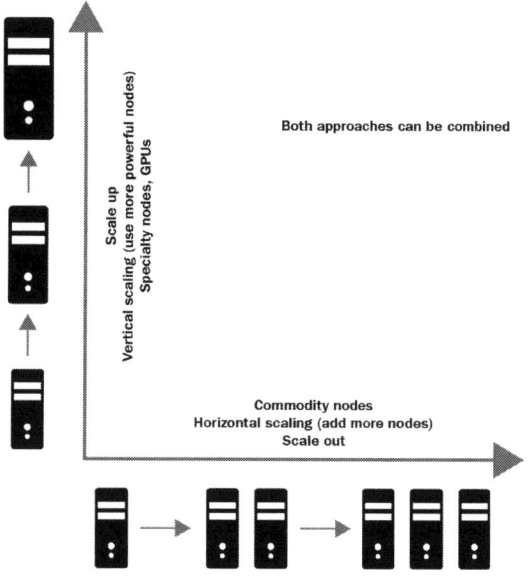

Figure 13.6 – Scaling up versus scaling out

Finally, all these scaling options can be used simultaneously to improve an application. In addition to adding more instances to handle traffic, bigger and more capable instances can be added to the cluster. Beware that many distributed applications recommend using uniform nodes in the cluster architecture.

In this section, we learned about the different ways we can scale. In the next section, we will learn the advantages of this scalability.

Advantages of cloud scalability

A scalable system provides many advantages, mainly the following:

- It enables customizable infrastructure to serve individual customers' needs.

- It allows for the possibility of quickly increasing or decreasing a system's capacity in order to precisely match the point-in-time demand.

- It assists in the implementation of SLAs in a cost-efficient manner.

- It provides significant cost savings because hardware and software licensing is only provisioned when needed and decommissioned when it's not, avoiding having costly capacity "on call" in case it's needed.

Now that we have learned about availability, reliability, and scalability in theory, let's see how we can apply these concepts in the context of AWS.

Availability in AWS

Most services, including compute, database, and storage services in AWS, are built from the ground up to provide high availability and reliability and to be massively scalable.

Let's look a little more closely at these three core types of services in AWS:

- **Compute services** – Amazon EC2, Amazon ECS, and other compute services allow the provisioning of computing resources. Enabling high availability and reliability as well as massive scalability can be fully automated and configured using available features such as Auto Scaling, load balancing, and auto-provisioning over multiple **AZs** and regions.

- **Database services** – Amazon DynamoDB, Amazon RDS, Amazon Redshift, and other managed database services give you a plethora of options to automate the deployment process for full-featured databases. Including multiple read replicas (within and across AZs) in the deployment is as easy as picking a few more options during the configuration stage while creating the database or after it has been provisioned.

- **Storage services** – AWS storage offerings, such as S3, CloudFront, EFS, and EBS, cannot be used without using the built-in high-availability options. High availability is a default feature. S3, CloudFront, and EFS automatically and transparently store data across AZs. EBS facilitates the deployment and replication of snapshots to multiple AZs.

Let's learn specifically how some of the most fundamental services in AWS handle availability, specifically, for these services:

- Amazon EC2

- SQL databases in AWS

- Storage services in AWS

Availability for Amazon EC2 instances

When creating, maintaining, and using Amazon EC2 instances, AWS has a variety of in-built capabilities to increase availability, as mentioned here:

- **Elastic Load Balancing** – This service automatically creates EC2 instances and distributes workloads using a variety of strategies.

- **AZ** – Instances can be deployed across AZs.

- **Auto Scaling** – Use Auto Scaling to detect when the load increases and you can transparently and elastically provision extra instances to handle the load and terminate instances when the demand subsides.

The **Elastic Load Balancer** distributes the load across provisioned EC2 instances. These instances can be deployed in separate subnets residing in separate AZs. Optionally, these instances can be part of an Auto Scaling group. Extra instances can be launched as needed.

Let's now learn how SQL databases in AWS provide high availability using some of the concepts we have already covered.

AWS high availability for Amazon RDS

Amazon RDS is a popular service when applications need a SQL database. Amazon RDS databases are AWS managed databases that can effortlessly enable high availability and failover by configuring them to use a **Multi-Availability Zone** (**Multi-AZ**) deployment. This signifies that RDS can automatically and transparently create a synchronous replica of all the data in another AZ. If the primary instance fails, traffic will be rerouted to the other AZ with little or no disruption and without any knowledge of the failure. If the primary instance fails, a secondary database instance is fully available that is completely in sync with the primary instance ready to take over the traffic. The failure could be so severe that a complete AZ could fail and users would still not be disrupted.

A Multi-AZ database deployment is shown in the following diagram:

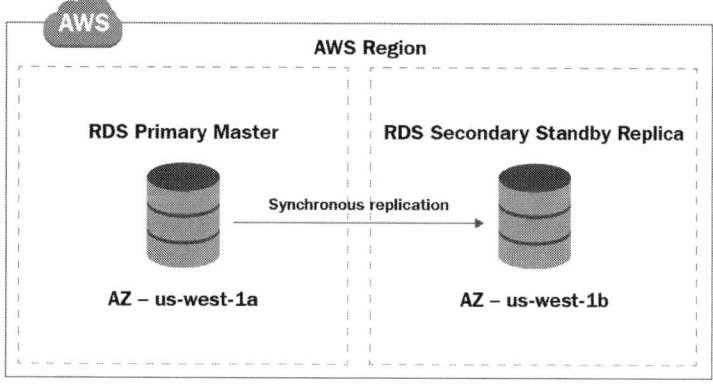

Figure 13.7 – Multi-AZ RDS architecture

Enabling a Multi-AZ Deployment is as simple as clicking on a checkbox when creating an RDS instance to turn on the capability. And like many other functionalities in AWS, this feature can also be enabled via the Amazon CLI or the Amazon SDK. Multi-AZ deployments are fully managed by AWS, relieving your staff of the burden and allowing them to focus on other tasks.

> **Important note**
> One caveat to note: Multi-AZ deployments, as of May 2020, are not supported for read-only instances. In that use case, read replicas should be used to achieve high availability.

RDS provides the following availability options:

- **For MySQL, PostgreSQL, Oracle, Aurora, and MariaDB** – High availability leveraging Amazon Multi-AZ technology.

- **For SQL Server** – High availability can be achieved by mirroring to another AZ, taking advantage of Microsoft's SQL Server database mirroring.

Now that we have covered high availability in AWS database services, let's learn about how AWS provides high availability in its storage services.

AWS high availability for storage services

Let's quickly overview how Amazon can provide high availability in its storage services:

- **Amazon S3** – S3 delivers 99.999999999% (eleven 9's) durability. It does this by making multiple copies of the same file across multiple devices in at least three AZs within the same Amazon region.

- **Amazon EFS** – EFS delivers 99.9% availability. Files stored using EFS are also redundantly stored across multiple AZs.

- **Amazon EBS** – Unlike S3 and EFS, EBS volumes are provisioned in one AZ. Volumes can be provisioned in one AZ and they can be attached to EC2 instances residing in the same AZ. To make a volume accessible outside the AZ, or to provide redundancy, a snapshot can be created and then restored in a different AZ in the same region or other regions. As you can imagine, this method will not provide real-time replication and the data will not be as fresh as the frequency of your snapshot replication strategy.

We have learned in the previous sections that horizontal scaling is a powerful and efficient way to increase the amount of traffic that an application can handle. In the next section, we will learn about one of the many services that AWS offers to implement horizontal scaling.

Amazon Elastic Load Balancing

Elastic Load Balancing (ELB) in AWS allows you to assemble arrays of similar EC2 instances to be able to distribute incoming traffic among these instances. ELB can distribute this application or network traffic across EC2 instances or containers within the same AZ or across AZs.

In addition, to help with scalability, ELB also increases availability and reliability. A core feature of ELB is the ability to implement health checks on the managed instances. An ELB health check is used to determine the *"health"* or availability of registered EC2 instances and their readiness to receive traffic. A health check is simply a message or request sent to the server and the response that may or may not be received. If the instance responds within the 200 range, everything is fine. Any other response is considered *"unhealthy"*. If an instance does not return a healthy status, it is considered unavailable and ELB will stop sending application traffic to that instance until it returns to a healthy status. To learn more about return statuses, see `https://docs.aws.amazon.com/elasticloadbalancing/latest/classic/ts-elb-http-errors.html`.

Before we delve into the nitty-gritty of the different types of ELB services, let's understand some fundamental concepts.

ELB rules

ELB rules are comprised of the following:

* Conditions
* Target groups
* Priorities

Rules drive what action will be performed when a rule is matched by a request. You can define up to 10 rules per **Application Load Balancer (ALB)**. Let's go into more detail about the parts that make up a rule:

* **Conditions** – A condition is a regular expression indicating the path pattern that needs to be present in the request in order for the traffic to be routed to a certain range of backend servers.

- **Target groups** – A target group is a set of instances. Whenever a condition is matched, traffic will be routed to a specific target group to handle requests. Any of the instances in the group will handle the request. Target groups define a protocol (for example, HTTP, HTTPS, FTP, and others) and a target port. A health check can be configured for each target group. There can be a one-to-many relationship between ALBs and target groups. Targets define the endpoints. Targets are registered with the ALB as part of a target group configuration.

- **Priorities** – Priorities are definitions to specify in which order the ALB will evaluate the rules. A rule with a low number priority will have higher precedence than a rule with a high number. As the rules are evaluated by priority, the rules get evaluated. Whenever a pattern is matched in a rule, traffic is routed to a target group and evaluation stops.

Like many other AWS services, an ALB can be created and configured via the AWS console, the AWS CLI, or the Amazon API.

Let's now analyze the different types of routing available for ELBs.

Host-based routing

Host-based routing enables the routing of a request based on the host field, which can be set in the HTTP headers. It allows routing to multiple services or containers by using a domain and path.

Host-based routing provides the ability to transfer more of the routing logic from the application level to the Application Load Balancer, therefore, allowing developers to focus more on business logic. It allows traffic to be routed to multiple domains on a single load balancer by redirecting each hostname to a different set of EC2 instances or containers.

Path-based routing

Simply put, path-based routing is the ability to route traffic from the ELB to particular instances on the ELB cluster based on a substring in the URL path.

An example would be the following path-based routing rules:

```
/es/*
/en/*
/fr/*
*
```

We could use these rules to forward the traffic to a specific range of EC2 instances. When we deploy our servers, we could ensure that the `en` servers are using Engish, the `es` servers have the Spanish translation, and the `fr` servers are using the French strings. This way, not only will the users be able to see our content in their desired language but the load will be distributed across the servers. In this particular example, it might be beneficial to constantly monitor traffic by language and deploy enough servers for each language, or even more powerfully, we could create rules that automatically launch new servers for the different language clusters based on demand by language.

Elastic Load Balancer types

In August 2016, AWS launched a new service called **ALB**. ALB allowed users of the service to direct traffic at the application level.

The old ELB service offering can still be used and it was renamed Classic Load Balancer. As if things were not confusing enough, a third type of ELB was later launched, named the Network Load Balancer. In this section, we will try to understand the differences between all of them and when to use one versus the others.

Classic Load Balancers

A **Classic Load Balancer** (**CLB**) can route traffic using the transport layer (Layer 6, TCP/SSL) or the application layer (Layer 7, HTTP/HTTPS). CLBs currently have a requirement where the load balancer needs a fixed relationship between the instance port of the container and the load balancer port. As an example, you can map the load balancer using port `8080` to a container instance using port `3131` and to the CLB using port `4040`. However, you cannot map port `8080` of the CLB to port `3131` on a container instance and port `4040` on the other container instance. The mapping is static and it requires the cluster to have at least one container instance for each service that is using a CLB.

CLBs can operate at the request level or the connection level. CLBs don't use host-based routing or path-based routing.

CLBs operate at Layer 4 of the OSI model. This means that the CLB routes traffic from the client to the EC2 instances based on IP address and TCP port.

Let's go through an example:

1. An ELB gets a client request on TCP port `80` (HTTP).
2. The request gets routed based on rules defined in the AWS console for the load balancer to direct traffic to port `4040` to an instance in the provisioned pool.

3. The backend instance processes the instructions from the request.

4. The response is sent back to the ELB.

5. The ELB forwards the payload for the response to the client.

To get a better idea of how traffic is handled with CLBs, look at the following diagram. As you can see, all traffic gets directed to the load balancer first, which in turn directs traffic to instances that the load balancer decides are ready to handle traffic:

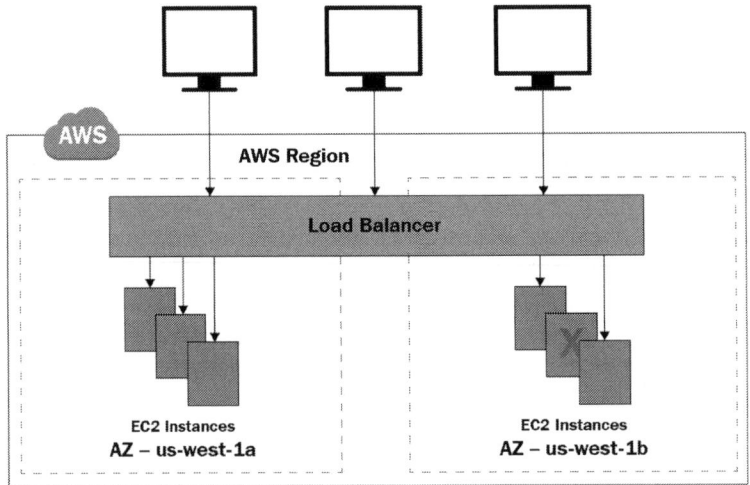

Figure 13.8 – CLB architecture

From the client's perspective, the request appears to be fulfilled by the ELB. The fact that the request was actually handled by the backend servers beyond the ELB will be completely transparent to the client.

Even though it is absolutely possible to set up an ELB with only one EC2 instance supporting the load, it defeats the purpose of having an ELB. Additionally, it is best practice to set up your supporting EC2 instances across AZs in case of an AZ disruption.

Under the default configuration, the load will be distributed evenly across the enabled AZs. When using the default configuration, it is recommended to use a similar number of instances per AZ.

Application Load Balancers

An **ALB** is similar to a CLB but it operates on a different level in the network stack. An ALB is designed to handle HTTP and HTTPS traffic so it's ideally suited for web applications.

Using the OSI model terminology, ALBs operate in Layer 7, otherwise known as the application layer.

ALBs deliver advanced routing features that can provide host-based routing and path-based routing (previously explained in this chapter in the sections of the same names) and they can support containers and microservices. When you operation in the application layer (a HTTP or HTTPS request on Layer 7), the ELB can monitor and retrieve the application content, not just the IP and port.

This facilitates the creation of more involved rules than with a CLB.

Multiple services can be set up to share an ALB, taking advantage of path-based routing.

ALBs also can easily integrate with the **EC2 Container Service** (**ECS**) by enabling a Service Load Balancing configuration. Doing so enables the dynamic mapping of services to ports. This architecture can be configured in the ECS task definition. In this case, several containers are pointing to the same EC2 instance, with each container executing multiple services on multiple ports. The ECS task scheduler can seamlessly add tasks to the ALB.

Network Load Balancers

The **Network Load Balancer** (**NLB**) operates at the network (Layer 3) and the transport layer (Layer 4) of the OSI model. In this layer, there is no opportunity to analyze the request headers so the network load balancer blindly forwards requests.

When using network load balancing, the availability of the application cannot be determined. Routing decisions are made exclusively on TCP-layer and network values without knowing anything about the application. In general, an NLB determines *"availability"* by using an **Internet Control Message Protocol** (**ICMP**) ping and seeing if there is a response or by completing a three-way TCP handshake.

An NLB cannot distinguish whether certain traffic belongs to a certain application or another. The only way this could be possible would be if the applications use different ports. For this reason, if one of the applications crashes and the other one doesn't, the NLB will continue to send traffic for both applications. An ALB would be able to make this distinction.

Now that we have learned about the three types of load balancers offered in AWS, let's understand what makes each type different.

CLB versus ALB versus NLB comparison

The following diagram illustrates the differences between the three types of ELBs. This will help in our discussion to decide which load balancer is best for your use case:

Feature	Application Load Balancer	Network Load Balancer	Classic Load Balancer
Protocols	HTTP, HTTPS	TCP, UDP, TLS	TCP, SSL/TLS, HTTP, HTTPS
Platforms	VPC	VPC	EC2-Classic, VPC
Layer	Layer 7	Layer 3 & 4	Layer 4
Generation	Newer Tech	Newer Tech	Old Tech
Performance	High	Highest	High
Health Checks	✔	✔	✔
Cloudwatch metrics	✔	✔	✔
Logging	✔	✔	✔
AZ fail-over	✔	✔	✔
Load balancing to multiple ports	✔	✔	✔
IP addresses as targets	✔	✔	
Cross-zone load balancing	✔	✔	✔
Sticky sessions	✔	✔	✔
Static and Elastic IPs		✔	
Path/Host based routing	✔		
Redirects	✔		
SSL offloading	✔	✔	✔
Server Name Indication	✔	✔	
User authentication	✔		

Figure 13.9 – ELB comparison

As a general rule of thumb, it is normally better to not use a CLB on a new project and only use them in legacy applications that were built when CLBs were the only option.

CLB and ALB commonalities

Even though there are differences, CLBs and ALBs still have many features in common. All these features are supported by both:

- **Security Groups** – Leveraging a **Virtual Private Cloud** (**VPC**) architecture, a security group can be mapped with AWS services including EC2 instances and ELBs to provide extra security to the overall architecture.

- **SSL termination** – Terminating the SSL connection at the ELB level offloads the processing of SSL traffic from the backend instances to the ELB. This removes load from the backend instances and enables them to focus on handling application traffic. It also simplifies the management of SSL certificates by centralizing the management of the certificates in one place (the ELB).

- **Idle connection timeout** – ALBs and CLBs both support the configuration of the idle connection timeout period. Connection timeouts enable the termination of connections that exceed a predefined threshold when no traffic is received by the server from the client.

- **Connection draining** – Connection draining allows you to gracefully terminate instances and remove them from the ELB while allowing existing transactions to complete. Connections are not terminated until all pending traffic has been processed.

Now that we understand the different characteristics of the three ELB types, let's understand when it's best to use each.

The best choice of ELB by use case

One item of note when using AWS is the fact that you don't see version numbers. There is no such thing as S3 version 1.0 and S3 version 2.0. At any given point in time, AWS offers the best version of a given service and upgrades happen transparently. This puts a tremendous responsibility on AWS but it makes our job easy. The fact that AWS still offers three load balancers instead of just one tells us that they see value in offering all three. And the reason that all three still exist is, depending on the use case, each one of them could be the best for the job.

And that's the perfect segue. CLBs are probably the best option for legacy applications where a CLB is already in place. Many deployments were done when CLBs were the only option (at that point, they were called ELBs when that was the only option). Only later were they renamed CLBs to distinguish them from the new ALBs.

If your deployment already uses CLBs but you are considering migrating to ALBs, these are normally some of the features that might compel you to migrate because they are not supported on a CLB:

- Support for **AWS Web Application Firewall** (**AWS WAF**)
- Support for targets for AWS Lambda
- Support for targets for IP addresses
- The ability to add several TLS/SSL certificates using **Server Name Indication** (**SNI**)

If you have a greenfield deployment and you are considering which ELB to use, most likely, the best option will be to use an ALB. ALBs integrate with the following:

- **Amazon Elastic Container Service** (**Amazon ECS**)
- **Amazon Kubernetes Service** (**Amazon EKS**)
- AWS Fargate
- AWS Lambda

You should have a really compelling reason to choose a CLB as your option during a brand new deployment. A good reason to use NLBs is if performance is one of your utmost priorities and if every millisecond counts. Other reasons to choose an NLB are as follows:

- The ability to register targets using IP addresses, including a target that is outside of the VPC that contains the load balancer.
- Support for containerized applications.
- NLBs support directing requests to multiple applications that are deployed on the same EC2 instance. Each instance or IP address can be registered with the same target group by assigning different ports.
- Support for traffic with high variability and high volume (millions of requests per second) for inbound TCP requests.
- Support for static or elastic IP addresses. Elastic IPs enable you to keep using the same IP address even if a physical instance goes down.

It would not be surprising if CLBs are eventually phased out (as the name suggests). Expect AWS to drop this service in the future.

Summary

In this chapter, we reviewed some basic but powerful concepts about the cloud and why it is so popular. Mainly, the concepts of availability, reliability, and scalability. We also learned about three different types of architecture, each one offering different levels of availability. As expected, an architecture that offers higher availability is a more expensive solution that requires more resources.

We also explored the concepts of RPO and RTO, which are useful ideas to track and measure system availability. Additionally, we analyzed the differences between scaling up and scaling out. And finally, we went over some highly available services in AWS, including Amazon ELBs.

ELBs are especially useful when application traffic is highly variable. They enable you to treat your compute resources like a special computer that can expand and contract depending on demand.

In the next chapter, we will learn about the five pillars of a well-architected framework.

Section 4:
Hands-On Labs

In this section, we will go through a hands-on exercise based on a real-world scenario and we will reinforce the key knowledge we have learned.

This part of the book comprises the following chapter:

- *Chapter 14, Hands-On Labs and Use Cases*

14
Hands-On Lab and Use Case

In this chapter, we will put together many of the concepts that we learned about in previous chapters to build a practical, generic web UI serverless architecture. After reading this chapter, you should be able to use the concepts to build your own application using some or all of the components that we will review in this chapter.

For many of the services, you will be able to plug and play and pick and choose the services that will be used in the applications you develop. For example, your application may be more user-centric and may not require any asynchronous services. In this case, you can pull the asynchronous component out of your architecture. However, for some of the services, it is highly advisable that you make sure you include them in your architecture. For example, if your application is going to have a frontend, you will want to ensure that you have an authentication component so that every user is authenticated before using any of the other services in the application.

In this chapter, we will first review the list of available AWS programming languages and learn about the serverless AWS microservice architecture and setup services. We will then learn about frontend **user interfaces** (**UX**), learn to authenticate and manage users, look at the concepts involved in content delivery networks, and learn about the asynchronous communication service. Toward the end of the chapter, we will learn about file uploads and the AWS API Gateway.

To achieve this, we will cover the following topics:

- Reviewing the list of available AWS programming languages
- Understanding the serverless AWS microservice architecture
- Setting up services
- Learning about frontend user interfaces (UX)
- Authenticating, authorizing, and managing users
- Grasping **Caps for acronym introduction** (**CDN**) concepts
- Understanding the asynchronous communication service
- Learning about file uploads
- Covering the AWS API Gateway
- Reviewing business APIs
- Understanding state-machine services
- Exploring backend persistence service
- Learning about asynchronous activities

An introduction to the use cases

This chapter will allow you to combine and put into practice many of the concepts that we have covered throughout this book. For some of the components of this example, you may be able to use other AWS services. For example, in this case, we will choose AWS Lambda for our implementation, but as we saw in *Chapter 9, Serverless and Container Patterns*, AWS offers a few other services that can be used instead of or in conjunction with AWS Lambda.

Two reasons why AWS Lambda is popular are listed here:

- The ability to quickly and effortlessly scale in and scale out
- The pay-per-call pricing model; users only pay when calling a Lambda function

Keep in mind that in order to take full advantage of AWS Lambda, we should pair up our solution with other AWS solutions that offer similar flexibility when it comes to scalability.

Now that we have an overall high-level architecture, the next step is to decide which services to use to implement these components. AWS offers a wide variety of services and solutions, and there is some overlap across services, which means that it is not always clear which one is the best solution. Some of examples of such solutions are listed here:

- Should you use CloudFormation or the AWS Cloud Development Kit, or should you create the resources from the console?

- Should you use Amazon DynamoDB, or should you use Amazon DocumentDB?

- Should you use Postgres or MySQL?

- Should you use AWS Fargate or AWS Lambda?

This only highlights the potential choices that are going to be made using AWS *native* services. A decision must also be made as to whether the architecture will only use AWS services or whether we will use third-party tools, many of which are available in the AWS Marketplace. For example, consider the following:

- Should Amazon Redshift be used or should we go with Snowflake instead?

- For graphics and charts, should we use Amazon QuickSight or Tableau?

- Should we use Neptune or Neo4j?

There is a case to be made for all these alternatives. In this design, we will have certain preferences and make a definite choice, but make sure that you research all the services and tools available and try to align them with your particular use case. The right decision can often depend on the individual use case and your company culture and capabilities, and not just the features available.

For example, if your company has a long history of using Microsoft products, then using SQL Server instead of MySQL as the choice for your RDS instances may be the right decision if you have a big library of stored procedures that use a lot of SQL Server proprietary syntax. The alternative would be to translate and migrate all these stored procedures to MySQL stored procedures.

Since this is a book about AWS, in our sample microservice architecture, we are going to recommend using the AWS service option whenever possible. As discussed above, you should perform your own research and decide whether going with a third-party vendor makes more sense for any component in your implementation.

Before we lock down the services that we are going to use for our architecture, let's ask a critically important question. What language should we use for our application?

Reviewing the list of available AWS programming languages

As we design our microservice architecture, we need to decide which programming language to use for development. As we saw in *Chapter 9, Serverless and Container Patterns*, and *Chapter 10, Microservice and Event Driven Architectures*, microservices make it easy to use different languages for different microservices since they all communicate through the common RESTful protocol by passing JSON back and forth. As we also learned in these chapters, just because we can use different languages doesn't mean that we should have a mishmash of services, all written in different languages.

Let's spend some time exploring the advantages and disadvantages of the various options. First, AWS offers a version of the SDK in a limited number of languages, so unless you have a compelling reason to go with a different choice, you probably want to stick to one of the supported languages. The supported languages as of May 2020 are as follows:

- Java
- Python
- C++
- .NET
- JavaScript
- Node.js
- Ruby
- Go
- PHP

Next to religion and politics, there may not be a more controversial topic than which programming language to use for projects. Some folks in the software industry can be quite dogmatic when it comes to programming language selection. The truth of the matter is that languages are not static, as they continuously obtain new features and steal ideas from each other to make them better. The list of languages that AWS supports is no accident. They realize that these languages are popular with a segment of the development community, and that's why they made the cut to be supported. As other languages also gain support, don't be surprised if the list of supported languages continues to grow. For example, it would not be a big shock if AWS added support for Scala sometime soon. This makes choosing a language that much more difficult.

In this section, we will go over the characteristics, advantages, and disadvantages of these offerings, but the truth of the matter is that there is no best language for all situations, and the best language is going to be different for different organizations. The question that you will have to answer is *What is the best language for my organization or for my individual project?*

Interpretive versus compiled languages

The languages that we are going to cover fall into two broad classifications:

- Statically compiled and strongly typed languages
- Dynamic interpreted languages

Most older languages fall in the former camp. Compiled or *strongly typed* languages can provide syntax errors during the compilation process. This means that some errors can be caught sooner and potentially provide safer code. The drawback is that compiling code can take time and increases the development cycle. In general, older languages are compiled and newer languages tend to be interpreted. Some cases fall somewhere in between, such as Java. Java has a compiler that creates bytecode that is later interpreted by a **Java Virtual Machine (JVM)**.

The advantages afforded by compiled languages over interpreted languages have narrowed over the last few years. Today's interpreted languages can provide high-quality code and are commonly used for rapid prototyping. There does seem to be a shift toward using interpreted languages more and more for new development efforts.

An example of a compiled language is C++. An example of an interpreted language is Ruby.

Let's now delve a little deeper into the available choices, especially in the context of how they can be used to develop microservices.

Java

Java was created by *James Gosling* at *Sun Microsystems* in 1995, and since then it has become a popular choice for creating mission-critical enterprise applications. That is a lifetime in computer years. This long life has produced a robust pipeline of services and open source projects, starting with the Apache web server and the Tomcat application server. Another advantage of this long shelf life is the deep bench of experienced developers. Java received another boost by being the language of choice for the Android operating system.

One of the original design goals of Java was to give developers the ability to write their code once and be able to run it anywhere—*write once, run everywhere*. However, this goal has proved to be somewhat elusive, and while Java is supported in many platforms and devices, at the very least, it is highly recommended that you test the code in as many devices as possible to ensure that the code runs as expected across the devices.

One hiccup that the Java language encountered was when *Oracle* bought *Sun Microsystems*. This caused some friction among the Java community. As an example, and without picking sides, we have the example of the lawsuit *Google versus Oracle America*.

This court case is a pending copyright law legal battle between Google and Oracle. The disagreement revolves around the use of certain parts of the Java programming language's **Caps for acronym introduction (APIs)**. Google used some of them to initially develop the Android operating system. Java is now owned by Oracle. While Google admits to using the APIs and has since moved to using code that does not fall under dispute, it is still arguing that the original use of the APIs was well within fair use.

Without getting into too many details, one can argue that cases like this have stifled innovation in the language and have reduced adoption.

Right around the time of this lawsuit, other languages emerged that took advantage of the JVM architecture without using Java. The most popular example is **Scala**. Scala runs on a virtual machine.

Another drawback with Java is that running a JVM can be resource intensive, and depending on the application, it can require significant amounts of computer memory, especially compared with compiled languages.

Another disadvantage of Java is that it tends to be verbose and not as compact as other languages (Python comes to mind). But the support of an annotation syntax is a Java feature that enables the development of microservices. Annotations were not always supported in Java, but they are a welcome addition, and they do tend to make the code more compact.

Some libraries that you may want to consider using for the development of microservices in Java are as follows:

- **Spring Boot** – Spring Boot is a framework that leverages aspect-oriented programming concepts, as well as the **inversion of control (IoC)** paradigm.

- **Restlet** – Restlet is another package that enables the development of RESTful services.

- **Dropwizard** – Dropwizard is a popular development framework that can be used to assemble simple and lightweight microservices.

- **Service discovery solutions** – Such as Consul, Netflix Eureka, and Amalgam8.

- **Spark** – Spark may be the most popular open source project today and is often used to develop microservices as well.

- **Other options** – Such as Ninja Web Framework, Play Framework, RestExpress, and RESTX.

Python

Python has gained tremendous popularity in the last five years or so. Together with Java and JavaScript, Python is an open source interpreted language that has gained consistent mindshare among the development community. Python is a high-level programming language that provides a wide range of powerful libraries. It is also very popular among the data analyst, network engineer, and data scientist community.

Even though Python was first conceived in the late 1980s, it has only become popular in the last decade or so. It was created by *Guido van Rossum* at **Centrum Wiskunde & Informatica** (**CWI**) in the Netherlands. Its predecessor is the ABC language. The actual implementation started in 1989. Amazingly, *Van Rossum* was the lead developer and committer for Python until 2018.

As is the case with other languages, Python is not immune to the inconsistencies across operating systems. There are instances of libraries and drivers working properly in a Linux environment, but not working in Windows, for example. If you require your services to work across various operating systems, it is highly recommended that you test all the different configurations.

It should also be noted that Python has trouble scaling on multiple cores on a single machine. But it usually scales smoothly when using horizontal scaling across commodity servers.

Python is often used to build prototypes that can then be leveraged and enhanced to increase functionality.

Because of these benefits, Python is a good candidate for building robust microservices. Some of the Python libraries that are most commonly used to create microservices are as follows:

- **Flask** – Flask may be the most popular Python package to build microservices. Flasks enables the development of RESTful endpoints. It is based on *Jinja2* and *Werkzeug*.

- **Nameko** – Nameko creates a layer of abstraction for Python microservices enabling developers to focus more on application logic and less on the microservice plumbing.

- **Django** – Django is a Python framework used by many popular content sites, including Instagram, Pinterest, and EventBrite.

- **Falcom** – Falcom is used to generate proxies, APIs, and backend services.

- **Bottle** – Bottle is a lightweight WSGI microservices framework.

C++

C++ was invented by Bjarne Stroustrup in 1979. While doing his PhD thesis, Stroustrup was working with a language called **Simula**, which, as you can imagine, was mainly used for simulations. Simula 67, a flavor of Simula, was the first programming language to provide object-oriented programming. Stroustrup liked the benefits of object-oriented programming, but Simula was too slow to be practical.

Other people would have quit, but instead of doing so, Stroustrup took the ideas he liked from Simula and incorporated them into a new language. The new language kept the speed, compilation ability, and portability of C and combined it with the object-oriented paradigm of Simula.

In addition to all the features available in the C programming language, C++ also offered the following:

- Inlining

- Default function arguments

- Basic inheritance

- Strong type checking

C++ is a compiled object-oriented language. Because it's compiled, it can be highly optimized and can run faster in production environments than other interpreted languages. It is quite popular to this day for database applications, robotics, and IoT devices.

On the flip side, C++ is not that popular for web development projects. Some of the reasons that this might be the case are as follows:

- C++ requires the application developer to handle memory management.

- The language is seen as more complicated than Java or Python.

- Since it's compiled, it takes a little longer to get compilers, linters, and other code creation services set up.

Cross-platform microservices can be built using C++. Like other languages, these services can have a RESTful interface that allows them to interoperate with other services, even if those services use other languages. Some libraries that are often used in C++ to create microservices are as follows:

- **CppMicroServices** – CppMicroServices is an open source project to develop and manage modular microservices based on ideas from the OSGi Alliance. The OSGi Alliance is a global company consortium created to promote processes to create open specifications that facilitate the modular assembly of Java software. All the CppMicroServices code is available on GitHub. The code can be found at `https://github.com/CppMicroServices/CppMicroServices`.

- **POCO C++ libraries** – The POCO C++ libraries are popular with developers when building automation systems, IoT platforms, mission-critical systems, and enterprise applications. C++ shops have been using the POCO C++ libraries for over 15 years, and they have been installed in millions of platforms and devices.

.NET

ASP.NET and .NET Framework for application development are also a popular choice for web applications, as well as the creation of APIs and microservices. It goes without saying that this is a solid choice for companies that have made a strong commitment to Microsoft technologies, since .NET is a Microsoft product. With the advent and popularity of open source software, you must tread lightly before locking yourself to one vendor. However, every day many project managers take the plunge and commit to this technology. This says a lot about the capabilities and features of the software.

Just because it's a Microsoft technology does not mean that AWS is necessarily going to treat it as a less important technology when it comes to supporting it in its platform. Amazon realizes the importance of this technology, and provides a full feature set SDK to support it.

Microsoft began developing .NET Framework in the late 1990s. You can think of .NET as Microsoft's answer to Java, which started gaining popularity about this time. In the latter half of 2000, the first beta version of .NET was published.

In August 2000, Microsoft collaborated with its longtime partner Intel to standardize a core component of .NET called the **Caps for acronym introduction (CAI)**, as well as a new language called C#.

For many years up until this point, Microsoft held what some would call a monopolistic share of the operating system market, and therefore could dictate development standards. Around this time, Linux started to take off, especially for hosting web servers, and Microsoft had to pivot and adjust to an environment where they were no longer the only option.

Since then, Microsoft has tried to perform a delicate dance between open sourcing some of its software and keeping some of its software proprietary. For example, Microsoft has a patent for the CLI and C#, but these technologies have also been blessed by the organizational standards of the **European Computer Manufacturers Association (ECMA)** and **International Organization for Standardization (ISO)**. ECMA and ISO require that all patents essential to a standard supported by their standards are to be made available under "reasonable and non-discriminatory terms".

Microsoft agreed to these terms and has allowed access to these patented technologies without a license fee. However, other parts of .NET Framework are not covered by the ECMA-ISO standards, and therefore Microsoft reserves the right to charge for them and in some cases does charge a fee. Some examples of the technologies that do not conform to ECMA-ISO standards are Windows Forms, ADO.NET, and ASP.NET. Microsoft realizes that making code open source in the current environment is critical to boosting adoption, and the trend will be to make more and more parts of .NET Framework open source.

In addition, Microsoft for its part recognizes the importance of open source software, and it is constantly making sure that .NET and its related technologies interoperate seamlessly with these open source technologies.

.NET fully embraces the microservice architecture, which allows developers to use a swath of different technologies for each microservice. Committing to .NET for one part of your application does not necessarily mean that you have to commit to using .NET across the enterprise. .NET microservices can be intermingled with other applications written in Java, Node JS, Ruby, PHP, or any other language that supports microservices. Using this approach, a company can gradually start adapting .NET or migrate away from .NET.

Another important consideration is that even though .NET is a Microsoft technology, it doesn't just support Windows for development and deployment; other operating systems such as Linux and macOS are also supported. Similarly, AWS is not the only cloud provider that provides support for .NET; all leading cloud providers also provide support for this technology.

However, don't assume that porting .NET applications from Windows to Linux will always be seamless. As you can imagine, Microsoft does give a higher weight to the Windows platform. If you have a hybrid environment with both Linux and Windows servers, it might be best to use another development environment.

C# is the main programming language used by .NET developers. C# and other components of .NET are open source, but .NET is a proprietary ecosystem controlled solely by Microsoft.

.NET's CLI virtualized system functions as a language-independent platform, and so allows developers to code in a variety of languages. C# is the most common choice, but other alternatives include the following:

- VB.NET
- C++
- Python
- Ruby

Microsoft, as well as some third-party vendors, offer extensive documentation and a wide variety of tools to develop microservices in the .NET environment.

If your company has traditionally been using Microsoft technologies, then using .NET as one of your development environments may make sense. If you are starting a new project and you don't have a big investment in Windows servers and Microsoft mindshare, then other platforms may be a better choice to avoid licensing fees and vendor lock-in.

The **Convey** package is a popular set of helper libraries that are designed specifically to create microservices. They can (for the most part) be used independently to develop these microservices.

Convey is a set of extensions and a layer of abstraction that handles lower-level functionality commonly needed to create microservices, such as the following:

- Routing
- Service discovery
- Load balancing
- Tracing
- Asynchronous messaging

JavaScript

Depending on who you ask, **JavaScript** may be the most popular programming language today. It was born as a client-side scripting language, but it has moved over to the server as well, and many highly trafficked sites run using JavaScript as the server-side scripting language.

One place where we can check out the popularity of languages is the pervasive versioning site, GitHub. According to GitHub, JavaScript has consistently been the most popular language since at least 2014.

Here are the most recent available statistics (as of the first quarter of 2020). As you can see, JavaScript (**18.703%** share) has a slight edge over Python (**16.238%** share) and a bigger lead over Java (**10.938%** share):

Year	Quarter
2020 ▼	1 ▼

# Ranking	Programming Language	Percentage (Change)	Trend
1	JavaScript	18.703% (-1.466%)	
2	Python	16.238% (-1.654%)	
3	Java	10.938% (+0.538%)	
4	Go	9.005% (+0.978%)	
5	C++	7.423% (+0.040%)	
6	Ruby	6.812% (+0.342%)	
7	TypeScript	6.769% (+1.522%)	∧
8	PHP	5.127% (-0.468%)	∨
9	C#	3.835% (+0.141%)	
10	C	3.181% (-0.203%)	
11	Scala	1.947% (+0.468%)	∧

Figure 14.1 – Pull requests on GitHub by language. Source: Github.com

With this popularity in development comes a large development community, which translates into many available packages and libraries, as well as a huge user base of available talent.

One of the most popular JavaScript libraries for microservice development is **Feathers**. Feathers is a lightweight JavaScript framework specifically designed for the creation of REST APIs.

If your staff has JavaScript expertise, perhaps obtained by creating a lot of frontend web development, you may be better off leveraging the power of Node.js and not trying to write in native JavaScript.

Node.js

Node.js is a JavaScript runtime environment that supports asynchronous event-driven programming. It is used more and more every day to build massively scalable applications.

The popularity of JavaScript for client-side scripting is indisputable. However, even though other server-side solutions that used JavaScript for server-side development existed before Node.js, Node.js solidified JavaScript as a valid alternative language to use for server-side development.

Some examples of companies that heavily rely on Node.js for their development are as follows:

- Netflix
- LinkedIn
- Trello
- Uber
- PayPal
- Medium
- eBay
- NASA

Node.js is not really a language but a development environment. The language used by Node.js is JavaScript.

Given its popularity and its maturity, it is hard to believe that the development for Node.js only started in 2009. It was initially created by Ryan Dahl. One of its predecessors was a product by Netscape called LiveWire Pro Web, which was one of the first server-side JavaScript application servers.

Dahl identified that one of the most popular environments at the time had difficulty in handling many concurrent connections (when you got around the 10,000-connection range) and the solutions to mitigate this problem were lacking.

Dahl demonstrated one of the first versions of Node.js at the inaugural European JSConf in November 2009. The first version of Node.js leveraged the Google V8 JavaScript engine.

As adoption started to take hold, a package manager was released in January 2010, dubbed npm. The package manager facilitated the deployment and publication of Node.js. npm vastly simplified the installation and maintenance of Node.js libraries and packages.

Initially, Node.js only supported Linux and macOS X, but in June 2011, Microsoft and Joyent released a native Windows-complaint version, which only added to the popularity of the environment.

Despite its relative *new kid on the block* status, Node.js has become an extremely popular platform in the past few years for enterprises and startups, both for web development and for the creation of microservices.

Node.js is a good choice for the development of your microservices, especially if you have access to a stable of solid Node.js developers. It offers a good combination of speed, performance, and productivity, which makes it a solid alternative.

Because Node.js is a newer technology, finding people with a strong Node.js background might be a difficult task. However, a lot of developers exist that have client-side experience with JavaScript, and the learning curve to convert these folks to proficient Node.js developers will be less steep than trying to train someone who doesn't have the JavaScript background.

Let's look at an analogy to help you gain a better understanding about JavaScript, if you have a background in Java.

Java has a **Java Runtime Environment** (**JRE**), which provides an environment to run (but not compile) Java code. Another important component in Java is the **Java Virtual Machine** (**JVM**). A JVM enables a computer to run Java programs.

Conversely, with JavaScript, Node.js is analogous to the JRE and the JSVM (V8 engine) is analogous to the JVM.

Some of the most common libraries used to create Node.js microservices are as follows:

- **Seneca** – Seneca is sponsored by Voxgig, and currently, its lead maintainer is Richard Rodger. Seneca is a powerful set of tools to create microservices and to organize the business logic of your application.

- **ClaudiaJS** – ClaudiaJS is a development toolkit that specializes in helping you to convert existing Node.js routines into AWS Lambda services. It has an active GitHub community.

- **Restify** – As the name implies, Restify is a service framework with the goal of enabling the creation of RESTful production-quality scalable web services.

- **Sails** – Sails was developed by Mike McNeil and released in 2012. Sails is one of the most popular MVS frameworks for Node.js and can therefore be used for more than just the creation of microservices. Full-fledged UI-enabled applications can be created with Sails.

Ruby

Ruby is an open source programming interpreted language. It has a heavy focus on simplicity and productivity. It has a heavy emphasis on configuration rather than focusing on procedural programming. Once you master the language, it is easy to create powerful and feature-rich applications, including microservices, but there is a learning curve to achieve this mastery level. When writing Ruby, many of the features for a program may be implicit. This can result in compact code that can be quickly written, but it can be difficult for a newbie to understand.

There is quite a bit of online support for this language on the web, and it has an active and passionate community. Because it's so popular, there are many great libraries and packages to enable the creation of microservices.

Ruby's libraries are called Ruby gems, or gems for short. Like other languages, Ruby has its own idioms and lexicon. Ruby can also be integrated with Docker, Puppet, Chef, and other DevOps tools. Some of the companies that have made a sizable commitment to Ruby are shown in the following list:

- Airbnb
- Crunchbase
- Soundcloud
- Fiverr
- Zendesk
- Yellow Pages
- Slideshare
- GitHub
- Groupon

One justified concern that is often heard is that the Ruby language does not scale up well when it's deployed at a massive scale. A commonly cited example is the case of Twitter. Twitter made the decision to migrate from Ruby to Scala in 2010. Its Ruby-enabled backend at that point was having trouble handling Twitter's exponential growth. Ruby is open source, and an argument against using open source software is that you don't have a vendor's neck that you can wring in order to get support. Some "for profit" organizations often fill this void by charging for support for open source tools. The most famous example of this type of company is perhaps RedHat, which was recently acquired by IBM.

Another mark against Ruby is that it is relatively easy to get started with it, but it becomes harder and harder to maintain as the number of lines of code increases.

A good place to start to see what libraries are available to develop microservices in Ruby is the Awesome Ruby collection, which can be found at `https://awesome-ruby.com/`.

Go

The **Go** language is a cross-platform, compiled programming language. Go also offers language-level support for concurrency. From its inception, Go has been open source. Like the C programming language, Go also provides memory management, garbage collection, and structural typing. You may also see the name Golang used (because its domain name is golang.org), but the correct name is Go.

Go is a fairly new language. It was created in 2007 by a team at Google led by Robert Greisemer, Rob Pike, and Ken Thompson. It was first publicly announced in November 2009, and was first released in March 2012. As you can imagine, one of the main users and proponents of the Go language is Google.

Other companies that have taken a liking to the Go language are listed here:

- Facebook
- Twitter
- Netflix
- Soundcloud

One of the main drivers for the creators of Go was their shared hatred of the C++ syntax. I can't say I necessarily blame them; C++ syntax can be tricky and nonintuitive. Go has a clean and simple structure and syntax. It does not support type inheritance and it relies heavily on functions. It is easy to get up and running with Go. Like C, C++, and Java, Go has an efficient concurrency model.

Some of the disadvantages of Go are as follows:

- Less flexibility than an interpreted language.

- Because it's fairly new, there are not as many third-party libraries as there are with other, more mature languages, but that is probably going to change over time.

- It currently doesn't and may never support generics. Generics can result in more compact and flexible implementations. Like any language that makes tradeoffs, the developers decided to choose simplicity instead of supporting generics.

The Go language continues to gain mindshare. It is not as pervasive as Python, Java, and others, but it continues to gain adherents quickly every day.

Some of the commonly used Go libraries that are used to create microservices are as follows:

- **Go kit** – Go kit is an elegant programming toolkit that is used to create microservices using the Go language. It provides a framework that provides much of the necessary underlying plumbing and allows the users of the toolkit to focus on delivering business value.

- **Go Micro** – Go Micro is quite a popular library for the development of Go microservices. There are many online examples and tutorials showing how to use it, and it has an active user community. Out of the box, Go Micro offers load balancing, service discovery, and synchronous and asynchronous communication, as well as message encoding. There are other third-party developers that offer plugins for the framework that can integrate seamlessly with the tool.

- **Gizmo** – Gizmo is another microservice toolkit surprisingly first created by the New York Times. It's surprising because nontechnology companies are not well known for creating frameworks. Gizmo relies heavily on a pub/sub model.

- **Kite** – Kite is another Go toolkit that is used to develop microservices. It provides both RPC client packages and server-side packages. The service discovery service for Kite is called Kontrol. Kontrol is also a Kite service. If you don't use the Kontrol service discovery service, you may find it difficult to integrate with other service discovery services.

PHP

Almost as soon as the web finally took hold in the 1990s and the HTML language started to be used to develop static web pages, another language used for dynamic content started gaining in popularity. That language was **PHP**.

The initial version of the PHP language was created by Rasmus Lerdorf in 1994.

PHP was built from the C language by Lerdorf to replace snippets of Perl code in his personal website to track visitors. In 1995, he released the first formal and public version of the language. Interesting tidbit, back then it wasn't called PHP; the name used was Personal Homepage Tools. At that point, it was still more a set of tools than a language.

In 1997, Andi Gutmans and Zeev Suraski in Israel performed major surgery on the language to enable PHP to be used for e-commerce. This version was dubbed PHP 3.0, and it is much closer to the language we have today.

In 2000, Gutmans and Suraski released version 4.0 of the language. The same duo later created version 4.0. And in 2004, another major version was released—PHP 5.0. Today, even though PHP is considered a legacy language by many, it is still used to power millions of websites.

Unless you use a compiled version of PHP (such as Hack), you will probably have a hard time scaling a production-level workload at a massive scale.

Because, in internet years, PHP is an ancient language, and because of the different versions of PHP that exist, the quality of PHP code can vary greatly. PHP's syntax is pretty forgiving, especially when compared to compiled languages or languages with strict standards, such as Python. For this reason, it is not difficult to create code quickly, which can be great at the beginning but makes the maintenance of the code difficult. PHP now supports object-oriented programming, but the initial versions didn't. Much of the code out there is legacy code that did not leverage this feature, so this only increases the complexity in maintaining the code.

Some of the early and heavy adopters of PHP reads like a *who's who* of technology, as you can see from the following list:

- Facebook
- WordPress
- Twitpic
- Flickr
- Imgur

Of note is the fact that, to this date, Facebook relies on PHP for some of its development. But much of its code is also now written in C++. In order to make PHP more performant, Facebook created a PHP compiler to turn the code into native code. The version of PHP that Facebook uses is called *Hack*.

Swagger

A special mention goes to **Swagger**. Swagger is not a language, but it can be an essential tool to create microservices regardless of what language you decide to use. When you write a book, it is advisable to first write an outline and then fill in the blanks of the outline with the content of the book. Swagger can be used to write the *outline* of your microservice design and implementation. Swagger standardizes the process of API design for microservices and any other API service. You can create your service API with Swagger and Swagger will produce stubs for your documentation and stubs for your APIs. Using Swagger ensures that you have a consistent model and standards across your design, regardless of the individual styles of your team members.

Deciding which is the best language

As we noted at the beginning of the chapter, some friendships have been lost during arguments about what language is best. A better question to ask is what language is best for you, for your project, and your company. As a general rule of thumb, if you have a greenfield project where you have a wide berth about what language to pick, it may be best to go with one of the newer languages, and it also makes sense to pick a language that is popular.

This choice is not always simple and clear cut. A language's popularity is not static. As an example, Perl was one of the most popular languages in the 1990s, but its popularity has severely waned. So it's not enough to consider the popularity of a language, but also how fast it's growing or fading away.

If a language is popular, you will have an easier time finding resources to staff your project. Some other considerations to keep in mind are shown in the following list:

- **Compiled versus interpreted** – If you don't expect your project to become the next Airbnb and you know that the number of users or the workload will be capped, you might be better off using an interpreted language rather than a compiled language. Interpreted languages allow you to quickly prototype and ramp up your application. Being able to fail fast is key in order to eventually succeed fast. Fast development cycles allow us to test our ideas quickly and discard the ones that don't perform as expected. Normally, the development life cycle is quicker with an interpreted language because the code doesn't need to be compiled every time there is a code change. If your application has strict security requirements, a compiled language may also be a better choice.

- **Problem domain** – If you have a small project and you are not working in the context of a company, the better choice may hinge on what other people have already done. You may be a highly experienced Java developer, but perhaps someone already solved 90% of the requirements that you are trying to cover. In this case, you may be better off teaching yourself a little Python and save yourself a ton of work in the process.

- **Staff availability** – After doing your research, you may conclude that Ruby is the best language ever and that it has everything you need. But if you expect the application to require a sizable team to take it to completion and Ruby developers are in short supply (and therefore command high rates), it may be best to settle for second best and not be a language purist.

Regardless of your language selection, if you design your application properly and leverage the advantages of a microservice architecture, you will be well on your way to a successful implementation. The combination of a microservice architecture with a serverless deployment in AWS or a similar environment has been the recipe for many recent hits, some of them so successful that billion-dollar companies have been created around these products and services.

Now that we have reviewed the language choices available in AWS and hopefully decided on a language to use for our application, it is now time to start putting some components together using the microservice architecture we learned about in *Chapter 10*, *Microservices and Event-Driven Architectures*.

Understanding the serverless AWS microservice architecture

Now that we have thoroughly covered the different languages that can be used to implement our microservice architecture and the pros and cons for each, let's analyze how we can implement a microservice architecture in AWS that fully takes advantage of the many serverless services offered by AWS. We will keep the design high level and will not prescribe a specific language for the implementation. You should be able to transfer the concepts covered and use this design in your project regardless of the programming language that you or your firm favors.

Let's start looking at the design for our serverless microservice application. First, we'll present the high-level architecture and afterward, we'll analyze each individual component or *domain* independently in detail:

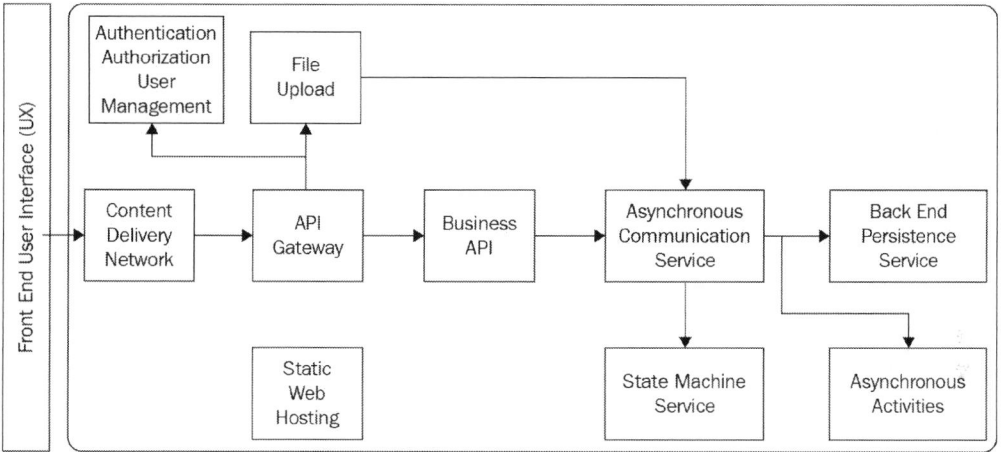

Figure 14.2 – Serverless web-application architecture

As you can see, the architecture provides services for static web hosting, business services, an asynchronous service, a state-machine service, and file uploads, among other components. In the next sections, we will go into detail about each one of these components.

In the preceding figure, each block represents clearly delimited domains and technical functionality that can be found in many serverless implementations. Depending on the methodology used and whether we decide to use a microservice architecture, each one of these boxes will represent one or more microservices. For example, the business API should probably be broken down into a series of microservices and not just one; you might have a microservice to handle *accounts* and another microservices to manage *companies*.

Setting up services

The first thing we must do in order to start creating our application is to set up the necessary services. Since we decided that we are going to go all-in with AWS services, all these services can be set up through the AWS Console. However, this is not the only way that services can be set up. There are a variety of ways to start up the services and they each have distinct advantages and disadvantages. Depending on your requirements, one method will be better than another. First, let's list out some of the available methods (we won't focus on non-AWS methods, such as Chef, Puppet, Ansible, and others).

AWS Command Line Interface

Any action that you can perform via the AWS Console can be performed via the **Command Line Interface** (**CLI**) as well.

If you are testing the configuration of resources or creating a **proof of concept** (**POC**), you might be better off creating your resources via the AWS Console, especially if you are not that familiar with the CLI. The AWS Console is somewhat more intuitive; however, as you start getting more familiar with the CLI, you will probably find yourself using the CLI more and more and creating scripts for common tasks, such as spinning up an EC2 instance.

AWS CloudFormation

CloudFormation is a popular AWS service to provision infrastructure. CloudFormation is a declarative language that specifies which resources will be created. You can use the console to execute the same action, but using the console implies the use of manual intervention with the possibility of human error.

AWS CloudFormation enables users to model infrastructure and application resources with code. All the instructions to set up the resources can be specified in a YAML or JSON file. The AWS CloudFormation Registry and CLI simplify the process of managing non-AWS resources. CloudFormation can also be thought of as a single source of truth for all system resources and enables the standardization of infrastructure components. This reduces the time it takes to troubleshoot problems and increases compliance with company security policies.

With CloudFormation, once you test your script and successfully deploy all the resources in one environment, you can reuse the script to deploy the same resources in another environment with the assurance that the resources will be deployed in an identical manner.

In fact, all the tools listed in this section allow consistent repeatability of resource provisioning.

AWS Cloud Development Kit

CloudFormation was one of the first ways that AWS offered to define **infrastructure as code** (**IaC**). To be fully honest, it can be painful developing CloudFormation scripts. They can be verbose and difficult to read and maintain. Fortunately, there is a new service that provides a layer on top of CloudFormation that makes it easier to define infrastructure with code.

The AWS **Cloud Development Kit** (**CDK**) service allows you to define infrastructure without having to learn a new templating language.

AWS CDK was released in 2019. AWS CDK is a framework that enables the definition of cloud infrastructure using your favorite programming language and the provisioning of this infrastructure through AWS CloudFormation.

Users of the service can use the following supported languages:

- TypeScript
- JavaScript
- Python
- Java
- C#/.NET

AWS CloudFormation was the original offering from AWS to create IaC. While it has been used successfully for many years now, it has some disadvantages. It can be cumbersome to use, it is difficult to modularize it, and its lack of abstraction constructs can result in verbose scripts.

The AWS CDK can overcome these disadvantages. The AWS CDK supports the languages that are listed previously. Developers can use their favorite language to develop scripts instead of the CloudFormation JSON and YAML templating language.

Both CloudFormation and CDK can be used to spin up and tear down most of the AWS infrastructure services. Some examples are shown in the following list:

- S3 buckets, folders, and files
- EC2 instances
- VPC configurations

- Relational database service instances
- Route 53 configurations
- API endpoints

However, YAML and JSON files are declarative and can be hard to read, especially if you are not familiar with them. For complex installations that require a high degree of infrastructure integrations, it can become quite verbose and difficult to work with these files. CloudFormation templates do not support a high level of abstraction, and so reusability and modularization are not easy when working with CloudFormation.

The AWS Console is a simple way to create and configure AWS resources, but every time a resource is configured, it involves manual intervention. It cannot be automated, which opens the possibility of creating resources in an inconsistent manner. CloudFormation and the AWS CDK close this gap and enable the automation of this process.

Let's go deeper into the components that support the AWS CDK. All basic components in the AWS CDK are known as **constructs**. Constructs can be used to represent a range of architectures, from a single EC2 instance to a complex system to be deployed across multiple AWS regions. A construct can contain other constructs that can be leveraged to achieve modularization.

The AWS CDK has an AWS construct library, with a variety of simple and advanced constructs. The simple constructs, known as CFN resources, can facilitate the provisioning of resources. A second level of constructs can support common procedures—standard code used by CFN resources. Finally, users of the AWS CDK can leverage advanced constructs, called *patterns*, to perform infrastructure deployments consisting of a combination of AWS services.

In the following figure, you can find an example of a popular pattern provided by the AWS CDK. This particular pattern can be useful when creating web applications that require a persistence layer:

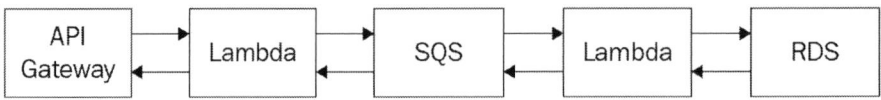

Figure 14.3 – AWS CDK pattern example

The AWS CDK is ideally suited to create and combine multiple services that require integration. Advanced constructs allow users to create resources easily. The AWS CDK supports the use of default values that will be used for unspecified parameters. In addition to advanced constructs, AWS CDK also offers type checking, autocompletion, and advanced tooling, including a command-line interface.

Since AWS CDK increases the number of resources that developers can provision through code, it can be a better alternative to CloudFormation and Hashicorp TerraForm. In short, AWS CDK simplifies the creation, verification, and testing process of resource provisioning, which will result in a more secure and consistent infrastructure.

AWS CodeDeploy

AWS CodeDeploy is a code deployment service that is fully managed by AWS to automate code deployment to a range of services and locations, such as the following:

- Amazon EC2
- AWS Lambda
- AWS Fargate
- On-premises servers

It facilitates the rapid deployment of features and is well suited for prototyping. By using CodeDeploy, downtime can be minimized because deployments are quicker, simpler, and more consistent.

As with CloudFormation, using CodeDeploy minimizes or completely eliminates erroneous code deployments because manual operations are eliminated, and provisioning 1,000 servers is just as easy as provisioning only one.

AWS Config

Occasionally, a video pops up on YouTube with a dash cam footage of either a hilarious fall or a fatally serious accident. If the dash cam had not been present, it would be up to witness testimony to ascertain what transpired. And humans are notoriously bad and forgetful witnesses.

Similarly, if we make any changes to AWS through the AWS Console, it would not be unlikely that if we try to remember what the changes are, we will miss some things. That's where AWS Config can help. AWS Config records and monitors every change to the AWS environment regardless of who and how the change was made. It doesn't matter if we created an EC2 instance from the console, via CloudFormation, or using the CLI, AWS Config will record it and it can later be audited. We can then easily find out when the change was made, who made it, and whose neck we need to wring.

AWS Config continuously tracks and saves changes to the AWS resource configurations and enables users to automate and test changes to configurations against a desired configuration.

AWS Elastic Beanstalk

Sometimes, a simple solution is the best solution. Sometimes, you need more control, and the solution becomes more complicated, but necessarily so. In mathematics, engineering, and software development, the definition of an elegant solution is a solution that solves a problem in the simplest and most effective manner while yielding the correct answer or providing the required functionality.

Elastic Beanstalk is one of those simple solutions that may be able to solve many of today's use cases.

Elastic Beanstalk leverages Auto Scaling and the Elastic Load Balancing service to scale and balance workloads. It also takes advantage of the Amazon CloudWatch service to determine when it should scale up or scale down. You can set customized CloudWatch alerts that will be used to add capacity when a certain metric is reached. For example, a rule can be set to add EC2 instances when the average memory utilization exceeds 80% for more than five minutes. This simple amalgamation of services creates a powerful combination that can solve many problems.

AWS Elastic Beanstalk also provides a secure development environment. It transparently runs workloads on an independent VPC separated from other resources. HTTPS endpoints can be enabled to provide access and use of this service can be easily restricted to authorized users only, leveraging the IAM service. Additionally, a **demilitarized zone** (**DMZ**) can be created using Amazon VPC to create a private subnet to provide additional security.

AWS Service Catalog

Do you remember how you felt the first time you logged into the AWS Console? If your experience was anything like mine, you were probably overwhelmed. As of 2020, AWS offers 212 services, and the number keeps on growing. Could you imagine if companies gave every one of their clients' team members unfettered access to the console? Developers and admins need access to AWS to create services that enable them to perform their job, but giving them unlimited access may result in a hefty monthly bill.

AWS Service Catalog goes a long way toward solving this problem. The AWS Service Catalog enables you to restrict the services that a user can launch and even the type of service. For example, you can use it to specify that users can only launch EC2 instances that are *small T2* instances. Go back to the section *EC2 instance types* in *Chapter 6*, *Amazon Athena – Combining the Simplicity of Files with the Power of SQL*, if you want to refresh your memory on EC2 instance types.

AWS Service Catalog enables IT admins to define and manage a menu of IT services that users can create and use in AWS. The menu can specify which machine images can be created, which services to show, and more. AWS Service Catalog simplifies and centralizes the management of commonly deployed resources, and aids in the implementation of consistent governance policies that help you meet compliance requirements while allowing developers, analysts, and other users to perform their job.

Now that we have covered how to set up the core services, let's move on and learn about the frontend development of our architecture.

Learning about frontend user interfaces (UX)

Now that we have analyzed the languages that we can use for our microservice and we understand the environments that we can use to deploy our service, let's delve further into the architecture.

Let's start by looking at a critical component of the architecture—the frontend user interface. It is possible to create a microservice that does not have a frontend. The reason to do this would be if our application is not meant to be used by humans—in other words, all our service clients are other computing services. However, many microservices will need some form of frontend, even if it's only for some parts of the service.

Since smartphones and tablets took hold some time ago (let's say in 2007, with the release of the iPhone), it is no longer enough to create your frontend so that it focuses on desktop development. There are all kinds of form factors that need to be considered—from a small phone to a big-screen TV.

In this section, we focus on browser-based UIs. For quite a while, most browser-based development was done using native JavaScript. Later, jQuery became a popular library written on top of JavaScript. For the last few years, three other libraries have dominated the browser development market. They are listed as follows:

- React
- Angular
- Vue

Let's look at some statistics to see the popularity of these frameworks. Popularity is not everything, but it is an indicator of adoption. Here are the number of downloads from GitHub for these frameworks as of 2020:

- **React** – Downloads: around 7,000,000; Stars: around 150,000; Forks: around 29,000
- **Angular** – Downloads: around 1,000,000; Stars: around 165,000; Forks: around 25,000
- **Vue** – Downloads: around 1,000,000; Stars: around 61,000; Forks: around 16,000

As you can see, React also dominates by a wide margin, with the greatest number of downloads, stars, forks, and comments.

A huge percentage of today's most popular websites are **single-page applications (SPA)**. The three web UI technologies we presented in this section are SPAs. SPAs are feature-rich dynamic web applications that are assembled into a package of static files that will need to be downloaded the first time a web user hits the access URL, which but will be cached during subsequent visits. When using AWS to host SPAs, the files are hosted on an S3 bucket and can then be served using the **CDN** service CloudFront.

A more recent trend that is picking up some steam is **server(less)-side rendering (SSR)** technologies such as Next.js. To configure an SSR application, `Lambda@Edge` can be used within CloudFront. Using this service can enable server-side rendering, leveraging AWS Lambda functions that will be deployed as close as possible to the final end user.

In the same way that CloudFront enables the deployment of static files close to the end user, `Lambda@Edge` allows you to deploy AWS Lambda functions close to all your website visitors, greatly enhancing the performance of your site and reducing latency.

Unless your application is extremely simple, you will not want users to visit your application without making sure that they are authorized to use the application and authenticate their identity.

In the next section, we will learn best practices in AWS for user authentication and authorization.

Authenticating, authorizing, and managing users

Unless you are making the most basic microservice, the service you create will need to have a security wrapper around it to ensure that only authorized users can access it. Before we can determine whether a user is authorized to access a resource, we need to authenticate the user (make sure that they are who they say they are) – or, in other words:

- Authentication verifies credentials.

- Authorization verifies permissions.

As you can imagine, AWS has offerings to cover these requirements, many of which have been around since AWS first launched. Let's briefly review them.

AWS Identity and Access Management

AWS offers many varied services. One thing that they have in common is that they can all be managed and controlled to determine who can access them via the **Identity and Access Management (IAM)** service.

Like many other security frameworks and services, it establishes a series of components to enable security, which we will look at now.

Users

A user can be a process or an actual human user, and they can access AWS services through a variety of ways, including the AWS Console, AWS CLI, AWS SDKs, and application APIs.

Groups

A user can be assigned to one or more groups. Doing so simplifies security management so that permissions don't have to be assigned individually to each user.

As an example, an administrator group can be created and assigned permission that would typically be given to an administrator, such as creating EC2 instances, databases, and so on. If a user is assigned to the administrator group, they will have all the permissions allocated to that group. If a new employee joins your firm and is hired as a system administrator, they could just be assigned to the group and they would get all the permissions. Similarly, if the same person ever leaves the company, you can remove their access by simply removing them from the group.

Permissions

Permissions in AWS are used to allow access to certain resources and services. They can be extremely granular. Permissions can be given to an entity that can be either a user, a group, or a role. When you log in with the root account, by default, it has full access to all AWS services, including the ability to create other users. When another non-root user is created, by default, they do not have access to anything, and permissions need to be granted explicitly.

To assign permissions to entities, a policy can be attached to determine the type of access, the actions that such an entity can perform, and which resources those actions can be performed on. Policies are extremely flexible. For example, a conditional statement can be specified in a policy that gives the conditions under which a certain permission can be achieved. As an example, you can specify a condition that gives permission to a user to only spin up T2 micro instances and no other instance type.

Roles

IAM roles enable the delegation of access for users or services to AWS resources. A user or a service can assume a role to get temporary security credentials that can then in turn be used to access a resource or make an API call. By doing this, it is not necessary to share long-term credentials, such as a user password, and we don't need to assign permissions for each individual user.

The following are use cases that can be resolved by using roles.

Granting applications access to other AWS resources

If an application is deployed on an Amazon EC2 instance and it needs access to other AWS services, one solution may be to store the necessary credentials on each EC2 instance. However, as you can imagine, this can be a nightmare to manage and creates opportunities for hackers to get access to these resources if they get access to the EC2 instances. Using roles, eliminates the need to store the credentials in each individual EC2 instance, and instead, the EC2 instance can assume a role that is assigned to it without storing the credentials.

Cross-account access

It is a common scenario to want to restrict access to various resources. Here's a quick example. Say that you have 10 EC2 instances: 5 belong to the development environment and the other 5 are production instances. Obviously, we want to restrict access to these two types of EC2 instance and we want to simplify the management. One way to manage this is to create the development machines using one AWS account and the production machines using another AWS account. However, there may be some instances where access from one account is needed by the other account. For example, a user in DEV might need access to the PROD environment to push an update from the DEV environment to PROD. One way to solve this is to give the user access to both accounts, but this can get complicated quickly so an alternative that can also simplify management is to grant that user cross-account access by assigning them the appropriate IAM role granting this access.

Granting permissions to AWS services

Before an AWS service can execute operations, permissions must be granted for it to perform these actions. IAM roles can be used to grant these permissions so that AWS services can call other AWS services.

Policies

A **policy** in AWS is a document that specifies at a granular level the permissions that a user, group, role, or resource will have. For the policy to take effect, it needs to be attached to the entity that is using it. As is the case with many other AWS functions, a policy can be created via the AWS Console, AWS CLI, or the AWS API. Let's look at the definitions of some basic concepts regarding policies.

Customer-managed policies

A **customer-managed policy** is a standalone policy that is created without having to associate it directly with an identity right away. Later, it can be associated with groups, users, or roles.

AWS-managed policies

An **AWS-managed policy** is a type of standalone policy maintained by AWS. Standalone policies have a unique **Amazon Resource Name** (**ARN**).

Inline policies

An **inline policy** is a type of policy that has been embedded into a group, user, or role. This creates a coupling with that identity.

Policy types can also be classified based on the type of entity that they are associated with:

Identity-based policies

Identity-based policies allow you to associate managed and inline policies with IAM groups, users, or roles. Identity-based policies give permissions to an identity.

Resource-based policies

Resource-based policies allow you to associate inline policies with resources. An example of a resource-based policy is an Amazon S3 bucket policy. Resource-based policies give permissions to a principal. The principal is something that is spelled out in the policy.

It is recommended that you use customer-managed policies and not inline policies whenever possible. Customer-managed policies are easier and cleaner to maintain.

It's also recommended that you leverage customer-managed policies and not use AWS-managed policies whenever possible. AWS-managed policies normally give administrator or read-only permissions. Customer-managed policies, as you can imagine, provide greater control and granularity as to exactly which users can perform which actions on what resources. To achieve a higher degree of security, always grant the least privilege. Least privilege only gives the necessary permissions to perform a specific task and no more.

So now that we have understood how we can control access to users and secure AWS services and resources, let's continue learning about other critical components of our sample architecture.

Grasping CDN concepts

Having a **CDN** is another commonly used component with microservices. However, we covered CDNs, Amazon CloudFront, and other AWS storage services in *Chapter 8*, *Best Practices for Application Security, Identity, and Compliance*, so we recommend that you refer to that chapter to learn more about the options available.

Understanding the asynchronous communication service

An essential component to a microservice architecture is the ability of the components to communicate asynchronously. Some of the components are going to produce data that then needs to be consumed by other components.

Having a centralized area where the communication can take place might be the single most important decision to keep the architecture simple. If we allow services to communicate among each other, the combinatorial explosion of those connections and the complexity that will result from it will soon bury us and doom the project. The following figure illustrates how many more connections are needed if we don't have a centralized communication mechanism:

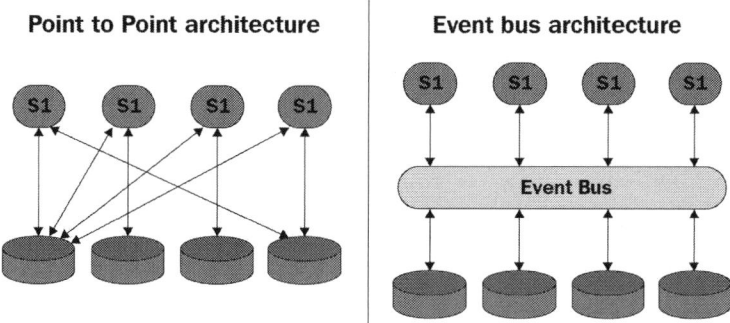

Figure 14.4 – Point-to-point architecture versus event bus architecture

On the left of the figure where the point-to-point architecture is illustrated, there are many more connections that need to be made if an event bus is not used. And many connections are still missing in the point-to-point architecture. However, as we can see in the image on the right-hand side, every component is connected via the event bus, and they require much fewer connections.

Now that we have learned about these two important architectures, let's learn how we can implement an application event bus using AWS services.

Amazon EventBridge

It is difficult to overestimate the importance of **Amazon EventBridge**. It can be argued that Amazon EventBridge was one of the most important service announcements since AWS Lambda. An application event bus is a critical component of a microservice architecture, and Amazon EventBridge provides a powerful yet simple implementation of an application event bus.

Amazon EventBridge is a fully managed, serverless event bus service that facilitates the connection of applications through a common touchpoint. The data from the producer services is placed on the bus so that consuming services can read and process it. EventBridge can be run on a real-time basis with other AWS services, as well as third-party vendor applications and tools. Routing rules can be intuitively set up to filter out which services receive which messages.

A precursor to Amazon EventBridge is Amazon CloudWatch Events. CloudWatch Events was introduced in 2016.

In some ways, EventBridge is a rule-driven event router. It enables the definition of event patterns. These patterns can be routed based on the content of the event to determine which subscribers or targets receive the generated events from the event bus. An event target can be a variety of services, such as the following:

- An AWS Lambda function

- An Amazon Kinesis stream

- An Amazon SQS queue

- Another event bus in a different AWS account

The wide variety of targets makes EventBridge a powerful service to create multiservice, multidepartmental decoupled communications.

EventBridge simplifies the creation of event-driven applications by handling these tasks:

- Event ingestion

- Event delivery

- Message security

- User authorization and authentication (via IAM)

- Error handling

In a point-to-point architecture, it is not uncommon to have different formats for different endpoints. This problem is easily avoided when using Amazon EventBridge. It provides a schema registry that can store schemas in a shared centralized location with a standard naming convention, making it much easier to use and maintain. These schemas can be mapped to Python, Java, and JavaScript. Users can interface with the registry via the AWS Management Console, AWS CLI, and a variety of SDKs available for quite a few languages, such as Java, Ruby, and Python.

EventBridge events and event patterns

Out of the box, EventBridge provides two types of events, which we will look at now.

Scheduled events

A **scheduled event** can be triggered at regular intervals using a rate. A rate is a number given in a unit of time. The event will be repeated every X units of time. The valid units of time for a rated event are as follows:

- Minutes
- Hours
- Days

Another way to trigger scheduled events is to use *cron* type expressions. Cron expressions have been around for a long time, ever since the Unix operating system. Cron expressions are much more flexible than using the rate option.

Pattern event

Pattern events provide a flexible way to generate events from different actions and have them occur in AWS services. Some examples of AWS actions that generate a pattern event are as follows:

- A file being placed in an AWS bucket
- An Amazon EC2 instance starting
- A record being added to a table

Filters can be used to ensure that only a subset of the events triggers an action. Some examples of filtered events are as follows:

- A file with a size greater than 10 MB is placed in the bucket named `MySpecialBucket`.
- A P3 Amazon EC2 instance starts in the us-east2 region.
- A record with a value of `Error` for the `Status` column is added to the table called `AppLog` in the schema called `Application`.

These are powerful ways to process events, but there is a third type of event that increases the flexibility of the EventBridge, as we shall see next.

Custom events

Custom events provide the ability to create and configure EventBridge events. Third-party applications and companies have started to take advantage of this functionality and have started placing their own events to offer them for consumption. You can also place your own custom events. The type of events that can be created are basically limited only by your imagination.

Learning about file uploads

Uploading files from your computer or a local system to the cloud is going to be quite a common occurrence as you develop applications. You will need to upload static data files, HTML files, code, database snapshots, PDF files, logs for analysis, and so on.

Each one of these file types may need different treatment based on the frequency of use, security requirements, user type, and other factors. For this reason, different methods are best for different use cases. As an example, if you are uploading a static HTML file to display on your website, you may want to use one way to upload the file. But if the file that is getting uploaded is a bank statement that is being uploaded by one of your website users, you will want to use a completely different method.

Fortunately, AWS provides a variety of ways to upload files that cover the majority, if not all, of the different use cases that you may have. We'll try to cover most of them.

Uploading to an AWS service via the AWS console

Uploading to an AWS service via the AWS Console probably has the smallest learning curve. A common service to which static files are uploaded is S3, but it's not the only one. Other services that have a console UI to upload files are Amazon SageMaker, Amazon Rekognition, and AWS CodeDeploy.

Uploading with signed URLs

Amazon S3 can be combined with AWS Lambda to produce a signed and secured upload URL that can be leveraged by frontend applications to upload files to Amazon S3. Once the file is uploaded, an additional asynchronous AWS Lambda function can be set up to listen for S3 file changes and perform operations that can interact with the newly uploaded file.

Uploading files using the File Transfer Protocol

Another standard way to upload files in general is using the **File Transfer Protocol** (**FTP**). AWS unsurprisingly provides support for this common protocol in a variety of ways.

A simple example where FTP can be used is with the EC2 service. After starting an EC2 service, it is possible to upload files to the ephemeral store or the EBS volume attached to the instance using any FTP client.

A slightly more complicated example is to use Amazon S3 to implement an FTP server. Using S3 to implement an FTP server is an elegant solution. FTP requires block storage, and that normally would mean spinning up an Amazon EC2 instance and attaching an EBS volume to it. But Amazon S3 stores files as objects (without using blocks), and communication with S3 happens at the application level via an API interface. This means that you can't mount Amazon S3 directly at the operating-system level. A package exists to help us bridge that gap called S3FS-Fuse. S3FS-Fuse enables users to mount an S3 bucket as a local filesystem with read/write permissions. Once you install S3FS-Fuse, you can now interact with the mounted bucket via a Unix command, such as mv, cp, del, and so on, as well as connecting to this mount point via FTP.

> **Important note**
> FTP is an unencrypted protocol and should only be used with nonsensitive data. If the data is sensitive in nature, it is recommended that you use encrypted protocols, such as SFTP and SCP.

Uploading to an AWS service via the CLI

Files uploaded via the console will generally be uploaded in this way when we don't need to upload them consistently and repetitively. Manual uploads are prone to human error. If the requirement calls for periodic and consistent uploads, we are better off using a different method. A semi-automated, and perhaps fully automated, way to upload files is via the CLI. Using the CLI allows us to create scripts that can be run multiple times, giving us consistent results, and these scripts can be invoked via a tool such as cron to perform the actions on a schedule.

As with any other way to access Amazon S3, when using the CLI, you will first have to authenticate yourself through AWS to ensure that you have the authority for the commands you are trying to invoke.

Once authenticated, and assuming that you have the right level of privileges, it is simple and straightforward to invoke a command via the CLI with a syntax loosely following Unix commands—for example, the command to remove a file via the CLI is as follows:

```
aws s3 rm s3:// <<name of the bucket>>/<<name of the file>>
```

Let's now learn how we can perform the same action using the AWS SDK.

Uploading files to AWS via the AWS SDK

As it does for many other operations and supported languages, AWS offers a series of API calls to manage the upload of files using SDK calls. For example, in the AWS SDK for Ruby, there are two ways to upload files. The first method is using the file uploader:

```ruby
require 'aws-sdk-s3'


s3 = Aws::S3::Resource.new(region:'us-east-1')
obj = s3.bucket('the-name-of-the-bucket').object('the-key')
obj.upload_file('/file/path/filename')
```

Another way is useful for uploading long strings or I/O objects that are not a file on disk:

```ruby
require 'aws-sdk-s3'


s3 = Aws::S3::Resource.new(region:'us-east-1')
obj = s3.bucket(' the-name-of-the-bucket ').object('the-key')


# I/O object
File.open('/file/path/filename', 'rb') do |file|
  obj.put(body: file)
end
```

We can also upload files using a REST API. Let's proceed to see how it can be used.

Uploading files to AWS using REST

Much of the communication between microservices is done via REST services. AWS provides an easy-to-use REST interface for the uploading of files. Here is an example of what a REST PUT request may look like:

```
PUT /sample_image.jpg HTTP/1.1
Host: sampleBucket.s3.us-east1.amazonaws.com
Date: Sun, 28 June 2020 19:45:00 GMT
Authorization: authorization string
Content-Type: text/plain
Content-Length: 17211
x-amz-meta-author: Joe.Smith
Expect: 100-continue
[17211 bytes of object data]
```

Yet another method to upload files is by using a glorified removable hard drive. In the AWS lingo, they are called Amazon snowballs. Let's learn about them.

Uploading files using AWS Snowball

Another way that seems slow on the surface but can be the right solution in some situations is the use of **AWS Snowball**. Let's go through an example to understand what they are and how they can be used. Say that your boss comes to you with a requirement to move some data from your "on-prem" data center to an AWS AZ. You know your options are to upload the files using a connection over the internet or using a hard drive and then shipping the drive via FedEx. One can easily assume that the faster solution would always be to use a direct connection. But that answer would be wrong. In some cases, for extremely large files you are better offloading and shipping the files.

This section concludes some of the various options that AWS offers to upload files for our solution. Let's now start looking at some of the AWS services that we can use to create microservices and a RESTful API for our application.

Covering the AWS API gateway

We have already discussed AWS Lambda at length throughout the book. AWS Lambda functions can be called in a variety of ways including the following:

- Directly from the Lambda console in the AWS Console
- Using the Lambda API

- Invoking AWS Lambda functions with the AWS SDK
- Invoking AWS Lambda functions with the AWS CLI
- Using AWS toolkits
- Configuring other AWS services to call AWS Lambda functions
- Configuring AWS Lambda to read data from a stream or items from a queue and invoke an AWS Lambda function depending on the contents.

But another powerful way to invoke AWS Lambda is by using the AWS API Gateway. Invoking AWS Lambda in this way is a popular method to create publicly available and private RESTful API services.

The invocation of an AWS Lambda function can be done synchronously or asynchronously. When the function is invoked synchronously, the response from the function can be retrieved in the same code fragment that has the function invocation. Depending on how long the function takes to return a response, this may take some time. If the function is invoked asynchronously, the function invocation will take much less time at the expense of having to receive the response in a different code segment because it will not be immediately available after the function call returns.

In the case of our particular use case, the AWS API Gateway and AWS Lambda can be combined to create HTTP endpoints and implement a RESTful API to support website functionality, such as retrieving and updating backend data.

In this case, the AWS Lambda functions will implement the business logic necessary to support our application, as well as retrieving and updating the data in the data store we choose for persistence of our application.

Depending on the logic that needs to be implemented, we will have to make some decisions as to whether it makes more sense to implement the AWS Lambda function asynchronously or synchronously. In many cases, the decision to use one method over the other is more of an art than a science. The main driver for the decision is how long the function will take to complete and how long the invoker of the function is willing to wait.

Some examples of functions that it may be better to implement synchronously are as follows:

- Retrieving an individual record from the database
- Updating one record in the database

- Simple, basic, and short-running calculations and computations
- Operations that require an ordered execution of steps because there are dependencies between the steps

Some examples of functions that should probably be implemented asynchronously are as follows:

- Generating a report that retrieves data from multiple sources.
- Sending out an email or an SMS message and getting a response.
- Batch operations.
- Writing to a log.
- Application functionality when we don't want the UI to freeze for an extended period. In these cases, we invoke the function asynchronously and refresh the screen with the function response when the response is available.

This section covered some of the critical AWS services that can be used to connect to microservices. In the next section, we will cover technologies that can be used to create the internal business logic for these microservices.

Reviewing business APIs

In some ways, the **business API** component will be the heart of the application. If we implement the logic correctly, the business logic and validation will be applied regardless of how the application is being accessed. For example, we could allow users of our application to access it via a web browser, an Android interface, and via the RESTful API being invoked by a third-party application. Regardless of the invocation method, the same business logic should be applied. This is one of the places where microservice architectures shine. They can encapsulate the business logic and make sure it is applied fully and consistently.

A concept that is often used to enhance the implementation of the business APIs and microservices is the concept of a business rules engine. Let's explore what this is.

Business rules engine

A **business rules engine** is a software component that can evaluate rules at runtime in a production environment. The most common implementations of a business rules engine provide a simple interface so that non-technical users can add and modify rules in the system.

The rules may implement the following:

- **Legal regulations** – Implementing country-specific laws. For example, a US-based employee may not be dismissed because of their sex, race, or country of origin.

- **Company policies** – Implementing company-specific rules. For example, if an expense is submitted into the time-keeping system with a value of $25.00 or greater, it must be accompanied by a receipt.

- **Operational and departmental decisions** – Some rules may only apply at the department level. For example, employees in the warehouse belonging to the union cannot work more than 50 hours per week.

A business rules engine supports the creation, definition, testing, maintenance, and execution of these business rules.

Business rules engines typically support the definition of the following:

- Rules

- Facts

- Priorities

- Preconditions and postconditions

There is no AWS service specifically designed for the definition of business rules, but it is certainly possible to integrate existing solutions with other AWS services to create a full solution wrapped into a microservice. Several business rules engine implementations exist. Some of the most popular ones are as follows:

- RedHat Decision Manager (formerly JBoss BRMS)

- Progress Corticon **Business Rules Engine** (**BRE**)

- Drools open source software

- Visual Rules BRM

- Computer Associates Aion

- SAS Business Rules Manager

Hopefully, it is now clear to you that there are a range of technologies that we can use to create business rules and business logic. Business rules allow you to create simple static rules, but in some cases, you need to enable workflows where the current state of certain attributes determines how to move things along in a process. In that case, using a state-machine service may be more appropriate. We will learn more about them in the next section.

Understanding state-machine services

In some cases, the application logic and data flow may be complex, and just using AWS Lambda to try to implement the logic may prove difficult. In those situations, we may want to use another AWS service that is better suited to implementing this logic and flow. A service that can implement a state machine and keep track of its state. AWS has a service that fits this bill and can help to fill this gap—**AWS Step Functions**.

AWS Step Functions is a service that provides the coordination of individual pieces in applications. The coordination can be specified in a simple way using a visual editor. Applications can be put together by assembling these individualized software components. Each of the components specializes in one or a few tasks.

AWS provides a graphical editor to display and edit the system components. These are displayed as a series of steps. AWS Step Functions can trigger and track these steps and retry a task a specified number of times if an error occurs. AWS Step Functions brings deterministic execution to your application by executing steps or instructions in a precise order during each execution. As is the case with most AWS services, AWS Step Functions leverages AWS CloudWatch to log the step progress, so if there is a problem, it can easily be diagnosed and debugged efficiently.

Step Functions is fully managed by AWS, ensuring performance regardless of volume and scale.

Tasks for AWS Step Functions don't have to run in the AWS environment. They can also be tracked if they run in other environments if there is connectivity back to AWS. Like other AWS services, Step Functions can be invoked and managed via the following:

- The AWS Step Functions console
- The AWS SDKs
- Using HTTP API calls

Some key features of AWS Step Functions include the following:

- Step functions leverage the concepts of tasks and state machines.
- State machines are defined by using the JSON-based Amazon States Language.
- A graphical view of a step function state machine's structure can be displayed via the Step Functions console, allowing you to visually verify a state machine's logic for a given step function and enable the monitoring of step function executions.

Once step functions have been tested and validated in the AWS Console, it is not a bad idea to formalize the creation of your step function using CloudFormation.

This section concludes the middleware portion of our generic application. We will now move on to the backend services of the application, such as how we can implement an asynchronous service.

Exploring backend persistence services

As you can imagine, only the simplest applications will not require a persistence layer to store application activity, domain data, and application transactions. We covered databases extensively in *Chapter 5, Selecting the Right Database Service*, so we encourage you to visit that chapter to decide which of the many data persistence services that AWS offers is best for your particular application.

Summary

In this chapter, we were able to piece together many of the technologies, best practices, and AWS services that we have covered in this book. We weaved it together into a generic architecture that you should be able to leverage and use for your own projects.

As fully featured as AWS has become, it is all but certain that AWS will continue to provide more and more services to help enterprises large and small to simplify their information technology infrastructure.

You can rest assured that Amazon and its AWS division are hard at work creating new services and improving the existing services by making them better, faster, easier, more flexible, and more powerful, as well as by adding more features.

As of 2020, AWS offers a total of 212 services. That's a big jump from the 2 services it offered in 2004. The progress that AWS has achieved in the last 16 years has been nothing short of monumental. I personally cannot wait to see what the next 16 years will bring for AWS and what can kind of solutions we will be able to deliver with their new offerings.

I hope you are as excited as I am about the possibilities that these new services will bring.

Other Books You May Enjoy

If you enjoyed this book, you may be interested in these other books by Packt:

AWS Penetration Testing

Jonathan Helmus

ISBN: 978-1-83921-692-3

- Set up your AWS account and get well-versed in various pentesting services
- Delve into a variety of cloud pentesting tools and methodologies
- Discover how to exploit vulnerabilities in both AWS and applications
- Understand the legality of pentesting and learn how to stay in scope
- Explore cloud pentesting best practices, tips, and tricks
- Become competent at using tools such as Kali Linux, Metasploit, and Nmap
- Get to grips with post-exploitation procedures and find out how to write pentesting reports

AWS Certified Security – Specialty Exam Guide

Stuart Scott

ISBN: 978-1-78953-447-4

- Understand how to identify and mitigate security incidents
- Assign appropriate Amazon Web Services (AWS) resources to underpin security requirements
- Work with the AWS shared responsibility model
- Secure your AWS public cloud in different layers of cloud computing
- Discover how to implement authentication through federated and mobile access
- Monitor and log tasks effectively using AWS

Leave a review - let other readers know what you think

Please share your thoughts on this book with others by leaving a review on the site that you bought it from. If you purchased the book from Amazon, please leave us an honest review on this book's Amazon page. This is vital so that other potential readers can see and use your unbiased opinion to make purchasing decisions, we can understand what our customers think about our products, and our authors can see your feedback on the title that they have worked with Packt to create. It will only take a few minutes of your time, but is valuable to other potential customers, our authors, and Packt. Thank you!

Index

Made in the USA
Middletown, DE
22 September 2021